# TABLE OF CONTENTS

*(Continued inside back cover.)*

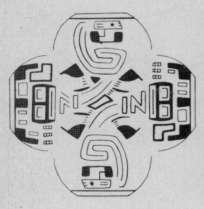

# PERUVIAN ARCHAEOLOGY

*Selected Readings*

## ROWE and MENZEL

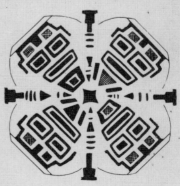

A  PEEK  PUBLICATION

# PERUVIAN ARCHAEOLOGY

*Selected Readings*

## JOHN HOWLAND ROWE

### and

## DOROTHY MENZEL

*Department of Anthropology*
*University of California*
*Berkeley*

**Peek Publications · Box 11065 · Palo Alto, California 94306**

# Introduction

This reader comprises a selection of articles in English on Peruvian arch-aeology designed for the use of students. The field of Peruvian archaeology is developing with great rapidity; new discoveries which alter the general picture are made almost every year, and publication lags far behind research for simple eco-nomic and social reasons. The editors note with a mixture of pleasure and dismay that their own interpretations of five and six years ago are obsolete on points of major importance, and the same is true of other contributions. This situation makes research in the Peruvian field very exciting but has its drawbacks when one attempts to present the subject to students. It is impossible to provide a selection of articles which gives a picture of the subject which is at once well rounded and up to date. This selection is neither, but it represents the best approximation the editors could devise within the limits of space available. There is, of course, much important work in longer monographs which could not be represented in a reader of this kind.

The fact that the selection had to be made from the literature in English was a severe handicap. There are very important articles in other languages, particularly Spanish, French, and German, which could not be considered. Peru-vian archaeology is a truly international effort in which Peruvian scholars have naturally played a leading role, but little of their recent work is available in English.

Inca history and historical ethnography are not represented in this reader. The best available general accounts of Inca culture at the time of the Spanish con-quest are those by Rowe (Handbook of South American Indians, Bureau of American Ethnology, Bulletin 143, vol. 2, pp. 183-330, published in 1946) and J. Alden Mason (The Ancient Civilizations of Peru, Pelican Books A395, first published in 1957). Both these works are out of date. For the conquest and the Colonial period the latest general survey is Rowe's "The Incas Under Spanish Colonial Institutions," Hispanic American Historical Review, vol. XXXVII, no. 2, May, 1957, pp. 155-199.

## COMMENTS ON INDIVIDUAL ARTICLES

The editors have been working for some years to develop a very precise method of relative dating for Peruvian archaeology. Article 1 provides a discus-sion of the theory behind this method. Article 2 presents the evidence on which we base our dating in years. The ages suggested in this article will probably be obsolete within two years as a result of refinements in the radiocarbon method of age determination. Because, in the present state of the art, estimates of age based on radiocarbon determinations can only be tentative, we consider it important to keep relative dating as nearly as possible independent of radiocarbon results. Thus, in the chronological charts which follow this introduction, the placement of the styles listed is based on archaeological associations and comparisons, influenced by radiocarbon determinations only in a few cases involving isolated sierra styles. The charts provided should be used to correct the earlier estimates of age found in many of the articles, for example Rowe's 1958 guess as to the date of Pucara (article 10) and the short scale dates appearing in article 23.

# CHRONOLOGICAL TABLE OF THE PERUVIAN COAST

| Comments | North Coast | Central Coast | Master Sequence Ica (South Coast) | | Relative Chronology |
|---|---|---|---|---|---|
| | | | Ica 10 | | Colonial Period |
| accounts, bronze tools | Inca Influence | Inca Influence | Inca Influence Ica 9 | 1500 | Late Horizon |
| | | | 8 | 8 | |
| | | | 7 | 7 | |
| | | | 6 | 6 | |
| | Chimu | Chancay | Ica 5 | 5 | Late Intermediate Period |
| | | | 4 | 4 | |
| | | | 3 | 3 | |
| corbel vault | | | 2 | 1000 2 | |
| | | | 1 | 1 | |
| bronze jewelry | Derived Huari-Pachacamac | Derived Huari-Pachacamac | Derived Huari-Pachacamac | 4 | Middle Horizon |
| | | | | 3 | |
| | Huari Influence | Pachacamac Huari Influence Nieveria | Huari Influence | 2 | |
| silver, lead | V | 9 | Nasca 9 | 500 1 | |
| molded adobes | IV | 8 | 8 | 8 | |
| | | 7 | | 7 | |
| | III | Moche (Mochica) 6 | Lima (Interlocking) | 7 | |
| (end fortified towns) | | 5 | 6 | 6 | Early Intermediate Period |
| | II | 4 | | 5 | |
| | | 3 | Nasca 5 | 5 | |
| | | 2 | | | |
| | I | 1 | 4 | A.D. 4 | |
| pottery molds | Gallinazo | Miramar (White-on-red) D | 3 | B.C. 3 | |
| | | C | | | |
| | | B | 2 | 2 | |
| | Salinar | A | 1 | 1 | |
| gold and copper metallurgy | Tembladera (Tecapa) | | 10 | 500 10 | |
| | | | 9 | 9 | |
| fortified towns | | ? | 8 | 8 | |
| | | | Ocucaje (Paracas) 7 | 7 | Early Horizon |
| | | | 6 | 6 | |
| large cities (may be earlier) | Cupisnique (Chavin) | Ancon (Chavin) | Chavin Influence | 1000 5 | |
| | | | 4 | 4 | |
| | | | 3 | 3 | |
| | | | 2 | 2 | |
| | | | 1 | 1 | |
| | ? | | Consuelo | 1500 | |
| | Guañape | Haldas | | | Initial Period |
| | | | Erizo | | |
| | | | | 2000 | |
| pottery (South Coast) maize (Central Coast) | | | | | |
| formal temples adobes, llamas | Huaca Prieta | Rio Seco (Chuquitanta) | Casavilca | 2500 | Preceramic |
| permanent buildings cotton cultivated | | | | 3000 | |

## CHRONOLOGICAL TABLE OF THE PERUVIAN SIERRA

| Relative Chronology | North Ancash | North-Central Ayacucho | South-Central Cuzco | South Puno | Bolivia La Paz |
|---|---|---|---|---|---|
| Colonial | | | Colonial Inca (K'uychipunku) | | |
| Late Horizon | Inca Influence | Inca Influence | Imperial (Cuzco) Inca | Inca Influence | Inca Influence |
| Late Intermediate Period (8 7 6 5 4 3 2 1) | Local Styles | Tanta 'Urqo | Early Inca (K'illki) ↓ | Local Styles | "Chullpa" |
| Middle Horizon (4 3 2 1) | Huari Influence | Huari | Huari Influence | Tiahuanaco ↓ | Tiahuanaco ↓ |
| Early Intermediate Period (8 7 6 5 4 3 2 1) | White-on-red ↑ Recuay ↓ | Huarpa ↓ ? ? | ? | ? ? | ? Early Tiahuanaco (Qeya) |
| | | Derived Chanapata | | Pucara | |
| Early Horizon (10 9 8 7 6 5 4 3 2 1) | ? ↑ Chavin | Rancha ? EF Wichqana ? D C AB | Chanapata Marcavalle | Qaluyu | Chiripa ↓ |
| Initial Period | | | | | Huancarani ↓ |
| Preceramic | | | | | |

Precise relative dating is essential for sound cultural inference and the reconstruction of events. How much detail can be recovered when the dating is sufficiently precise is illustrated by the two articles by Menzel (12 and 16) and the one by Lyon (14). Lyon's article also provides an example of the kind of detailed analysis of style that makes precise relative dating possible and enables the investigator to see the cultural processes which ancient pottery reflects.

One 19th century article is included because it still remains one of the best descriptions of an individual tomb we have from the point of view of cultural reconstruction (15). It deserves rescuing from the oblivion into which it has fallen.

Much of ancient Peruvian art is so highly conventionalized that it appears unintelligible to modern viewers. If we are to grasp the meaning, usually religious, of this art we must learn to see through the conventions. Two of the articles in this reader are attempts to understand elaborate systems of conventions (7 and 13).

The combination of archaeological work with historical research in early Spanish documents is a potential source of much valuable information regarding the later periods of Peruvian antiquity. Article 17, on Inca bridges, illustrates this approach.

One article on the archaeology of the tropical forest zone of eastern Peru (19) has been included in order to call attention to the potential importance of this area, currently being explored by D. W. Lathrap and his students. The article chosen is Lathrap's pioneer publication; his sequence has been much extended by later work.

The persistence of native traditions after the Spanish conquest is illustrated by articles 18 and 21. The latter article is also an example of a fruitful use of ethnographic information to throw light on archaeological problems.

COMMENTS TO THE CHRONOLOGICAL TABLES

Two chronological tables, one for the Peruvian coast and the other for the sierra, are provided on facing pages for an up-to-date overview of the stylistic sequences in selected areas and for cross dating. In both chronological tables thick horizontal lines indicate divisions of time in the relative sequence. Narrow horizontal lines indicate stylistic divisions in different regional sequences. Thick broken horizontal lines are used as a visual aid to show the divisions of relative time in some style sequence columns, for areas where precise stylistic divisions have not yet been worked out or where much of the evidence has not yet been discovered. A broken narrow line in the Initial Period section of the north coast column is intended to show that a style phase corresponding to the earliest Chavin influences on the central coast may exist there although it has not yet been found. Narrow horizontal lines with a central space indicate that a style is found at least as late or as early as that point in the relative sequence, with successors or antecedents which must be there but have not yet been discovered. Thick question marks in the Early Intermediate Period sections of the sierra columns indicate lack of information. Question marks following Early Horizon style names in the north-central sierra column indicate that the placement in the relative chronology is only very approximate. Arrows indicate a continuation of the stylistic tradition for an as yet undetermined span of time.

TERMINOLOGY

One of the more obvious problems presented by the literature on Peruvian archaeology is that there is great variation in the terminology used in talking about pottery styles and dating, both among different writers and in earlier and later works of the same writer. Most of the differences in terminology are not capricious but reflect important differences or changes in research methods, knowledge of the subject, or interpretation of the evidence.

For example, before chronological distinctions began to be made in the archaeological record it was noted that pottery styles differed from one area to another. Many writers yielded to the temptation to identify each regional style with the nation or tribe known from historical records to have occupied the area where the style was found. Because of such identifications many pottery styles were given names of tribes or languages. With further research and the establishment of sequences of styles for different areas it was frequently found that the style to which the historic tribal name had been given belonged in fact to a much earlier time, while the style actually associated with the historic tribe was quite different. In order to avoid confusion of this kind, most archaeologists now prefer to name their styles for sites or regions rather than tribes. Sometimes a style is named for the first site at which it was found, and sometimes for another site where it is considered to be particularly characteristic. In Peru most of the tribal names used earlier have now been replaced.

This kind of change in naming practice is illustrated by Kutscher's discussion of names for one of the ancient styles on the north coast of Peru (9). The earlier names "Proto-Chimu" and "Early Chimu" were intended to refer to the historic kingdom, Chimu or Chimor, which occupied the area, while "Mochica" is the name of one of the languages spoken in the kingdom, also called "Muchik." The name, "Moche," proposed by Kutscher, is preferable to all these alternatives and is now coming into general use.

As research proceeds and more evidence is accumulated, it is often possible to make new classifications of familiar materials which reflect more accurately the changes which have taken place in pottery style and other aspects of culture. If the new categories are not just subdivisions of the old ones but radically different groupings, as is commonly the case, it would obviously be misleading to use the same names for the new categories as for the old ones.

An example of changes in terminology made necessary by reclassification is provided by the Ica pottery style from the south coast of Peru. Kroeber and Strong, who studied this style in 1922-23, divided it into categories which they called Middle Ica I, Middle Ica II, Late Ica I, and Late Ica II. Their intent was to make divisions with chronological significance, and the names themselves suggest a sequence. However, Kroeber and Strong admitted that at least some of the pottery classified as Late Ica I had to be later than Late Ica II, because it was found associated with Spanish glass trade beads. Subsequently, the same collection studied by Kroeber and Strong was restudied by Dorothy Menzel, who paid greater attention to the associations of the specimens. She was able to sort out two units in Kroeber and Strong's "Late Ica I" of which one was earlier than their "Late Ica II" and one was later. At the same time, she found many inconsistencies in the way Kroeber and Strong had classified other parts of the Ica sequence. In order to call attention to the differences between her classification and that made by Kroeber and Strong, she called her phase of the Ica style by site names: Chulpaca A and B, Soniche, and Tacaraca A and B. Chulpaca A and B corresponded roughly to Kroeber and Strong's Middle Ica I and II, but with several gravelots differently classified. Her Soniche and Tacaraca B together correspond roughly to Kroeber and Strong's Late Ica I, while her Tacaraca A is more or less Kroeber and Strong's Late Ica II. This classification was arrived at in 1954. Further work by Dorothy Menzel and others has filled in gaps in the sequence and made possible the subdivision of some of the 1954 phases. We can now distinguish ten successive phases of the Ica style and decided in 1966 to simplify a terminology which was becoming unwieldy by numbering the phases, Ica 1-10. Of the numbered phases, Ica 1 corresponds to the older Chulpaca A, Ica 2-4 to Chulpaca B, Ica 6 to Soniche, Ica 9 to Tacaraca A, and Ica 10 to Tacaraca B.

The older Kroeber and Strong divisions and terminology appear in this volume in an article by Lothrop (20) which was written in 1949 and published in 1951.

References to the latest terminology of numbered phases occur in this volume in Lyon's article (14), written in 1966.

Another example of changes in terminology made necessary by reclassification concerns the styles of the Middle Horizon. Max Uhle many years ago was impressed by the similarity between the Huari style group of Peru and the Tiahuanaco style of Bolivia and treated them as a single style, applying the term "Tiahuanaco" to both. Menzel's analysis of the Middle Horizon styles points to important differences between the Tiahuanaco and Huari styles, and the distinction in terminology reflects these differences (12). The terminology introduced by Uhle is followed by Sawyer in his discussion of Huari style textiles from the coast of Peru (13). The materials that Schaedel calls "Tiahuanacoid" also belong to the Huari style (8). His use of the suffix "id" implies a recognition that stylistic differences exist between the objects discussed by him and the Tiahuanaco style proper. In the older literature the term "Coast Tiahuanaco" is commonly used to reflect a recognition of the differences between Huari style objects from the Peruvian coast and the Tiahuanaco style of Boliva.

The article by Samuel K. Lothrop on Peruvian metallurgy (20) reflects several other obsolete terms besides those noted for Ica. "The Necropolis culture discovered at Paracas," which is mentioned by Lothrop, is a local style of the Pisco area dating to Early Horizon Epoch 10 and Early Intermediate Period Epoch 1. The style that Lothrop calls "Early Ica" is approximately equivalent to what Menzel calls "Ica Epigonal" in her Middle Horizon paper (12). "Epigonal" is an older name for this style, being the one introduced by Max Uhle. Lothrop's "Early Tiahuanaco Period" represents the style of the later part of the Early Intermediate Period at Tiahuanaco.

A third reason for diversity of terminology is disagreement regarding the framework in which Peruvian archaeology should be discussed and interpreted. Since 1946 most writers of general works on Peruvian archaeology have presented their discussion in a framework of cultural stages, but there is very little agreement among them regarding the division points between stages or the names applied to them. The drawbacks to the use of stages for archaeological interpretation are discussed by Rowe in an article of 1962 reprinted in this volume (1). Rowe's article also presents the alternative, which is to use a system of periods instead of stages.

## ADDITIONAL READING

The following are some other recent articles of particular interest:

Bird, Junius Bouton
    1965   The concept of a "pre-projectile point" cultural stage in Chile and Peru. American Antiquity, vol. 31, no. 2, October, pp. 262-270. Salt Lake City.

Heiser, Charles Bixler, Jr.
    1965   Cultivated plants and cultural diffusion in nuclear America. American Anthropologist, vol. 67, no. 4, August, pp. 930-949. Menasha.

Lanning, Edward Putnam
    1965   Early Man in Peru. Scientific American, vol. 213, no. 4, October, pp. 68-76. New York.

Menzel, Dorothy, and Rowe, John Howland
    1966   The role of Chincha in late pre-Spanish Peru. Ñawpa Pacha 4, pp. 63-76. Berkeley.

Readers interested in keeping up to date with new developments in Peruvian archaeology should consult especially the annual publication Ñawpa Pacha, published by the Institute of Andean Studies, 2137 Rose Street, Berkeley, California 94709. Numbers 1-4 of this publication can be ordered from the Institute for $3 each. Important articles and reviews in this field also appear fairly frequently in the journals American Antiquity and Archaeology.

# STAGES AND PERIODS IN ARCHAEOLOGICAL INTERPRETATION

## JOHN HOWLAND ROWE

STAGES and periods are different kinds of units used to organize archaeological evidence so that it can be interpreted in terms of cultural change. The difference is that stages are units of cultural similarity, while periods are units of time, or, more specifically, units of contemporaneity. Within a single small area, cultural units which are closely similar are usually also nearly contemporary, so that stages are equivalent to periods. When the problem is one of matching local sequences over a large area, however, stages established on the basis of uniform criteria can be expected to give a different matching from periods, because of the effects of diffusion. An examination of the problems involved in the organization of archaeological sequences suggests that periods provide a more useful basis for cultural interpretation than stages, provided that the periods are defined with reference to some single local sequence which is known in precise detail.[1]

Stages, as we have said, are units of cultural similarity. Cultural units are assigned to the same stage because they share one or more features which have been selected as diagnostic for that stage and lack other features which are considered diagnostic of other stages. What distinguishes stages from other kinds of classificatory units based on similarity is the fact that stages are supposed to follow one another in a fixed order. When stages are used their order is still sometimes determined in the 18th and 19th century manner by deducing it from the theory of progress, but in archaeological practice the order is usually controlled by empirically established sequences.

There are two kinds of stages which can be used to relate local archaeological sequences to one another, and I propose to call them "simple stages" and "complex stages" respectively. Simple stages are those defined on the basis of the presence or absence of a single feature. For example, we may find, in a particular area, that cultural units which include pottery everywhere follow other cultural units which lack pottery. We can then use this observation as the basis for defining two stages, a non-pottery or pre-ceramic stage and a ceramic one. It is not necessary

1 An earlier version of this paper was read at the Fifth Annual Meeting of the Kroeber Anthropological Society, Berkeley, May 13, 1961. It is a byproduct of research on Peruvian archaeology being carried out on a grant from the National Science Foundation, and the Foundation's support is gratefully acknowledged. The argument has profited from the criticisms and suggestions of Theodore D. McCown, Dorothy Menzel, John V. Murra, Mildred Dickeman and Thomas C. Patterson.

Reprinted from SOUTHWESTERN JOURNAL OF ANTHROPOLOGY, Vol. 18, No. 1, 1962. pp. 40-54

to assume that any other specific cultural features must accompany pottery; the relationship of other features to the one used in defining the stages can be made the subject of direct inquiry. Complex stages are stages defined on the basis of several different features which are supposed to occur together. If, for example, we note a frequent correlation of pottery with evidence for farming, animal husbandry, and loom weaving in the area we are studying, we may be tempted to use all four of these features together as criteria for a single cultural stage.

The limitations involved in the use of stages for organizing archaeological data can be brought out by examining the relationships between the two kinds of stages and what we can determine about how cultural change occurs. In the large body of historically documented cases which is now available it is apparent that each cultural change which takes place starts with an act of a single individual and spreads by a process of imitation. Cases in which the same change is initiated independently by more than one individual occur but are not very common. Once a new kind of behavior is in existence, however, many people can imitate it simultaneously, and the change can spread with any degree of speed. Usually changes spread slowly enough so that there is a perceptible delay in transmission when any substantial distance is involved.

There is a further complication in the fact that the changes which take place in a particular area begin in different parts of it, whether as a result of local invention or of transmission from neighboring areas. Changes having different points of origin naturally spread in different directions. In interpreting the archaeological record in terms of cultural change, it is therefore important to determine in which direction each change spread and, as nearly as possible, where it originated within the area being studied.

The use of any system of simple stages to relate local archaeological sequences to one another enables the investigator to study the order in which changes took place but not to determine differences in point of origin and direction of spread. The stage boundary is the constant element which must be shown as a straight line on the chart of relationships. This difficulty can, of course, be avoided if the investigator can refer to absolute dates or to an independent system of relative periods for a control of contemporaneity. In either of these cases, however, there is no need to resort to stages to relate the local sequences to one another, and nothing is gained by introducing them.

Complex stages work like simple stages as long as the features which are supposed to be diagnostic of a particular stage are in fact introduced at the same time and place and spread together. If the diagnostic features have different origins and spread separately, as frequently happens, the investigator using complex stages finds himself working with transitions between stages in which some but not all of the diagnostic features are present. The disadvantages of this situation, particularly when the transitions turn out to be several centuries in length, are so obvious as to require no comment.

The reason why such a situation can arise is that archaeologists who adopt a system of complex stages as a framework for organizing their data usually do so at a very early stage in their research on the area involved. They have, perhaps, one good sequence, the units of which range from 300 to 500 years in length, and are wrestling with the problem of relating to it a number of isolated cultural units from other parts of the area. The units of the known sequence are too long to betray differences of a century or two in the appearance of new features, and the lack of other sequences for comparison eliminates the possibility of finding that the diagnostic features appear in a different order in different parts of the area. The inherent weaknesses of the method of using complex stages as a framework for interpretation appear only much later when the relative chronology can be made more precise and other local sequences are established. Unfortunately, by this time everyone is accustomed to thinking in terms of the traditional stages, and it is very difficult to give them up and start afresh with a more productive system.

If, when the archaeological record begins to be well known, it turns out that several features of culture are indeed always found associated with one another in the area in such a way as to suggest that they were introduced together, the fact may be very significant for cultural interpretation. The association of several features in this way is very unlikely to occur in the area in which they were invented, even if they were all invented in one place, because invention is a rather rare process. The usual situation is that inventions are made one at a time. However, once a series of inventions has been made and the new items have spread over a large area, they may become associated with one another as parts of a single cultural pattern, as has happened in the case of Christianity, monogamy, and trousers. Then the associated features are very likely to be transmitted as a unit. The association of several features in an area should therefore suggest to the investigator that he is dealing with a pattern introduced from some outside source.

It follows from this argument that a system of complex stages should give better results in an area which has several times been under heavy outside influence than it would in the area which was the source of the influence. If it is easier to fit the archaeological record of Europe into the Three Age System of stages than it is the archaeological record of the Near East, the reason may be that Europe was generally on the receiving end of influences from the Near East, and that these influences sometimes came in comparatively massive doses.[2]

The source of the long continued popularity of complex stages as aids to archaeological interpretation lies in man's persistent hope of getting something for nothing. The method offers two sorts of inducements. In the first place, if we can assume that cultural change does in fact take place through a series of uniform stages over a large area, the establishment of a single local sequence provides us at once with the outline of the cultural development of the area as a whole. There is no need to seek other sequences except to fill in minor details, and a great deal of laborious research can be saved. Of course, if the saving is accepted and the research is not done, the weaknesses of the original assumption will never be discovered.

In the second place, the use of complex stages seems to promise a shortcut to more extensive cultural interpretation. It does so, not because of anything inherent in the idea of complex stages as stages, but because of an old and persistent association of complex stages with the theory of cultural evolution, a legacy of 18th century social philosophy. The theory of cultural evolution begins by assuming that all human culture develops through a series of more or less uniform complex stages, the most advanced of which is represented by present day Western culture. Present day non-Western cultures represent less advanced stages of the same development. Each stage is supposed to be characterized by a certain pattern of institutions, so that a certain kind of technology is associated with a certain kind of social organization and certain economic, political, and religious ideas. It is this last aspect of evolutionary theory which is particularly attractive to archaeologists looking for a short-cut to cultural interpretation, for it provides a method for reconstructing those aspects of culture for which the archaeological record provides no direct evidence. A particularly clear and honest example of the combination of complex stages and evolutionary theory for archaeological interpretation is provided by the following quotations from a general paper on the archaeology of the eastern United States:

The general trend of cultural growth in the eastern United States is a familiar one to all who possess a knowledge of human history [*read* cultural evolution]. . . .
From our knowledge of the general cultural stage of these early Archaic people we may assume that they lived as groups or bands of closely related people who probably

2 Even in Europe the fit does not appear to be very good. Childe's 1951 discussion of the problem is particularly interesting (see especially Ch. XII). The European situation is complicated by a chronic confusion between stage and period against which Glyn Daniel has been protesting since 1943.

reckoned descent through the father and were probably patrilocal . . . the local bands were usually exogamous. . . .[3]

The camp sites of the people referred to naturally provide no direct evidence for line of descent, rule of inheritance, or marriage customs. This information is derived, as the author is careful to state, from the assumptions of evolutionary theory regarding the kind of social organization which should be associated with the subsistence patterns and technology observed in the archaeological record.

The evolutionary notion of complex stages characterized by the association of particular customs, institutions, and ideas did not arise from any consideration of archaeological evidence but belongs rather to sociological and ethnological theory. Its validity is chiefly an ethnological problem, and the obvious way to test it is to inquire whether the associations claimed do in fact occur regularly in the cultures on which ethnographic information is available. The essence of Boas' criticism of evolutionary theory was that they do not, and the evolutionists have never offered a satisfactory answer to this criticism.

The disadvantages and temptations of using stages to construct a framework for archaeological interpretation can be avoided by the use of periods for this purpose. Some writers have attempted to secure this advantage by a simple change of name, setting up what is in fact a system of stages but calling their stages "periods" and assuming that cultural units falling on the same stage are more or less contemporary. The result, of course, is only to compound confusion. In order to avoid this mistake the difference in meaning between the two terms must be kept sharply in mind.

At the beginning of this paper I defined periods as units of contemporaneity. This definition means that any two archaeological monuments or cultural units are to be assigned to the same period if there is some reason for regarding them as contemporary, regardless of how different they may be from one another. If there is some reason to think that a non-ceramic unit in one part of the area is contemporary with a ceramic unit in another, the two must be assigned to the same period in spite of the contrast in inventory. In historical terms, terminal native culture in Tasmania belonged to the same period as early Victorian culture in England, in spite of the differences between the two cultures.

The idea of using periods of relative time instead of stages to construct a framework for archaeological interpretation is not new in archaeology, but it has had a somewhat limited use. The idea was first proposed by W. M. F. Petrie at the turn of the century as a solution to the problem of organizing the archaeologi-

---

3 Griffin, 1952, pp. 352, 354.

cal data for Predynastic Egypt.[4] Petrie's scheme consisted of a series of numbered periods which he called "sequence dates." The basis of the scheme was a seriation of a very large number of Predynastic grave lots according to the selection of pottery types they contained. Other monuments were assigned to sequence date on the basis of their association with Petrie's pottery types.

Shortly after the publication of Petrie's method of sequence dating Max Uhle organized the results of his archaeological explorations in Peru and Bolivia in a system of six periods. This system is presented most clearly in a popular article which he published in Harper's Monthly Magazine in 1903. The text describes the cultures of the Peruvian coast in order by period but provides no names or numbers by which the periods can be designated. In the captions to the illustrations, however, the periods are referred to by names or numbers: "Earliest Period," "Third Period," "Sixth Period," etc. Uhle's use of periods may have been influenced by Petrie's paper of 1900, for Uhle cites Petrie's work in another article which he published in 1902.

The cross-dating of local sequences in Uhle's system was done by reference to two "chronological horizons," as Uhle called them, periods in which relatively uniform artistic styles spread over the whole area studied. He designated these "the chronological horizon of the culture of Tiahuanaco," and "the chronological horizon of the Inca culture," and they corresponded to the Second and Sixth periods of the numbering system. Uhle assumed that the spread of the "horizon" styles took place rapidly enough so that all occurrences of the same "horizon" style could be considered approximately contemporary.[5]

After his experiment with numbered periods in 1903 Uhle dropped the idea, and in his later work he preferred to discuss chronological relationships with reference to approximate absolute dates, even though the absolute dates were based on pure guesswork.[6]

In 1922, however, A. L. Kroeber undertook to study Uhle's archaeological collections and review his work, with the assistance first of W. D. Strong and later of other students. Kroeber at once noted the phenomenon of the existence of two widespread styles which Uhle had used to define his "chronological horizons," and by reference to these styles he devised his own system of four periods, Kroeber's third period corresponding to the Third, Fourth, and Fifth Periods of Uhle's 1903 scheme. The four period system was first published in 1924 in a joint report by

4 Petrie, 1900, 1901.

5 Uhle first used the expression "chronological horizon" in an article published in 1913 (p. 341), but he was using the idea of stylistic uniformities for cross-dating at least as early as 1899 when his correspondence with Mrs Phoebe Hearst begins.

6 See, for example, Uhle, 1920, and compare Daniel, 1951.

Kroeber and Strong on the Uhle collections from Chincha; in this report the periods are called "general horizons" or simply "horizons," and they are designated as Pre-Tiahuanaco, Tiahuanaco, Pre-Inca, and Inca.[7] In Kroeber's report on Moche pottery, published the following year, these periods are called "general periods" or "eras," and the same names are used for them.[8] The use of the terms "horizon," "period," and "era" as alternates in these two reports suggests that the general inspiration of Kroeber's scheme was the kind of periodization which is current in geology. In the Moche report Kroeber emphasized the importance of making a systematic distinction between time and style and used his period scheme as a device for doing so.[9] This is a discussion of the greatest theoretical importance.

In 1929 Kroeber renamed his periods, perhaps in consultation with L. M. O'Neale, with whom he was then working on Peruvian textiles. The new names were Early Period, Middle Period or Tiahuanaco-Epigonal Horizon, Late Period, and Inca Period (or Horizon).[10] No change in the definition of the periods was involved. Kroeber's scheme, with the 1929 period names, was widely used by other Peruvianists until Kroeber himself abandoned it in 1943.[11]

Another system of periods was devised in 1924 by V. Gordon Childe as a framework for interpreting the archaeology of central Europe.[12] Childe constructed a generalized archaeological sequence for Moravia, Silesia, Hungary, and northern Serbia and labelled the cultural units of this sequence Danubian I, II, III, and IV. Then he set up four periods, corresponding to these cultural units, which he labelled Periods I to IV. In a later study, published in 1929, the period system is extended so that a total of seven periods is recognized, while the numbered units of the Danubian cultural sequence are reduced to two. It is quite evident from the way the period designations are used in these publications that Childe was making a conscious effort to distinguish between cultural similarity and time, just as Kroeber was.

Childe stated in his professional testament, published in 1958, that his scheme of periods for central Europe was inspired by Wace and Thompson's periodization of Thessalian archaeology, which was published in 1912, and by Arthur Evans' system of "periods" for Minoan Crete which was first published in 1905 and 1906. The fact is, however, that neither Wace and Thompson nor Evans made any distinction between cultural similarity and time. Both their schemes referred to small

7 Kroeber and Strong, 1924, p. 53.
8 Kroeber, 1925, pp. 231-232.
9 *Idem,* pp. 229-231.
10 O'Neale and Kroeber, 1930, especially p. 24; Kroeber, 1930, pp. 108-113.
11 Kroeber, 1944, pp. 105-106.
12 Childe, 1925b and 1925a.

areas in which there was no need to do so. Childe's distinction in 1924 was an innovation in European archaeology.

As Glyn Daniel has pointed out, Childe did nothing to call attention to his use of periods, and they are easily overlooked in his discussions of the details of central European archaeology.[13]

The use of periods is a somewhat more prominent feature of Childe's later study of the archaeology of Britain.[14] This work covers a longer span of time, and the number of periods used is accordingly increased to nine. However, while other writers have generally begun with stages and confused them with periods, Childe began with periods and then confused them with stages. His periods are defined with relation to changes in pottery on the chalk lands of southern England, and he complains of finding no "counterparts" to some of them in Yorkshire and Scotland.[15] It is quite clear that he was thinking of cultural similarity and not of contemporaneity in this discussion.

Still another tradition of period use was initiated by J. A. Ford in Louisiana and Mississippi in 1935 and applied in the Caribbean, with some modifications, by Irving Rouse.[16] Ford based his period scheme on the frequency of occurrence of ceramic types in the sequence with which he was concerned, while Rouse used the frequency of occurrence of "modes" (taxonomically defined features). Both Ford and Rouse refer to their systems as "time scales." A system of periods based on Ford's practice was used in Peru in a limited fashion by the archaeologists participating in the Virú Valley Project of 1946.[17] The cultural interpretations resulting from this project were presented in terms of stages, however.[18]

Kroeber abandoned his scheme of periods for Peruvian archaeology in 1943 because new discoveries had extended the cultural sequences back in time, so that the period names he had been using seemed no longer appropriate. The "Early Period" had become too long, and the "Middle Period" no longer fell near the middle of the known sequence. It occurred to me in 1955 that Peruvian archaeology had lost a valuable tool when the period system was abandoned, and that a simple adjustment of names would take care of the difficulties which had led Kroeber to give it up. According to the criteria which Kroeber had used in formulating the original scheme, there were now six periods to be provided for instead

---

13 Childe, 1925a and subsequent editions; 1925b, and 1929. See Daniel, 1951, p. 35.

14 Childe, 1940.

15 Compare Childe, 1940, pp. 8, 9 and chart on p. 11, and see also Childe, 1956, pp. 101-102.

16 Ford, 1935, 1936; Rouse, 1939.

17 E.g., Ford, 1949.

18 E.g., Strong, 1948; Bennett and Bird, 1949.

of four, and the Chavin culture, falling in the second period of the new series, clearly marked a "chronological horizon" in the same sense that the Inca and "Tiahuanaco-Epigonal" cultures did. I therefore proposed the period names Initial Period, Early Horizon, Early Intermediate Period, Middle Horizon, Late Intermediate Period, and Late Horizon.[19] Subsequent experience has confirmed the utility of this scheme.

It soon became clear, however, that the periods of this scheme, as Kroeber had defined them, could be considered to be true periods only because we had been working with a vague and approximate relative chronology. The Horizons were defined by the appearance, respectively, of Chavin, Tiahuanaco (or Huari) and Inca influence in local sequences. Their definitions therefore rested on criteria of cultural similarity, a fact which, according to the definitions advanced in this paper, gives them the character of stages. Uhle and Kroeber, however, assumed that the unifying influences which defined the Horizons spread sufficiently rapidly so that the appearance of these influences in local sequences could be taken to indicate contemporaneity. This assumption was tenable, because the length of the divisions then recognized in the local sequences was so great as to mask any delay that may have taken place in the transmission of stylistic influences. As more precise subdivisions of the sequences have become established, however, the question of delay has become important. In effect, we found our periods dissolving into stages.

The situation can be illustrated by reference to the spread of Inca influence. According to their own historical traditions, it took the Incas about forty years to conquer most of what is now Peru, not counting the tropical forest area.[20] Kroeber could treat the appearance of Inca influence as contemporaneous in all parts of the area, for archaeological purposes, because there was no local sequence in Peru with sufficiently precise divisions to pick up a time difference of forty years. The work of Dorothy Menzel on late south coast pottery styles has made this difference significant for that area, especially when an attempt is made to cross-date the south coast with Cuzco.

As the precision of our chronology increased beyond the point where the appearance of "horizon styles" could be taken as a sufficient indication of contemporaneity, some new basis for defining the periods had to be found. The solution proved to be to relate the system of periods to the local sequence of one particular valley. The sequence of this valley then becomes the master sequence to which all relative dates in the area are referred. The idea of relating a general system of

19 Rowe, 1960 (read in 1956).
20 Rowe, 1945.

periods to a single master sequence is a new one and, in fact, represents the only original contribution to the theory of archaeological periods reported in this paper. Childe came very close to anticipating this idea, particularly in basing his British "periods" on the sequence for southern England, but he let it slip through his fingers by treating his "periods" as stages in extending them to other areas. He related other sequences to that of southern England on the basis of cultural similarity rather than contemporaneity.

The use of a master sequence to control a system of periods can be illustrated from Peruvian data. In applying the idea to Peru I chose the Ica valley as the most convenient point of reference, because we had made the best start toward establishing a detailed chronology of the pottery styles of that valley. We could then say that the Initial Period begins at the time of the introduction of pottery in Ica. The Early Horizon is the time from the first appearance of Chavin influence at Ica until polychrome slip painting replaces resin painting in that valley. The Middle Horizon is the time from the beginning of Phase 9 of the Nasca style at Ica to the beginning of Phase A of the Chulpaca style. The Late Horizon is the period from the beginning of Phase A of the Tacaraca style at Ica until the beginning of Phase B of the same style. Since we believe that the beginning of the Tacaraca A style coincided in time with the beginning of the Inca occupation of the Ica valley, we assign the traditional date of the Inca conquest of this area, about 1476 AD, to the beginning of the Late Horizon.

With the system of periods thus defined in terms of the master sequence, relative dating can be put strictly on a basis of contemporaneity. A particular cultural unit in some other part of Peru will be assigned to the Early Horizon, for example, because there is some reason for thinking that it is contemporary with a cultural unit at Ica which is dated to the Early Horizon, and without regard to whether there is any stylistic or technological resemblance between them.

The new procedure focuses attention on the problem of cross-dating and makes necessary some systematic thinking about the theory of contemporaneity. This subject deserves a separate paper. For present purposes it is sufficient to point out that there are a number of different ways in which contemporaneity between cultural units can be established.

1. The most obvious method is by reference to absolute dates. For most areas some radiocarbon dates are now available, and they occasionally provide a check on the cross-dating of cultural units. In Peru, for example, the Pucara style is dated in the Early Horizon by a series of radiocarbon determinations; there is little other evidence by which to place it.

2. Trade pieces provide some of the best evidence of contemporaneity, and

some trade is likely to occur between neighboring areas even in times of relative isolation. The most convincing argument for contemporaneity is provided by the repeated and consistent association of a particular style of trade pieces with a particular style of local pieces, as, for example, the association of Late Inca and Tacaraca A pieces in burials at Ica.

3. Contemporaneity is usually indicated if it can be shown that one local style has influenced another, although the possibility of archaism provides a complication in the argument. The best case for influence can be made when two styles show the same patterned combination of features, but the pattern does not remain the same for very long in either style.

Often an argument for contemporaneity depends on a combination of different kinds of evidence. Each problem of cross-dating has its own peculiarities, and any proposed solution should be judged on its individual merits.

The use of a master sequence to provide chronological control for a system of periods has a number of consequences. In the whole area to which the system of periods applies, the precision possible in relative dating is limited by the detail in which stylistic changes in the master sequence have been studied. The method works best if research on the master sequence is continuous, so that it is always the best known local sequence in the area. As other local sequences are tied firmly to the master sequence they can be used as secondary standards of reference, but opportunities for direct cross checks with the master sequence should always be sought in order to avoid accumulation of error.

The basic periods of the Peruvian system are quite long, except for the Late Horizon which lasted only about 58 years. The earlier periods range from 300 to 700 years in length. It is generally convenient in any area to have time units of about this order of magnitude available for approximate relative dating. For more precise cross-dating the basic periods can be subdivided, and the chronological subdivisions can be made as fine as the stylistic subdivisions which can be distinguished in the master sequence. In the Peruvian system, for example, the Early Intermediate Period represents the time covered by Phases 1 to 8 of the Nasca style at Ica. We can therefore divide the Early Intermediate Period into eight subdivisions ("epochs"), each corresponding to one of the Nasca phases. Thus, Epoch 7 of the Early Intermediate Period (or, more briefly, EIP 7) is the span of time corresponding to Nasca 7 at Ica. If the Early Intermediate Period lasted about 650 years, as now seems likely, its epochs average less than a century in length. When we can secure more precise archaeological associations it should be possible to subdivide some of the longer epochs. Such subdivisions can be designated by capital letters: for example, EIP 7A, EIP 7B, etc.

The use of a system of periods rather than stages to organize archaeological data is a valuable aid to clear thinking in cultural interpretation. It has both positive and negative advantages. Its positive advantage is that it provides a close control of relative dating which permits the investigator to identify delays in the spread of cultural features and hence to determine the direction in which the spread took place and ultimately the area of origin of the feature studies. Information on the nature of cultural influences and the direction in which they move in turn throws light on prestige relationships, since people tend to imitate those whom they respect.

Some interesting and unexpected patterns of cultural influence are beginning to appear in Peru as a result of recent refinements in relative dating associated with an organization by periods. The evidence available is still very incomplete, but it suggests that pottery reached the Peruvian coast from the north, maize was introduced to the coast from the central sierra, and copper metallurgy came from the south, perhaps from as far away as Chile or northwestern Argentina. Maize appears on the central coast at the beginning of the Initial Period or even before, while it is not found on the north coast until the later part of the Initial Period. Pottery, on the other hand, appears on the north coast before the beginning of the Initial Period and is later than maize in the center. Copper metallurgy was present all along the south coast before the end of the Early Horizon, but it does not appear on the central and north coasts until well after the beginning of the Early Intermediate Period. Each of these cultural features diffused over most of the Andean area in a few centuries, so that close chronological control is necessary to follow the process.

The negative advantage of using periods rather than stages to organize archaeological data is that the investigator runs much less danger of assuming what he ought to be trying to prove. Because of the close association of stages with the theory of cultural evolution, virtually every archaeologist who uses stages to organize his data thereby builds into them certain assumptions about cultural development without being aware that he is doing so. Later, in making his cultural interpretations, he discovers the pattern of cultural development which was assumed in his system of organization and thinks that he is deriving it empirically from the data. The argument becomes perfectly circular. The danger of circularity in cultural interpretation is avoided when the data are organized in terms of periods, because the period system involves no assumptions about cultural patterns. There is at least a chance that the investigator may see new patterns emerging from his data which he would not have thought of at the beginning of the investigation.

The method of basing archaeological interpretation on a framework of periods keyed to a local master sequence could be applied elsewhere in the world just as profitably as in the Andean area. In Europe, for example, it would be worth while trying to take the stage element out of the system of "periods" proposed by Childe by using an appropriate local sequence in southern England as the master sequence and relating cultural units elsewhere to it on the basis of arguments of contemporaneity.[21]

## BIBLIOGRAPHY

BENNETT, WENDELL C., AND JUNIUS B. BIRD
    1949    *Andean Culture History* (American Museum of Natural History, Handbook Series, no. 15, New York).

CHILDE, V. GORDON
    1925a   *The Dawn of European Civilization* (Alfred A. Knopf: New York).
    1925b   *When Did the Beaker-folk Arrive?* (Archaeologia, vol. 74, 1923-24, pp. 159-180, London).
    1929    *The Danube in Prehistory* (Clarendon Press: Oxford).
    1940    *Prehistoric Communities of the British Isles* (W. and R. Chambers, Ltd.: London and Edinburgh).
    1951    *Social Evolution* (Watts and Co.: London).
    1956    *Piecing Together the Past; the Interpretation of Archaeological Data* (Frederick A. Praeger: New York).
    1958    *Retrospect* (Antiquity, vol. 32, no. 126, pp. 69-74, Newbury).

DANIEL, GLYN E.
    1943    *The Three Ages; an Essay On Archaeological Method* (University Press: Cambridge).
    1951    *The Chronological Framework of Prehistoric Barbarian Europe* (Man, vol. 51, articles 63-81, no. 64, pp. 34-37, London).

EVANS, ARTHUR
    1905    *La classification des époques successives de la civilisation minoenne* [summary] (Comptes rendus du Congrès International d'Archéologie, 1re Session, Athènes 1905, p. 209, Athens).
    1906    *Essai de classification des époques de la civilisation minoenne; résumé d'un discours fait au Congrès d'Archéologie à Athènes* (Édition revisée, B. Quaritch: London).

---

21 The periodization of European archaeological data which Daniel suggested in 1951 represents a different solution to the problem. Daniel's periods are periods of absolute time, while mine are periods of relative time which can be set up in the absence of any absolute dates whatsoever. Both systems avoid the drawbacks of stage schemes; mine has the additional advantage of making the determination of relative time a separate problem from that of determining absolute time.

FORD, JAMES ALFRED
1935 *Ceramic Decoration Sequences at an Old Indian Village Site near Sicily Island, Louisiana* (State of Louisiana, Department of Conservation, Anthropological Study no. 1, Louisiana State University Study no. 24, New Orleans).

1936 *Analysis of Indian Village Site Collections from Louisiana and Mississippi* (State of Louisiana, Department of Conservation, Anthropological Study no. 2, New Orleans).

1949 *Cultural Dating of Prehistoric Sites in Virú Valley, Peru* (Anthropological Papers, American Museum of Natural History, vol. 43, part 1, New York).

GRIFFIN, JAMES B.
1952 "Culture Periods in Eastern United States Archeology" (in *Archeology of Eastern United States,* James B. Griffin, ed., pp. 352-364, University of Chicago Press: Chicago).

KROEBER, A. L.
1925 *The Uhle Pottery Collections from Moche* (University of California Publications in American Archaeology and Ethnology, vol. 21, no. 5, Berkeley).

1930 *Archaeological Exploration in Peru. Part II, The Northern Coast* (Field Museum of Natural History, Anthropology Memoirs, vol. 2, no. 2, Chicago).

1944 *Peruvian Archeology in 1942* (Viking Fund Publications in Anthropology, no. 4, New York).

KROEBER, A. L., AND WILLIAM DUNCAN STRONG
1924 *The Uhle Collections from Chincha* (University of California Publications in American Archaeology and Ethnology, vol. 21, no. 1, Berkeley).

O'NEALE, LILA M., AND A. L. KROEBER
1930 *Textile Periods in Ancient Peru* (University of California Publications in American Archaeology and Ethnology, vol. 28, no. 2, Berkeley).

PETRIE, W. M. FLINDERS
1900 *Sequences in Prehistoric Remains* (Journal, Anthropological Institute of Great Britain and Ireland, vol. 29, pp. 295-301, London).

1901 *Diospolis Parva; the Cemeteries of Abadiyeh and Hu, 1898-9* (Special Extra Publication [Twentieth Memoir] of the Egypt Exploration Fund, London).

ROUSE, IRVING
1939 *Prehistory in Haiti; a Study in Method* (Yale University Publications in Anthropology, no. 21, New Haven).

ROWE, JOHN HOWLAND
1945 *Absolute Chronology in the Andean Area* (American Antiquity, vol. 10, pp. 265-284, Menasha).

1960 "Cultural Unity and Diversification in Peruvian Archaeology" (in *Men and Cultures; Selected Papers of the Fifth International Congress of Anthropological and Ethnological Sciences,* Philadelphia, September 1-9, 1956, pp. 627-631, Philadelphia).

STRONG, WILLIAM DUNCAN
1948 *Cultural Epochs and Refuse Stratigraphy in Peruvian Archaeology* (Memoirs, Society for American Archaeology, no. 4, Menasha).

UHLE, MAX
1902 *Types of Culture in Peru* (American Anthropologist, vol. 4, pp. 753-759, New York).
1903 *Ancient South American Civilization* (Harper's Monthly Magazine, vol. 107, October, pp. 780-786, New York and London).
1913 *Zur Chronologie der alten Culturen von Ica* (Journal de la Société des Américanistes de Paris, n.s., vol. 10, pp. 341-367, Paris).
1920 *Los principios de las antiguas civilizaciones peruanas* (Boletín de la Sociedad Ecuatoriana de Estudios Históricos Americanos, vol. 4, no. 12, pp. 448-458, Quito).

WACE, A. J. B., AND M. S. THOMPSON
1912 *Prehistoric Thessaly; Being Some Account of Recent Excavations and Explorations in North-eastern Greece from Lake Kopais to the Borders of Macedonia* (Cambridge Archaeological and Ethnological Series, University Press: Cambridge).

UNIVERSITY OF CALIFORNIA
BERKELEY, CALIFORNIA

# AN INTERPRETATION OF RADIOCARBON MEASUREMENTS ON
## ARCHAEOLOGICAL SAMPLES FROM PERU

John Howland Rowe

The radiocarbon method is the only one available for determining absolute or chronometric ages in Peruvian archaeology prior to the second half of the 15th century of our era. There are no inscriptions, because writing was unknown in ancient Peru, and no attempt has been made to set up a chronology based on tree rings. In evaluating radiocarbon measurements from this area, therefore, the only available standard is the degree of consistency observed among the measurements themselves.

Except when the question is one of consistency among different measurements on portions of the same sample, consistency among radiocarbon measurements can only be determined with reference to archaeological associations and the system of relative chronology which has been set up for the area. In order to be useful for evaluating radiocarbon measurements, associations must be specific and the system of relative chronology both precise and independent of radiocarbon evidence.

Associations provide the basis for any inference that certain kinds of objects are contemporary with a radiocarbon sample or that two samples are of the same relative age. It should be obvious that two samples from the same storage pit or the same burial are likely to be of very nearly the same age; on the other hand, two samples from the same arbitrary 25 cm. level in an excavation in a habitation site are much less specifically associated. If the level is cut by a floor, or if the deposit is a fill, the two samples may be hundreds of years apart. Both conditions noted are common in Peruvian sites.

To compare measurements made on samples from different associations it is necessary to refer them to a system of relative chronology. Two measurements yielding the same radiocarbon age are judged consistent if they were made on samples assigned to the same minimum unit of relative time, while two measurements yielding different radiocarbon ages are judged consistent if they fall in the sequence predicted from the relative ages of the samples and a proportionate distance apart. Obviously, if the system of relative chronology is itself based on radiocarbon evidence, there is serious danger of being caught in a circular argument.

The importance of precision in relative dating is best illustrated by an example. Let us consider a case in which the minimum units of relative time that can be distinguished are each about three times as long as the standard deviations of the available radiocarbon measurements.

Reprinted from Proceedings of the Sixth International Conference, Radiocarbon and Tritium Dating, held at Washington State University, Pullman, Washington, June 7-11, 1965, pp. 187-198. U. S. Atomic Energy Commission, Division of Technical Information, CONF-650652 Chemistry (TID-4500). Springfield, Va., 1966.

This is a fairly common situation in archaeology. Now let us suppose that one sample, which actually dates from near the beginning of a particular relative time unit, is measured and yields an erroneous value which is just under one standard deviation later than the end of the time unit. Then let us suppose that another sample, which actually dates from near the end of the same time unit, is measured and yields a value which is equally erroneous in the opposite direction, falling just under one standard deviation earlier than the beginning of the time unit in question. Both samples are known to belong to the same unit of relative time, and the first standard deviation of each overlaps an end of the unit. On the evidence available, the two measurements would have to be judged consistent and acceptable within one standard deviation. The facts that the values obtained are in the wrong order and that each is accurate only in the fourth standard deviation cannot be detected for want of precision in the relative chronology. If the units of relative time were half as long as in the hypothetical case just described, the samples in question would be assigned to different time units, and the reversal of order would be evident.

The conditions for evaluating consistency in radiocarbon measurements are better in Peru than in most other areas without an alternative chronometric scale. Fifteen years of work by University of California archaeologists on the pottery of the valley of Ica have resulted in the most carefully studied ceramic sequence in the New World, now in process of publication. This ceramic sequence serves as a reference standard for a general system of relative chronology applicable to a large part of Peru. Objects or events are assigned to one or another unit of this system on evidence of their contemporaneity with one or another phase of the Ica ceramic sequence. In so far as possible, the argument for contemporaneity is based on trade pieces and stylistic influences, rather than on general cultural similarity or radiocarbon measurements. Cross-ties are reasonably satisfactory with most areas except Cuzco and the basin of Lake Titicaca.

The system of relative chronology we are discussing covers the span of time from the introduction of pottery at Ica to the end of the 16th century A.D. when the ancient sites were abandoned. This time span is divided into seven major time units, of which the second, fourth, and sixth are called "horizons" and the rest are called "periods." The intent of the contrast in names is to call attention to the fact that in the horizons Ica was subject to influences from remote parts of the country, while in the periods it was relatively isolated. The three horizons are designated Early, Middle, and Late. The outside influences felt at Ica in the Early Horizon are from Chavin in northern Peru; those of the Middle Horizon are from Huari, and perhaps ultimately from Tiahuanaco; while those of the Late Horizon are from Cuzco and represent the imperial rule of the Incas.

The period between the introduction of pottery at Ica and the beginning of the Early Horizon is called the Initial Period, a name which simply indicates that this period is the earliest one to which ceramic dating can be applied. The period between the Early and Middle Horizons is called the Early Intermediate Period, and the one between the Middle and Late Horizons is called the Late Intermediate Period. The Late Horizon ends with the Spanish conquest and is followed by the Colonial Period.

Two of the horizons and two of the periods are divided into epochs, which are designated by Arabic numerals. The Early Horizon comprises 10 epochs, the Early Intermediate Period 8, the Middle Horizon 4, and the Late Intermediate Period 8. The Late Horizon is too short to divide, and the Initial Period is too little known. A few of the epochs can be sub-divided, the subdivisions being designated by capital letters. The beginning of each unit in the system is marked by a change in the pottery style of Ica.

It is fortunate, and not altogether coincidental, that a high proportion of the radiocarbon measurements from Peru with precise associations were made on samples from Ica or other south coast areas near enough to it to be related easily to the system of relative chronology just described. Consistencies in these measurements are particularly easy to demonstrate.

In reviewing radiocarbon measurements one expects to find a single pattern of consistency to which most of the measurements conform, with the remainder scattered in a more or less random manner. The Peruvian measurements, however, show not one pattern of consistency but two, and the two are in direct contradiction to one another. One pattern appears in measurements made between 1955 and 1957, the other in measurements made since 1962.

My attention was first called to this anomaly in 1963 when the measurements made in 1962 became available. Most of us working in the Peruvian field had for some years been using a set of estimated dates based primarily on a consistent series of radiocarbon measurements made at the Lamont Geological Observatory, Columbia University, before 1957. Most of the measurements in this series which had precise archaeological associations were made on samples from burials from the south coast of Peru, including some from Ica. The south coast series of samples with burial associations comprised seven Lamont measurements made by the carbon dioxide method, and six of them formed a remarkably consistent sequence. This sequence was supported directly by two other measurements, one made at Groningen in 1955 and the other at Yale in 1956, and indirectly by two Lamont measurements made on samples from the north coast (see Table 1). The supporting measurements were also made by the carbon dioxide method, and the samples were all from burial associations. The Lamont and Yale measurements in question were all corrected for the Suess effect before publication, while for the Groningen measurement the laboratory later published a correction of 0. The situation thus was that ten of the eleven best controlled radiocarbon measurements available for ancient Peru supported the estimated dates we had been using.

The measurements we have been discussing all referred to the ceramic stage. There were also available four New Zealand measurements for refuse-associated samples from the cotton-using preceramic stage which had, or were thought to have, reasonably satisfactory associations. Of these measurements three were consistent among themselves and all were consistent with the Lamont series (see Table 1).

There were also available numerous measurements made by the solid carbon method at Chicago and Lamont and some additional measurements on samples with debatable refuse associations made by the carbon dioxide method at the Lamont laboratory. It was and is difficult to know how to interpret these measurements, because the ones with reasonably precise archaeological associations show no clear pattern of consistency. Many have large standard deviations, and all were made before the discovery of the Suess effect. Neither the Chicago nor the Lamont laboratory had, or has, published Suess effect corrections for its early measurements.

The estimated time scale for Peruvian archaeology based on the best measurements of 1955 to 1957 put the introduction of pottery on the Peruvian coast somewhere between 1200 and 1450 B.C. in radiocarbon years based on the 5568 year half-life. For convenience of reference I shall call this the short scale.

After 1957 it was not until 1962 that any new measurements were made which were comparable to those of 1955-57. Since 1962, however, fifteen more measurements have been made on south coast samples with reasonably precise associations (see Table 2 and Appendix). Twelve of these measurements form a sequence which is just as consistent as the one formed by the 1955-57 measurements but quite different from it. The estimated time scale based on the measurements made between 1962 and 1964 puts the introduction of pottery on the Peruvian coast before 1900 B.C., again on the basis of the 5568 year half-life. I shall refer to this scale as the long scale.

Of the three 1962-64 measurements which do not fit the pattern, one (UCLA-153) is 800 to 1000 years too young to fit the long scale and 200 to 400 years too young to fit the short scale. Another (P-516) is 400 to 600 years too young to fit the long scale but corresponds reasonably well to the short scale. The third (GX-0187) is 200 to 400 years too old to fit the long scale. The inconsistent measurements thus form no pattern of their own. The fact that one of them fits the short scale is probably just a coincidence.

The difference between the two scales varies from 14 to 25%, depending on the age at which the comparison is made and the way in which the relative dates are adjusted to the radiocarbon measurements. I thought at first that it might be possible to calculate a single correction factor which would bring the short scale measurements into line with the long scale ones, but further figuring shows that the differences between the scales are not so consistent. The most direct contrast is between the long scale and short scale measurements for Early Intermediate Period 3. This epoch, which is probably 100 to 150 years in length, has a short scale date of third to fifth century A.D. and a long scale one of first to second century B.C.

It should be pointed out that the measurements supporting the long scale are the work of four different laboratories. The oldest measurements with pottery associations are two based on parts of the same charcoal sample (GX-0185 and GX-0186); they are very close together and can reasonably be averaged. There are three measurements for Middle Horizon 2, all on samples believed to be from the same association and with a satisfactory overlap (I-1041, I-1042, I-1043); they can also be averaged.

Of the radiocarbon measurements made on samples from other parts of Peru since 1962, many of those with the best associations also support the long scale. A scattering of individual measurements could be construed as consistent with the short scale, but there is no post-1962 short scale series. The lack of archaeological evidence to relate the sequences of the Cuzco and Titicaca Basin areas with the system of relative dating based on Ica makes it impossible to evaluate the radiocarbon measurements from these areas effectively.

The anomaly of two patterns of consistency in the Peruvian radiocarbon measurements obviously calls for some explanation. Because the measurements comprising the long scale pattern were made seven years after the ones comprising the short scale pattern, it seems most reasonable to seek an explanation in some improvement in laboratory technique.

Several colleagues have suggested to me that the differences in the measurements might be the result of a change in the chemical pretreatment to which the samples were subjected before measurement, and I have investigated this possibility. The most widely used chemical pretreatment is one which employs hydrochloric acid to remove carbonates which might have contaminated the sample with older carbon. In 1958 Olson and Broecker of the Lamont laboratory called attention to the possibility of humic acid contamination, which would introduce younger carbon. They suggested a method of pretreatment with sodium hydroxide to eliminate this type of contamination and stated in their report that the Lamont laboratory had been using the new pretreatment for about a year. Several other laboratories adopted the Lamont method of pretreatment or devised variations on it. There are some spectacular cases, notably those involving samples from the Abri Pataud in France and Cape Krusenstern in Alaska, which indicate that the sodium hydroxide pretreatment may, in some cases, result in much earlier measurements (Movius, 1963, pp. 134-135; Schultz and others, 1963, p. 342. The correct values of the Pennsylvania measurements cited by Schultz are P-400, 3678 $\pm$ 53, and P-404, 2829 $\pm$ 63). The sodium hydroxide pretreatment was introduced after the Peruvian short scale measurements were made, and its effect is potentially great enough to explain the difference between the long scale pattern and the short scale one. However, a check with the laboratory records shows that not a single one of the samples which gave the measurements comprising the long scale pattern was given a sodium hydroxide pretreatment. The pretreatment explanation must be eliminated.

The search for other possible explanations should be undertaken by someone who is more familiar than I with the techniques used in radiocarbon laboratories and who has a better background in chemistry and mathematics. The archaeologist has done his job if he can provide the evidence for deciding which measurements are consistent and which ones are not. As one who is, in a sense, an innocent victim of inconsistencies in the radiocarbon method as it is currently practiced, I might add that I am somewhat appalled by the lack of attention paid by most laboratories to the consequences of improvements in laboratory technique. We need less indiscriminate measurement of samples of unknown age and a great deal more research on the effects of various factors on measurement results.

There remains my archaeological problem, which is what estimates of absolute age to use in discussing Peruvian archaeology. On present evidence the only reasonable solution appears to be to accept only those measurements which are consistent with the long scale pattern and to be very cautious in accepting any synchronism based on radiocarbon evidence alone.

------------------

Acknowledgements. It is a pleasure to express my appreciation to the following persons and institutions for permission to use unpublished radiocarbon measurements on Peruvian samples: Dr. Adolfo Bermúdez Jenkins, the Museo Regional de Ica, Peru; Mr. Douglas Newton and Miss Julie Jones, the Museum of Primitive Art, New York. I am sincerely grateful to the following persons who provided information, criticism or advice at different stages in the writing of this paper: Junius B. Bird, Thomas C. Patterson, Edward P. Lanning, Patricia J. Lyon, Gary S. Vescelius, Alejandro Pezzia, Patrick H. Monaghan, Hallam L. Movius, Robert Stuckenrath, Jr., Rainer Berger, David Kleinecke, Frederick Johnson, John A. Graham, Robert F. Heizer, and Eugene A. Hammel. I hope I have profited from all the advice I have received, even though I have not always followed it.

Berkeley, California

May 23, 1965

# BIBLIOGRAPHY

Menzel, Dorothy

1963    Style and time in the Middle Horizon.  Ñawpa Pacha 2, pp. 1-105.
        Berkeley.


Movius, Hallam Leonard, Jr.

1963    L'age du Périgordien, de l'Aurignacien et du proto-Magdalénien
        en France sur la base des datations au Carbone 14.  Aurignac
        et l'Aurignacien; centenaire des fouilles d'Edouard Lartet.
        Bulletin de la Société Méridionale de Spéléologie et de Pré-
        histoire, tomes VI à IX, années 1956-1959, pp. 131-142.  Toulouse.


Olson, Edwin A., and Broecker, Wallace S.

1958    Sample contamination and reliability of radiocarbon dates.
        Transactions of the New York Academy of Sciences, series II,
        vol. 20, no. 7, May, pp. 593-604.  New York.


Schultz, Hyman, and others

1963    Pretreatment of wood and char samples (abstract).  Hyman
        Schultz, L. A. Currie, F. R. Matson, and W. W. Miller.
        Radiocarbon, vol. 5, p. 342.  New Haven.

# TABLE I

## PERUVIAN RADIOCARBON MEASUREMENTS:  SHORT SCALE PATTERN

### South coast burials

| Date | Sample | 5568 yr. half-life | List |
|------|--------|--------------------|------|
| EIP 8 | L-335F (1956) | 1200 ± 90 (AD 756) | IV |
| EIP 7 | Y-126 (1956) | 1320 ± 60 (AD 636) | III |
| EIP 5 | L-335E (1956) | 1430 ± 90 (AD 526) | IV |
| EIP 3 | L-335G (1956) | 1620 ± 100 (AD 336) | IV |
| EIP 1 | GrN-618 (1955) | 1765 ± 155 (AD 190) | II |
| EIP 1 | L-115 (CO$_2$) (1956) | 1750 ± 90 (AD 206) | III |
| EIP 1 | *L-311 (1956) | 2050 ± 100 (95 BC) | IV |
| EH 10 | L-335C (1956) | 1840 + 100 (AD 116) | IV |
| EH 9 | L-335D (1956) | 1940 ± 100 (AD 16) | IV |

### North coast burials

| Date | Sample | 5568 yr. half-life | List |
|------|--------|--------------------|------|
| EIP 7 | L-335A (1956) | 1300 ± 80 (AD 656) | IV |
| EIP 7 | L-335B (1956) | 1300 ± 80 (AD 656) | IV |

### Preceramic refuse with cotton

| Sample | 5568 yr. half-life | List |
|--------|--------------------|------|
| NZ-208 (1957) | 3270 ± 100 (1314 BC) | 4 |
| **NZ-209 (1957) | 3740 ± 100 (1784 BC) | 4 |
| **NZ-210 (1957) | 3800 ± 100 (1844 BC) | 4 |
| NZ-212 (1957) | 3800 ± 80 (1844 BC) | 4 |

---

* Measurement does not fit the pattern.

** NZ-209 and NZ-210 are too close together; both cannot be right.

## TABLE 2

### PERUVIAN RADIOCARBON MEASUREMENTS:  LONG SCALE PATTERN

### South coast measurements made 1962-64

| Date | Sample | 5568 yr. half-life | 5730 yr. half-life |
|------|--------|--------------------|--------------------|
| MH 4 | P-512 (1962) | 1058 ± 52 (AD 892) | 1090 ± 52 (AD 860) |
| MH 3 | O-1664 (1962) | 1150 ± 105 (AD 800) | 1184 ± 105 (AD 766) |
| MH 2 | I-1041-43 (1963) | 1227 ± 69 (AD 723) | 1264 ± 69 (AD 686) |
| MH 1 | P-511 (1962) | 1345 ± 118 (AD 605) | 1385 ± 118 (AD 565) |
| EIP 4 | P-513 (1962) | 1986 ± 62 (19 BC) | 2027 ± 62 (78 BC) |
| EIP 3 | **P-515 (1962) | 2014 ± 62 (65 BC) | 2074 ± 62 (125 BC) |
| EIP 3 | **O-1689 (1962) | 2125 ± 110 (176 BC) | 2189 ± 110 (240 BC) |
| EH 9 | O-1692 (1962) | 2400 ± 110 (451 BC) | 2472 ± 110 (523 BC) |
| EH 3 | *P-516 (1962) | 2408 ± 214 (459 BC) | 2480 ± 214 (531 BC) |
| late IP | *GX-0187 (1964) | 3745 ± 165 (1796 BC) | 3857 ± 165 (1908 BC) |
| early IP | GX-0185-86 (1964) | 3854 ± 61 (1905 BC) | 3970 ± 61 (2021 BC) |
| early IP | *UCLA-153 (1962) | 2960 ± 90 (1011 BC) | 3049 ± 90 (1100 BC) |

---

* Measurements do not fit the pattern.

** P-515 and O-1689 are from the same mummy.

Pennsylvania measurements are from Pennsylvania VI (Radiocarbon, vol. 5, 1963, pp. 97-99); the UCLA measurement is from UCLA II (Radiocarbon, vol. 5, 1963, p. 16).  The rest are unpublished (see Appendix).

TABLE 3

## THE ARCHAEOLOGICAL CONTRAST

Estimated beginning dates for the periods of the Peruvian relative chronology based on the short scale and long scale patterns respectively. In each case the first figure given is the estimated date based on the Libby half-life value of 5568 years; the equivalent based on the Cambridge or 5730 year half-life value is added in parentheses. The beginning of the Late Horizon is dated historically at 1476, a figure which is unlikely to be more than 10 years in error.

|  | short scale | long scale |
|---|---|---|
| LIP | AD 1100 $\pm$ 20 (1075) | AD 930 $\pm$ 20 (900) |
| MH | AD 800 $\pm$ 20 (775) | AD 580 $\pm$ 20 (540) |
| EIP | AD 150 $\pm$ 20 (95) | 300-350 BC (370-420) |
| EH | 600-800 BC (675-880) | 1200-1400 BC (1300-1500) |
| IP | 1200-1450 BC (1295-1550) | 1930-2000 BC (2050-2120) |

The Cambridge half-life values for the long scale estimates constitute the best chronology now available for Peruvian archaeology.

# APPENDIX

## Radiocarbon measurements with precise associations from the

## south coast of Peru, made since 1962

The date in parentheses following a laboratory number is the date the measurement was made. Age measurements are given in radiocarbon years on the basis of the Libby half-life value of 5568 ± 30 years, followed by a notation in parentheses of the median age converted to the Cambridge half-life value of 5730 ± 40 years (conversion factor 1.03). The standard deviation is the same. The Cambridge half-life value is regarded as the best value now obtainable. The following measurements are unpublished: GX-0185, GX-0186, GX-0187; I-1041, I-1042, I-1043; O-1664, O-1689, O-1692. Sample descriptions of published measurements have been revised and expanded. Comments are provided only for inconsistent measurements (GX-0187, P-516, UCLA-153).

GX-0185 (1964)    Erizo, Callango, Ica    3890 ± 90 (4007)

1941 B.C. (2058)

Charcoal fragments probably representing cooking fires from undisturbed refuse in the Erizo site (PV62-191) in the desert bordering the Hacienda Callango, Ica, Peru (14° 26' 45" S. Lat., 75° 39' 40" W. Long.). The site has been subjected to severe wind erosion. Sample was collected from a depth between 5 and 30 cm. in a roughly circular depression some 2 m. in diameter where uneroded refuse was preserved. The refuse contained Hacha style pottery, the earliest pottery reported from the south coast of Peru, together with textile fragments and abundant vegetable remains. Squash, beans, peanuts, capsicum, guava, gourds, and cotton were present, but no maize was found. Relative date, early Initial Period. Collected August, 1963, by J. H. Rowe and P. J. Lyon. Submitted by J. H. Rowe, University of California, Berkeley.

"The charcoal was examined for impurities and treated with hot dilute HC1 to remove carbonates and other soluble matter prior to analysis." The uncertainty quoted is one standard deviation judged by the analytical data alone.

GX-0186 (1964)    Erizo, Callango, Ica    3820 ± 85 (3935)

1871 B.C. (1986)

Another portion of the same sample measured as GX-0185.

Average of GX-0185 and GX-0186    3854 ± 61 (3970)

1905 B.C. (2021)

GX-0187 (1964)     Mastodonte, Villacurí, Ica     3745 ± 165 (3857)

                                                1796 B.C.   (1908)

Charcoal fragments probably representing cooking fires from undisturbed refuse in the Mastodonte site (PV59-23), near the edge of the Pampa de Villacurí, west of Ica, and near Km. 267 on the Panamerican Highway south of Lima (about 13° 15' S. Lat. 76° 1' W. Long.).  The sample was collected at a depth of 5 to 30 cm. in an area not over 2 m. across.  The refuse contained vegetable remains, including maize, and pottery of a style believed to date to the latter part of the Initial Period or the beginning of the Early Horizon.  Collected August, 1962, by J. H. Rowe and T. C. Patterson.  Submitted by J. H. Rowe, University of California, Berkeley.

"The charcoal was examined for impurities and treated with hot dilute HCl to remove carbonates and other soluble matter prior to analysis. Carbonates were abundant."

Comment (J.H.R.):  Measurement is 200 to 400 years too old with relation to GX-0185 and GX-0186.  The most reasonable explanation of the discrepancy is that the acid pretreatment failed to remove all the carbonates carrying older carbon which were present in the sample.

I-1041 (1963)     Blue and yellow feather hanging     1305 ± 120 (1344)

                                                A.D. 645    (606)

Section of vicuña wool band from a feather hanging (Museum of Primitive Art, N. Y., no. 59.194).  The specimen is believed to have formed part of a cache or offering deposit of some 96 nearly identical feather hangings found in 1942 at the site of Corral Redondo, on the Hacienda Hispana, near La Victoria, in the valley of the Churunga River, an upstream affluent of the Ocoña River (15° 56' S. Lat., 73° 8' W. Long.).  The hangings were rolled up and buried in large face-neck jars of a style dating to Middle Horizon 2 (see Menzel, 1964, p. 86, note 196).  If the specimen dated is not from the Corral Redondo deposit, it must nevertheless be of nearly the same age, because it is closely similar in construction and dimensions to fully documented pieces from this lot.  Submitted by the Museum of Primitive Art, New York.

The only pretreatment was a thorough rinse in distilled water.

I-1042 (1963)     Blue and yellow feather hanging     1165 ± 120 (1200)

                                                A.D. 785    (750)

Section of vicuña wool band from a feather hanging (Museum of Primitive Art, N. Y., 59.193).  Same data as for I-1041.

I-1043 (1963)     Blue and yellow feather hanging     1212 ± 120 (1248)

                                                A.D. 738    (702)

Section of cotton base fabric from a feather hanging (Museum of Primitive Art, N. Y., 58.85). Same data as for I-1041.

Average of I-1041, I-1042, and I-1043          1227 ± 69 (1264)

                                                A.D. 723  (686)


O-1664 (1962)    Montegrande, Nasca            1150 ± 105 (1184)

                                                A.D. 800  (766)


Loose cotton from a mummy bundle found in 1960 in a tomb containing 24 mummies on the Hacienda Montegrande, lower Nasca drainage (14° 57' S. Lat. 75° 25' W. Long.). The pottery associated with the mummies in this tomb is all of the Soisongo style, dating to Middle Horizon 3 (see Menzel, 1964, p. 63 and note 385). Submitted by Adolfo Bermúdez Jenkins, Museo Regional de Ica.

The sample was "treated with hydrochloric acid only ... then rinsed with distilled water until all the acid was removed, dried, and burned. We do not believe that such pretreatment alters the ages determined on samples" (letter from Patrick H. Monaghan, Geochemistry and Basin Geology Division, Esso Production Research Company, Houston, Texas, May 17, 1965).

O-1689 (1962)    Cerro Max Uhle, Ocucaje, Ica   2125 ± 110 (2189)

                                                176 B.C.   (240)


Carbonized cotton cloth from a mummy from a burial in a cemetery on the west side of Cerro Max Uhle, Hacienda Ocucaje, Ica (14° 22' 15" S. Lat., 75° 41' W. Long.), excavated by Alejandro Pezzia, Duncan M. Masson, and Gerd Glaessner for the Museo Regional de Ica on June 28, 1957. The associated pottery corresponds to the early Nasca 3 style, dating to Early Intermediate Period 3. Submitted by Adolfo Bermúdez Jenkins, Museo Regional de Ica. Same pretreatment as O-1664.

O-1692 (1962)    Cerro Max Uhle, Ocucaje, Ica   2400 ± 110 (2472)

                                                451 B.C.   (523)


Loose cotton from the stuffing of a mask from a mummy from Tomb 6 in a cemetery on the west side of Cerro Max Uhle, Hacienda Ocucaje, Ica (14° 22' 15" S. Lat., 75° 41' W. Long.), excavated in 1953 by personnel of the Museo Regional de Ica. The associated pottery corresponds to the Ocucaje 9 style, dating to Early Horizon 9. Submitted by Adolfo Bermúdez Jenkins, Museo Regional de Ica. Same pretreatment as O-1664.

Measurements O-1664, O-1689, and O-1692 courtesy of the Exploration Department and the Geochemical Laboratory, Humble Oil & Refining Company, Houston, Texas.

P-511 (1962)     Cahuachi, Nasca                    1345 ± 118 (1385)

                                                     A.D. 605    (565)


     Cotton cloth from a mummy from Tomb 2 in the López cemetery at
Cahuachi, Nasca (14° 50' S. Lat., 75° 7' W. Long.), excavated by personnel
of the Museo Regional de Ica in 1952 in collaboration with W. D. Strong of
Columbia University.  The associated pottery belongs to the Nasca 9 style,
dating to Middle Horizon 1 (see Menzel, 1964, p. 25, note 116, and figs.
14-16).  Submitted for the Museo Regional de Ica by Dwight T. Wallace,
University of Oregon.  Reported in Pennsylvania VI, Radiocarbon 5, 1963,
p. 99.

     "Pretreated with HCl."

P-512 (1962)     Ulluhaya, Callango, Ica            1058 X 52 (1090)

                                                     A.D. 892   (860)


     Loose cotton and cotton cloth from the interior of a cylindrical
mummy bale from a tomb in the Ulluhaya section of the Hacienda Callango,
Ica (14° 36' S. Lat., 75° 37' W. Long.), found in 1956 by Frédéric Engel
and given by him to the Museo Regional de Ica.  The associated pottery
corresponds to the Ica Epigonal style, dating to Middle Horizon 4.  Submitted for the Museo Regional de Ica by Dwight T. Wallace, University of
Oregon.  Reported in Pennsylvania VI, Radiocarbon 5, 1963, pp. 97-98.

     "Pretreated with HCl."

P-513 (1962)     Cahuachi, Nasca                    1968 ± 62 (2027)

                                                     19 B.C.    (78)


     Piece of a woolen mantle from Tomb 3 in the López cemetery at Cahuachi,
Nasca (14° 50' S. Lat., 75° 7' W. Long.), excavated by personnel of the
Museo Regional de Ica in 1952 in collaboration with W. D. Strong of
Columbia University.  The associated pottery corresponds to the Nasca 4
style, dating to Early Intermediate Period 4.  Submitted for the Museo
Regional de Ica by Dwight T. Wallace, University of Oregon.  Reported in
Pennsylvania VI, Radiocarbon 5, 1963, p. 98.

     "Pretreated with HCl."

P-515 (1962)     Cerro Max Uhle, Ocucaje, Ica       2014 ± 62 (2074)

                                                     65 B.C.    (125)


     Loose cotton and carbonized cotton cloth from the same mummy as O-1689.
Submitted for the Museo Regional de Ica by Dwight T. Wallace, University of
Oregon.  Reported in Pennsylvania VI, Radiocarbon 5, 1963, p. 97.

P-516 (1962)      Cerrillos, Ica                    2408 ± 214 (2480)

                                                   459 B.C.   (531)


     Vegetable remains from refuse in Cut 2, Pit C, Level 3, at the site of
Cerrillos (PV62-63), Ica (13° 58' 15" S. Lat., 75° 41' 50" W. Long.),
excavated in 1958 by Dwight T. Wallace under the auspices of the University
of San Marcos and the U.S. Educational Commission in Peru. The associated
pottery corresponds to the Ocucaje 3 style, dating to Early Horizon 3.
Submitted by Dwight T. Wallace, University of Oregon. Reported in Pennsylvania VI, Radiocarbon 5, 1963, p. 98.


     "Pretreated with HCl."


     Comment (J.H.R.):  Measurement is 400 to 600 years too young to fit
the pattern of other measurements made since 1962 but corresponds reasonably well to the scale of measurements made between 1955 and 1957 (short
scale).


UCLA-153 (1962)      Hacha, Acarí                    2960 ± 90 (3049)

                                                   1011 B.C. (1100)


     Charcoal fragments, probably representing cooking fires, from refuse
at the Hacha site (PV74-6) in the desert behind the Hacienda Cerro Colorado,
Acarí (15° 28' 15" S. Lat., 74° 37' 10" W. Long.). The refuse deposit
contains shells, vegetable remains including squash, beans, peanuts, guava,
capsicum, gourds, and cotton, but no maize. The sample was collected in
1959 by Gary S. Vescelius, Hernán Amat Olizábal, and Dorothy Menzel. The
associated pottery belongs to the Hacha style, the earliest style of
pottery on the south coast, dating to early in the Initial Period. Submitted by J. H. Rowe, University of California, Berkeley. Reported in
UCLA II, Radiocarbon 5, 1963, p. 16.


     Comment (J.H.R.):  This sample should be roughly contemporary with
the samples from Erizo, Ica, which have a radiocarbon age of 3854 ± 61
(average of GX-0185 and GX-0186, 5568 year half-life). The result obtained is 800 to 1000 years too young to fit the pattern of post-1962
measurements and 200 to 400 years too young to fit the pattern of the
measurements made between 1955 and 1957.


                         ----------------


     The associations of the following measurements are not sufficiently
precise for the purposes of the present review:  I-1346, I-1347, P-517,
P-518, UCLA-154.

# EARLY CULTURAL REMAINS ON THE CENTRAL COAST OF PERU[1]

## Thomas C. Patterson

On the basis of investigations carried out during the early months of 1963, Patterson and Lanning reported the occurrence of three early cultural assemblages in the lower part of the Chillón Valley on the central Peruvian coast.[2] These were the Chivateros I and II assemblages, found in a stratified quarry-workshop site on Cerro Chivateros, and the Oquendo complex which was found isolated at another site located about three kilometers away. The chronological relationship of the Chivateros I and II assemblages was immediately clear from the stratigraphy at the site. Artifacts of the Chivateros I assemblage were found in a zone of gray eolian sand with a salitre formation in the upper 2-5 cm of it; immediately overlying this zone of the soil profile was a later zone of fine-grained, gray-brown eolian sand that contained Chivateros II implements. Similarities between some of the more common artifacts in the two assemblages, as well as the nature of the soil profile itself, suggested that the Chivateros I and II complexes were fairly close to one another in age. The problem still remained, however, of relating the Oquendo complex which not only occurred in another locality but also contained artifacts that were quite different from those of either assemblage found at the site on Cerro Chivateros. After three years of examining the data collected at Oquendo, it was still impossible to say with any degree of certainty whether the Oquendo assemblage preceded Chivateros I in time or was later than Chivateros II. Since equally unconvincing arguments could be made to support both placements in time for the Oquendo complex, we decided that the only way this question might be answered would be by new excavations at the Oquendo and Chivateros sites. These excavations were made by members of the Seventh Peabody Museum, Harvard University, Archaeological Expedition to Peru in August, 1966 under the auspices and at the direction of the Museo Nacional de Antropología y Arqueología. What I propose to do in this paper is report the preliminary results of this investigation.

A small excavation with a maximum depth of 80 cm was made in the upper part of the Oquendo site. This excavation revealed two distinct zones in the soil profile. The upper zone consisted of a layer of fine-grained eolian sand with an average depth of 45 cm below the present surface and contained large quantities of Oquendo artifacts and chipping debris and a few fragments of salt water mussels tentatively identified as Mytilus magellanicus and M. chorus. Immediately underlying this layer was a thick zone of eolian sand that contained fragments of foliating quartzite and an unidentified metamorphic rock and lacked artifacts, chipping debris, and shell fragments; this zone, which had a more granular texture and appearance than the later zone of the soil profile, was sealed off by a 2-3 cm thick salitre layer that formed along its upper edge.

The artifacts and chipping waste of the Oquendo assemblage are made of a distinctive, fine-grained quartzite that is grayish-

Reprinted from ÑAWPA PACHA 4, 1966. pp. 145-153.

green in color and outcrops in the area of the site. The basic chipping technique was direct percussion flaking with small river or beach cobble hammerstones. The cores in this assemblage have unprepared striking platforms and multiple flakes, flake-blades, and blades removed by blows directed usually at one flat surface of a tabular fragment; these cores resemble the pyramidal cores found in other lithic assemblages in the New World. The majority of the cores was discarded when a sufficient number of flakes had been removed from them, although a few were apparently made into keeled scrapers, by removing small chips with blows directed at the original striking platform, or into core burins. The flakes removed from the pyramidal cores of the Oquendo assemblage typically have a small part of the original striking platform at their proximal ends near the bulb of percussion.

Most implements in the Oquendo assemblage have unifacial chipping along one or more edges of a flake or flake-blade. The most common implements in the Oquendo assemblage are burins; these include simple burins made by removing a spall along the longitudinal axis of a flake from a flat edge so that the resulting angle is slightly less than 90°, burins on a notch, which were made by making a concave area on one edge and removing a spall along the longitudinal axis from one or both sides of the notch, burins on a notch, in which the spall was removed from a scraper edge on the longitudinal axis of the flake, and right angle burins which were made by removing spalls at approximately 90° angles to each other. Many pieces in the Oquendo assemblage have more than one burin on them or consist of burins combined with another kind of tool; for example, one flake has three simple burins and a scraper edge and another has a simple burin on one edge and a denticulate on the other.

Other implements that occur in the Oquendo sample include asymmetrical denticulate tools which were made by removing flakes and chips along an edge with blows directed on one surface, keeled denticulate tools which have triangular to diamond-shaped cross-sections and unifacial chipping on the widest surface, pointed tools which are made at the intersection of two edges by removing small chips from both edges in order to emphasize the point, side scrapers made by unifacial chipping along a straight or convex-curved edge, notched tools which are made on a latitudinal edge of a flake, and steep-nosed end scrapers.

Two small test excavations were made in the vicinity of the short trench excavated in 1963 at Cerro Chivateros. The first excavation was adjacent to the deepest square of the 1963 trench and revealed four major zones in the soil profile that were separated from each other by salitre formations along the upper edges of the second and fourth zones and by the different consistency of the third zone. The most recent zone of the soil profile was composed of a fine-grained, gray-brown eolian sand that varied in depth from 6 to 15 cm below the present surface and contained large quantities of Chivateros II artifacts and chipping debris made from green to blue-gray quartzite. The second zone, which is a slightly compacted gray eolian sand varying in depth from 8 to 18 cm, is capped by a 2-6 cm thick salitre and contained quartzite artifacts and chipping

debris of the Chivateros I assemblage. The third zone was composed of
a compacted gray eolian sand with a maximum depth of 15 cm and contained quartzite artifacts and chipping debris. The earliest zone in
the deposit is a highly compacted reddish-brown eolian sand with a
maximum depth of 40 cm which is capped by a 1-2 cm thick salitre layer
and immediately overlies a zone of quartzite foliating from the bed-
rock; interspersed through this zone are quartzite implements and
chipping debris that have heavily stained or patinated surfaces varying in color from nearly yellow through tan to a grayish-brown.

The second excavation was made on the northeast corner of the
1963 trench, about five meters uphill from the first one. It revealed
three of the four soil zones encountered in the first test excavation.
The most recent zone in the soil profile of the second excavation
was a gray-brown eolian sand with a maximum depth of 8 cm which contained rootlets, traces of Tillandsia sp., and Chivateros II artifacts
and chipping debris. The second zone was an uncompacted gray-brown
eolian sand with a maximum depth of 22 cm, the upper 10 cm of which
was a salitre formation; this zone corresponds to the second major
zone encountered in the first excavation and contained Chivateros I
artifacts and chipping debris. The lowest zone, which varied between
17 and 25 cm in thickness, was composed of a compacted brown eolian
sand and contained artifacts and chipping debris that were similar
to those of the lowest zone in the first excavation.

Two main conclusions can be drawn from the two test excavations made at Cerro Chivateros. One is that the soil profile found
in the deep square adjacent to the first excavation was atypical of
the site as a whole in that the third soil zone was found immediately
overlying a quartzite outcrop, and the fourth, or red, zone was
absent. As a result of this misfortune of sampling, the remainder
of the 1963 trench was excavated only to the top of the red soil
zone. The second major conclusion is that the assemblage found in
the red zone is not only different from the Chivateros I complex,
which was defined on the basis of materials from the second and
third soil zones, but also stratigraphically earlier than the
Chivateros assemblages.

All the chipped stone at Chivateros is fine-grained quartzite
which outcrops in the quarry-workshop area. The outcrops are composed of tabular pieces with quadrangular cross-sections and flat
faces resulting from the natural fracture pattern of the stone.
Unworked pieces with triangular, pentagonal, or hexagonal cross-
sections and flat faces also occur as a result of secondary fracture or shearing. The angle of natural fracture on the unworked
material is between 35° and 55°.

The basic chipping technique used during the period when the
lowest, or red, zone of the soil profile formed was direct percussion with beach or river cobble hammerstones. The cores have
unprepared striking platforms and multiple flakes removed from one
face of a tabular fragment by blows directed at approximately the
same striking angle to the surface; occasionally, however, flakes
were removed from more than one surface. When a sufficient number

of flakes were removed, most of the cores were apparently discarded, though a few were made into implements by percussion chipping along the edge of a previous flake scar. The cores in this assemblage resemble the so-called polyhedral cores that have been reported in other early lithic assemblages in the New World. The flakes removed from the cores are quite variable in length, width, and thickness; many are short and thick with triangular or trapezoidal cross-sections while a few are long, thin triangular blades that were probably burin spalls.

Most implements in the red zone are made on flakes struck from cores or on small, naturally fractured pieces of quartzite which resemble flakes and occur in the vicinity of the outcrops. The tools in this assemblage were made by direct percussion chipping along one or more edges of the flake or tabular fragment, and nearly all the chips were removed by blows delivered at approximately the same angle to a single striking surface. Among the implements occurring in the Chivateros Red Zone assemblage are simple and right angle burins which are similar to those of the Oquendo complex, notched tools which were made by removing a series of uniform chips on either side of three or four small flakes on the longitudinal edge of a fragment, pointed tools which are made in the same way as those in the Oquendo assemblage, double pointed tools which are made on either end of a steeply chipped notch, unifacially chipped side scrapers made on straight or convex-curved edges, and steep-nosed end scrapers made with unifacial chipping on the latitudinal end of a fragment.

An innovation in chipping techniques occurred during the period when the third, or earliest gray, zone of the soil profile was formed, and the method persisted as the predominant one through-out the time represented by the three later soil zones in the deposit. The basic chipping technique was still direct percussion flaking with cobble hammerstones that were apparently larger on the average than those occurring in either the Oquendo or Chivateros Red Zone assemblages. Flakes were removed bifacially from tabular fragments and large flakes in order to make the cores into implements; this kind of chipping contrasts markedly with the techniques used in the Chivateros Red Zone and Oquendo assemblages, which produced flakes that were then made into tools. In the Chivateros I and II assemblages, flakes were struck from both prepared and unprepared striking platforms and typically have small areas of the platform at their proximal ends near the bulbs of percussion. Flakes of all sizes are much more common in the chipping debris than in the earlier red soil zone; the flakes range from a few to more than 25 cm in length, and pieces with lengths of 10-15 cm are quite common.

Among the objects occurring in the third soil zone are keeled bifaces made on tabular fragments of quartzite, large denticulates which were made by bifacially flaking the edge of a tabular fragment, large side and end scrapers made on tabular frag-ments and large flakes by removing flakes from one surface, small notched tools with unifacially chipped notches on either a longi-tudinal or latitudinal edge of a tabular fragment, pointed tools made on small flakes, and a number of long thin triangular blades that may possibly be burin spalls.

The collection from the part of the second soil zone below the salitre formation was fairly small and included large flakes with prepared and unprepared striking platforms, large side scrapers with unifacial chipping on straight or convex-curved longitudinal edges of tabular fragments and flakes, notched tools with unifacially chipped notches on the latitudinal edges of tabular fragments and flakes, pointed tools made at the intersection of two edges of a tabular fragment, steep-nosed end scrapers, and a keeled denticulate similar to those of the Oquendo complex.

The salitre formation in the upper part of the second soil zone yielded bifaces with both keeled and lenticular cross-sections that were made on tabular fragments and large flakes, large denticulates with both unifacial and bifacial chipping along the edges of tabular fragments and large flakes, large scrapers with unifacial chipping along the longitudinal edges of tabular fragments or flakes, notched tools with unifacially chipped notches on both the longitudinal and latitudinal edges of tabular fragments, a keeled denticulate, and a bifacially chipped "thrusting spear" point.

The most recent zone of the soil profile contained a bifacially chipped "thrusting spear" point, a keeled denticulate with unifacial chipping, two fragments of small points with diamond-shaped cross-sections, unifacially chipped denticulates made on flakes and tabular fragments, notched tools with unifacially chipped notches on the longitudinal edges of tabular fragments, and unifacially chipped scrapers on the longitudinal edges of tabular pieces.

The discovery of the Red Zone assemblage at Cerro Chivateros sheds new light on the problem of placing the Oquendo complex in the local cultural sequence.[3] It is now possible to make a plausible seriational argument that the Oquendo assemblage is intermediate in age between the Chivateros Red Zone and Chivateros I units, because it shares features with both complexes. The Chivateros Red Zone and Oquendo assemblages share several varieties of burins that are apparently absent from the two later complexes at Cerro Chivateros. On the other hand, the Oquendo and Chivateros I and II assemblages share a number of specific tool types--such as denticulates, keeled denticulates, and implements with notches on their latitudinal edges--which are absent from the Red Zone complex at Cerro Chivateros. An impressionistic examination of the four assemblages suggests that the Oquendo and Chivateros Red Zone artifacts are similar to each other in that they have chunky appearances, and that the chipping wastes of the Oquendo and Chivateros I and II complexes are more similar in that they contain high proportions of flakes with small areas of striking platform at their proximal ends.

The seriational argument for the placement of the Oquendo complex between the Chivateros Red Zone and Chivateros I assemblages is also supported to some extent by additional data obtained in the Lurín Valley by members of the Peabody Museum, Harvard University Expedition in August, 1965. Three distinctive, early cultural assemblages have been found in the lower part of the Lurín drainage. One of these, the Cerro Tortuga complex, shares tool types and chipping techniques with both the Chivateros Red Zone and Oquendo complexes. The second complex, which is called Cerro Achona, shares tool types and chipping techniques with both Oquendo and the later Chivateros assemblages, though its artifacts are made from a poor quality quartzite. The Conchitas assemblage shares tool types and its chipping technique with the Chivateros I and II complexes, though the artifacts are again made from a quartzite that does not chip very well.

During the 1963 excavation at Cerro Chivateros, a small, un-worked and uncharred piece of wood and a number of distinctive Chivateros I artifacts were found in the salitre formation at the top of the second soil zone. The wood fragment, which was submitted to the Institute of Geophysics of the University of California at Los Angeles, yielded a measurement of 10,430 ± 160 radiocarbon years (UCLA-683) before A.D. 1950 and dates the later part or end of the period when Chivateros I artifacts were made.[4]

Data collected from the soil profiles at Cerro Chivateros and Oquendo indicate that the Oquendo and Chivateros II assemblages were incorporated entirely into eolian deposits, and that the Chivateros Red Zone and Chivateros I complexes were incorporated into eolian deposits covered with salitre formations. The cultural sequence pre-sented in this paper suggests that the upper soil zone at Oquendo is slightly later than the fourth zone at Chivateros and earlier than the third zone; if this is the case, then there was an interval at Cerro Chivateros when soil formation was either lacking or occurred at a slow rate. Such a situation might easily be produced by slight changes in the prevailing wind directions.

If the salitre formations at the tops of the second and fourth soil zones at Cerro Chivateros and on the upper edge of the second zone at Oquendo correspond to slightly wetter phases on the Peruvian coast that are contemporary with periods of glacial advance at higher elevations and latitudes,[5] then it is possible to make some estimates of the ages of the Chivateros Red Zone and Oquendo assemblages. The radiocarbon measurement obtained from the wood incorporated into the salitre at the top of the second soil zone at Chivateros suggests that the formation may be contemporary with the Valders Readvance and Younger Dryas in the northern hemisphere and that the eolian deposit underlying the salitre was formed during a slightly warmer, drier interval that corresponds to the Two Creeks Interstadial and the Allerod Oscillation. The salitre layer covering the fourth soil zone at Chivateros would represent a wet phase cor-responding to the Port Huron or Older Dryas glacial advance in the northern hemisphere. If this is the case, then the Chivateros Red Zone assemblage would have an age of slightly more than 12,000 radiocarbon years, and the Oquendo complex would date between 11,000 and 12,000 radiocarbon years.

## NOTES

[1]This paper is a by-product of research that was carried out by the Seventh Peabody Museum, Harvard University Archaeological Expedition to Peru and was financed by Grant GS-1111 from the National Science Foundation. The paper has profited considerably from the comments of Edward P. Lanning, Lucille G. Lewis, Richard S. MacNeish, Elizabeth O. Patterson, John H. Rowe, and Alan J. Westcott. I also wish to acknowledge the assistance that I have received from Jorge C. Muelle, Hermilio Rosas, Elizabeth Holtzman, and Edward M. Franquemont.

[2]Patterson and Lanning 1964, p. 113

[3]Patterson and Lanning 1964, p. 113; Lanning 1963 and 1965.

[4]Two counts were made on this sample; one yielded an age of 10,420 + 160 radiocarbon years and the other an age of 10,440 + 160 years. The average of the two counts was published by Berger, Fergusson, and Libby 1965, p. 347. The radiocarbon ages cited are based on the Libby or 5568 + 30 yr. halflife.

[5]Patterson and Lanning ms.

## BIBLIOGRAPHY

Berger, Rainer, Fergusson, Gordon J., and Libby, Willard Frank
    1965    UCLA radiocarbon dates IV. Radiocarbon, vol. 7, pp. 336-371. New Haven.

Lanning, Edward Putnam
    1963    A pre-agricultural occupation on the central coast of Peru. American Antiquity, vol. 28, no. 3, January, pp. 360-371. Salt Lake City.

    1965    Early man in Peru. Scientific American, vol. 213, no. 4, October, pp. 68-76. New York.

Patterson, Thomas Carl and Lanning, Edward Putnam
    1964    Changing settlement patterns on the central Peruvian coast. Ñawpa Pacha 2, pp. 113-123. Berkeley.

    ms.    Late glacial and post-glacial environments in South America. typescript, 24 pp.

## KEY TO ILLUSTRATIONS

Figs. 1-9. All specimens from the lowest soil zones in the two excavations at Cerro Chivateros.
    1. Two double pointed tools.
    2. Three pointed tools, all made on thin tabular fragments.

3.  Two steep-nosed end scrapers with unifacial chipping on the latitudinal ends.
4.  Two notched tools with triangular cross-sections.
5.  Simple burin made by removing a blade along the longitudinal axis of the fragment.
6.  Three spalls.
7.  Two polyhedral cores with percussion chipping along the edges of previous flake scars.
8.  Two unifacially chipped scrapers with curved edges.
9.  Unifacially chipped side scraper.

Figs. 10-15.  All specimens from the third soil zone of the first excavation at Cerro Chivateros.
10. Keeled biface made from a tabular fragment.
11. Denticulate with bifacial chipping along the edges of a tabular fragment.
12. Unifacially chipped side scraper made on a tabular fragment with a triangular cross-section.
13. Three spalls.
14. Two notched tools made by unifacial chipping on the edges of tabular fragments.
15. Pointed tool made on a flake.

Figs. 16-21.  All specimens from the part of the second soil zone below the salitre cap in the first excavation at Cerro Chivateros.
16. Two tabular fragments with notches on their latitudinal ends.
17. Notched tool made on a tabular fragment with a triangular cross-section.
18. Two spalls.
19. Two tabular fragments with scraper edges on their latitudinal ends.
20. Two scrapers with curved edges.
21. Keeled denticulate.

Figs. 22-26.  All specimens from the salitre cap of the second soil zone in the first excavation at Cerro Chivateros.
22. Fragment of a biface with a lenticular cross-section.
23. Fragment of a "thrusting" spear point.
24. Keeled denticulate.
25. Scraper with unifacial chipping on the longitudinal axis of a tabular fragment with a triangular cross-section.
26. Unifacially chipped notch on the latitudinal end of a tabular fragment.

Figs. 27-33.  All specimens from the most recent soil zone in the first excavation at Cerro Chivateros.
27. Small biface with a lenticular cross-section.
28. Fragment of a "thrusting" spear point.
29. Two fragments of small points with diamond-shaped cross-sections.
30. Keeled denticulate.

31. Two notched tools on the longitudinal edges of tabular fragments.

32. Unifacially chipped denticulate made on the longitudinal edge of a tabular fragment.

Figs. 34-41. All specimens from the upper soil zone at Oquendo.

34. Pyramidal core.

35. Three fragments of keeled denticulates.

36. Large flake with unifacially chipped scraper edges.

37. Unifacially chipped denticulate made on a tabular fragment with a triangular cross-section.

38. Burin core with a simple burin.

39. Burin made on a notch.

40. Spall.

41. Double pointed tool combined with a notched tool.

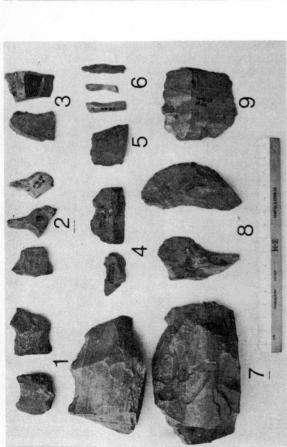

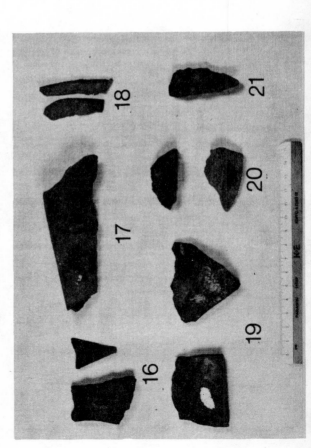

Plate XIX. Specimens from the lowest soil zones in the two excavations at Cerro Chivateros (figs. 1-9); specimens from the third soil zone of the first excavation at Cerro Chivateros (figs. 10-15); specimens from the part of the second soil zone below the salitre cap in the first excavation at Cerro Chivateros (figs. 16-21).

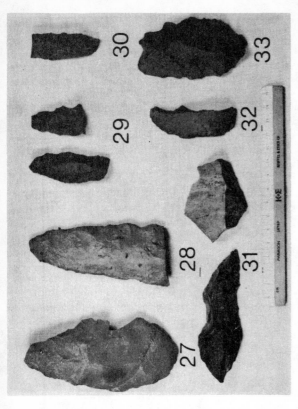

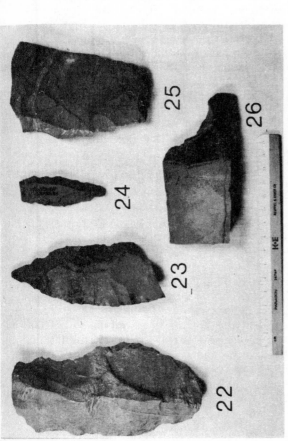

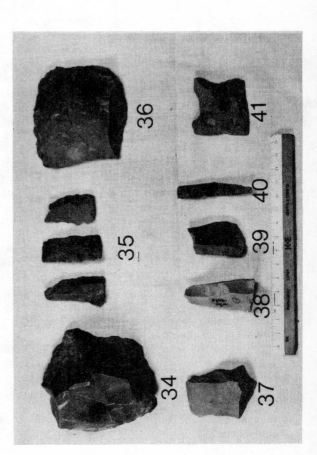

Plate XX. Specimens from the salitre cap of the second soil zone in the first excavation at Cerro Chivateros (figs. 22-26); specimens from the most recent soil zone in the first excavation at Cerro Chivateros (figs. 27-33); specimens from the upper soil zone at Oquendo (figs. 34-41).

# A PRE-AGRICULTURAL OCCUPATION ON THE CENTRAL COAST OF PERU

Edward P. Lanning

### ABSTRACT

More than 50 campsites, quarries, and workshop sites belonging to the pre-agricultural stage have been explored at Ancón on the central coast of Peru. The sites are located in areas of extinct fog vegetation, which was exploited not only for its seeds and roots, but also for grazing animals. The sites are winter camps. Six different lithic industries have been identified and seriated in a tentative sequence which may reach back to the Pleistocene. The earliest industry almost entirely lacks projectile points and other fine stone work. The next two industries are characterized by their stemmed projectile points and distinctive scrapers, while the three latest assemblages have stemless points and lack scrapers. The pre-agricultural stage came to an end around 2500 or 2000 B.C. with the establishment of permanent villages near the shore as a result of the retreat of the fog vegetation and the enrichment of the sea.

THE EXISTENCE of a pre-agricultural stage in the human occupation of Peru was until recently a hypothesis based on essentially undated finds on the Pampa de los Fósiles on the North Coast and in rockshelters near Huancayo in the Central Highlands. In 1958, excavations by Rosa Fung de Lanning showed that the Huancayo lithic industry was contemporary not only with agriculture but with ceramics as well (Fung de Lanning 1959). In the same year, Augusto Cardich's excavations at Lauricocha established the existence of a pre-agricultural hunting culture in the Central Highlands and indirectly supported the supposed antiquity of the Pampa de los Fósiles workshops (Cardich 1958; Lanning and Hammel 1961: 148).

Since August of 1961 the author has been engaged in an archaeological survey of the Ancón area on the central coast of Peru. The work has been sponsored by the Fulbright Commission and the Universidad Nacional Mayor de San Marcos. The principal result of the survey has been the recording and exploration of over 50 campsites, quarries, and workshop sites attributable to the pre-agricultural stage. These sites have provided evidence of six different cultural complexes, all of which seem to antedate the introduction of cotton and cultivated food plants on the central coast.

Most of the sites are located in areas of extinct *lomas* — the hardy desert vegetation which extracts its water from the thick winter fogs. Today the *lomas* plants are found only above 300 meters altitude and usually in relatively small patches, although some large areas remain, such as Lomas Lachay north of the Chancay valley. Formerly, however, they were far more extensive and reached down to an altitude of about 75 meters above sea level, always on gentle hillslopes. These ancient *lomas* have left abundant evidence in the form of rootlets — which do not decompose in the Peruvian desert — and shells of the snails which inhabited them.

The *lomas* seem to have provided most of the livelihood of their ancient inhabitants. Grinding tools, both milling stones and small mortars, are common on the campsites, and grasses and seeds are found in the refuse deposits. Though the seeds have not yet been specifically identified, they come from the *lomas* grasses. Projectile points and scrapers indicate hunting as an important economic activity. Deer and guanaco graze in the *lomas* today, and must have been more abundant when their pastures were more extensive. If the beginning of the archaeological sequence should go back to the Pleistocene, we can reasonably expect to find horses, sloths, and perhaps other animals available as game. In addition, such other foods as wild potatoes, lizards, and field owls would be available for exploitation. It is also possible that the larger land snails so abundant in the *lomas* were eaten.

The sea was also exploited, though apparently to a lesser degree. The refuse deposits contain both sea shells and fish bones, and the wind has concentrated broken sea shells on the surface of the sites. The sites range from 500 meters to 7 kilometers from the shore, and the Bay of Ancón cannot have extended much further inland when the sites were occupied. Yet even the most distant 'campsite has its share of sea food which must have been carried in skins, baskets, or other containers.

Gourds and sedges are also found in the refuse deposits and could not have been collected in the *lomas*. These plants could have been collected along the banks of the Chillón River to the south or the Chancay River to the north, or, with the additional moisture implied by the greater extent of the *lomas*, there may

---

Reprinted from **AMERICAN ANTIQUITY**, Vol. 28, No. 3, 1963. pp. 360-371.

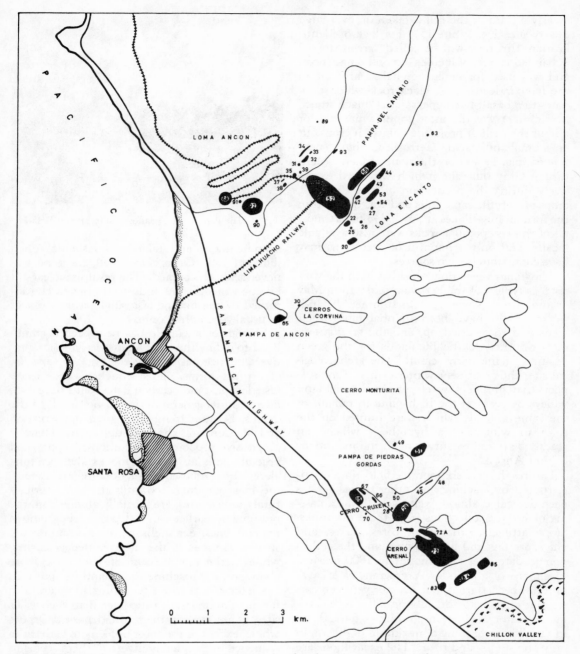

FIG. 1. Map of the Ancón area, showing location of archaeological sites mentioned in the text. Based on the 1:200,000 map of the Servicio Geográfico Militar, with principal errors corrected. The prefix PV45–, indicating the Ancón area, has been omitted from the site numbers. Stippling indicates beaches; hatching, modern towns; solid black, archaeological sites; narrow lines, edge of hills; wide lines, roads.

have been seep springs on the Pampa de Ancón near the bay.

The raw materials for stone artifacts were available locally. The most popular rocks were metamorphic. A fairly fine-grained green rock with a tendency to hinge fracture was used almost exclusively for percussion-flaked artifacts in the earlier industries. It crops out all over a long, low hill, which we have baptized Cerro Cruxent, on the Pampa de Piedras Gordas.

Nearly a third of the hill is taken up by a large quarry site (Fig. 1, Site 15). For lack of identification, this rock will be called "green stone." A banded variety of it crops out on Loma Ancón and was used for percussion-flaked artifacts in the later industries. A black rock which patinates to a basalt-like appearance ("black stone" hereinafter) was the most popular material for all but the earliest projectile points. It crops out on a small hill facing Cerro la Corbina (near Site 65, Fig. 1) and on the slope of Cerro Monturita. Gray quartzite, which was used extensively during the occupation of Site PV45-20, crops out on the same hills and was quarried in the form of huge flakes at Site PV45-65. Almost all of the less popular rocks were also available locally, and only a handful of specimens may have come from foreign sources.

The *lomas* vegetation flourishes with the winter fogs typical of the Peruvian coast, from May or June until November. In summer the hillslopes would have been uninhabitable, their seeds and roots dried up, and the grazing animals returned to the highlands for the green pastures of the rainy season. The archaeological sites thus represent winter camps. One suspects that summers were spent in the highland valleys or even on the high *puna* in pursuit of the same animals which were hunted on the coast in winter — a hypothesis which can readily be tested by surveying in the mountains behind Ancón.

During the last six months, field time — interrupted by teaching and other duties — has been dedicated almost exclusively to the amassing of surface collections from these campsites. Stone artifacts, other than cores, flakes, and chips, are few and hard to find, and the collection to date does not amount to 1000 finished specimens of all kinds. A program of excavation has been started, but has not yet been carried far enough to add substantially to the artifact inventory. The refuse is thin — 5 to 20 cm. in most sites, reaching a maximum of 40 cm. in only one site — and poor. The excavations are producing an average of one artifact per 2 cubic meters of refuse. Stratigraphy is out of the question.

The disadvantage of artifact scarcity is offset by a remarkably faithful isolation of different cultural complexes in different sites or on different hills. Evidently there was only one group camping at Ancón each winter, returning regularly to the same zone each year but eventually

Fig. 2. The Pampa del Canario, seen from Site PV45-44.

abandoning it and taking up residence on a different hill. Once abandoned, the zone was never again reoccupied. The result is a clear-cut isolation of different industries only rarely disturbed by the finding of a single artifact out of its usual geographic context.

Enough of a sample has now been accumulated to define the stone industries, and a tentative sequence has been worked out by seriation of artifact forms. This sequence needs to be tested against radiocarbon dates, but I have confidence in its general outline if not in all of the details, because trends of artifact preservation and of economic changes support it. There is progressively poorer preservation of bones and vegetal materials as one moves back in time along the proposed sequence. Mussel shells, the most common foodstuff in later (agricultural) village sites, are virtually absent from the presumably earlier camp deposits, abundant in the later ones. Sea shells in general occur in only small quantities in the sites seriated as earlier, while in the more recent sites they are more abundant, approaching the quantities found in the later village sites. Grinding tools are also far more abundant on the later than the earlier sites, as are seeds in the refuse deposits. On the whole, except in the most unlikely case that the sequence is completely inverted, there seems to have been a steadily increasing reliance on gathering, both of seeds and shellfish, through the course of time.

There are two major areas of early campsites in the Ancón area, one to the south on the Pampa de Piedras Gordas and the watershed between Ancón and the Chillón Valley, the other to the north on both sides of the Pampa del Canario (Fig. 2). The entire southern group of sites should be earlier than the northern group. There are certain gross differences between the artifact assemblages in these two areas. Stemmed projectile points and all scrapers except for a few tiny side scrapers come from the southern group; nonstemmed points come from the northern group. Choppers are abundant and grinding tools scarce in the southern group, and their proportions are reversed in the northern group.

The industry seriated as earliest is found on the Pampa de Piedras Gordas and the adjoining slopes of Cerro Cruxent and Cerro Monturita (Fig. 1, Sites 28, 29, 45, 48–51, 66, 67, and 70). The most outstanding feature of the sites in this area is the great quantity of large flakes of green stone on the surface. Since these flakes were only rarely made into shaped artifacts, and often show edges dulled by use, they were evidently struck off for use as tools without further modification. Of the same material, of course, are the cores from which they were struck, and also a series of round cores with wavy bifacial cutting edges and flat butts. The latter form often shows light battering of the edges and was evidently made for use as a tool (Fig. 4 a, b). Accompanying these round choppers are a few large, heavy scrapers made on thick flakes or tabular pieces of green stone. Extensive search has turned up only two fragments of crudely percussion-chipped projectile points and one well-made round scraper of the type found in the next complex (Fig. 4 d). The general scarcity of fine chipping debris on the Piedras Gordas sites is certainly a function of the rarity of such finer artifacts.

Another type of artifact made from green stone is a small percussion-flaked tool with a protruding point which is usually not very sharp (Fig. 4 c). These pointed tools can be used for working bone, though they are not as efficient as a piece of sandstone, and they make excellent pressure flakers. The sharpest of them can also be used as awls or perforators. Since there is no clear evidence of pressure flaking in this earliest industry, this tool form probably began its career as a bone scraper, though later evidence suggests that it came to be used as a pressure flaker as well.

Other artifacts include beach and river cobbles used as hammerstones; a few large, thick, milling stones, small mortars with unshaped exteriors and basin-shaped bowls, and cobble pestles (Fig. 3); and a series of plain and retouched large flakes struck from beach cobbles. These cobble flakes are found in quantity throughout the sequence. They can be found not only on the living sites but also scattered in areas of extinct *lomas* where no camps were ever established. This special association with the fog vegetation suggests that they were used as sickles for harvesting seed-bearing grasses.

The second industry is found on sites in the Ancón-Chillón watershed, southeast of Cerro Arenal and east of a small farm known as the Estancia Luz (Fig. 1, Sites 72, 83, 84, and 85). It has been named the Luz complex. The Piedras Gordas green stone industry is found on these sites, but with some modification. Pointed tools occur with the same frequency, but round choppers and large utilized flakes are much less common. The large amorphous scrapers of Piedras Gordas type are replaced by neatly made round scrapers, sometimes with intentionally serrated edges (Fig. 4 e, f). There are also a few notched scrapers and a single pointed scraper of Arenal type (Fig. 4 o). Other elements carried on from the Piedras Gordas industry are cobble hammerstones, plain and retouched cobble flakes, milling stones, small mortars, and cobble pestles. Manos for the milling stones may be either plain, flattish cobbles or may be shaped by pecking around the edges and across the ends.

The most distinctive artifacts of the Luz complex are its projectile points and related implements. The most common of these are stemmed points of Paiján-Pampa de los Fósiles type. These are exceptionally large, flat specimens with long triangular blades and slender stems bulged at the base (Fig. 4 j–l; cf. Lanning and Hammel 1961, Fig. 3 a, b). The largest of them

Fig. 3. Mortar and pestle, Piedras Gordas complex, Site PV45-29.

FIG. 4. Artifacts of the Piedras Gordas and Luz complexes. Piedras Gordas complex (Site PV45-29): *a–b,* choppers; *c,* pointed tool; *d,* scraper. Luz complex (PV45-72: *e, h–j, m;* PV45-84: *f–g, l, n–o;* PV45-29, intrusive Luz workshop: *k):* *e–f,* round scrapers; *g,* dart point; *h–i,* awls; *j–l,* spear points; *m–n,* percussion-flaked blades; *o,* pointed scraper.

are over 15 cm. long, and the smallest must have had twice the bulk of any other projectile point from Ancón. While later points are all of moderate size, presumably for use with spear-throwers, these Paiján-type specimens were more probably attached to hand-held or hand-thrown spears. Finished specimens show edge rubbing on the stem and lower part of the blade.

Accompanying the spear points are a few smaller points which may have been used with the spearthrower. One of the latter, with barbs and a contracting stem, is probably ancestral to Arenal dart points (Fig. 4 g). There is also a group of large, thick, leaf-shaped blades made by neat percussion flaking (Fig. 4 m, n). An-other series of distinctive artifacts consists of fragments of long, slender, pointed objects, re-markably well-made in view of their needle-like shape (Fig. 4 h, i). Finished specimens of this sort have heavy-use polish on the faces together with some wearing down of the edges, but none shows the marked rotatory abrasion of the edges characteristic of stone drills. They seem to have been awls. Luz spear points, percussion-flaked blades, and stone awls are made primarily of light-colored rocks, in contrast to the predom-inantly dark projectile points of all later assem-blages at Ancón. The only case of a projectile point found completely out of geographical con-text is a Canario-type bipointed specimen from a Luz site (Fig. 5 n).

Arenal complex, the third and latest industry in the southern group, is found only on two small sites on the Ancón-Chillón watershed just northwest of the previous group (Fig. 1, Sites 71 and 72A). Fortunately, Site PV45-72A is one of the richest at Ancón, so that the sample, if somewhat biased, is quite large. The outstand-ing features of this industry are the abundance and variety of its scrapers. Three-fourths of all the scrapers found at Ancón come from PV45-72A. Round and notched scrapers continue from the previous complex (Fig. 5 k), and are now accompanied by thick flake side scrapers, hump-backed pointed scrapers (Fig. 5 j), large, neatly made oval scrapers (Fig. 5 a), and beau-tifully finished small end and snub-nosed scrap-ers (Fig. 5 g–i). The latter are particularly abundant. These new types of scrapers are gen-erally made of black stone and other dark-colored rocks, only occasionally of green stone.

The few projectile points found at Sites 71 and 72 are distinctive. The standard forms are stemmed, with triangular blades, either single shouldered (Fig. 5 b, c) or with two shoulders and contracting stems (Fig. 5 d). Both forms show neat bilateral pressure retouch, which is also characteristic of the nonstemmed points of succeeding industries, and basal edge smooth-ing. Chipped stone awls continue from the Luz complex (Fig. 5 e), but not Paiján spear points or leaf-shaped blades.

Other artifacts are continuations of earlier types. The green stone industry shows the same range of form as in the preceding complex: large flakes, round choppers, residual cores, round scrapers, and pointed tools (Fig. 5 f, k). The latter form is especially abundant. Cobble ham-merstones and cobble flakes are the same as in previous complexes. Grinding stones are limited to four manos, but a larger sample could be ex-pected to include the usual milling stones, mor-tars, and cobble pestles.

The next three complexes are found on sites on Loma Ancón and Loma Encanto, the two large hills which flank the Pampa del Canario. The differences between these three complexes are less marked than those between the earlier industries, but they are well isolated from each other and certainly represent three different, if brief, periods of time. Scrapers disappear so abruptly from the sequence, immediately after reaching a peak of abundance and variety, that one suspects a lapse of time between the early complexes on the southern sites and the later ones on the northern sites.

The seriation of these later industries is based on their projectile points, pointed tools, and mortars. The most recent of them, Encanto, is easy to identify because of the excellent preser-vation of bones and vegetal material in its refuse and because it has the same form of projectile points as a cotton-using preceramic village near the shore. The oldest, Canario, has mortars, green stone choppers and pointed tools, and one stemmed point, all carried over from the Luz-Arenal group.

The Canario complex is found on the east slope of Loma Ancón (Fig. 1, Sites 31–35, 37–39, 58, and 89–93). Its rough stone industry shows the first significant change since Piedras Gordas times. While there are still a few round, green stone choppers, very large flakes with uni-facially step-flaked and battered edges are more common. These flakes, together with most of the large unretouched flakes, are of a banded

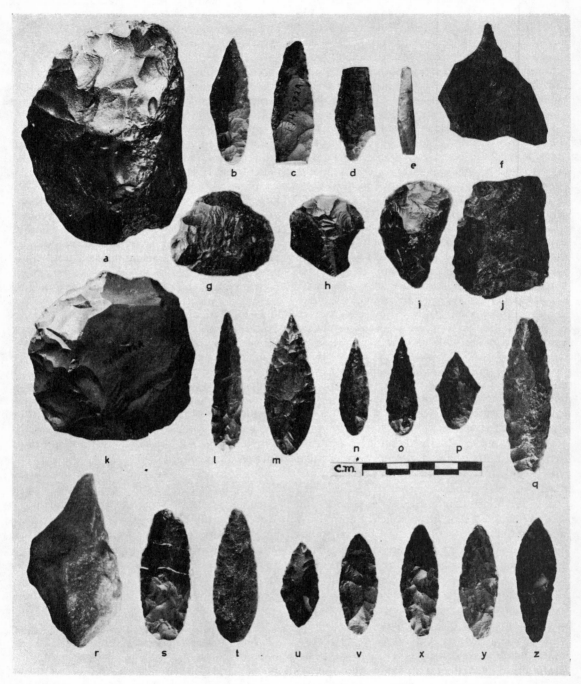

FIG. 5. Artifacts of the Arenal, Canario, Corbina, and Encanto complexes and from Lomas Lachay. Arenal complex (PV45-72A): *a, g–k,* scrapers; *b–d,* projectile points; *e,* awl; *f,* pointed tool. Canario complex projectile points: *l–m, o* (PV45-31), *n* (PV45-84), *p* (PV45-92). Corbina complex (PV45-20): *r,* pointed tool; *s,* projectile point. Encanto complex projectile points: *q, z* (PV45-26); *u* (PV45-42); *y* (PV45-53). Lomas Lachay: *v–x* (PV43-7A); *t,* willow leaf point (PV43-4).

variety of green stone which outcrops on Loma Ancón in the middle of the Canario habitation area.

Milling stones, shaped and unshaped manos, mortars, and cobble pestles are indistinguishable from those of the earlier complexes. Green stone pointed tools also continue without change. Cobble flakes, both plain and retouched, are more abundant at Canario sites than in any other complex. Cobble hammerstones continue, but are now accompanied by ordinary hill stones used as hammers. There are no scrapers whatever.

Canario projectile points are made primarily of black stone and of dark-colored siliceous rocks. They have long pointed bases with maximum width behind the mid-point. There are two varieties: one large and broad, usually made on selected flat flakes which may have concave faces (Fig. 5 *m*), the other small and thick (Fig. 5 *n, o*). Both show basal edge smoothing. The one stemmed point is a reworked piece originally of the broad bipointed form, but with tiny lateral barbs at the point of maximum width (Fig. 5 *p*). A unique specimen, long, slender and thick, approaches the form of projectile points in the succeeding Corbina complex, but is proportionately longer and narrower (Fig. 6 *l*).

The next complex, tentatively named Corbina, is represented at one campsite on the low, flat top of Loma Encanto (PV45-20) and at a quartzite quarry (PV45-65). Site PV45-30, at the foot of Cerro la Corbina, may also belong, but has not produced enough artifacts to allow certain identification. The distinctive characteristics of Site 20 are its projectile points and a quartzite industry which is not found in any other complex. The projectile points, which include the only quartzite points from Ancón, are long and parallel-sided with round or very short pointed bases (Fig. 5 *s*).

The surface of Site 20 is littered with hundreds of flakes and cores of gray quartzite which was quarried at Site 65 in the form of huge thick flakes. This material is almost exclusively the residue of artifact manufacture; very rarely a flake shows dulled edges, but none of the quartzite cores can be classified as choppers. Quartzite artifacts include not only projectile points but also pointed tools, all of which are larger than their green stone counterparts in earlier industries (Fig. 5 *r*).

There remain only traces of the green stone industry — a single core which may be a chop-

per and a few flakes. If Site 30 should prove to belong to this complex, then it also includes large flakes with unifacially step-flaked edges like those common at Canario sites. As in the Canario complex, there are no scrapers whatever, and hammerstones may be either cobbles or field stones. Site PV45-20 has produced a fair number of manos and a couple of milling stones, but no mortars or pestles, and the latter type of grinder may no longer have been in use. Cobble flakes continue as in previous assemblages.

The last of the pre-agricultural complexes, Encanto, is found on the west slope of Loma Encanto, facing the Pampa del Canario (Fig. 1, Sites 22, 25–27, 42–44, 52–56, and 63). Sites 22, 52, and 56 are areas of scattered small workshops; the other ten sites are ancient camps. The most striking feature of these sites is the large number of milling stones and manos — more than on all other sites together (Figs. 6–7). On the other hand, there are no mortars, and rough chipped stonework is very scarce. There are no bifacial choppers and only a very few green stone flakes and cores, a few flakes with step-flaked edges of Canario type, and a few cobble flakes. Hammerstones are now mostly hill stones, though they still include some river cobbles.

Encanto projectile points are smaller than in any other complex, bipointed, and made by percussion flaking only (Fig. 5 *u–z*). They show considerable variety of profile, with the maximum width varying from near the point to near the base, and are often bilaterally asymmetric. Being small and thick, they do not break easily, and there is a correspondingly high proportion of complete specimens in the collection. One

Fig. 6. Milling stones, Encanto complex, Site PV45-26.

Fig. 7. Manos, Encanto complex, Site PV45-26.

unusual specimen is a large spearpoint or knife of the same form and workmanship as the small points (Fig. 5 *q*). Of some 50 points and fragments collected to date, not one shows the fine bilateral pressure flaking typical of the earlier complexes. This abandonment of the pressure-flaking technique is accompanied by the disappearance of pointed tools from the artifact inventory, which implies that pressure flaking was the primary function of that tool form.

Scrapers make a brief reappearance in the Encanto complex, rarely and in specialized form. They consist of little flakes with short, straight edges worked by unifacial flaking.

So far excavation in Encanto sites has been limited to two small test pits, but these have shown substantial differences in refuse content from the earlier complexes. The refuse at PV45-26 is 40 cm. deep and stratified. Sea shells, grasses, and seeds are more abundant. With better preservation there are more fragments of gourds and of mammal bone, and sedge cordage is common. Although no pieces of mats have yet been found, there are sedge stems with binding marks, indicating that twined mats were made.

Similarities with early lithic industries in other areas are less frequent than one would expect. Piedras Gordas shows no particular similarity to any other industry. Its round choppers and amorphous large scrapers differ both from the cobble cores of later Peruvian coastal preceramic sites (Bird 1948: Fig. 11) and from the large plano-convex artifacts of such non-projectile-point industries as Ghatchi in Atacama (Le Paige 1960). Luz spear points, leaf-shaped blades, and round scrapers are of the same types as those from the Pampa de Paiján and Pampa de los Fósiles on the north coast of Peru (Bird 1948: 27; Lanning and Hammel 1961: Fig. 3 *a*, *b*). Stemmed points of similar form but much smaller are found in early context at El Inga in Ecuador (Bell 1960: 2 *a–h*). From the same site there are pointed tools resembling those from Ancón (Bell 1960: Fig. 2 *v*, *w*).

The hump-backed pointed scrapers which occur occasionally in Luz and Arenal complexes are somewhat similar to Jobo scrapers from Venezuela (Cruxent and Rouse 1956: Fig. 3). Arenal end and snub-nosed scrapers can probably be duplicated from many parts of America and from many time periods. Their peculiar feature at Ancón is that they are limited to a single brief period of time. Arenal projectile points cannot be matched in the literature for South America.

One complete point of the Canario large bipointed variety practically duplicates a point found with the second mammoth at Santa Isabel Ixtapan in Mexico (Aveleyra 1956: Fig. 7, No. 2). Whether this similarity is historically significant or simply a coincidence, I do not know. Canario small bipoints and Corbina lanceolate points are both clearly related to Ayampitín and Lauricocha II forms, though neither achieves the classic willow-leaf form found in the highlands (González 1952: Pl. 13; Cardich 1958, Fig. 13 *a*) and at Lomas Lachay (see below). The highlands willow-leaf point has an estimated age of 6000–3000 B.C. (Cardich 1958: 20, Fig. 9; Lanning and Hammel 1961: 150).

Encanto points seem more similar in form and workmanship to those of the Shell Fishhook culture of Pichalo in northern Chile than to any other (Bird 1943: Fig. 34 *b*), though they average somewhat larger. The one large Encanto point (Fig. 5 *q*) is remarkably similar to Jobo points from Venezuela (Cruxent and Rouse 1956: Fig. 2), but the similarity is certainly a coincidence, since the Encanto complex must be thousands of years more recent than El Jobo. Finally, Encanto micro-side scrapers are duplicated in obsidian at the cotton-using preceramic village site of Casavilca at the mouth of the Ica valley.

At present there is no way to date the earlier industries in this sequence. The presence of grinding tools from the beginning argues for conservative dating, since grinding tools are not usually found in exceptionally ancient contexts in America. On the other hand, occasional similarities to El Inga in Ecuador, El Jobo in

Venezuela, and Santa Isabel Ixtapan in Mexico suggest dates on the order of 10,000 years and more. My guess is that at least Piedras Gordas goes back to the Pleistocene, but this guess cannot be substantiated without the results of radiocarbon determinations or association with extinct animals.

Whatever dates are finally assigned, both Piedras Gordas and Luz should be very ancient. I am convinced that Hammel and I guessed wrong in assigning Paiján points to the period 6000–3000 B.C., and that they, like Jobo points, are older than we had realized. The presence of large stemmed points in the Andes on so ancient a time level should be no surprise. Fishtail points, which also show flat sections, great size, and long stems, date to nearly 10,000 B.C. in Patagonia and Ecuador (Lanning and Hammel 1961: 150; Bird 1938: 270; Bird 1951: 44–5; Mayer-Oakes and Bell 1960: 1806).

The end of the pre-agricultural stage at Ancón came with the abandonment of the winter camps in the *lomas* and the establishment of permanent villages near the shore in the hills just above the present town of Ancón. There are two principal preceramic village sites here, the Yacht Club (PV45-5) and Tank (PV45-2) sites. The former was excavated by the author in August and September of 1961. The latter has been excavated, under the direction of Jorge C. Muelle, by the Museo Nacional de Arqueología y Antropología and the Universidad de San Marcos. Both sites have evidence of cultivated plants in the form of cotton — used for string, netting, and twined textiles — and *ají*, and both have gourds in quantities which suggest that they were now cultivated and not simply gathered. Guava fruits also appear in these sites for the first time. The Yacht Club is the earlier village, as evidenced by the presence of Encanto points. Projectile points at the Tank site are larger and very crudely chipped. The preceramic deposit at the latter site is overlain by the great early ceramic midden deposits discovered by Max Uhle and studied by countless archaeologists.

Three fundamental changes thus took place at about the same time: the introduction of cultivated plants, above all, cotton, and of twined textiles, and the settlement in permanent villages. With these came a fourth and equally important change — the substitution of the sea for the *lomas* as a primary source of food. Though there are still a few milling stones to be found, indicating a continuation of the ancient seed-grinding pattern, the middens are packed with sea shells, fish bones, and the bones and feathers of shore birds. Even hunting patterns changed, so that sea lion bones replace land mammal remains in the refuse.

These changes are evidently related to a modification of the circulation pattern of the Pacific Ocean off the coast of Peru. The retreat of the *lomas* to their present position implies a lifting of the fog belt from a formerly lower position, or a general decrease in the moisture content of the fog. Either case suggests increased activity of the cold Peru Current, either increased upwelling or a shoreward movement of the Current from a previously more seaward position, with a corresponding decrease in temperature and water-carrying capacity of the air, and increased warming as it moves in over the land. In a study of guano deposition patterns, Hutchinson (1950: especially 65–71, 109–112, 364–5, 481) concludes that such a change in circulation pattern took place in the first or second millenium B.C., at which time the guano formerly deposited in the area from Paracas southward along the Chilean coast began to be deposited on the central Peruvian coast instead. Broggi (1961) has presented evidence of the renewed growth of giant sand dunes associated with the retreat of the fog belt to higher altitudes. Yazawa (1960) and Sato (1960) also cite evidence of decreased precipitation and increased wind velocities on the Peruvian coast in relatively recent times.

The archaeological evidence clearly indicates a desert climate since the time of the earliest human habitation. The most abundant remains in the pre-agricultural sites — *Tillandsia* and *lomas* snails — are those of desert dwellers. Climatically, however, the Peruvian coast is in a state of delicate balance, and even a slight change of oceanic circulation pattern affecting the humidity of the air would be sufficient to cause the retreat of the *lomas*. Any increase in the activity of the Peru Current would also lead to an enrichment of the sea, multiplication of schools of anchovies, immigration of guano birds, more fish and shellfish. Thus, the phenomenon which destroyed the means of livlihood in the *lomas* opened up a new life on the beach.

With the introduction of cultivated plants it was no longer possible to leave the area in summertime, because summer is the growing season when the rivers run full and the water table rises — at Ancón, the season when shallow wells would produce and seep springs would be active. This factor, together with the year-round livelihood now provided by the sea, can be adduced as the reason for the abandonment of nomadic life and the establishment of permanent villages.

Hutchinson proposes a date in the first or second millenium B.C. for the critical change in the Peru Current (Hutchinson 1950: 65–71). The preceramic shore villages on the north and central coast of Peru were founded in the third millenium or, at the latest, at the beginning of the second millenium B.C. The long series of radiocarbon dates for Huaca Prieta indicates a beginning around 2500 B.C. (Bird 1951: 37–43), and dates from other sites fall within the same range (Engel 1957: 143; 1958: 3–4). Hutchinson's date is based on calculations of rate of deposition and is subject to the uncertainties which plague the use of that method, even when it is employed with the skill and caution found in Hutchinson's study. Thus there need be no temporal discrepancy between the climatological change and the founding of the shore villages.

Confirmation of a sort comes from Engel's excavation of a preceramic cemetery with a radiocarbon date of around 3000 B.C. near Paracas (Engel 1960). This cemetery, said to pertain to a textile-twining but pre-agricultural culture, should be contemporary with the Encanto complex at Ancón. The fact that it is a concentrated burial ground suggests association with a village rather than with the campsites of nomads. Paracas is almost on the northern limit of the area of ancient guano deposition, and should therefore be the locus of villages older than those of the central and north coast. It is to be hoped that Engel will soon have his collection examined by biologists in order to determine whether the textiles are indeed non-cotton, and whether the skins found on some of the burials are vicuña, as he suggests, or sea lion, as is to be expected at a shore village. It seems useless to pose the question of farming in this culture until a midden has been excavated.

In order to examine the significance of *lomas* as areas of habitation in pre-agricultural times, extinct *lomas* have been visited in the area of Lomas Lachay north of the Chancay valley. The situation here resembles that at Ancón: modern vegetation above 300 meters altitude, with the snail shells and rootlets of extinct vegetation following the slopes down nearly to the sea. The area of extinct vegetation is full of early lithic sites, some of them several kilometers long. Those explored so far show two culture complexes isolated at different sites. One, with Canario and Ayampitín-like points (Fig. 5 t), numerous small pointed tools, mortars and milling stones, corresponds to the fourth and fifth complexes at Ancón, but has substantial local differences of raw material and of artifact inventory. The other is Encanto complex, exactly as at Ancón. In general the Lachay sites are larger and richer than their Ancón counterparts. Patient search should produce a more complete sample, at least for these later industries, than can be acquired at Ancón.

New problems have already arisen as a result of the present research, and others are sure to follow. Some shifting of concepts will certainly be necessary. Discussion of these problems will have to wait, however, until radiocarbon dates have tested the sequence and given an idea of its antiquity. In the meantime, we have a new field to explore on the Peruvian coast.

*Acknowledgments.* My gratitude is due, first of all, to the Fulbright Commission in Peru, which is financing the project, and to the Universidad Nacional Mayor de San Marcos for its material and personal assistance in the research. Jorge C. Muelle and Junius B. Bird have been extremely helpful, examining the sites and collections, evaluating evidence, and suggesting interpretations and new lines of research. A. Lyndon Bell, Víctor Benavides, and John Wilson have all helped in settling the question of the relation between the campsites and the Bay of Ancón in ancient times. Emilio Rosas Lanoir, student of archaeology at San Marcos, has assisted tirelessly and skilfully in the field. My thanks to all.

Aveleyra A. de Anda, Luis
    1956 The Second Mammoth and Associated Artifacts at Santa Isabel Ixtapan, Mexico. *American Antiquity*, Vol. 22, No. 1, pp. 12–28. Salt Lake City.

Bell, R. E.
    1960 Evidence of a Fluted Point Tradition in Ecuador. *American Antiquity*, Vol. 26, No. 1, pp. 102–6. Salt Lake City.

Bird, J. B.
    1938 Antiquity and Migrations of the Early Inhabitants of Patagonia. *Geographical Review*, Vol. 28, No. 2, pp. 250–75. New York.

    1943 Excavations in Northern Chile. *Anthropological Papers of the American Museum of Natural History*, Vol. 38, Part 4. New York.

    1948 Preceramic Cultures in Chicama and Virú. In "A Reappraisal of Peruvian Archaeology," edited by W. C. Bennett, pp. 21–8. *Memoirs of the Society for American Archaeology*, No. 4. Menasha.

1951 South American Radiocarbon Dates. In "Radiocarbon Dating," edited by Frederick Johnson, pp. 37–49. *Memoirs of the Society for American Archaeology*, No. 8. Salt Lake City.

BROGGI, J. A.

1961 Las ciclópeas dunas compuestas de la costa peruana, su origen y significación climática. *Boletín de la Sociedad Geológica del Perú*, Tomo 36, pp. 61–6. Lima.

CARDICH, AUGUSTO

1958 Los yacimientos de Lauricocha, neuvas interpretaciones de la prehistoria peruana. *Studia Praehistorica* I. Centro Argentino de Estudios Prehistóricos, Buenos Aires.

CRUXENT, J. M. AND IRVING ROUSE

1956 A Lithic Industry of Paleo-Indian Type in Venezuela. *American Antiquity*, Vol. 22, No. 2, pp. 172–9. Salt Lake City.

ENGEL, FRÉDÉRIC

1957 Sites et établissements sans céramique de la côte péruvienne. *Journal de la Société des Américanistes*, n.s., Vol. 46, pp. 67–155. Paris.

1958 Algunos datos con referencia a los sitios precerámicos de la costa peruana. *Arqueológicas*, No. 3. Museo Nacional de Antropología y Arqueología, Lima.

1960 Un groupe humain datant de 5000 ans a Paracas, Pérou. *Journal de la Société des Américanistes*, n.s., Vol. 49, pp. 7–35. Paris.

FUNG DE LANNING, ROSA

1959 Informe preliminar de las excavaciones efectuadas en el Abrigo Rocoso No. 1 de Tschopik. In *Actas y Trabajos del II Congreso Nacional de Historia del Perú (Epoca Pre-Hispánica), 4–9 de Agosto de 1958*, Vol. 1, pp. 253–74. Lima.

GONZÁLEZ, A. R.

1952 Antiguo horizonte precerámico en las Sierras Centrales de la Argentina. *Runa, Archivo para las Ciencias del Hombre*, Vol. 5, pp. 110–33. Buenos Aires.

HUTCHINSON, G. E.

1950 Survey of Contemporary Knowledge of Biogeochemistry. 3. The Biogeochemistry of Vertebrate Excretion. *Bulletin of the American Museum of Natural History*, Vol. 96. New York.

LANNING, E. P. AND E. A. HAMMEL

1961 Early Lithic Industries of Western South America. *American Antiquity*, Vol. 27, No. 2, pp. 139–54. Salt Lake City.

LEPAIGE, GUSTAVO

1960 Antigua cultura atacameña en la cordillera chilena: época paleolítica (2° artículo). *Revista Universitaria, Anales de la Academia Chilena de Ciencias Naturales*, Años 44–45, No. 23, pp. 191–206. Universidad Católica de Chile, Santiago.

MAYER-OAKES, W. J. AND R. E. BELL

1960 Early Man Site Found in Highland Ecuador. *Science*, Vol. 131, No. 3416, pp. 1805–6. Washington.

SATO, HISASHI

1960 Geomorphology of the Western Lowlands of the Central Andes. In *Andes, Report of the University of Tokyo Scientific Expedition to the Andes in 1958*, pp. 414–7. Andean Institute, University of Tokyo, Tokyo.

YAZAWA, TAIJI

1960 Climatological Survey in the Central Andes. In *Andes, Report of the University of Tokyo Scientific Expedition to the Andes in 1958*, pp. 412–4. Andean Institute, University of Tokyo, Tokyo.

UNIVERSIDAD NACIONAL MAYOR
DE SAN MARCOS

Lima, Peru

July, 1962

# PRECERAMIC CULTURES IN CHICAMA AND VIRÚ

## Junius B. Bird

THIS is a tentative résumé of the work done on the preceramic horizons in Chicama and Virú valleys as a part of the Virú Valley Project of 1946. Before summarizing the results of excavations in the old midden deposits, mention should be made of the recent physiographic changes in the Virú Valley. These have a definite connection with the prehistory.

The drainage of the south arm of the valley starts at an elevation of slightly over 4000 meters with the two highest forks on the flanks of a 4200 meter peak. This section is today completely ice free, but as the general level for glacial moraines in this part of Peru runs between 3200 and 3400 meters, with one moraine in the Callejón de Huaylas down to 1800 meters, it is obvious that the physiography of the valley was once influenced by water either discharged directly from glaciers or draining from a greater area of condensation.

The recent erosion of the present drainage channels has in places exposed the coarse waterworn gravels and large boulders which must have been deposited when that discharge occurred. This recent erosion has also exposed several good soil profiles, the best extending from 200 meters above the Virú bridge downstream for a kilometer below the bridge. The exposure is good and reveals a record of what has occurred. Unfortunately the cutting has not exposed the coarse boulder gravel valley fill at this point though I believe the Virú River is here running on or near its surface.

By pitting at the base of the exposure, Webster McBryde and I secured a 21-foot profile. Starting at the bottom, there is waterworn sand which blends upward into clay and clayey soil. Above this is evidence of a long period of aggrading accompanied by five or six major flood periods, marked by light-colored silty bands, which seemingly occurred at rather regular intervals. Above each light band the soil gradually darkens, becoming darkest below the next

light band. The aggrading ultimately ceased and erosion reversed the process. What factors were involved in this reverse trend I do not know, but it is clear that they are still effective for the erosion is continuing at the present.

I have mentioned all this simply because the record of human occupation is involved. Sixteen feet below the top of the bluff were found sherds of the type of Cupisnique ware made just before the appearance of Salinar ceramics. Within the uppermost soil zone are the La Plata-Chimu sherds indicating that the heavy erosion is a late feature in the valley record. The sherd distribution and the relative uniformity of the soil must mean that the elapsed time since the laying down of the coarse valley bottom fill, namely, the time of heavy discharge up into the period of Cupisnique ceramics, is far less than the interval between Cupisnique and the present. It is likewise obvious that the valley bottom structure has changed considerably since the beginning of occupation and that these changes can ultimately be correlated with the cultural record. For the moment it is sufficient to remember that the early record to be reviewed here has to be fitted into the period represented in this soil profile by what lies between the 16-foot level and the coarse detritus.

In treating this phase of the cultural record, I will start with what was found at the Huaca Prieta at the mouth of the Chicama Valley. This well-known site, with a reputation among the local *huaqueros* as a place which would yield nothing, had been visited by the Larcos, Tello, Kroeber, Bennett, Lothrop, and other archaeologists. None however was able to devote much time to it, so its contents have remained in doubt. Even after seven months of sifting with a ten-man crew we can report only on the contents of a small portion of the deposit and have left the problem of clearing the subterranean structures which abound in its upper portion to someone else.

Reprinted from "A Reappraisal of Peruvian Archaeology", MEMOIRS OF THE SOCIETY FOR AMERICAN ARCHAEOLOGY, AMERICAN ANTIQUITY, Vol. XIII, No. 4, 1948. pp. 21-28.

The midden, a flat-topped, roughly oval mound about 125 meters long by 50 meters wide by 12 meters thick, lies by the shore at the southern tip of a low triangular plateau of conglomerate rock. This outcrop rises only a few meters above the level of ground water but this has been long enough to keep the deposit dry some miles to the north, at Milagro (Fig. 4); hence I believe, though the evidence cannot be presented here, that these sites were first occupied during the last period of relatively static tectonic conditions. Since their abandonment another period of coastal rise has started.

By taking advantage of the erosion, we

FIG. 3. Huaca Prieta, Preceramic Agricultural Period Mound near El Brujo, Chicama Valley.

FIG. 4. Huaca Palpur, Preceramic Agricultural Period Mound at Milagro, Chicama Valley.

FIG. 5. Excavation of Lowest Strata on the Eroded Western Side of Huaca Prieta, Chicama Valley.

with the result that perishable plant and other remains have survived.

The steep slope of the west side (Fig. 3) is the result of erosion produced by the cutting away of the underlying conglomerate by wave action. A slight uplift of the coast has stopped this process so that erosion today is limited to wind and infrequent rains. This situation is duplicated at another contemporary midden examined the lowest strata with a minimum of work and found that the mound started to form west of its present limits (Figs. 5, 6).

To avoid the confusion of working among the subterranean structures in the central part of the mound another test was made in its lee on the northern flank. The compact nature of the accumulation, consisting mostly of fine ash, firestones, sea urchin spines, and a small percentage by volume of shell, permitted steep cutting so the bottom was reached without difficulty. All debris to be examined was removed following strata lines and sifted.

The results were surprising. For one thing there was no evidence of major cultural change from top to bottom. This might suggest rather rapid build-up though the nature of the deposit indicated the reverse.

to oval, with short narrow entrances forming a step down from the surface. Walls are of cobbles from the adjacent beach set in a hard mortar made by simply mixing the midden dirt with water (Fig. 7). Short roof beams of wood and whalebone were covered with stone and dirt flush with the surrounding surface. Floors are of dirt and bear no evidence of fire hearths. The use of these structures appears to be limited to

FIG. 6. Close-up of Strata shown in Figure 5, taken Several Months later. Cords intersect at Meter Intervals. (Courtesy of John Collier, Jr.)

When the mound had grown to about one-third of its present height a low retaining wall had been constructed more probably to stabilize a level surface than as a defensive measure. As the debris outside accumulated three more walls were added from time to time. The uppermost has been so nearly destroyed by exfoliation and wind erosion that it is certain that, when abandoned, the mound was somewhat higher than it is today.

The subterranean structures mentioned were small, with one and two rooms, roughly square

the upper half of the accumulation. In view of the local climate they were thoroughly satisfactory and provide a much more uniformly comfortable temperature than the houses built in the vicinity today. Were it not for the erosion of the mound sides one could make a very accurate population estimate of the community at any one time by plotting all the houses. At most it could not have been more than a few hundred, providing further reason to suppose a long period of occupation.

These people supported themselves in part by

agriculture, in part by fishing and the gathering of wild plants and fruits. As cultivated plants they had cotton, gourds, squash, aji peppers, beans (*Canavalia*), two varieties of "frijol de guava," and what may be the "lenteja bocono" (*Dolichos lablab*).

Some of these plants might have grown wild, others would not have required very much attention; considering the plants as a group, there is little reason to doubt that we are dealing with

FIG. 7. Lower Portion of Cut in North Side of Huaca Prieta, showing the First and Second, and Bottom Edge of the Third, Retaining Wall.

at least rudimentary agriculture. In addition to the species listed, various other plants were utilized as food. Quite important was the achira (*Canna edulis*), of which we secured a good many tuber fragments and leaves. This might well be included among the cultivated plants.

Truly wild, but eaten in abundance, were: junco tubers (*Scirpus*—?), cattail roots, and a small tuber locally known as "Cocos" or "barra de San José" (*Cyperus esculentum?*). Several other species occur sporadically.

The fruits gathered were: lúcuma, ciruela de fraile (*Bunchosia armeniaca*), guayaba (*Psidium guaba*), and one yielding an unidentified seed, resembling those from the zapote, but definitely not zapote. All identification of plant remains is

tentative pending the arrival and study of the collection.

Other foods were fish, sea urchins, mollusks, sea lion, porpoise, and birds. No land mammal bones were encountered, and the marine species were relatively infrequent. No ceramics were made and cooking was done with firestones. No

FIG. 8. Woven Matting from Huaca Prieta.

FIG. 9. Twined Basket from Huaca Prieta.

fire drills or hearths were found though hundreds of stick and twig fragments survived.

The material culture was exceedingly simple. Cotton textiles were common with twining predominant. Warp-face weaving occurs with occasionally simple-warp float patterns. These are sometimes twined in part and in some short wefts were used and knotted on the side selvages. No garments were made, the fabrics possibly serving as shawls or pubic covers. Dry red pigments appear on some fabrics and a little dyeing in blue was done. Coiling, looping, and netting are common. Matting is mostly twined though a little was woven of reeds using a cord weft (Fig. 8). Basketry was common and is entirely twined, with several variations in construction (Fig. 9). Bark cloth was made but as yet we have no knowledge of the sources of the material. No ornaments were found. Floats for fish nets (Fig. 10) and containers were made from gourds. Rarely was there any attempt at decoration and this was almost limited to crude scratches in the soft epidermis of the gourds before drying.

No weapons of any type with the exception of a few toy slings were found. This supports the inference of the faunal remains that they were not a hunting people and further suggests that they led a peaceful existence.

Their stone working provides another surprise. Either they had lost the art of pressure flaking before settling here or had never known it, for not a single pressure-flaked artifact occurs. Thousands of coarse stone flakes were recovered, some showing wear or slight nicking but with almost no intentional retouching of the edges. Cores (Fig. 11) and hammerstones are common, some of the former suggesting hand axes, but in the aggregate appearing as cores. Holes were pecked in small cobbles and, though these resemble loom weights, one was found attached to the fish net (Fig. 10). Though one fragment of a stone bowl appeared well down in

FIG. 10. Fish Net, Floats, and Sinker, as found at Huaca Prieta.

the debris, I hesitate to include this as a trait. If only the stone artifacts had survived one would be forced to think of these people as exceedingly primitive culturally, so that it is

well that a more complete listing of artifacts is possible.

From the nature of the accumulation on the mound slope it was obvious that the mound

FIG. 11. Stone Cores from Huaca Prieta, showing Range in Size and Form.

had been abandoned before the introduction of ceramics. What may have been a tidal wave deposited beach cobbles and gravel well up on the mound flanks. This rests on windblown dust eroded from the top of the mound and so could have had nothing to do with the abandonment which may well have been occasioned by the erosion of the western side.

Though the preceramic to ceramic juncture was found a short distance north of the base of the Huaca Prieta, further data on the late phase of the preceramic people were found near the little settlement of Guañape at the northern side of the Virú Valley mouth. This is located in the only suitable place for a fishing community in Virú and further emphasizes the importance of fishing in this early period.

There are three separate mounds of preceramic debris here, none approaching the Huaca Prieta in size, though all run to over eight meters in thickness. Unfortunately all are based on sand in which there is considerable fluctuation in ground-water level and all have a high content of wind-blown sand. The result is that almost no perishable material survives and this is limited to the later levels. In the northernmost of the three mounds the preceramic refuse slopes down and is in part covered by sherd-bearing debris. It was here that Strong and Evans secured the pottery type designated "Guañape" and in nearby pits encountered preceramic levels.

The scarcity of perishable material makes it difficult to compare the early Guañape occupation with Huaca Prieta. It is further complicated by the contrast in local settings. Both are near sections of beach which are good for net fishing but not for hand lines; both are located by land which can be cultivated without irrigation but while at Huaca Prieta an abundance of cobbles are at hand for building material, the beach at Guañape is pure fine sand. No cobble

cesses built in the walls in at least one example. The purpose of the other walls is obscure, as erosion has been irregular and destroyed a great deal. No sherds were found with them so they are definitely preceramic. The only textile scraps recovered fit into the Huaca Prieta series so it seems that they mark a late preceramic phase not clearly defined at the Huaca Prieta. Contemporary refuse has shell beads and jet mirrors, both unknown earlier.

Fig. 12. Cupisnique Period House in Foreground, intersecting Conical Adobe Wall resting on Earlier House made with Cylindrical Adobes, Chicama Valley.

deposits exist nearby and the nearest rock outcrop is two-and-a-half kilometers away at the inner end of the Cerro Prieto promontory. Cobble firestones are thus rare but many small irregular bits of burned stones occur, showing that they made use of what they could rescue. Instead of stone-lined structures there are similar constructions lined with large rectangular adobes laid on edge. The use of such structures was here ultimately outmoded, and above them is a network of clay walls originally standing above the surface and made without adobes. Some are rectangular houses with squarish re-

Near the Huaca Prieta, as mentioned, what appears to be an unbroken sequence carries through into the Cupisnique level. The oldest pottery is a plain utilitarian ware similar to the Guañape type but with a minor difference in rim form in some pieces. They first occur in association with firestones, as though that custom was still a strong trait even when cooking pots were being used. With these sherds are clay retaining walls and above-ground clay houses, both made with vertical cylindrical adobes and small biscuit-like adobes stacked in piles, then filled in with mud (Fig. 12). Over walls of this

construction are others of roughly conical adobes laid with their long axes horizontal. Associated with these last are Cupisnique sherds and for the first time evidence of the cultivation of maize. Also new to the site are warty squash, pacay, and brown cotton. Various new techniques are apparent among the cloth scraps, but the earlier types of twining are still abundant. Further evidence of cultural continuity or blending of the new elements with the old is the basketry and the survival of stone-lined subterranean structures which intersect, cut through, and are thoroughly mixed in among the adobe walls, some older and some later (Fig. 13). The situation strongly suggests the peaceful settling here of a new people, who at first held to their own methods of construction but who finally realized the advantages of the local type.

With the oldest sherds are jet mirror fragments; bird bone, shell, and stone beads; weaving implements; pottery roller and plain stamps; figurine fragments; rectangular bone snuff tablets and bird bone snuff tubes; and probably stone bowls.

As the Cupisnique complex has been well described by Sr. Rafael Larco Hoyle[1] and others, there is little to add to what has already been mentioned—the plants new to the region, new textile techniques, and common use of pyro-engraving on gourds.

In addition to the work mentioned, a check was made of the most promising locations from Casma to Puemape, near Pacasmayo, looking for evidence of a strictly fishing culture but without success. A search for traces of nomadic hunter remains was somewhat more successful. Several years ago, Professor Otto Welter of Lima had found some interesting stone artifacts just north of the Chicama Valley. He kindly showed me the location which proved to be dotted with the workshop sites on which are an abundance of pressure flaked objects. Similar sites were found by Sr. Larco in Cupisnique quebrada and I located another in the Río Seco Valley between Moche and ·Virú. All are on fairly static surfaces, only rarely accidentally associated with sherds. All lack camp refuse and, though scraps of elephant and other extinct animal remains are present on the same type of surface, there is nothing to imply direct association. The lack of sherds with the pressure flaked blades and the absence of pressure flak-

ing in the Huaca Prieta and later cultures indicate that we are dealing with an earlier, unrelated group, probably nomadic hunters, and possibly the oldest remains yet encountered in this part of Peru.

Fig. 13. Subterranean House with Roof removed. Cupisnique Period, Chicama Valley.

Until the collections are available for study, it is premature to generalize on the results of this field work. Enough has been covered here to show that Peruvian prehistory goes much further back than previously supposed, whatever that may be in actual years.

### APPENDIX

As an appendix to this article, I would like to add some of the points to be considered in estimating time span in this region. My own estimates are presented here not with any idea of finality, but merely to stimulate discussion.

The position of the earliest sherds in the 21-foot soil profile, mentioned at the beginning of this article, suggests that the elapsed time since the Cupisnique ceramics is about five-sevenths of the total time since the drying up of the heavy discharge from the retreating ice. If Cupisnique goes back only 2000 years, the total profile would thus represent 2800 years. Into these first 800 years we must crowd·the following:

---

[1] Larco, 1941.

1) Sufficient time to permit the formation of a ground cover similar to the present vegetation on uncultivated ground. Let me assign 100 years for this, for the sake of argument.

2) Sufficient time to permit the formation of the 40-odd feet of fine debris at Huaca Prieta, ignoring any additional deposits which may have eroded away. Allowing an average rate of deposit of about one-half inch per year gives 1000 years.

3) To the above must be added the period of clay wall construction at Guañape with its 8 to 12 feet of sand mixed soil. With little strain on the imagination this might amount to 200 years.

4) Since our earliest sherds in the valley profile are of Cupisnique style, we must add the early ceramic period before Cupisnique, which is represented by about six feet of debris and disintegrated adobe dirt accumulated on a fair sized area at El Brujo. This might again amount to 200 years.

The summation of these considerations gives an estimated total of 1500 years, rather than the 800 previously allotted. If 1500 years is used as a scale for the lower two-sevenths of our soil profile, we arrive at an estimate of 3750 years since the introduction of Cupisnique ceramics and a total of 5150 years since the establishment of agriculture on this part of the coast.

American Museum of Natural History
New York City

# PRE-CERAMIC ART FROM HUACA PRIETA, CHICAMA VALLEY

## Junius B. Bird

While excavating pre-ceramic debris at the Huaca Prieta in the Chicama Valley just north of Trujillo two small carved gourds were found with a burial, a shallow, simple interment in the side of the community refuse dump.[1] Both were inside a woven cotton pouch which measured 12 by 21 cm. The gourds were so rotted that they were scarcely stronger than cigar ash and would have been abandoned except for the fact that they showed traces of carving. It required much painstaking work to harden the fragments and reconstruct the gourds for study.[2]

The results fully justified the effort, for these specimens were the only items of their kind encountered among the 10,770 gourd fragments and objects of gourd found in the same pit. Out of this total only thirteen pieces show any trace of decoration. Some pieces are crudely decorated by scratching away the outer surface or epidermis before the fruit was thoroughly dry, but the scratches in no instance form a recognizable design or pattern. Two fragments have fine incised line hatching. Five others show pyroengraving, but all are too incomplete to reveal the nature, quality, or extent of the design. None of the fragments show the careful cutting and combined use of fine and broad lines found on the two items from the burial. The lack of similar decorated pieces in the refuse suggests that the two containers were not made on the site but were importations.

The more complete of the two, fig. 1, b and c, measures 6.5 cm. in diameter and is 4.5 cm. high; the other, fig. 1 a, is slightly smaller. Both had lids cut from larger gourds, each with a yarn-whipped flange fitting inside the container opening.

The decoration of the better preserved gourd consists of four faces occupying equal segments of the surface, shown in flat projection in fig. 1 b. Its lid, though simply marked, may have been so fitted that its markings coincided with the quadrant plan of the design below it.[3]

The second gourd, fig. 1 a, has a more complex theme, two human figures with their faces visible on opposite sides of the gourd, while their bodies and limbs are cleverly adapted to the small area across the bottom. It is, in fact, difficult to recognize the import of these lines on the original specimen, and they were not understood until Miguel Covarrubias showed me how they separate to form the two figures. Even he, however, could not interpret the lines in the remaining spaces on the sides. These are areas where cleaning was stopped, and in them the course and relationship of all the lines is not clear. The lid of this specimen bears an S-shaped incised figure with bird heads at each end. Although the adaptation to small areas may have modified the proportions of these heads, the shape of the beaks and the projections above them suggest the male condor.

Reprinted from ÑAWPA PACHA 1, 1963. pp. 29-34.

The two containers have been shown to various artists and art historians who were asked for comments. All were in agreement on two significant points: that the work is not that of a beginner or someone experimenting in gourd carving, and that the character of the designs indicates a well established traditional art style. None could suggest a source or even a close parallel. The burial, No. 99.1/903, with which these specimens were found did not differ in arrangement from others above and below it, except that it was the only one in which artifacts other than matting had been deliberately placed with the body.

The position of the burial indicates that it was contemporary with Excavation Layer 0. It was located exactly two thirds of the distance down from the surface to the bottom in sloping strata which expand nearby to a present thickness of 13.7 m. As this large mound is and has been eroding for about 3,000 years, the original depth of refuse may well have been 3 m. greater. The whole mound consists of occupational debris resting on a flat surface, and all of it was deposited prior to the appearance of ceramics in this part of Peru.

The first C-14 measurements on samples from Huaca Prieta were made by the Chicago laboratory in 1950 using the solid carbon method.[4] The mean ages for the samples nearest to the burial (C-313 and C-316) suggest a date in the twenty fourth century B.C. for the burial. However, later measurements suggest that this date is too early. In 1955 the Lamont Laboratory ran two samples from the base of the deposit at Huaca Prieta using the newer carbon dioxide method (L-116A and L-116B).[5] Since publication of the results, the laboratory has corrected the age determinations by adding 200 years to each, because of the Suess effect. The earliest date which fits both of the revised Lamont measurements is 2125 B.C. The standard deviation figures for the earlier solid carbon dates are so large that these dates can be adjusted to the results of the Lamont measurements. If we accept 2125 B.C. as the most probable date for the beginning of the deposit at Huaca Prieta, the burial in question would be dated about 1950 B.C. Whatever the absolute date turns out to be, we have the positive evidence of stratigraphy that these carvings were made long before the appearance of pottery on this part of the coast.

Since the gourds were reconstructed, a study of the fabrics from the preceramic deposit has revealed far more patterning and design than we had previously expected. The commonest construction technique is twining with spaced wefts and exposed warps. Other pieces are woven, knotted, or looped. In the last two categories patterned examples are fairly common, but the techniques limit the design to structurally created diamonds variably spaced with bars or rows of small squares.

In the woven pieces patterning, except for stripes, is accomplished with warp floats. The most elaborate of these pieces, found above the level of the gourds, shows a bird figure, inverted and reversed in a repeat (fig. 2). The design was reconstructed by using a microscope to determine the position of the floats and then plotting them on graph paper.

In the twined fabrics warp stripes are common, though only rarely is their presence indicated by surviving color differences. Structural patterning was done by warp manipulation, the warps being shifted or transposed laterally and from face to face in various ways. A few patterned pieces, while technically complex, apparently made no use of color. The decoration consists of structurally contrasting areas in simple geometric arrangements. In the remaining twined specimens the manipulation of the warp was for the control and distribution of color. These are the specimens pertinent to the present topic.

Recognition of the designs in pieces where color contrast was used is difficult because of loss of dyes, pigments and natural fiber shades. Only in rare instances do color contrasts survive. Where the color is gone, special photographic techniques can help, but in most cases one must work with a microscope and plot each and every warp yarn movement in order. In this way the original shifts of color position can be determined, and, if enough of the fabric survives, the pattern or figure can be reconstructed.

Some of the designs are purely geometric assemblages of small diamonds and lines to form bold chevrons and squares. Others are representations of people, birds, or animals. These designs are achieved by two basic systems. One, in which the design shown in fig. 3 is executed, is technically identical with the construction of certain Woodland twined bags of North America. In the other system the warp pairs are handled somewhat differently, giving more solid color areas and sharper color divisions. The use of the latter system has not survived into historic times anywhere, as far as I know.

Both methods have technical limitations which give specific characteristics to the designs. In the first method, if the vertical lines of a figure parallel the warp, the horizontal color divisions, running across the warp, are clear, sharp, and straight. Deviations from a continuous horizontal have to be stepped by at least the space between weft rows and are clearly visible. Verticals are inevitably slightly zigzag but can be shifted less abruptly than the horizontals. Diagonals with minimum angles away from the vertical, determined by the ratio of the warp-weft count, are jagged and become increasingly serrated as the angle increases.

The second method produces serrated lines for both verticals and horizontals but has straight diagonals along the angle of the warp shift movement. Any other diagonal shift will be stepped.

In both methods, curves could be indicated as a series of steps but would be effective only in larger figures than those encountered. All figures done in these techniques are markedly angular, and faces shown in front view could have a stylistic resemblance to those on the gourds.

The degree to which such structural factors affect an art style will be directly proportional to the frequency with which the medium is used. At the Huaca Prieta the available media, in addition to textiles and gourds, include bark cloth, matting, basketry, wood, shell, bone, and stone. No decoration has been found executed in any of these materials, a situation which forces us to the conclusion that textiles were the major medium used in artistic expression. What is more, textiles were the major medium from the beginning of the occupation of the site. The complex techniques appear in the earliest levels and were already fully developed. Curiously, in the upper strata there is a suggestion of cultural, or at least artistic, degeneration. Production of the elaborate fabrics ceased completely, and there was no continuity of this form of expression into the later times.

What happened at Huaca Prieta need not have happened in other areas. Frédéric Engel has published a figured twined fabric from a pre-ceramic burial in the valley of Asia, about 660 km. south of the Huaca Prieta, which may date to late pre-ceramic times.[6] The design consists of large, angular double headed snakes. The construction of the Asia specimen is not exactly duplicated in the Huaca Prieta collection.

Perhaps more significant as a suggestion of continuity is the recurrence and distribution of the double headed snake theme. It appears in fig. 4 with crab appendages. Versions of the same motif are commonly executed in Paracas Cavernas (T-3) embroideries, double cloths and gauze weaves.[7]

Our sample of the other representations is too small to indicate preferences. I doubt that the use of the condor and of animal figures which might be cats has any more significance than the depiction of the crabs. The artists were representing the creatures they were familiar with, and if we find that their preference ran to the more impressive ones in each category, is that grounds for any but broad comparisons? What we should note is the absence of the type of emphasis on fangs which is so strongly apparent in the subsequent art of Chavín and wherever Chavín influence was felt.

This limited evidence suffices to extend the known antiquity of artistic expression in Peru and indicates at least some continuity with the work of later times. It shows that an angular, highly conventionalized style can be an outgrowth of technique and does not have to fit into any theoretical sequence of art forms starting with naturalistic treatment. There is as yet no basis for suggesting the origin or antecedents of this art style. As it is primarily a textile art, the chances of solving the question of its origins are exceedingly remote and will, in any case, involve an understanding of the rise and development of twined fabric technology in various parts of the world.[8]

## NOTES

[1]The excavations at Huaca Prieta were made for the American Museum of Natural History in 1946-47. For a general account of the site, see Bird, 1948.

[2]The initial field conservation was effected by slipping the gourd fragments from the pouch to wire screening and dipping them several times in a very dilute cellulose acetate, acetone and amyl acetate solution with no attempt at cleaning. Later each fragment was lined on its inner surface with bits of rice paper and, as contacts were established, the breaks also were covered. This procedure resulted eventually in the formation of a complete paper shell inside each specimen.

Next, over a period of weeks, very small amounts of the hardening solution were injected through the paper into the gourd material. Cleaning of the outer surface was left to the last and was the most delicate step, for the hardened dirt and dust had to be softened and removed without converting the gourds to a paste. In one case the work was completely successful; in the other it had to be stopped before all details were exposed.

[3] This gourd was illustrated by Covarrubias, 1954, fig. 2, p. 16.

[4] Bird, 1951.

[5] Kulp and others, 1952, p. 410; Broecker and others, 1956, p. 163.

[6] Engel, 1959, pl. 2.

[7] O'Neale, 1942.

[8] In using the illustrations to this paper it must be borne in mind that figs. 4, 5, 6 and 7 are plotted reproductions of yarn movements, laid out on graph paper at a warp-weft ratio of two to one. When this ratio differs radically from the warp-weft ratio of the specimen there is distortion. In fig. 6 the wing spread of the bird would be about one twelfth greater if the diagram were drawn in true proportion.

## BIBLIOGRAPHY

Bird, Junius Bouton
  1948     Preceramic cultures in Chicama and Virú. Memoirs of the Society for American Archaeology, no. 4, pp. 21-28. Menasha.

  1951     South American radiocarbon dates. Memoirs of the Society for American Archaeology, no. 8, pp. 37-49. Salt Lake City.

Broecker, W. S., and others
  1956     Lamont natural radiocarbon measurements III. W. S. Broecker, J. L. Kulp, C. S. Tucek. Science, vol. 124, no. 3213, 27 July, pp. 154-165. Lancaster, Pa.

Covarrubias, Miguel
  1954     The eagle, the jaguar, and the serpent; Indian art of the Americas. North America: Alaska, Canada, the United States. Alfred A. Knopf. New York.

Engel, Frédéric
  1959     Algunos datos con referencia a los sitios precerámicos de la costa peruana. Arqueológicas, 3. Pueblo Libre.

Kulp, John Laurence, and others
  1952     Lamont natural radiocarbon measurements, II. J. L. Kulp, Lansing E. Tryon, Walter R. Eckelman, and William A. Snell. Science, vol. 116, no. 3016, October 17, pp. 409-414. Lancaster, Pa.

O'Neale, Lila Morris
  1942     Textile periods in ancient Peru: II. Paracas Caverns and the Grand Necropolis. University of California Publications in American Archaeology and Ethnology, vol. 39, no. 2, pp. i-vi, 143-202. Berkeley and Los Angeles.

# KEY TO ILLUSTRATIONS

Fig. 1 (Plate II), a, b, projections of the carved decoration on two small gourd containers and their lids. The solidly dark areas and heavy lines have been carved or excised; the finer lines incised or scratched. The two figures shown separately, upper left, interlock across the bottom of gourd a. Below, c is a side view of gourd b and d is a top view of the cover. The two gourds were found together at Huaca Prieta in Excavation 3, Layer O. Cat. No. 41.2/2555, 2554.

Fig. 2 (Plate III). Two bird figures created with a single faced, warp float, weave of two ply cotton yarn. Huaca Prieta, Excavation 3, Layer $H_2I_2$. Loom width of fabric, 10 cm. Cat. No. 41.2/1205.

Fig. 3 (Plate III). Two incomplete human figures from a twined construction fabric. The transposed warp technique of this specimen is the same as that used in some Woodland twined bags. Both figures lack heads, as that portion of the fabric is missing. Between the two, in a blue stripe, are an S-shaped figure with bird (?) heads at each end and a small bird seen in profile; both figures are in red. Huaca Prieta, Excavation 3, Layer F. Cat. No. 41.1/9613.

Fig. 4 (Plate IV). A double-headed figure with appended rock crabs, created in a twined fabric with a transposed warp technique. The shaded background indicates the extent of the surviving textile, beyond which all portions of the figure are reconstructed. Huaca Prieta, Excavation 3, Layer G. Original length perhaps 40.5 cm. Cat. No. 41.1/9826.

Fig. 5 (Plate IV). A plotting of the figures in a small, rectangular twined fabric of transposed warp technique. The area, measuring 18.3 x 28.7 cm., is divided into four separate units, the first containing two rock crabs, the other three of uncertain interpretation because sections are missing. Huaca Prieta, Excavation 3, Layer M. Cat. No. 41.2/1711.

Fig. 6 (Plate V). Figure of a male condor with a snake in his stomach, from a transposed warp technique, twined fabric. As plotted, the height is exaggerated; the dimensions of the original figure are 17.2 x 10.5 cm. Huaca Prieta, Excavation 3, Layer K. Cat. No. 41.2/1501.

Fig. 7 (Plate V). Bird figures in twined, transposed warp construction from two specimens. Fig. 7a, incomplete stylization of the male condor in profile, repeated in a pattern stripe. Original length of figures, beak to tail, 18 cm. Color, blue against natural cotton. Huaca Prieta, Excavation 3, at juncture of the M and N layers. Cat. No. 41.2/1716. Fig. 7b, a reconstruction of a possible placing of the bird figures of 7a within the stripe area. Fig. 7c, succession of parrot-like bird figures, each 5.6 cm. long, within a pattern stripe. Huaca Prieta, Excavation 3, Layer M. Cat. No. 41.2/1695.

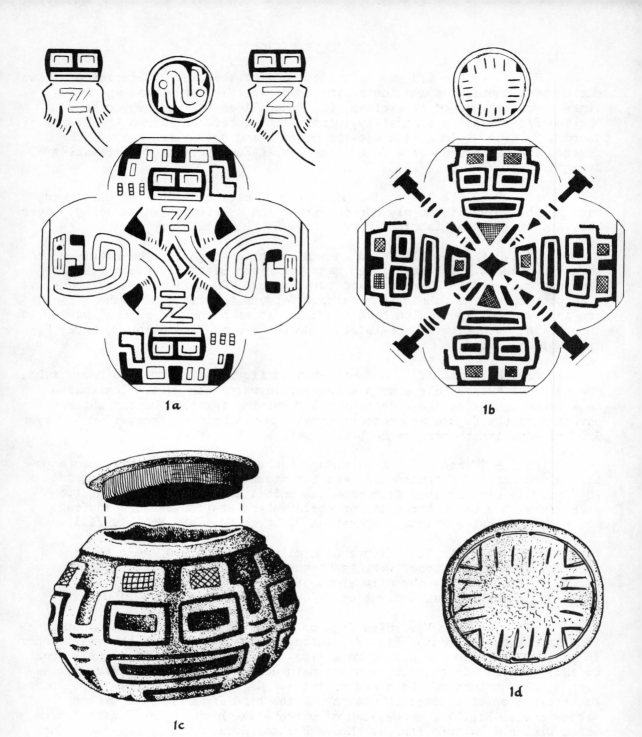

1a

1b

1c

1d

Plate II. Fig. 1, carved gourds from Huaca Prieta. a,b, projections of the designs; c, side view of gourd shown in b; d, cover of same gourd. (See key to illustrations for explanation.)

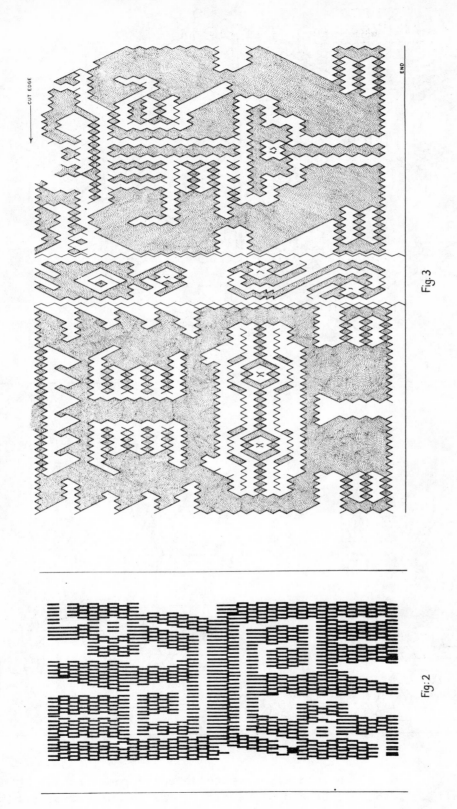

CUT EDGE

END

Fig.3

Fig:2

Plate III.  Fig. 2, bird figures on woven textile from Huaca Prieta; fig. 3, human figures from twined fabric.
(See key to illustrations.)

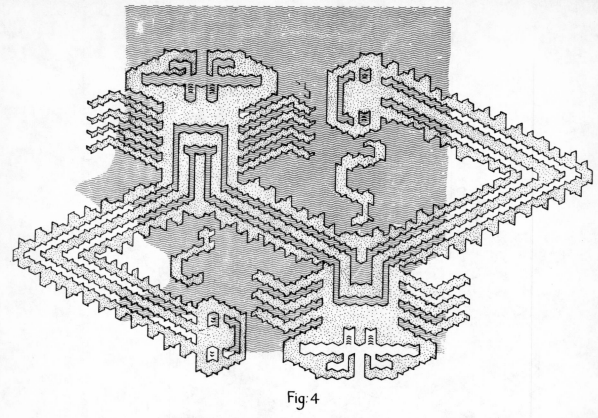

Fig: 4

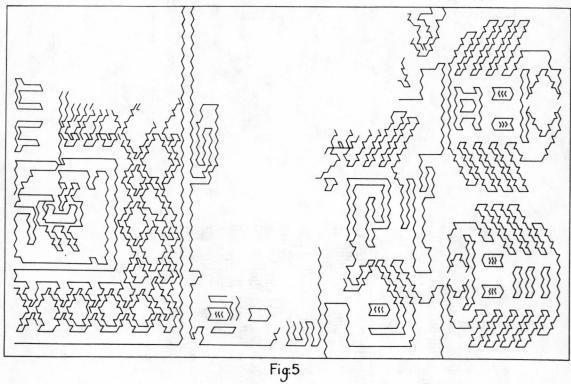

Fig: 5

Plate IV.  Fig. 4, double headed figure with appended rock crabs from a twined fabric; fig. 5, rock crabs and unidentified design units from a twined fabric.  (See key to illustrations.)

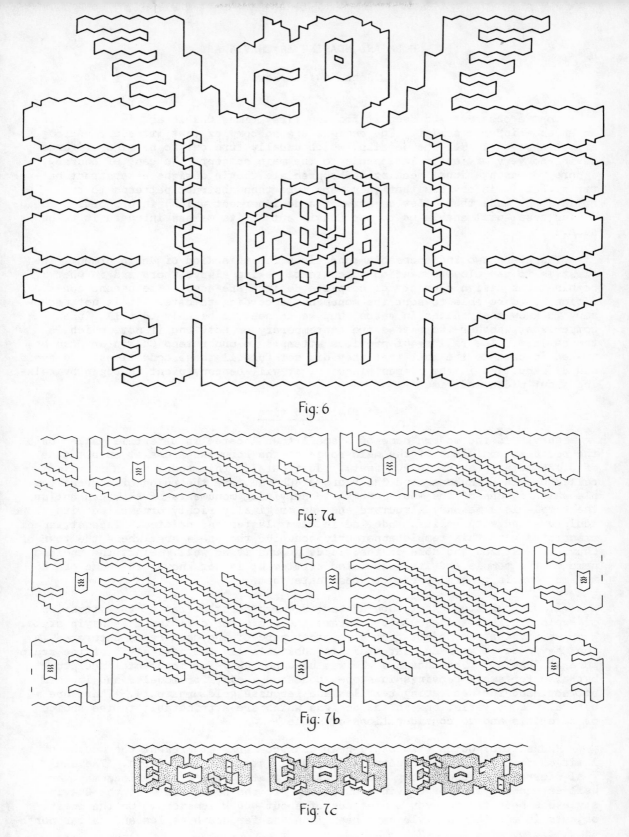

Fig: 6

Fig: 7a

Fig: 7b

Fig: 7c

Plate V.  Fig. 6, figure of male condor with a fish in his stomach (height exaggerated); fig. 7a, incomplete bird figure design; 7b, suggested reconstruction of 7a; 7c, band of parrot-like birds, all from twined fabrics.

# FORM AND MEANING IN CHAVIN ART

## John Howland Rowe

To the observer who sees it for the first time, Chavin art is as puzzling as an undeciphered script. The designs are so complex that it requires close attention even to see the details, which usually turn out to be minor figures having no very obvious relationship to the main subject. We can, of course, ignore representational meaning and appreciate Chavin designs as abstract patterns, but it is obvious that they were more than abstract patterns to the artists who made them. Let us attempt a decipherment which, in proportion to its success, will enable us to see Chavin art as its makers intended it to be seen.[1]

There are two indispensable conditions for this kind of decipherment. The first is to pay close attention to context, asking always where and in what combinations design elements or complete designs are used. The second condition is to be able to sort the monuments according to date. It is not necessary to know their dates in years, but we do need to be able to tell, in any comparison, whether two pieces are contemporary or not, and if not, which is the earlier. The failure of previous attempts to understand Chavin art can be traced in part to the fact that they did not fulfill these conditions. To avoid old difficulties in the present inquiry, it will be convenient to begin by talking about place and time.

## Place and time

Chavin is the modern name of a small town located in a fertile valley on the northeastern slope of the main range of the Peruvian Andes at an altitude of 3,135 meters (about 10,200 feet). Just outside this town, which is also called Chavin de Huántar and San Pedro de Chavin, are the ruins of a great temple which is one of the most remarkable surviving monuments of American antiquity. The temple is a masonry structure and was originally richly ornamented with stone sculpture and with reliefs modelled in clay plaster and painted. The settlement associated with this temple apparently occupied the whole area where the town of Chavin now stands and some of the fields around it as well. Since the ancient name of the temple and its associated settlement is not known, the name of the modern town is generally used to designate them.

It was the stone sculpture at Chavin which first attracted the attention of explorers, and this sculpture became the basis for defining the Chavin style. When we say that an object from some other part of the country is decorated in the Chavin style we mean that it is in substantially the same style as the sculpture at Chavin.[2] The Chavin style was used not only for monumental sculpture but also for small carvings in stone, bone and shell, for modeled and incised pottery, and for decorating textiles and repoussé gold ornaments. There are naturally some variations in the designs which are attributable to the choice of materials and to considerations of scale.

The site of Qotus ("Kotosh") near Huánuco marks at present the southern limit of discoveries of objects in the Chavin style in the sierra. The central sierra is so poorly explored, however, that future explorations may very well extend the area of Chavin occupation. To the north and west the Chavin style has been traced over a distance of about 400 kilometers. On the coast, objects in the Chavin style have been found as far south as Ica and as far north as Chiclayo.

The site of Chavin is not the only one with an imposing temple in the Chavin style. Two more are known in the sierra, one at La Copa ("Kuntur Wasi"), west of Cajamarca, and the other at Pacopampa near the northern edge of known Chavin territory. On the coast there is a great temple at Garagay, 7 km. north of Lima, the plan of which is very similar to that of Chavin, and other famous shrines at Mojeque and Pallca in the Casma Valley and at Cerro Blanco in the valley of Nepeña. In the present state of our knowledge we cannot say that Chavin was the ultimate center of origin of the Chavin style, although the style presumably originated somewhere in the area of its distribution. The available evidence suggests, however, that Chavin became an important center for the distribution of ideas of religious art.

At the same time that the Chavin style dominated the art of northern Peru a different style, called Paracas from the place where it was first recognized, was flourishing to the south of it. The Paracas style, with many local variations, has been found along the coast from Cañete in the north to Yauca in the south, and in the sierra near Ayacucho. Its full extent has not yet been traced. The Paracas style had close relations with Chavin, although it had many distinctive characteristics. No Paracas stone sculpture is known, but Chavin influence is evident in designs on pottery vessels, pyroengraved gourds, and textiles.

Dates in years for the decorative styles of ancient Peru are based on radiocarbon measurements. None of the results of measurements made on samples supposedly having Chavin style associations inspires much confidence, but the determinations made on earlier and later materials indicate the general order of antiquity of the Chavin style. On the basis of this kind of evidence it now appears that the Chavin style flourished between about 1200 and about 300 B.C. Its origins have not yet been found and may go back considerably further.

Constant change is apparently a universal characteristic of art styles, and it is not surprising to find that there were substantial changes in Chavin art in the nine hundred years or so of its existence. By determining the order of these changes we can establish a scale which will enable us to determine which monuments are earlier and which are later. Much research remains to be done on this problem, but the general outlines of the sequence are already apparent.

Our best evidence for the order of changes in the Chavin style is derived from a study of the Chavin influences reflected in the Paracas style pottery of the Ica Valley. The development of the Paracas tradition in Ica was the subject of an important study made by Lawrence E. Dawson and Dorothy Menzel of the University of California at Berkeley in 1959 and 1960.[3] These investigators were able to distinguish ten successive phases in the Ica variant of the Paracas style. This variant they call Ocucaje, after a section of the Ica Valley in which remains of this type are abundant, so that the phases of the sequence are designated "Ocucaje 1," "Ocucaje 2," and so on. The influence of the Chavin style is strong from Ocucaje 1 to Ocucaje 8, chiefly in the most elaborate pieces. Dorothy Menzel made the crucial observation that the Chavin influence in the Ocucaje sequence is not uniform; the Chavin features vary from one phase to another in a very consistent fashion, and features which are restricted to certain phases at Ica are found only on certain Chavin monuments. The order of changes in the Chavin influences in the Ocucaje sequence can be expected to reflect at least approximately the order of changes in Chavin art.

Among the features of Chavin origin present in the Ocucaje sequence which
have proved most useful in establishing time differences in Chavin art we may
mention a decorative point at the corner of the mouth which appears at Ica
first in Ocucaje 4, earlier Chavin influenced mouths having simple rounded
or square corners.  The mouth with this point should therefore be a relatively
late feature at Chavin.  Another useful feature is the treatment of twisted
geometric figures.  The curvilinear guilloche occurs early in the Ocucaje
sequence, while the angular twined fret occurs only very late and can be shown
to have developed out of the guilloche.  Decorative curls acquire longer and
longer stems.  There is an increasing tendency to accommodate the design to a
framework of parallel bands like the spaces on lined paper, with a consequent
replacement of curved lines by straight ones.

Using these features and a few others which occur in the Ocucaje sequence
as guides, it has been possible to arrange the stone sculpture from Chavin in
a consistent order which also makes sense in terms of other features not found
on Ica pottery, or occurring there under circumstances which do not permit
placement in time.  Features of this sort which occur only in a relatively late
context in Chavin art are eyes with angular eyebrows, the presence of a central
fang on profile faces, triangular teeth in the mouths of principal faces, small
snake heads in which the mouth is a continuation of the eyebrow line instead of
being drawn separately, and the extension of lip and teeth over the profile of
the face.

While I was working at Chavin in 1961 it occurred to me that it might be
possible to derive some independent evidence for the relative age of Chavin
sculpture from the relationship of individual pieces of sculpture to successive phases in the construction of the temple.  The inquiry turned out to be more
valuable for establishing context than for finding evidence of time differences,
but the results have some value for both purposes.

Largely because of vandalism beginning in the Colonial period and lasting
until the early years of the present century, most of the sculpture at Chavin
has been removed from its original position. Much has been destroyed, and much
is preserved only in battered fragments used as building stone in the village
church and in private houses.  There are, however, a few fragments remaining
in or near their original locations which enable us to visualize how sculpture
was used in the construction of the temple.

The temple consists of a number of rectangular structures up to 12 meters
in height which appear to be platforms of solid masonry designed to support
shrines built on top of them (fig. 2).  These rectangular structures are not
solid, however, but are honeycombed with interior passages and small rooms,
roofed with large slabs of stone and connected with each other and with the
open air by an effective system of ventilating ducts.  There are traces of painted plaster on the walls of these passages, and in one of the rooms three of the
slabs forming the ceiling have traces of low relief carving, now badly damaged.
Most of the roofing slabs were not carved, however.

The outside walls of the temple fabric were adorned with a row of human
and animal heads, carved in the round, which projected from the facade.  These
heads were provided with stone tenons, rectangular in section, which fitted
into sockets provided in the masonry.  Above the row of heads was a projecting
cornice of flat slabs with squared edges.  The under side of this cornice, and

in places the outer edge as well, was decorated with figures carved in low relief. Only one slab of this cornice is now in place, but others were found at the foot of the wall, presumably not far from where they had fallen. A number of rectangular stone slabs have been found, each with one side well finished and carved with a figure in relief with a frame around it. These slabs were apparently designed to be set in walls, but none has been found in its original position.

One of the interior passages leads to a great image which was evidently a cult object of major importance, one of the few cult objects of ancient Peruvian religion which can still be seen in its original setting (fig. 5). It is a shaft of white granite, some 4.53 meters long, set upright in a gallery crossing. The stone has been carved in low relief to represent a figure in human form with the right hand raised. The scale of this Great Image and its setting in a dark passage give it an awe-inspiring quality which can be felt even by a present day unbeliever, but which photographs and drawings fail to communicate.

The Great Image, infelicitously called "the Lanzón" in the earlier literature, was probably the principal cult object of the original temple at Chavin, for it stands close to the central axis of the oldest part of the temple structure. The original temple seems to have been a U-shaped structure consisting of a main building and two wings enclosing three sides of a rectangular court, the open side being on the east. The whole structure occupied an area of some 116.30 by 72.60 meters (fig. 2).

Subsequently the temple was enlarged several times and its center shifted. The two principal additions affected only the south wing, enlarging it until it formed a solid rectangular structure 70.80 by 72.60 meters in plan. The enlarged south wing was then treated as the main building of the temple; a new and larger court was laid out in front of it with flanking buildings on the north and south sides, again providing a U-shaped arrangement open to the east. The east front of the new main building, facing the court, was provided with a monumental portal, the south half of which was constructed of white granite and the north half of black limestone. We can call it the Black and White Portal (figs. 3 and 4).

The expansion of the south wing of the old temple until it became the main building of the new one probably reflected an increase in the importance of a deity which had originally been worshipped in the old south wing, an increase no doubt accompanied by a decline in the prestige of the deity of the Great Image. The original image of the deity of the south wing has not been found, probably because it was destroyed centuries ago. As we shall see, there may be a later representation of it, however.

We cannot use the sequence of additions to the old south wing to establish the order in which the cornices and tenon heads of this part of the structure were carved, because there is evidence suggesting that older sculptures were reused when a new addition was built, and that damaged slabs in the older parts of the temple were replaced long after the original date of construction. The evidence is stylistic; some of the cornice blocks found by the walls of the second major addition are almost identical in style with the earliest ones from the old south wing, while the most advanced style cornice slab in the whole temple was found near a much earlier one at the foot of the wall of the old south wing.

The sculptures associated with the Black and White Portal, however, do have some value in establishing a sequence of style changes in Chavin art. The Portal sculptures consist of two cylindrical columns, each carved with a single large figure in flat relief, and a short cornice decorated with a frieze of standing birds, also in relief (figs. 8, 9, 15, 16).[4] The columns supported the lintel of the entrance, and the cornice must have rested on top of the lintel. The close structural relationship of these carved members, the dimensions of which indicate that all were cut for the positions they occupied in the Portal, suggests that they were all carved at the time the Portal was built. This inference is supported by the fact that the style of all three is virtually identical. We can therefore treat the Portal sculptures as a stylistic and chronological unit for purposes of comparison. From its position the Portal cannot be earlier than the construction of the second addition to the south wing, and it may be later; its sculptures, therefore, should represent a relatively late phase in the sequence of Chavin carvings. The evidence of Chavin influence at Ica also suggests a relatively late date for the style of the Black and White Portal, so there is no conflict in the evidence.

The evidence now available is sufficient to suggest only the general outlines of a chronology for the Chavin style, a chronology much less detailed than the sequence we have for the contemporary Paracas style from Ica. For the present we can distinguish only four phases of Chavin art based on stylistic differences in the sculptures at Chavin itself; we can label these phases AB, C, D, and EF for convenience of reference. The use of the double letters, AB and EF, for the first and last of these phases will serve to remind us that it should be possible to subdivide them when a little more evidence is available.

The anchor point in this sequence is Phase D, for which the sculptures of the Black and White Portal serve as a standard of comparison. There are many other pieces of sculpture at Chavin which can be assigned to this phase because of their stylistic similarity to the Portal reliefs. Chavin Phase D should be at least in part contemporary with the fourth and fifth phases of the Paracas sequence at Ica. For Phase C at Chavin the standard of comparison is the most elaborate single monument of Chavin art, the so-called "Tello Obelisk" (figs. 6 and 7).[5] Only a few other fragments of sculpture can be assigned to this phase. Phase AB includes all examples of Chavin art which are judged to be earlier than the "Tello Obelisk," while EF includes all those which are later than the Black and White Portal. Among the monuments assigned to AB by these criteria are the cornice blocks from the main structure of the new temple which are decorated with representations of eagles or hawks (figs. 11-13), except for one, mentioned earlier, which belongs in Phase D (fig. 14).[6] The Great Image in the old temple (fig. 5) can be assigned to Phase AB also, although it is possible that some of the details on this figure were added later. Phase EF includes the famous Raimondi Stone (fig. 10) and a number of other reliefs, mostly fragments.[7]

Turning to monuments from other sites and pieces without provenience, we can assign the temple reliefs at Cerro Blanco in Nepeña to Phase C, and the lintel found at La Copa to EF.[8] The superb jaguar mortar in the University Museum in Philadelphia, the provenience of which is unknown, is a Phase AB piece, while Phase C is again represented by a carved bone spoon from the Huaura Valley.[9]

Not all examples of Chavin art can be assigned to their proper phase in our present state of knowledge; only ones which happen to have some features

which we can recognize as significant for chronology can be placed in the
sequence. Naturally, the more complex and elaborate a Chavin design is the
more likely it is to contain features which we can use for dating. The
simple pieces are more likely to be difficult to handle. Nevertheless, for
purposes of understanding Chavin art it is not necessary to be able to place
every piece. What we need is enough of a sequence so that we can see what
kinds of changes took place in the style, and that much is now available.

## Convention and figurative expression

Chavin art is basically representational, but its representational meaning is obscured by the conventions which govern the Chavin style and, in many
cases, by the fact that representational details are not expressed literally
but in a figurative or metaphorical fashion. These matters need to be explained before we can ask what Chavin artists were trying to represent.

The most important conventions affecting the understanding of representation in Chavin art are symmetry, repetition, modular width, and the reduction of figures to a combination of straight lines, simple curves, and
scrolls. Except for the tenon heads at Chavin, some figures modeled in clay
at Mojeque, and a few stone mortars, conceived in the round, the task Chavin
artists set themselves was to produce a linear design on a surface which was
either flat or treated as if it were flat. The conventions must be seen in
this context.

The symmetry of Chavin designs is generally bilateral with relation to
a vertical axis. There are a few Chavin designs both halves of which are
exactly alike, but more commonly there is some difference; for example, the
head of a figure may be shown on the main axis but in profile, or a full-face
figure may hold different objects in his hands. It seems to be the balance
of the design which is most important. Individual figures shown entirely in
profile are not symmetrical, but there was a tendency to put figures facing
one another so as to achieve symmetric balance by grouping instead of within
each figure.

The repetition of details or even whole figures in rows is very characteristic of Chavin design and gives it a certain rhythm. When details are
repeated they are as nearly identical as space will permit, while when whole
figures are repeated the repetition need not be so mechanical. For example,
the cornice of the Black and White Portal is ornamented with a frieze of standing birds (cf. figs. 15 and 16). The birds are represented in profile and all
face the center line of the Portal, the two middle ones standing beak to beak.
All the birds are about the same general size and shape, but in details they
vary by pairs. There are two alike, then two more, alike but different from
the first pair, and so on. Repetition of details became increasingly common
in later Chavin art, and details came to be multiplied for the purpose of
repetition without much regard for the requirements of the representation.

Modular width is an expression which Lawrence E. Dawson has suggested
to designate a convention which is common to a number of art styles in ancient
Peru. By the convention of modular width a design is composed of a series of
bands of approximately equal width, and nonlinear features, such as eyes and
noses, are accommodated to the modular framework as well. In Chavin art the
bands tend to be adjacent and parallel, so that sections of a design look as

though they had been drawn to follow parallel ruled guide lines, like the lines on ruled paper, a convention also found in the Paracas style, as we noted earlier. The accommodation of designs to modular banding became increasingly strict in late Chavin art, the curved lines of earlier designs being replaced in Phase EF by straight ones which interrupted the banding less. In earlier Chavin designs several different modular widths might be used for different parts of the design, thus providing variety; band width is more standard in the later phases.

The reduction of figures to a combination of straight lines, simple curves, and scrolls led to the representation of anatomical features as more or less geometric figures. The pelage markings of jaguars, for example, are represented as quatrefoils or cinquefoils and crosses. These figures are reasonable approximations of the shape of jaguar markings in nature, though of course no natural jaguar marking would have the sharp corners and straight sides of the cross the Chavin artists used to represent it. It would be easy to mistake such geometric figures for abstract elements used simply to embellish empty spaces if we had to interpret them on the basis of a single example. Comparing many pieces, however, we find these particular figures occurring repeatedly on cats, while they are absent on representations of birds, snakes, and people. It is this kind of consistency in context which enables us to decide between alternate possible interpretations of ancient art. A similar argument based on the observation of context in many examples enables us to conclude that small scrolls or curls were common conventions for hair and for the down on birds. Eyes may be represented by circles, ovals, lens shaped figures, or rectangles, and some intermediate forms are also found.

It is the figurative treatment of representations in Chavin art which has caused the most difficulty to modern observers. The question of why figurative expression was used in Chavin art is one which we can consider more profitably after we understand how it was used.

The type of figurative elaboration which is characteristic of Chavin art is one with which we are more familiar in literary contexts; it is a series of visual comparisons often suggested by substitution. To give a literary example, if we say of a woman that "her hair is like snakes," we are making a direct comparison (simile). If we speak of "her snaky hair" we are making an implied comparison (metaphor). We can go even further, however, and simply refer to "her nest of snakes," without using the word hair at all, and in this case we are making a comparison by substitution. In order to understand our expression the hearer or reader must either share with us the knowledge that hair is commonly compared to snakes or infer our meaning from the context. Comparison by substitution was an especially fashionable device in Old Norse court poetry, and it was given the name "kenning" by the thirteenth century Icelandic scholar Snorri Sturluson (1178-1241). This term, which implies that some knowledge or thought was required to understand the allusion intended, is appropriate and applies equally well to the comparisons by substitution in Chavin art.

Figurative expressions, of course, lose their force as they become familiar and commonplace, and they may end by being no more than synonyms for the literal statement. In order to maintain the figurative character of the discourse, fading figures need to be strengthened by elaboration or replaced by new ones. The weakening to which popular figurative expressions are subject thus provides a motivation for changes.

In Old Norse court poetry kenning became the chief basis on which verse was judged. The poets responded to this development in taste by devising ever more complex and far fetched kennings as well as increasing the frequency with which they used these figures. The elaboration of kennings was of two kinds, the kenning of kennings and the introduction of kennings which depended on a reference to a story which the hearers were assumed to know.

Both kinds of elaboration can be illustrated from the celebrated "Head-ransom" poem composed by Egil Skallagrímssonar in honor of Eric Bloodax, king of Northumbria, about the middle of the tenth century. An example of the kenning of kennings can be found in the fifth verse of Egil's poem where, in speaking of a battle, the poet says:

> The seal's field roared in wrath under the banners;
> There in blood it weltered about.[10]

"The seal's field" is a common kenning for the sea which would have been recognized immediately by Egil's audience. The sea, in turn, is a kenning for the attacking force, sweeping forward against the king's battle line as the sea sweeps in to break in confusion on the rocks. Neither the attacking force nor the sea to which it is being compared is mentioned directly in this figure. In another place in the same poem Egil refers to poetry as "Odin's mead," using a kenning which involves a reference to a story, in this case the old Norse legend of the origin of poetry, not told in this poem.

The same kind of development in the direction of increasing figurative complexity which we have described for Old Norse poetry took place also in Chavin art. Kennings became more numerous and more far fetched, and we can identify cases of the kenning of kennings. We cannot identify kennings referring to stories in any specific way, because the literary tradition is lost, but no doubt some of the figures which are difficult to interpret as simple visual comparisons are in fact kennings of this type.

The way in which kennings and other comparisons were used in Chavin art can be seen most clearly in earlier pieces in which the comparisons are still relatively simple. Let us examine a few of the more common comparisons.

A projecting appendage to the body may be compared to a tongue and hence shown issuing from the mouth of an extra face which is inserted in the body for the purpose. The tongue comparison is applied to the tail and feet of cat figures, the legs and feet of human figures, and the tail, wings, and feet of birds. Since an extended tongue would cover the lower jaw, the faces used in this comparison are agnathic; that is, the lower jaw is not shown. The extra faces may be represented either in front view or in profile. Sometimes, when a front view face would seem to be called for, we find instead two profile faces, drawn nose to nose, combining symmetry with repetition.

The same bodily appendages which are compared to tongues may be compared simultaneously to necks and provided with a face at or near the end in consequence. A long appendage, such as a tail, may have an agnathic face part way down its length from which the rest of the appendage issues as a tongue.

Smaller bodily appendages are usually compared to snakes, and in this case they usually issue directly from the body or from a simple ring in the earlier style. The hair and whiskers of cats are represented as snakes, and

sometimes the ears as well.  In bird representations the down on the head and
the alula at the front of the wing may be shown in this way.  Individual
feathers usually end in faces, but it is not always clear whether they were
thought of as representing snakes or simply as necks with a head at the end,
snake heads not being always clearly distinguishable from other heads.  On
many of the tenon heads which represent human beings the hair is shown as
snakes, and sometimes the long wrinkles of the face as well.

Another common kenning is the use of greatly elongated mouths, best
described as continuous mouth bands, to mark the major structural lines of
the body.  In the earlier examples of Chavin sculpture this device is used only
to mark the main axis of the body, the axis of the backbone, in representations
of birds with the wings spread, and the continuous band has no eyes or nose
associated with it.  In later Chavin art the continuous mouth band was used
more freely, for example to mark the bony axis of bird's wings and the axis of
the tail, and there is often a nose and an eye associated with it.  The comparison intended by the continuous mouth band seems to be one between the
strong but flexible structure of a chain of bones and the lines of teeth set
in a pair of jaws.

The commonest figurative device in all of Chavin art is one in which the
mouth of almost any kind of creature may be represented as the mouth of a
snarling cat, with the teeth bared and long pointed canines overlapping the
lips.  The cat the artists had in mind was probably the jaguar, legendary
throughout tropical America for its courage and strength, because most of the
complete cat figures shown in Chavin art have jaguar pelage markings.  The cat
mouth appears not only in its natural context, in representations of cats, but
also as the mouth of human figures, of snakes, and, most incongruously, of birds.
Birds shown with the head in profile, in fact, often have not only a jaguar
mouth but a complete cat face with nose and forehead marking, the bird's beak
and cere being attached to the profile like an ill-fitting mask.  All faces used
to establish the kennings of tongues and necks have cat mouths, and the continuous mouth band is a cat mouth also, as indicated by the presence of long canines.
The cat mouth is not universal in Chavin art, however; there are some representations of human beings which do not have it.  It is interesting that these human
figures also lack kennings entirely.  Small snake heads used as kennings for
hair or down also lack the cat mouth, although larger snake heads have it.

The logic behind the figurative use of the cat mouth in Chavin art is obscure.  It is hard to see the cat mouth as a direct comparison, but on the other
hand it has a very intimate association with the use of kennings, being used in
all faces which establish kennings except for the small snake heads.  Perhaps
the most reasonable of several possible alternative explanations is that the cat
mouth is used to distinguish divine and mythological beings from ordinary creatures
of the world of nature, with the implication of a comparison between the power of
the jaguar and supernatural power.  If so, the cat mouth can be considered a kind
of kenning also, although it differs from the others in that it involves a comparison of quality; it becomes an allegorical figure.

The solution we have proposed for the problem of interpreting the significance of the cat mouth in Chavin art is supported by the further consideration
that there are some suggestions from the archaeological context of the art that
it is associated with religious ritual.  All of the sculpture at Chavin with
known provenience which uses the cat mouth figuratively is temple sculpture, and

the clay reliefs at Cerro Blanco in Nepeña have similar associations. One of the few lots of smaller objects in the Chavin style which has been found in some kind of association is a hoard of gold from the Hacienda Almendral, near Chongoyape, most of which is now in the Museum of the American Indian in New York.[11] The lot includes four crowns with elaborate designs, eleven ear spools and a pair of tweezers, an assemblage most reasonably interpreted as ritual paraphernalia. Both at Chavin and in the Chongoyape crowns the more prominent the main figure in a design is the more kennings (i.e., the more cat mouths) it has associated with it. Perhaps the use of kennings was even proportional to the supernatural importance of the figure involved.

The kennings we have discussed so far involve a single face for each kenning, and the faces themselves are treated more or less naturalistically. There is one comparison which involves a purely imaginative elaboration of figurative faces, however. Any long narrow feature such as a girdle or the body of a snake may be compared to a chain of connected profile faces; the girdle of the Great Image is a good example (fig. 5). The faces in the chain have two interesting peculiarities. In the first place, they are what we can call "dual faces"; that is, each mouth has an eye and a nose on each side of it, so that the mouth may be seen as shared by two faces, each upside down with respect to the other. In the second place, the faces are joined to one another by the device of a continuous lip band which runs from one mouth to the next across the profiles of the faces.

The chain of faces was subject to further elaboration as the Chavin style developed. In later phases the part of the continuous lip band connecting different mouths across the profile of the face was interpreted as the lip of an agnathic mouth at right angles to the original ones, and it was supplied with the appropriate teeth. There was also some tendency to run the lip and teeth of single faces up over the profile, probably by analogy with the faces in the chains.

As early as Phase AB we find front view agnathic faces provided with a pointed tooth in the center as well as the usual canines on each side. The central tooth is a pure product of the imagination which can be based on no observation of nature and represents simply the triumph of Chavin ideas of symmetry over the symmetry of nature. The idea later spread to other contexts. In Phase C the central tooth appears on profile faces with lower jaws, and this usage becomes standard in Phase D. The central tooth projects downward from the upper jaw and rests against the lower lip.

Although the Chavin style is predominantly representational, as we have already noted, it does include a few abstract and purely decorative elements. On the Great Image, for example, a two-strand guilloche appears on the back and under the feet of the principal figure. In the latest phase of Chavin art an angular twined fret was developed out of the rounded guilloche, although guilloches also continued to be made. Another late development was the use of three-strand guilloches and twined frets as well as two-strand ones.

As early as Phase C the guilloche acquired a representational meaning in some cases, being used to represent the twined bodies of two snakes. The difference is, of course, that such guilloches end in snake heads. Later the holes where the strands cross were supplied with eye pupils. Both of these developments represent reinterpretations of abstract shapes as representations, a type of reinterpretation made earlier by the fact that Chavin artists were accustomed to using geometric figures as representations of features of nature.

Abstract elements are, on the whole, commoner in the later sculpture from Chavin than in the earlier, and commoner on pottery than in sculpture. Some of them seem to be derived from earlier representational figures which came to be used out of context and were sufficiently ambiguous as figures so that their representational meaning was easily lost or ignored. For example, a simple figure like an S lying sideways is very common in later Chavin pottery and occurs also in later sculpture. It appears to be derived from a representation of an eyebrow with a curled end which is common in the earlier sculpture. An intermediate form appears on the bodies of the Phase AB cat figures which ornament the cornice on the southwest corner of the temple at Chavin (fig. 17). Here the S figure has a round eye in each end, and neither eye is in context as the eye of a face. The case of the S figure is, of course, the converse of that of the guilloche.

It should ultimately be possible to write a kind of grammar of Chavin art which would provide a complete explanation of the conventions and kennings of even the most complex of the later designs. The observations offered here fall far short of such a grammar, but they should be sufficient to enable the reader to make intelligent observations of his own when he looks at Chavin designs, and that is the purpose of the present survey.

## Representational meaning

Once we are able to recognize the elements in Chavin designs which are figurative or which represent purely decorative elaboration we can look behind such elements for the underlying representational meaning of the figures. For the most part, each figure is a separate problem; most Chavin compositions consist of a single principal figure which stands or acts alone, although it may have smaller subsidiary figures associated with it. The subsidiary figures are arranged according to the dictates of symmetry, however, and the arrangement does not necessarily reflect any narrative meaning.

When one learns to see through the figurative elaboration of Chavin designs a surprising proportion of them turn out to be representations of natural bird, animal, and human forms. Since most of these forms are supplied with cat mouths and other kennings, they are presumably the forms of supernatural beings, but the point is that they are seldom monstrous forms. Beings which are part human and part animal in form do occur in Chavin art, as we shall see, but they are much less common than is generally supposed.

The commonest natural forms represented in Chavin art are birds which can be identified as eagles and hawks. The recognizable features which permit this identification are the strong raptorial feet, the short, sharply hooked beak with a prominent cere over it containing the bird's nostril, and the fact that the birds are always shown with down or feathers on the head and sometimes under the chin as well. Hawks are distinguished by having a decorative line on the face curving back from the base of the eye, a convention for the cheek marking of natural hawks; eagles lack this marking. Contrary to widespread belief, there are no representations of condors in Chavin art. The figures which have been mistaken for condors are figures of eagles or hawks. The error originated in a misinterpretation of the Chavin convention for the cere with a nostril in it; this convention is a simple scroll at the top of the beak, and it was mistaken for a representation of the peculiar caruncle which projects above the beak of the male condor. Condors have no feathers on their heads, however, and do not have raptorial feet.[12]

Representations of cats are not particularly abundant in Chavin art and are virtually restricted to Phases AB and C. In most cases there is no question that the cat represented is a jaguar, the identification being given by conventionalized jaguar markings. On the cornice slab preserved at the southwest corner of the new temple at Chavin, however, there are two figures of cats, without the standard jaguar markings, which may be intended to represent pumas (fig. 17).

Representations of other animals are very rare as principal figures in Chavin compositions. At Chavin itself, there are two snakes on the same cornice slab with the "pumas," and one representation of a monkey, one of a bat, and one which may possibly be intended for a viscacha, these last three being on flat relief slabs originally set into a wall.[13] Representations of crabs are fairly common on the coast but have not been found in the sierra.[14] Fish occur only as secondary figures, but they are quite common in that context. It is interesting that there are no representations of food animals, such as the deer, guanaco, and guinea pig, and none of several other animals which are common subjects in other Peruvian art styles, such as the fox, the lizard, and the frog. Plants and vegetable products are rarely shown in Chavin art and then only as secondary figures.

The sculptured animal figures at the Chavin temple occur in three contexts, on cornices, on rectangular relief slabs made to be set in a wall, and in the form of tenon heads. In all three cases they serve as architectural decoration and are not given such emphasis that there is any reason to think that they may have served as cult figures. The eagles and jaguars wich predominate on the cornices may have been thought of as supernatural beings which served the gods, but they were clearly not deities themselves. The other animals less commonly shown are perhaps figures from mythology.

There are a few representations of men from the Chavin area which have no figurative elaboration of any kind. They are all on fairly small slabs and may also have served as architectural decoration. The most interesting one shows a man carrying a spear thrower and three darts in his left hand and a trophy head in his right (fig. 20). Perhaps a quarter of the tenon heads from the temple at Chavin represent human heads shown without kennings; there are also some which have natural mouths but hair and facial wrinkles kenned as snakes.[15]

Figures with a human or animal form depicted with elaborate kennings are the ones most likely to represent deities or important mythological beings, and our confidence that they do is increased by the contexts in which such figures occur.

There is only one animal figure which is represented in Chavin art in such a way as to suggest that it might be a deity or important mythological figure, and that is the alligator, or more properly cayman, which is represented on the so-called "Tello Obelisk" (fig. 6) and in two other sculptures, a granite frieze found at the foot of the Monumental Stairway at Chavin (fig. 19) and a relief from Yauya (fig. 18). In all three cases the caymans are shown with elaborate kennings, and in two of them accompanied by subsidiary figures. The "Tello Obelisk" is a rectangular shaft, carved on all four sides, and is more likely to have been a cult object than a simple piece of architectural decoration. The caymans are represented with fish tails, but this mythical detail may be no more than a misunderstanding on the part of artists who were not personally familiar with their subjects, caymans occurring only at a much lower altitude.

The Great Image in the interior of the old temple at Chavin certainly served as a cult object, and the principal figure shown on it can be taken to represent a deity. This figure (fig. 5) is human in form, apart from a moderate amount of figurative elaboration. The deity of the Great Image is represented standing, with his left arm at his side and his right arm raised. The hands are open and hold nothing. He wears ear pendants, a necklace, and apparently a tunic and girdle. His hair is kenned as snakes and his girdle as a chain of faces.

The most peculiar feature of this figure is the mouth, which is very large, has the corners turned up, and is provided with upper canines only. Ordinary human figures have mouths of more modest proportions, the corners of which are either straight or turned down, while the ordinary figurative cat mouth has both upper and lower canines. The peculiar features of the mouth of the Great Image are paralleled in three tenon heads belonging to an early phase of the Chavin style.[16] In the tenon heads, however, the mouth is agnathic and has no teeth in it, while the mouth of the Great Image does have teeth, together with a lower lip and a lower jaw. The teeth and lower lip seem out of context here, and on close observation it can be seen that they do not fit. The artist's conception of the deity he was representing may have demanded this incongruous combination, but it is also possible that the figure was first carved with a toothless agnathic mouth and then the teeth and lower jaw added.

A later representation of the same deity has also been found at Chavin on a beautifully finished relief slab found in a corner of the small patio in front of the Black and White Portal (fig. 21). The identification is based primarily on the mouth, which is large and has upturned corners, large backswept upper canines and no lower ones. This figure also has ear pendants which look as though they were copied from those of the Great Image. The figure on the relief slab holds a large spiral shell in the right hand and what appears to be a Spondylus shell in the left.[17] Shells such as these were common offerings in ancient Peru in many periods, and those which the deity holds very likely represent the offerings he expected from his worshippers. This cheerful deity deserves a name, and I propose to call him the Smiling God.

We were able to identify the Smiling God as a deity because the Great Image, which represents him, is clearly a cult object. There are some other figures represented in the temple at Chavin which occur in such contexts that we can recognize them as lesser supernatural beings; these are the figures represented on the columns which flank the doorway in the Black and White Portal (figs. 8 and 9). These columns are working architectural members and hence unlikely to have served as cult objects. Each column is ornamented with one great figure in low relief, and each figure has the body, legs, and arms of a man, but the head, wings, and claws of a bird of prey. The bird attributes of the figure on the south column are those of an eagle, while the figure on the north column has the cheek markings of a hawk. The figures are standing, and each holds what is apparently a sword club across his body. Both figures are represented with elaborate kennings, those of the eagle figure being somewhat the more elaborate of the two. The position of the columns suggests that these figures represent supernatural beings stationed to guard the entrance to the temple, "angels" in the original sense of the word; that is, supernatural messengers and attendants of the gods.

The guardian angels of the Black and White Portal were specifically
the attendants of the god who was worshipped in the new temple, presumably
the same one who had been worshipped in the south wing of the old temple.
As we remarked earlier, his cult image has not been found, but it is possible
to argue that we have other representations of him.  There are two parts to
the argument, the first involving the Raimondi Stone and the second a gold
plaque in the Museo Rafael Larco Herrera in Lima.

The Raimondi Stone is a beautifully finished granite slab carved with
a figure in relief which is so elaborated with kennings as to suggest that
it represents a deity (fig. 10).  It was found in the ruins of the temple
of Chavin about 1840, but no record of the precise location was made; it
has been exhibited in Lima since 1874.[18]  The slab is 198 cm. long and 74
cm. wide, making it the largest relief slab showing a single figure which has
been found at Chavin.  The deity represented on it is a being of human form
standing in full face position and holding a vertical staff in each hand.
He is not the Smiling God, because he has a mouth with turned down corners
and is provided with both upper and lower canines.  Furthermore, he lacks
ear pendants, although this feature is not necessarily as significant as
the mouth treatment and the position holding two staffs.  Let us call him
the Staff God.  The Raimondi Stone was meant to be set vertically, no doubt
in a wall.  The figure of the deity takes up only the lower third of its
total height, the rest of the length of the stone being filled with extra-
ordinarily elaborate figurative treatment of the Staff God's hair in which
a common late kenning, hair compared to a tongue coming out of a mouth, is
multiplied by repetition to fill the space.  The figure of the god could
not be elongated to fill the slab, because to do so would violate accepted
canons of proportion of the human body, and the multiplication of hair kennings was an ingenious solution to the artist's problem of making the representation of the god fit the stone.

The Raimondi Stone is carved with the same care and has the same unusually
fine finish as the relief slab from the terrace setback which represents the
Smiling God.  The relation between the latter slab and the Great Image seems
to be that the slab, which is later in style than the cult image, serves the
purpose of providing a representation of the Smiling God out in the open on
a wall of the temple where worshippers who would not be admitted to the
inner sanctum where the original image was could see it.  The first part of
my argument is that the Raimondi Stone is an analogue of the slab representing the Smiling God and thus a representation of another image worshipped in
the interior of the temple.  Since the Raimondi Stone is the larger of the
two slabs and the kennings on it are more elaborate, it should represent a
deity which, at the late period when the Raimondi Stone was carved, was more
important than the Smiling God.  The deity of the new temple was the one at
Chavin who became more important than the Smiling God, so the Staff God should
be the deity of the new temple.

The gold plaque in the Rafael Larco Herrera Museum which figures in
the second part of the argument lacks provenience but is in a pure and relatively late Chavin style (fig. 23).  It represents a figure which, from its
pose and treatment of the mouth, we can recognize as the Staff God of the
Raimondi Stone without the elaborated figurative treatment of the hair.  To
right and left of the Staff God are abbreviated figures of attendant angels
which combine human and bird attributes like the angels on the columns at

Chavin.  The combination on the plaque suggests that the angels shown on the columns are specifically attendants of the Staff God.  If so, the Staff God belonged in the temple behind them.

The Staff God was clearly more than just a local divinity at Chavin, for we find him represented also in gold on one of the crowns from the Almendral hoard at Chongoyape and on two pieces found in the territory of the Paracas style, at Ica.  One of the pieces from Ica is a painted textile in the collection of Michael D. Coe in New Haven, and the other is a ritual gourd cup, in the Paracas style but under heavy Chavin influence, in the collection of Paul Truel in Ocucaje (fig. 22).[19]  In later Andean religion gods who were worshipped so widely were nature gods, all others being of local or regional importance.  If, as seems likely, this fundamental distinction was an old one in Peru, the Staff God was probably a nature god.  His association with eagles and hawks in the temple at Chavin suggests that he was a sky god, but that is as far as our archaeological evidence will take us.  Perhaps he was a god of Thunder, like the Inca deity Illapa, who was pictured as a man holding a club in one hand and a sling in the other.  There is no particular reason to think that he was a creator god.[20]

The Staff God is the only deity of Chavin religion whom we can recognize on the basis of present evidence as having more than local importance.  The other gods we have been able to identify, the Smiling God and the cayman deity, are not known outside of the area around Chavin.  An image found at La Copa perhaps represents another local deity of this type.[21]  It should be remembered, however, that the evidence we have is still very fragmentary, and that future work may bring to light many other Chavin gods, some of whom may prove to be as widely popular as the Staff God.

We have now discussed the representational meaning of most of the complete figures which appear in Chavin art.  There are also many abbreviated figures, the meaning of which is much less clear, particularly on pottery and gold ornaments.  These abbreviated figures include human, cat, bird, and snake heads or simply generalized agnathic faces, and individual features out of context, such as eyes, hands, feathers, jaguar markings, and dotted circles which represent snake markings.  We can usually recognize a bird head as a bird head, for example when we find it on a Cupisnique bottle from the north coast, but we cannot yet tell whether the abbreviated figure is purely decorative or whether it is intended to convey also some religious meaning.

In spite of the problems that remain, we are now in a position to look at Chavin art with some understanding as well as to appreciate its purely aesthetic value.  It is a religious art, but it is also a highly intellectual one, produced for people who were willing to have their minds challenged as well as their emotions.  For us who approach Chavin art without knowing the language, the religious ideas, or the mythology of the men who made it, the problem of understanding what they meant to say is indeed comparable to the problem of deciphering an unknown script.

### The sequel

The Chavin style came to an end about 300 B.C., but we know little as yet about the attendant circumstances.  Perhaps its spread had been associated with military conquest and the central power collapsed, or perhaps a movement for religious reform developed and brought with it a simpler style. Perhaps the style itself simply became more and more abstract, so that the old rules disintegrated. At any rate, come to an end it did, and there followed a period characterized by the development of many distinctive local styles in the area which the Chavin style had once dominated. The Chavin style must have left some sort of a tradition, however, as Roman art left a tradition in the Middle Ages, because we find both imitations and derivatives of it in later times. Imitations of Chavin style are particularly prominent in the pottery style of Moche, while deities in the pose of the Staff God are found in the Middle Horizon religious art of Huari and Tiahuanaco.

The Moche style flourished on the coast between Pacasmayo and Nepeña, an important part of the old Chavin area, between about A.D. 1 and A.D. 580. The finest Moche pottery was naturalistically modeled or painted with lively narrative scenes executed in dark red on a cream background. Some of the scenes are clearly derived from myths, and a prominent figure in them is a personage with a human head but a jaguar mouth. His exploits remain to be studied in detail, but he appears in contexts which suggest that he may have been a culture hero.[22]

The shapes of the finer vessels in the Moche style and its emphasis on naturalistic modeling appear to represent a deliberate revival of the corresponding features of the Cupisnique style, the local variety of the Chavin style in pottery. This revival followed a period of some centuries during which the pottery of this area was quite different. In the third phase of the Moche style there are also a number of vessels which are decorated with remarkably faithful imitations of Chavin incised designs.[23] There is no question about the date and associations of these pieces, for several of them have been found in graves with ordinary Moche style pottery, and they display some characteristic Moche features mixed with the revived Chavin ones.

The Huari and Tiahuanaco styles of the Middle Horizon flourished about A.D. 580 to 930, the first in Peru and the second in northern Bolivia and neighboring areas. The two styles display variants of a common tradition of religious art the immediate origins of which are obscure. The Huari and Tiahuanaco styles have as one of their most prominent deity subjects a full face figure of human form holding two staffs, like the Staff God of Chavin. In fact, it seems likely that all deities in these styles were depicted in the Staff God pose. In the Huari style, but not at Tiahuanaco, deity figures have a jaguar mouth.[24] In both styles deities may be accompanied by attendant angels, sometimes with the heads of hawks.[25] These resemblances to Chavin are of a different sort from those of Moche, however; they represent a transmission of particular religious conventions. There are no known Huari or Tiahuanaco pieces which show an attempt to imitate the actual Chavin manner, like the attempt made by the Moche potters. One way or another, however, it is evident that Chavin art and Chavin religion cast a long shadow in ancient Peru.

[1] This study is a revision, written in 1967, of a paper originally written for a publication of the Museum of Primitive Art of New York (Rowe, 1962). The illustrations provided are a different selection from those which appeared with the 1962 version, and a selection which I believe is more appropriate to the text. Except as specifically acknowledged in the text, the ideas and interpretations presented here are my own and are based on direct examination of the original evidence.

My research on Chavin art was supported in part by a grant from the National Science Foundation. This study incorporates also data gathered on a trip to Peru in 1961, the expenses of which were met by grants from the American Philosophical Society and the University of California. Further data were gathered on another trip made in 1963 under the auspices of the University of California. It is a pleasure to acknowledge the hospitality and generous guidance provided by the Archaeological Commissioner at the ruins of Chavin, Marino Gonzáles Moreno, whose skillful and meticulously documented excavations, beginning in 1954, have thrown a flood of new light on Chavin architecture and sculpture. This study is dedicated to him in respect and admiration. I am also very grateful to Drs. Manuel Chávez Ballón and Jorge C. Muelle for information regarding their research at Chavin and to Toribio Mejía Xesspe and Julio Espejo Núñez for putting the Tello collections at the National Museum of Anthropology and Archaeology at my disposal.

The unsigned drawings are the work of the following illustrators: Zenon Pohorecky (figs. 10, 11, 15, 16); Janet C. Smith (figs. 6, 7, 8, 9, 12, 18); and Robert Berner (figs, 1, 14, 17, 19).

[2] This definition follows the one proposed by Gordon R. Willey in 1951 (p. 109). Willey's paper is a valuable guide to the earlier literature on Chavin and the Chavin style. The most important subsequent contribution to the subject is J. C. Tello's report on Chavin, written between 1940 and 1946 but not published until 1960. It includes a catalogue of the Chavin sculpture known before 1945.

[3] Menzel and others, 1964.

[4] See also Rowe, 1962, figs. 1, 3, 9, 10. The columns were found fallen and have been set up one step below their original position and further apart.

[5] For other illustrations of this monument see Rowe, 1962, fig. 6; Tello, 1923, fig. 72 and plate I; Tello, 1960, fig. 31. It is now in Lima, where I made a rubbing of it in 1961 which was the basis of the drawing presented here.

[6] See also Bennett, 1942, fig. 3; Tello, 1943, plate XXII; Valcárcel, 1957, figs. 6 and 7; Tello, 1960, figs. 36, 64, 66-67.

[7] Tello, 1960, fig. 69 (Bennett, 1942, fig. 24), and Tello, 1960, figs. 60 and 70. The piece illustrated by Tello, 1960, fig. 53, from the ruins of Qotus ("Gotush") on the opposite bank of the Mosna River, probably belong to this phase. The piece illustrated by Tello, 1960, fig. 52, is another fragment

of the same monument as that shown in fig. 53, or of another one very much like it.

[8] For Cerro Blanco, Nepeña, see Means, 1934, pp. 100-105; Tello, 1943, plate XIIIa (a reconstruction). I have cited the lintel from La Copa on the basis of a drawing published by Carrión Cachot, 1948, fig. 17.

[9] For the mortar, see Rowe, 1962, fig. 33; for the spoon, Lothrop, 1951, fig. 74d.

[10] Text from Gordon, 1957, pp. 112-114; my translation.

[11] Lothrop, 1941, pp. 251-258.

[12] This argument is an extension of one published by Yacovleff, 1932. The identification of the birds at Chavin as condors was first made by J. C. Tello in 1923.

[13] There is a good photograph of the snakes in Izumi, 1958, p. 7, top. For illustrations of the bat and the "viscacha" see Rowe, 1962, figs. 13 and 12. It was Marino Gonzáles who suggested the possibility that the last might be a viscacha. The lack of detail makes a positive identification of this animal particularly difficult.

[14] Kroeber, 1944, fig. 52, from Supe, is the clearest example.

[15] For reliefs of human figures, see Tello, 1960, pp. 245-250; for tenon heads see his pp. 259-263 and 268-283. Compare also Rowe, 1962, fig. 5.

[16] Tello, 1960, figs. 90-92.

[17] The identification of the object in the left hand of the deity was suggested by Junius B. Bird. I had thought previously that it might repre-sent a bunch of flowers, but this interpretation is most improbable, since there are only two "stems" corresponding to three "flowers." This repre-sentation of a Spondylus shell is unique in known Chavin art, and unique representations are always the most difficult ones to identify in so convention-alized a style. Spiral shells are more common; there is another one with a face on the "Tello Obelisk," fig. 7, A-21, for example.

[18] Polo, 1899, p. 195.

[19] See also Tello, 1959, figs. 31 and 33. The textile from the Coe collection is published in Rowe, 1962, fig. 29.

[20] On the late origin of Creator worship among the Incas, see Rowe, 1960.

[21] Carrión Cachot, 1948, plate XX.

[22] For examples, see Schmidt, 1929, pp. 160-168, 176-177, 202 and 204.

[23] Kroeber, 1926, figs. 3 and 4, are pieces from Moche III burials.

[24] Kelemen, 1943, vol. II, plate 165.

[25] Posnansky, 1945, vol. I, plates XLV-L.

# BIBLIOGRAPHY

Ayres, Fred D.
1961      Rubbings from Chavín de Huántar, Peru.  American Antiquity, vol.
          27, no. 2, October, pp. 238-245.  Salt Lake City.

Bennett, Wendell Clark
1942      Chavin stone carving.  Yale Anthropological Studies, vol. III.
          New Haven.

1944      The north highlands of Peru; excavations in the Callejón de Huaylas
          and at Chavín de Huántar.  Anthropological Papers of the American
          Museum of Natural History, vol. 39, part 1.  New York.

1954      Ancient arts of the Andes.  The Museum of Modern Art.  New York.

Buse, Hermann
1957      Huaras - Chavín.  Juan Mejía Baca & P. L. Villanueva, Editores,
          Lima.

Carrión Cachot, Rebeca
1948      La cultura Chavín; dos nuevas colonias:  Kuntur Wasi y Ancón.
          Revista del Museo Nacional de Antropología y Arqueología, vol. II,
          no. 1, primer semestre, pp. 99-172.  Lima.

Engel, Frédéric
1956      Curayacu - a Chavinoid site.  Archaeology, vol. 9, no. 2, June,
          pp. 98-105.  Brattleboro.

Gordon, Eric Valentine
1957      An introduction to Old Norse.  Second edition, revised by A. R.
          Taylor.  At the Clarendon Press, Oxford.

Izumi, Yasuichi
1958      Andesu no iseki.  Mizue, no. 22, Winter quarter, Supplement.  Tokyo.

Kelemen, Pál
1943      Medieval American art; a survey in two volumes.  The Macmillan
          Company, New York.

Kinzl, Hans, and Schneider, Erwin
1950      Cordillera Blanca (Perú).  Universitäts-Verlag Wagner, Innsbruck.

Kroeber, Alfred Louis
1926      Archaeological explorations in Peru.  Part I: Ancient pottery from
          Trujillo.  Field Museum of Natural History, Anthropology, Memoirs,
          vol. II, no. 1.  Chicago.

1944      Peruvian archeology in 1942.  Viking Fund Publications in Anthro-
          pology, number four.  New York.

Lothrop, Samuel Kirkland
1941      Gold ornaments of Chavín style from Chongoyape, Peru.  American
          Antiquity, vol. VI, no. 3, January, pp. 250-262.  Menasha.

1951        Gold artifacts of Chavín style.  American Antiquity, vol. XVI,
            no. 3, January, pp. 226-240.  Menasha.

Means, Philip Ainsworth
1934        Des commentaires sur l'architecture ancienne de la cote péruvienne.
            Bulletin de la Société des Américanistes de Belgique, no. 14,
            aout, pp. 75-110.  Bruxelles.

Menzel, Dorothy, and others
1964        The Paracas pottery of Ica; a study in style and time, by Dorothy
            Menzel, John H. Rowe, and Lawrence E. Dawson.  University of Cali-
            fornia Publications in American Archaeology and Ethnology, vol. 50.
            Berkeley and Los Angeles.

Polo, José Toribio
1899        La piedra de Chavín.  Boletín de la Sociedad Geográfica de Lima, año IX,
            tomo IX, nos. 4-6, 30 de septiembre, pp. 192-231; nos. 7-9, 31 de
            diciembre, pp. 262-290.  Lima.

Posnansky, Arthur
1945        Tihuanacu, la cuna del hombre americano; Tihuanacu, the cradle of
            American man.  I-II.  J. J. Augustin Publisher.  New York.

Rowe, John Howland
1960        The origins of Creator worship among the Incas.  Culture in history;
            essays in honor of Paul Radin, edited by Stanley Diamond, pp. 408-429.
            Published for Brandeis University by Columbia University Press.
            New York.

1962        Chavin art; an inquiry into its form and meaning.  The Museum of
            Primitive Art.  New York.

Schmidt, Max
1929        Kunst und Kultur von Peru.  Im Propyläen-Verlag zu Berlin.

Tello, Julio César
1923        Wira Kocha.  Inca, vol. I, no. 1, enero-marzo, pp. 93-320; no. 3,
            julio-septiembre, pp. 583-606.  Lima.

1943        Discovery of the Chavín culture in Peru.  American Antiquity, vol.
            IX, no. 1, July, pp. 135-160.  Menasha.

1959        Paracas.  Primera parte.  Publicación del Proyecto 8b del Programa
            1941-42 de The Institute of Andean Research de New York.  Empresa
            Gráfica T. Scheuch S.A.  Lima.

1960        Chavin; cultura matriz de la civilización andina.  Primera parte.
            Publicación Antropológica del Archivo "Julio C. Tello" de la Universi-
            dad Nacional Mayor de San Marcos, vol. II.  Lima.

Valcárcel, Luis Eduardo
1957        Nuevos descubrimientos arqueológicos en el Perú: Chavín.  Cuadernos
            Americanos, año XVI, vol. XCIII, no. 3, mayo-junio, pp. 180-184.
            México.

Willey, Gordon Randolph
    1951        The Chavin problem: a review and critique.  Southwestern Journal
                of Anthropology, vol. 7, no. 2, Summer, pp. 103-144.  Albuquerque.

Yacovleff, Eugenio
    1932        Las Falcónidas en el arte y en las creencias de los antiguos
                peruanos.  Revista del Museo Nacional, tomo I, no. 1, pp. 33-111,
                Lima.

Captions to illustrations


Fig. 1.  Location of some archaeological sites of the Chavin and Paracas cultures.  White circles, Chavin sites; black circles, Paracas sites.


Fig. 2.  Plan of the ruins of the temple of Chavin, surveyed in 1963 by J. H. Rowe and Marino Gonzáles Moreno.  The numbers indicate the places where some of the sculptures were found:  1, the cornice ornamented with felines and serpents, fig. 17; 2, the relief of the Smiling God, fig. 21; 3, the cornice ornamented with an eagle discovered in 1919, fig. 12, and fragments of other similar cornices discovered in 1958, fig. 13; 4, relief ornamented with caymans, fig. 19.


Fig. 3.  Plan of the Black and White Portal.  The dashed lines indicate details reconstructed in the drawing.


Fig. 4.  Vertical profile and elevation of the facade of the New Temple, with the Black and White Portal (reconstruction by the author).


Fig. 5.  Side view of the Great Image, based on a photograph made by Abraham Guillén.  Phase AB.


Fig. 6.  Roll-out of the reliefs on the "Tello Obelisk" based on rubbings made by the author.  Phase C.


Fig. 7.  Reference key to the figures on the "Obelisk."


Fig. 8.  Roll-out and reconstruction of the guardian angel figure from the north column of the Black and White Portal.  This angel has the facial markings of a hawk.  The drawing is based on a rubbing by Fred D. Ayres (Rowe, 1962, fig. 10) and on rubbings and drawings by the author.  Phase D.


Fig. 9.  Roll-out and reconstruction of the guardian angel of the south column of the Black and White Portal, with the face of an eagle. The drawing is based on a rubbing by Fred D. Ayres (Rowe, 1962, fig. 9) and on rubbings and drawings by the author.  Phase D.

Fig. 10.  The Raimondi Stone, ornamented with a representation of the Staff God.  The drawing is based on a photograph taken by Abraham Guillén and on a squeeze made by Max Uhle.  Phase EF.


Fig. 11.  Early style eagle reconstructed on the basis of fragments of a cornice found near the southeast corner of the New Temple (second addition).  Another fragment with the same figure was found in front of the east face of the old south wing.  Phase AB.


Fig. 12.  Eagle represented on a cornice found in 1919 at the place marked 3 on the plan (fig. 2), reconstructed on the basis of what remains of the original and of a plaster cast in the Museo Nacional de Antropología y Arqueología, Lima.  The body of the eagle, destroyed in the original (dashed outline), has been reconstructed to agree with the fragments of similar eagles found in 1958 (see fig. 13).  Phase AB, but later than fig. 11.


Fig. 13.  An eagle like that of fig. 12 but with one less figurative element in the wings.  Reconstruction on the basis of fragments of a cornice discovered in 1958 near the place marked 3 on the plan (fig. 2).  Probably contemporary with fig. 12.


Fig. 14.  Fragment of an eagle of a late style from a cornice stone found at the northeast corner of the old south wing of the temple of Chavin. Phase D.


Fig. 15.  Profile hawk from the cornice of the Black and White Portal. Phase D.


Fig. 16.  Profile eagle from the cornice of the Black and White Portal. Phase D.


Fig. 17.  Felines and serpents from the cornice at the southwest corner of the New Temple (no. 1, fig. 2), drawn on the basis of a rubbing made by the author.  The felines are on the under side of the cornice and the serpents on its edge.  Phase AB.

Fig. 18.   Roll-out of the figures of a relief found in Yauya.   The figures are an almost complete mythical cayman and part of the nose of a second one.   The drawing is based on a rubbing made by Fred D. Ayres (Rowe, 1962, fig. 31).


Fig. 19.   Reconstruction of the figures ornamenting two fragments of a granite lintel found in 1962 at the foot of the Monumental Stairway (no. 4, fig. 2).   Two profile caymans are represented.   The reconstruction is based on two rubbings and a photograph of the original.


Fig. 20.   Figure of a warrior which formed part of a frieze of similar figures.   The drawing is based on a rubbing made by the author.


Fig. 21.   Representation of the Smiling God from a slab found in the patio of the New Temple (no. 2, fig. 2).   The drawing is based on a rubbing made by the author.   Phase D.


Fig. 22.   The Staff God represented on a pyroengraved gourd found in a Paracas tomb in the Ica Valley.   The gourd is in the Paul Truel Collection. Drawing by L. E. Dawson and the author.


Fig. 23.   The Staff God represented on a gold placque without provenience in the Museo Arqueológico "Rafael Larco Herrera," Lima. The inlays which decorated the original are missing.   Drawing on the basis of a photograph in the Museum of Modern Art, New York (Rowe, 1962, fig. 27).

Figure 1

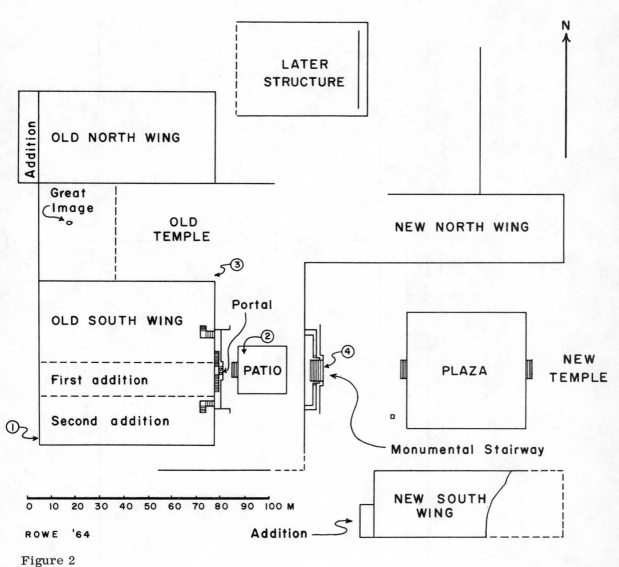

ROWE '64

Figure 2

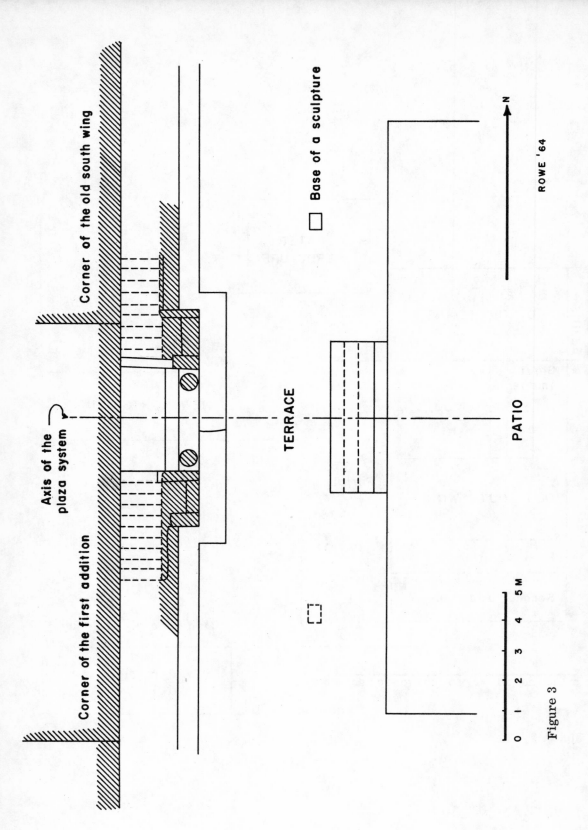

Figure 3

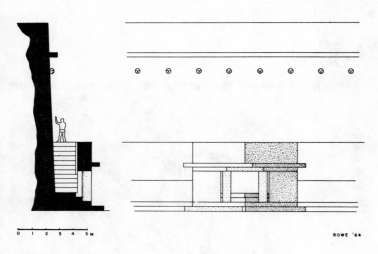

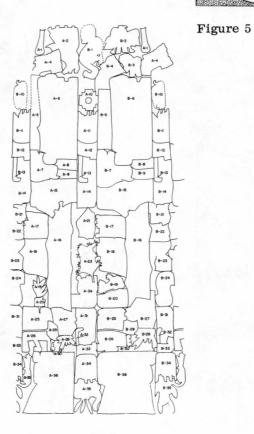

ROWE '64

Figure 4

Figure 5

Figure 6

Figure 7

Figure 8

Figure 9

Figure 10

Figure 11

Figure 13

Figure 15

Figure 12

Figure 14

101

Figure 16

Figure 18

Figure 17

Figure 19

Figure 20

Figure 21

Figure 22

Figure 23

103

Fig. 1. Aerial photograph of Pañamarca, Nepena valley, Peru. The main ruins measure c. 200 x 250 meters. The photograph was taken from directly overhead, but the sharp drop of the fields to the northwest (lower right) gives an oblique effect.
(Courtesy Servicio Aerofotografico Nacional, Peru)

# MOCHICA MURALS AT PAÑAMARCA

## By Richard P. Schaedel

OCHICA CULTURE HAS BEEN FAMOUS IN Peru for as long as its archaeology has been known, chiefly because of the excellence of Mochica ceramics. A red and white Mochica portrait-head jar or vase with painted figures (ARCHAEOLOGY 3.95) is generally the most typical item that one may look for in museum collections from Peru. Although the literature on Peruvian prehistory is studded with illustrations and descriptions of Mochica pottery, it is notoriously weak on other aspects of Mochica culture, notably architecture.

This is especially surprising in view of the fact that over fifty years ago MAX UHLE identified one of the largest mud-brick structures in Peru, known as the Huaca del Sol, near Trujillo, as of Mochica construction. In 1925, after the last big rain on the Peruvian coast, some wall paintings were discovered in an adjoining ruin, known as the Huaca de la Luna, which UHLE had also identified as Mochica. One of the purposes of the study of coastal architecture which the Institute of Anthropology of the University of Trujillo carried out last year, with the aid of a grant from the

Reprinted from ARCHAEOLOGY, Vol. 4, No. 3, 1951. pp. 145–154.

Colt Archaeological Institute of New York, was to locate all other traces of Mochica building activity, both in its presumed home valley of Moche, and to the north and south.

In this enterprise we were quite successful, and we can now demonstrate that the Mochicas had erected sizeable pyramids in the four valleys to the north and to the south of the Moche. It was in the southernmost valley, Nepeña, that we made our most felicitous finds, in what seems to have been a secondary center of the Mochicas, Pañamarca. Pañamarca, because of the loftiness of its adobe ruins, was known even to the travellers of the nineteenth century. A description of it was included in GEORGE EPHRAIM SQUIER'S *Peru*, published in 1877.

In the twentieth century the site received no attention until BENNETT, in *Archaeology of the North Coast of Peru*, published in 1939, described it briefly and referred to remains of badly preserved wall paintings. SORIANO INFANTE, in an article in the Peruvian *Revista del Museo Nacional* of 1940, referred to these remains, and to some others which were better preserved, but published no illustrations. When we arrived at Pañamarca in 1950 to make a study of the ruins, it still remained to be determined what people or peoples built Pañamarca and what was the extent and significance of the fragmentary murals.

Our reconnaissance crew consisted of one director-photographer, one student assistant of pure Mochica ancestry, two engineers from the University of Trujillo, and a student aide-de-camp whose chief job was to collect sherds and maintain liaison. We were operating from the Institute jeep out of our base in the nearby port town of Chimbote. Our schedule called for five days, but after the discovery of the well-preserved murals and a group of burials, we were obliged to remain another two days and to send a rush call to Trujillo for the artist, Sr. PEDRO AZABACHE, also of Mochica descent, who made tracings

of the paintings and executed reproductions which are exhibited in illustration of this article.

The site itself is reared on a rocky outcrop on the lower middle portion of the Nepeña river's north bank. At first glance the ruins resemble a monstrous accumulation of adobe bricks from which certain large walls and a pyramid emerge. Actually it is

Fig. 2. Pañamarca, Peru. A view of the main building, with the corner building to the right as seen from the northern approach. The wall crenelations are a Mochica architectural trait, reserved like the friezes for special buildings. Note the stone foundations of the exterior wall. The wall height averages seven meters.

composed of three principal structures, joined by a series of courtyards to a large plaza. Separated by a thin strip of vegetation from this group is a second outcrop, with a much more irregular surface. At its foot are remains of yet another large adobe structure and behind this building is the large cemetery used by the builders of the ruin. At various points on the lower periphery of rocky outcrops were circular depressions for grinding. On one of the rocks we found petroglyphs and another showed evidence of having been worn smooth by sliding. Slides like these have been found in the highlands and may not necessarily be prehistoric, but their proximity to ruins suggests that they were.

On most of the walls lining the courtyards and at various points in the buildings themselves we found

ARCHAEOLOGY

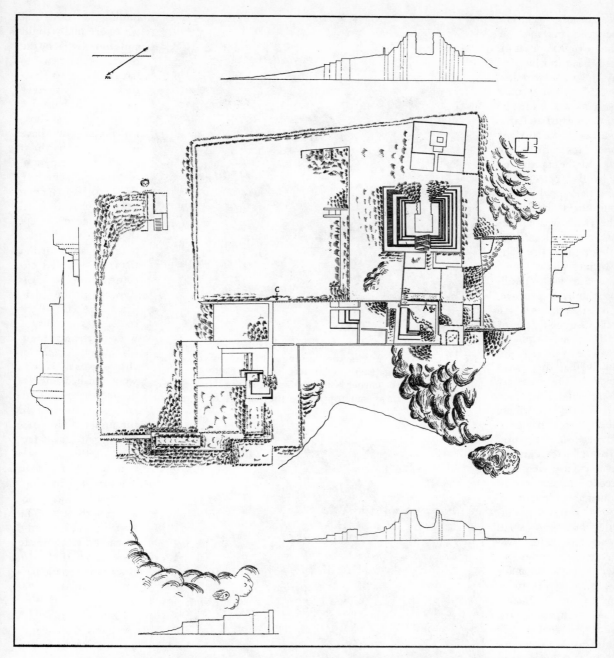

Fig. 3. Pañamarca, Peru. Ground plan of the ruins, done by the Institute of Anthropology of the University of Trujillo, Peru, under the direction of the author. The final copy was executed by Sr. Antonio Rodriguez Suy Suy. The scale is about 1 : 2000.

A indicates the spot where the frieze illustrated in color on the cover of this issue was found.

B shows the corner where the frieze illustrated in Figure 12 was discovered.

C is the point where the frieze of warriors and priests (Figures 13 and 14-18) was located.

remains of polychrome painting, but most of the original coating had been washed off by the periodic rains.

At least five distinct occupations could be distinguished at Pañamarca. The earliest one, to which we should hesitantly assign the petroglyphs and perhaps the small building at the foot of the plaza, was apparently by the local people of the valley. The Mochica phase, which was the most grandiose and impressive, followed, and we might suggest dates of *c.* 600-900 A.D. for their arrival. It is unlikely that they occupied the site for a very long time. To them we should attribute the three principal structures grouped about the central plaza. They were succeeded in turn by a Tiahuanacoid phase (*c.* 900-1,100 A.D.), during which time a small stone building was erected and certain alterations were made in the other structures. After the Tiahuanacoid occupation, the site apparently fell into disuse except for occasional dumping or as a burial place.

## The Mochica Occupation

The three principal structures with their

Fig. 4. Pañamarca, Peru. View from the summit of the main pyramid, looking across the rectangular court to the third principal building. In the near left is part of the ascending antechamber to the corner building. To the upper left is the extension of the rocky outcrop where the petroglyphs are.

Fig. 5. Rear view of the summit of Pañamarca. The large wall in the foreground is the inner surface of the rectangular enclosure which we called a "tank" but whose function we do not know.

joining courtyards that were originally built and embellished by the Mochicas appear to have had distinct functions, but at present we can only hazard a guess as to what those functions may have been. The highest building is the pyramidal one atop the hill. We could discern little about its original Mochica form except that it was roughly rectangular and smaller than the terraced circumstructure which is shown on the plan. The large cut in the center was mostly the work of treasure hunters, although some of the exposed walls were finished and indicated that the building was not solid throughout. The present zigzag ramp, facing northwest, was built at a later period. The original Mochica orientation was probably northeast. The stairway leading to the plaza indicates where the hypothetical Mochica ascent to the pyramid would have begun.

Opposite the zigzag ramp is the corner building, which has suffered even greater depredations than the first. Only the gross form of the terraced circumstructure could be plotted. Numerous cuts which had been

ARCHAEOLOGY

made into it reveal a hollow room of some partitional complexity as the likely Mochica prototype. Here we found three well preserved panels of mural decoration, one of which is shown on the cover of this issue. We have indicated on the plan the two possible entrances on the northeast and northwest. Both may have been used.

To the immediate northeast of this corner building is a rather complicated antechamber built on the ascent of the outcrop. At its lower extremity it leads via a door, past a terraced unit, onto the large rectangular courtyard which adjoins the southeast platform of the third principal edifice.

Fig. 6. Pañamarca, Peru. The rock with the petroglyphs. The drawings are not in Mochica style and are probably earlier. The notebook measures 22 x 17 centimeters.

Fig. 7. The small stone building to the southeast of the principal pyramid of Pañamarca. The regular coursing and smooth exterior facing are rarely found in coastal architecture and generally in association with Tiahuanacoid sites.

Fig. 8. The "slide" on the second rock outcrop, Pañamarca. Sr. Antonio Rodriguez Suy Suy is indicating the surface worn smooth in the center of the dark zone.

This building is essentially a graded series of platforms, with a small superstructure near the center. It appears to have been entered from the northeast corner by a long ramp. In contrast to the main pyramid and the corner building, this edifice has a maximum of open space at the top, and seems to have been a place where people could assemble in numbers. We could not ascertain whether this building had been of original Mochica construction except for its northwest face. It betrayed no later alterations at any rate.

The large central plaza originally had been sunken. On the inner facing of the wall lining the northwest side we discovered the procession of warriors and priests illustrated below.

To the west of the first two buildings described, and forming the back of the ruin, are a series of small structures and partitions, which may have served as

living quarters, since layers of refuse were found in this zone. The large empty enclosure which bounds the ruin on the northwest may have served as a gathering place for soldiers, prisoners, etc. Its exterior walls had been painted in polychrome, which proved that it was a Mochica structure.

Our group at Pañamarca gives a rough idea of what the general plan of the Mochica center was. The three main buildings and large court form the core which was generally oriented up-valley. The other large center already alluded to is in the Moche valley and consists of the Huaca del Sol and the Huaca de la Luna. It is larger and somewhat more spacious in layout but has the same architectural components. The inference is inescapable that these were not mainly dwelling sites.

The small amount of dwelling refuse indicates that at best only a few priests or persons of importance lived at the center along with their attendants and some artisans. The elaborate embellishment of the walls, with symbolic designs and figures in processional attitudes, indicates that the buildings were probably used for religious ceremonies, when the population which could be concentrated in the plaza area assembled from various parts of the valley. Ceremonial centers like these contrast strongly with later sites of a truly urban character, where emphasis was placed upon living quarters at the expense of elegant pyramid-temples.

### The Tiahuanacoid Occupation

The people who succeeded the Mochicas, as we have already indicated, were Tiahuanacoids. This term refers to a people of presumed south highland origin (near the southern end of Lake Titicaca), who either migrated to or conquered the central coast or perhaps did both, and then proceeded to move up the north coast as far as the Jequetepeque valley. Their polychrome textiles and ceramics share much iconographic content with the stone work of Tiahuanaco (ARCHAEOLOGY 1.66). Hence the name and the interpretation. They seem to have been responsible for the final shape of the buildings which we drew.

Their modifications of the main building were obvious since the later wall facings were covered with ochre paint and easy to follow. They consisted of the steep, zigzag ramp approach on the northwest face and the addition of the step terraces on all sides. The small stone edifice to the southeast was their only original contribution and it is typical of the masonry elsewhere found in association with Tiahuanacoid remains. In the center of this unit we found remains of another Mochica wall painting, but so far below the floor that only excavation will reveal its relationship to the substructure of which it is presumably part.

The Tiahuanacoids must have been responsible for some of the partitioning between the main and corner buildings, but we

Fig. 9. Pañamarca, Peru. A cluster of perforations for grinding, near the northwest corner of the ruin at the base. These holes were found at two other points in the ruin and occur at other sites of Tiahuanacoid occupation on the coast. These may be noted on the ground plan, Fig. 3, as circles at lower and upper left.

Fig. 10. A surprise find, a Tiahuanacoid burial practically on the surface, was discovered by the author too lazy to pick up a potsherd. He kicked away half of a polychrome bowl which was lying atop the four shown here. Just below these a group of Mochica burials was found. The "tank" is about fifteen feet away.

ARCHAEOLOGY

the friezes, it is difficult to explain away the architectural decapitation. In the pilfered refuse of the dumping ground we found, significantly enough, not a single Mochica potsherd; so that it is fairly clear that they did not use this zone for refuse.

Like the Mochicas the Tiahuanacoids used the area on the adjacent outcrop for burials although both groups also buried their dead outside the walls of the main ruin. We discovered this quite by accident while searching for potsherds. One of the large sherds which I carelessly kicked turned out to be half of a bowl, which together with three others formed the grave accompaniment of a Tiahuanacoid. Some twenty-five centimeters below him we found several Mochica burials.

The perforations in the rocks which occurred in clusters at various points in the ruin we have called grinding holes, since they show rotary abrasions. Similar holes have been found in other sites with Tiahuanacoid remains, so that they probably were made by the Tiahuanacoids although we do not know what substance was ground in them.

Fig. 11. Pañamarca, Peru: Mochica mural paintings. This is the hand-to-hand combat reproduced in color on the cover of this issue. Note how thoroughly it was covered. This panel was left untouched by the Institute except for some clearing away at the base.

Fig. 12. A second panel in the corner room, showing an anthropomorphic bird figure holding a conch shell.

could not determine how much. The corner building itself appears to have been filled in and covered up externally by the Tiahuanacoids, as we could determine by the courses of adobe covering the paintings. They apparently followed a similar procedure with the sunken plaza. In the area where we cleared away the material immediately in front of the friezes, we found that the friezes themselves had been covered up by two courses of adobes and that further toward the center the plaza seemed to be filled with miscellaneous refuse. This suggests that the Tiahuanacoids utilized the sunken plaza as a dumping ground. Although it is not clear as to their reasons, it would appear that they levelled the top of the wall lining the plaza so that the heads of all of the figures were destroyed. While it is conceivable that the Mochicas themselves may have placed the adobe covering against

On the basis of a few days' reconnaissance we are obviously not in a position to interpret the significance of the Tiahuanacoid occupation of this important Mochica center, but the cumulative evidence that we did uncover tends to indicate that the northward moving Tiahuanacoids met the southward expanding Mochicas at Pañamarca, and it is not improbable that a decisive struggle took place here which may have accounted for the abrupt disappearance of Mochica culture on the north coast. The rather significant alterations in the buildings at Pañamarca indicate that the Tiahuanacoids thought highly enough of the site to use it for their own purposes. When they in turn were

eventually displaced, declined, or what you will, the site fell into disuse, except for an occasional group of people who used its sacrosanct precincts for a cemetery, or its strategic heights as a watch tower.

Evidence for the post-Tiahuanacoid occupation was found in some burial remains in the plaza-dump area, indicating that its third and final function was that of

a cemetery. A more specifically post-Tiahuanacoid cemetery was on the northwestern fringe of the ruin where the modern thicket fence describes a rough, incomplete oval. Here ceramics of the Chimu and Inca periods had been dug up by the local huaqueros and were purchased for the museum of the University of Trujillo.

### The Polychrome Friezes

The friezes are best treated as two units: the panels in the corner room, and the procession of warriors and priests found in the interior of the wall lining the sunken plaza. The first group consists of three large

Fig. 14. A section of the frieze, which like the hand-to-hand combat scene had been discovered before we arrived. It shows the second warrior from the left. Note the top of the wall, which here more than decapitates the figure, and the superimposed adobes.

Fig. 15. The trench when we finished. The narrowness of the trench made photography difficult. The intersection of the northeast corner of the courtyard with the southern wall of the third building can be seen in the background.

ARCHAEOLOGY

112

...he complete frieze of warriors and priests, thirty on Figure 3). The small figures are valets or attend-...from a life-size copy, with minor restorations, made ...e had cleared a small trench in front of the friezes.

panels, one of which is shown on the cover of this issue of ARCHAEOLOGY, and see FIGURE 11. It measures 1.70 meters in height and 1.60 meters in width. The figures are approximately 1.40 meters high and 40 centimeters wide or life size. A clay coating was applied to the adobe walls as a primer. Upon this the outline of the design was incised and the colors were painted in. The scene obviously represents two individuals fighting, pulling each other's hair out by the roots. Although Mochica ceramics show motives similar to this, it is the first time it has been shown on a wall painting.

The other two panels, which are approximately the same size, portray a cat-demon with a conch shell on its back and an anthropomorphic bird figure (FIGURE 12), possibly a priest masked as a bird of prey. These two panels were found at right angles to one another, about twenty-five feet from the first.

The second unit consists of eight life-size figures (from the neck down), extending a total length of thirty feet. The maximum height of the figures is 1.50 meters. The full palette was employed on this frieze and consisted of white, the base color, red, yellow, brown, dark blue, black and gray.

The composition suggests some sort of procession or ceremony centered about a central figure. Our conjec-

Fig. 16 (above). The priest to the left of the head priest. The hands of the attendant can be distinguished grasping the tassels on his left side.

Fig. 17 (left). Pañamarca murals. The warrior figure on the extreme right, showing the continuation of the covering of the double course of adobes.

Fig. 18. The third warrior from the left and the attendant to the figure shown in Fig. 16. This view also gives a good idea of the surface texture of the painting and also the deeply incised outlines of the design.

tural interpretation is that the three figures on the left and the one at the extreme right are warriors. They are differentiated from the other major figures by what for lack of a better suggestion we call "knee guards" and shirts without tassels. The warriors at the left, to judge by their raised feet and joined hands, seem to be engaged in a dance. Three individuals, of a somewhat higher order of importance, may be distinguished to the right and left of the principal figure by the absence of the knee guard and the presence of tassels trailing from their shirts or tunics. We shall refer to them henceforth as "priests" if for no other reason than to avoid calling them "figures."

It will be noted that both the priests and warriors have a semi-lunar knife suspended from their belts by two thongs. On the basis of Mochica pottery scenes we can safely say that this knife was used principally for decapitation, and figures prominently in what might be interpreted as scenes of sacrifice. The typical offensive weapon of the Mochicas was the mace, the defensive the shield. The principal figure, whom we are calling henceforth the high priest, is shown in front view and wears a tunic with three serpentiform figures. He is the only man in the group not shown with the knife.

A possible interpretation of the otherwise puzzling figure to his left is that it represents an anthropomorphized knife in its sheath. This anthropomorphization of weapons occurs on the fragments of the only other

Mochica frieze, which was discovered at the Huaca de la Luna near Trujillo. (For a discussion and illustration of the only other Mochica friezes so far found see KROEBER's *Archaeological Explorations in Peru: the Northern Coast,* 1930.) It may of course be considered equally well as the dehumanization of the weapon-bearer. Such an explanation would accord with another feature of Mochica art, namely the reduction of minor figures of presumably inferior social status to something like half of their normal dimensions. On the other hand the intention may have been to represent dwarfs, in which case this would be our earliest document in Peru for the practice reported in Inca times of using hunchbacks, dwarfs, and other deformed people as court attendants.

The tiny figure above the "anthropomorphized knife" probably represents part of a background scene which has been destroyed.

The purpose of this brief description has been to present this magnificent document of Mochica mural painting in its prehistoric context without comment on its obvious aesthetic qualities. Our hope is that all the friezes so faithfully copied by Señor PEDRO AZABACHE may presently be reproduced in color, so that the full richness and vigor of Mochica art may be appreciated by the art historian. Even more, however, we hope that this description will serve as a timely note and warning to lovers of art and archaeology in Peru and elsewhere that this rich source of vivid mural decoration, which today only awaits the patience of the archaeologist to reveal, may tomorrow be irrevocably destroyed. If these still unrevealed documents of the human spirit are not to be forever lost to us, we must constantly keep in mind two ideals: as archaeologists, to devote our attention first and foremost to the adequate documentation of fragile paintings; and to create among the public in general an awareness of their aesthetic as well as their documentary value, so that the present apathy towards their preservation may be replaced by a sense of obligation towards their protection.

THE COVER: Two important Mochicas pulling each other's hair out by the roots, one of the polychrome panels of mural decoration found in 1950 at Pañamarca, Peru, by the Institute of Anthropology of the University of Trujillo.

The reproduction is from the life-size copy made by the Peruvian artist Sr. Pedro Azabache.

ARCHAEOLOGY

# ICONOGRAPHIC STUDIES AS AN AID IN THE RECONSTRUCTION OF EARLY CHIMU CIVILIZATION

*By* GERDT KUTSCHER†

For an appraisal of the ancient Peruvian Civilizations, two main sources of information are available. One is the written reports and records of the Spanish Conquistadores and christianized Indians, such as Guaman Poma de Ayala, and the other, the archeological discoveries and excavations, which are especially rewarding in the coastal regions. These two sources stand in marked contrast to each other when viewed in relation to the Incaic and Pre-Incaic periods. While the written records for the Incaic culture are abundant, the art forms and representations are relatively poor. A reconstruction of the Incaic civilization which would rely solely on the archeological finds would be a rather difficult task. Here, the early chronicles fill out the gap which would exist otherwise.

The situation is quite different for the reconstruction of the Pre-Incaic civilizations of the northern Peruvian coast. The number of reports recorded in early Spanish times is very small and can almost be counted on the fingers of one hand. One should mention the unique and extremely valuable report by Antonio de la Calancha on the civilization of the late Chimu, which can be gathered from his "Crónica Moralizada." Besides Calancha, there are

* This paper, illustrated with lantern slides, was presented at the meeting of the Section, March 27, 1950.
† The Free University and the Latin American Bibliotek, Berlin, Germany

Cabello de Balboa and an anonymous author in the year 1604. The historical importance of these sources has only recently been properly estimated by John Rowe.[1] On the whole, however, the information given by these writers on the Pre-Incaic civilizations is extremely poor. On the other hand, there is an immense amount of archeological material, obtained mainly from the very rich burial finds, material which gives an insight into the civilizations which created it.

This is especially true of the ceramics which were produced by the early Chimu or Mochica. This coastal civilization, which might have flourished in 600–800 A.D., had its main centers in the valleys of Chicama and Moche. Its northern borderline might have been the valley of Pacasmayo and its southern border, Nepeña. To Max Uhle, we owe the first stratigraphical work, which made it possible to fix approximately the historical position of the early Chimu civilization in the sequence of cultures of the northern Peruvian coast. Max Uhle called this civilization "Proto-Chimu" because of its "primordial character." A. L. Kroeber and P. A. Means used the term "Early Chimu," which seems appropriate, since there are many common links between this relatively early period and the Chimu period (called "Late Chimu" by Kroeber). This late Chimu can be considered as a sort of renaissance, after an interregnum or intermediate period of foreign styles.

What the people of the early period called themselves will never be found out, but it

Reprinted from the TRANSACTIONS OF THE NEW YORK ACADEMY OF SCIENCES, Series II, Vol. 12, No. 6, 1950. pp. 194-203.

is quite certain that they did not call themselves "Mochica." This name, given by
the old chroniclers, designates the language
spoken by the Chimu. To this author, the
application of this strictly linguistic term
as a name for the early period does not seem
too well justified. It might be more convenient to select a neutral term, such as
"Civilization of Moche" or "Mucheros,"
rather than to call them "Mochica." So
long as no neutral term has been proposed,
we are here calling them "Early Chimu," as
Kroeber and Means did.

The early Chimu, as was shown by Max
Uhle for the first time by his excavations
in Moche, made thousands upon thousands
of ceramics, painted in a characteristic bi-
color scheme, reddish brown on cream or
molded to represent entire figures, animals,
human heads, *etc.*

The extraordinary artistic and esthetic
value of these ceramics, especially of the
so-called "effigy" vessels in the form of
human heads, has been appreciated very
early by connoiseurs. This esthetic value
is paralleled, however, by its importance
as documentary source material. The vessels can be considered, thanks to their ornamentation, as a singular source for the reconstruction of the civilization of these
people. The unique position of the early
Chimu pottery rests on two facts: they
are unique in form as well as in content.
The form is extremely realistic, portraying
an enormous variety of topics. Nothing
seems to have been too low, vulgar, or re-
volting, nothing too high or sublime, that
it was not depicted.

At first sight, it seems almost impossible
to get any order into this extreme variety of
topics. Almost everything seems to have
aroused the interest of the sculptor and
painter of that time. Animals and
plants, hunting and fishing, war and trade,
dances and ceremonies, all are shown. Of
special interest is the large number of representations of their gods and demons.

The extraordinary importance of these
objects as anthropological documents has
been appreciated since the time of E. G.
Squier. Even in our day, however, these
works have too often been used as a means
of illustration for reports on the Incaic
period. Direct interpretations of this kind,
based on mere analogy, is not free from
dangers and pitfalls, as two examples may
show.

(1) Incaic religion was centered around
worship of the sun. On the other hand,
Antonio de la Calancha tells us that the
Chimu of the late period considered the
moon their supreme deity, which was called
Si. This god, regarded as the deity of all
crops and the boisterous sea, was venerated
in a big "huaca," called Si-An, the "house
of the moon." Opposed to the Incaic
sun-worship, the coastal people stuck to the
worship of the moon. This might be explained by the climatic conditions in this
part of the country.

(2) Another example is furnished by the
difference in the importance attributed to
the fox by the Incaic and by the Pre-Incaic
coastal civilizations. The fox (as well as
the skunk) was despised in the Incaic time,
as the myths of the region of Huatochin
show, whereas he had a very important
position in the highly developed religious
systems of the coastal peoples. The jaguar,
Tello's "dios felino," so important in the
Chavin civilization, is no equal to the fox
in Early Chimu religion and mythology.

These two short examples show quite
clearly that it is not possible to apply
ceremonies, ideas, customs, *etc.*, reported
to have been used by the Inca, by mere
analogy to the Pre-Incaic civilizations,
which were highly developed in their
*own* way.

It seems more plausible not to assay
these civilizations by mere analogy, but to
understand them out of themselves, *i e.*, by
their own works—by the way they have
depicted themselves.

Among the great number of Pre-Incaic
coastal civilizations, the Early Chimu seems
the most propitious for such a task for three
reasons, two of which have been mentioned
already: the realistic style and the wide
scope of representation. The third reason

is the large number of ceramics which have found their way into the museums of both America and Europe. To supplement the ceramics in this study, there are the buildings and the other contents of the rich grave finds: objects of stone, bone, metal, shell, and, more rarely in this period, textiles.

It is, therefore, rather tempting, with all this aid, to make an effort to classify and group this variety of representation and to try to reconstruct this ancient civilization. Iconographic studies afford the means for a cultural analysis which finally should lead to an understanding of this culture as a whole.

E. G. Squier was the first to recognize the value of the archaeological findings (especially the ceramics) as an aid in reconstructing this civilization. Twenty years later, Arthur Baessler became interested in the deeper meaning of the effigy vessels and vase paintings which he had collected and later published in his monoumental work on "Ancient Peruvian Art" in 1902–03. This study, however, was not a systematic one. Gösta Montell's excellent work on "Dress and Ornaments in Ancient Peru," which also dealt with the Early Chimu has not been followed by similar studies in other fields of culture. Of the gigantic work begun by Rafael Larco Hoyle, only two volumes have been published so far.[2] The present author, intrigued by the possibilities, has already attempted a further systematic reconstruction of the Early Chimu civilization.[3]

The enormous amount of material seemed to make it necessary to limit the iconographic study at first to selected, special aspects of this civilization and to study them more or less separately. In collecting the material, however, it became clear that this method could not be used, for the same reason that it cannot be used in modern social anthropological field work: the different aspects of the culture are related and connected with each other in the most intimate way. The warfare was, as we will see later, connected with religious ideas, while, on the other hand, an analysis of the demons and gods requires a study of the different animals, plants, etc. Therefore, it became inevitable to regard these representations more or less as parts of a whole and to consider these interrelations. This seems to be the only way to come to an understanding of the whole system of thoughts and ideas which gave origin to these representations.

Before giving a few practical examples to show how these iconographic studies work out, a few words should be said about the character of the ceramics.

The Early Chimu used three techniques for ceramic decoration with equal mastership; plastique, high relief, and painting. By "plastique" is meant that the vessel was cast in the form of a human being, a human head, an animal, etc. These works are more or less sculptured in the round, and only the stirrup-spout reminds us that they are vessels in practical use. The vessels decorated with reliefs and paintings in white and reddish brown form another group.

The easiest approach, of course, is found in the effigy vessels, which quite correctly are considered to be in the first row of ancient American art. They may also be regarded as anthropological specimens which yield a great deal of information. First of all, they tell us about the physical type of these people in a most naturalistic and sincere way. A comparison shows that this early civilization was built up out of a mixture of at least three different racial types. The physical appearance of the Early Chimu is therefore better known to us than that of most other Indian tribes. The vessels further inform us of the headdresses, the ear ornaments, and the facial paintings.

The same holds true, to an even greater degree, of the vessels which have been shaped in the form of an entire human being or an animal. They tell us about the costumes, ornaments, implements, and weapons used in this period. Usually, they depict a single sitting or standing figure, with little or no mobility (Plate 17[3]). On the other hand, there are occasionally groups which depict action: on the top of one vessel, a medicine man is treating a sick person stretched out before him (Plate 40[3]). Another vessel shows a group of three persons, a motif very popular in Early Chimu but also repeated in the late period: a drunkard being led home by his more sober friends (Plate 41[3]). As a rule, however, the effigy vessels stick to the one-figure representation and abhor eccentric, wild movement. They are more or less dominated by the "static" principle which characterizes all true plastic works.

Quite another tendency is to be found in low relief and in the vase paintings, which can be considered together. They are dominated by the principle of vivid and even dramatic action and by the representation of multifigured groups. Wild and quick movements, such as fast running, throwing a spear, *etc.*, are depicted in a masterly way. Furthermore, the number of figures which are painted on a vase may run up to more than sixty. These scenes afford an excellent opportunity to study the interrelations, the actions, and functions of the various beings, human or mythical, which might appear more or less isolated in other representations. In these dynamic paintings, we have an excellent chance for a deeper insight by functional analysis.

To estimate the vase paintings in a right and proper way and to the fullest extent, a precondition must be fulfilled. It is not sufficient to have a photographic reproduction; it is also necessary to have an "extension" or an "unrolling" made. The photographic reproduction can give but a detail, and even this detail will have fore-shortenings.

Some concrete examples should be considered here to give an idea of the abundant material for iconographic study. Furthermore, the should be mentioned, since the effigy vessels and vase paintings do not depict all aspects of life. This holds true for the primary source of existence: agriculture. Archaeological investigation leaves no doubt that the main subsistence was

won by a highly developed agriculture with artificial irrigation. The remains of these irrigation systems are still to be found everywhere. Many vessels are in the shape of, or decorated with, representations of Indian corn, beans, squashes, potatoes, manioc, *etc.* Nevertheless, representations of agriculturists at work seem to be extremely rare, if they exist at all.

On the other hand, even in this highly developed civilization, hunting, fishing, and even the gathering of snails must have played an important role, as all of this has been depicted many times. Admittedly, the hunting of the deer was more a kind of sport indulged in by the noble warriers. Not only the deer, but also the fox, was hunted in the deserts between the valleys, indicated in the drawings by little, sandy hills and

FIGURE 1.

cactus plants (FIGURE 1).[3] The characteristic trait of the fox is the furry, half-dark, half-clear tail, by which he can be identified without any doubt. This same principle applies to all other animals, as with the art of the northwest coast of North America, in which animals are always characterized by special features.

The two hunters wear short shirts and skirts which are decorated with little round metal discs. This rich dress, as well as the beautiful headdresses with the long eagle feathers, proves that they belong to the nobility. For weapons, they have, besides the sling, light javelins, which are thrown with an "atlatl." One of the hunters is just throwing his spear, the other appears in the same position, although he has already dispatched his spear. This is a kind of erroneous representation which can also be found in the Maya codices.

Since the waters of the Peruvian coast teem with fish, fishing was extremely important from the beginning. The Chimu used the same light rafts, made of reeds, which are still in use today on the northern coast. These "balsas" appeared to the fantasy of the Chimu as a kind of fish on whose "back" they embarked on the open sea. Thus the "balsa" in FIGURE 2 takes the form of a big fish: prow and stern of the raft-like boat are decorated with fantastic animal heads, and big fins appear on both sides of the craft.[2] The reeds used in the construction are fastened together with thick ropes. The fisherman sits in a Buddha-like way, holding a long rope in his right hand and the broad, board-like paddle in his left. Wave bands on all four sides give a solid frame to the composition. In

movie-strip like way. There are warriors on the march, approaching the enemy, and there are many battle scenes which are full of dramatic action. To this type belongs a scene which shows the flight of a warrior who is pursued by the victor (Figure 23[3]). The latter, protected by an armor of parallel staves, brandishes his bit war club. The fleeing enemy has already thrown away his club, armored shirt, helmet, and headdress. The large, bell-like ornament, which is the characteristic attribute of the warrior, starts to become unfastened from the belt.

An even better idea of the warriors dress and weapons is derived from another group of vase paintings which almost look like a kind of "Sears and Roebuck" catalogue. To the big war club are attached all the

. FIGURE 2.

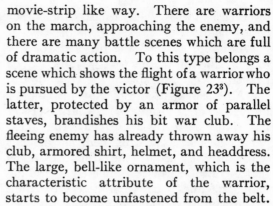

FIGURE 3.

the right corner, two houses are to be seen, which give a certain idea of the simple type of dwellings in which the fishermen lived.

A second big group of representations is devoted to the war-life. An effigy-vessel in the British Museum gives a good example of what the warriors of this time looked like (Plate 18[3]). Their equipment and weapons were rather standardized. The head is protected by the characteristic pointed helmet; under the short, armored shirt, which is decorated with spirals, the loin cloth is visible. The round shield is reinforced by small bands of copper, and the heavy war-club is furnished with a ring shaped knob. The vase paintings depict every phase of the war in an almost

trophies taken from the enemy: a helmet, the characteristic bell-shaped ornament, etc. (FIGURE 3).

After a battle, the victors would start for home, leading their naked captives by thick ropes tied around their necks. One of the large flaring rim bowls shows a column of this type. Three of the prisoners are trying in vain to stop the blood from pouring out of their noses, while the fourth turns back in an accusing gesture (Figure 25[3]). The warriors have shouldered the heavy war clubs, made heavier by the trophies attached to them. The column is headed by a kind of herald, whose belt ornament consists of the skin of a little fox-like animal. Humming birds surround the procession, which moves in quick tempo through the sandy hills, with their cactus and other desert plants.

What fate awaited the prisoners of war in the land of the victors is shown by a beautiful vase painting in the collection of the American Museum of Natural History in New York (FIGURE 4). Clark Wissler has quite correctly identified "the unexpected guests," as he calls them, as "officials with captives from 'the front'."[4] As a matter of fact, we see the chiefs of the defeated enemies carried in litters by their naked subjects. The bare head, as well as the strong rope around the third chief's neck, indicates that they are prisoners. The column approaches a great step-pyramid of the type so often encountered in

row, lies a severed human head. At least some of the prisoners, if not all of them, were sacrificed to the gods and demons, as is shown by a group in the upper row, above the litter bearers. There, we see two animal demons who are killing their victim with the typical sacrificial weapon: the tumi-like axe, which is never used in battle by the warriors but is reserved for ceremonies or for the gods in their fights.

In representations of this type, the close connection which existed between war and religious beliefs is indicated. As in Aztec Mexico, the main motif for the many wars seems to have been the winning of victims for human sacrifices, which were connected in some way with the "order of the world."

FIGURE 4.

these valleys. The platform of the pyramid is crowned by a richly decorated building. In the interior of this building, which might be the seat of a chief as well as a temple, a richly clad dignitary awaits the column, whose approach is announced by a smaller person, blowing a trumpet.

Whereas this group has been known for a long time, having been published by several authors, the smaller accompanying groups have never been published, although they are of no less interest in the continuity of the story. There is, for instance, in the lower row, a naked man, lying flat on his back, his extremities extended. This is the characteristic position, in the battle-scenes, for indicating a corpse. In the same

It is very interesting to note that the majority of these wars were of intertribal character. In general, both groups of warriors involved in a fight show the typical Chimu dress and weapons. This means that one group of the Chimu fought another, in the same way as among the ancient Greek city states. This intertribal fighting reflects the lack of a strong authority, dominating and uniting all the Chimu groups in the different valleys. The lack of political unification might also be the reason why the Early Chimu civilization did not spread as far to the north and south as did the late Chimu in its imperialistic phase.

In marked contrast to the primitive tribes, most of the higher civilizations of ancient America are noteworthy for a system of very severe punishments. The Early Chimu are no exception to this rule. The criminal was attached to a big pole and the skin of his face flayed to the point where it hung down like a mask. Then he was stoned to death and left to the birds of prey (Figure 29³). Seler suggested a long time ago that these representations might be connected with a very interesting astral myth reported by Antonio de la Calancha, telling about the severe punishment of thieves. Since a male and a female being are usually depicted, however, it could as well be punishment for adultery.

A decidedly more pleasant view of this civilization, in which the warriors played such an important role, is offered by the many dances and feasts. Here the warriors appear again in their full regalia, but without weapons. In addition to the typical helmet, the bell-shaped ornament, *etc.*, the dancers wore very tight gaiters with little bells or rattles affixed. The dancers always formed a long chain by holding the wrist of the next following man. The whole line was directed by two dancers who were especially richly dressed, one of them performing all steps backwards (Figure 31³).

Dances, music, and drinking bouts also filled the peaceful life after death. In one painting, the spirits form the characteristic chain, while two flutes and two pan-pipes furnish the music. Other death spirits stand before two enormous jars which contain the intoxicating beverage (Figure 33³). These representations of the dancing dead are rather unique in ancient American art and remind one in a surprising way of the medieval death dances of Western Europe.

Another group of vase paintings is devoted to a ceremony which must have been of special importance to this civilization. It seems to have been a kind of sacred race. The participants wore only their loin cloths and belts, but were adorned with beautiful head ornaments of special shape (Figure 36³) In almost every case, a very curious object is shown in one hand

of the racers. It is a little bag, fashioned out of a piece of cloth or leather, which is folded in such a way that two corners stand up vertically above the fingers. These sacred races stand in close relation to beans, which formed one of the most important staple foods. This connection is shown quite clearly in a vase painting from the Museum in Bremen, where a number of beans follow the runners (Figure 38³). This is to express in a graphic way the idea that the beans form the content of the little bags.

The big races, which played such an important role in this civilization, were certainly not just a mere sport; they also had a magical and religious significance. They may be considered as a kind of fertility ceremony to insure the growth and rich harvest of the beans. They might be compared to quite analogous ceremonial races among the tribes of the southwestern U. S. There is also a very interesting old Spanish report from the hinterland of Lima, dealing with an analogous ceremony which clearly was meant to insure the fertility of a certain fruit.

Among other plants, coca deserves a special mention. The chewing of coca must have played an important role also in the ceremonial and religious life, as is shown by a vase painting in the Stuttgart collection (Figure 5³). The three seated figures hold the typical containers carried by coca chewers, from which they dip small quantities of lime to add to their coca cuds. The fourth figure, his face turned upward and his hands in an adoring attitude, has a coca bag and a lime container clearly depicted. Partly surrounding him is a double-headed monster, which stands in some relation to the heavens. As Doering has indicated, the Chimu, as well as the ancient Mexicans and Maya, symbolized the heavens as a double-headed monster

From representations of this kind we gain a certain insight into the rich ceremonial life which centered around the "huacas," the big temple pyramides. Other effigy vessels and vase paintings give us an idea what the demons and gods looked like.

The vast number of mythical beings, much larger than could be imagined from the report given by Antonio de la Calancha for the later period, can be split up, as has been shown elsewhere, into several groups, among which the animal demons outnumber all other groups. The typical attributes are the big tusks, a motif pre-

uses helmet and armor, shield and club, and javelin and atlatl, whereas many other demons brandish a kind of "tumi," a very peculiar combination of axe and knife, also used in the human sacrifices. The same holds true for the plant demons, especially the bean demons, which are depicted as warriors wearing immense helmets. In the middle of the bean, a human face is inserted.

How much the mythology reflected the

FIGURE 5.

FIGURE 6.

FIGURE 7.

viously found in the Chavin civilization, and ear pendants in the form of serpent heads. Both attributes can clearly be seen in the beautiful crab demon, whose neck is encircled by a string of large pearls.

The extremely war-like character of these animal demons is made clear by their dress and other attributes. They use the same weapons as the warriors of this time did, as can be seen in the fox demon from a vase in the American Museum of Natural History in New York (FIGURE 6). The demon

real life of this period, which was crowded with wars, is shown by the many fights among the demons and gods. In these mythical battle scenes, there is a god of special importance, whose attribute consists of one or two snakes hanging down from his belt. This god, whose name is as unknown as those of his adversaries, is always victorious in the many fights in which he is engaged. His enemies are mostly crab and fish demons which he tries to subdue with his tumi or a long angler's line. A beautiful vase painting in the collection of the American Museum of Natural History in New York, published long ago by Squier, shows this god subduing a crab demon—grabbing him by the hair, the typical symbol of capture in war, in the Chimu civilization as well as in ancient Mexico (FIGURE 7).

Many scenes of fights among the gods, however, are not as simple as this. In a mythical battle scene from the Museum in Munich, there are more than sixty little beings represented (Figure 43³). Two groups of demons are involved in a fight: the animal demons fight against other demons which are personified objects, such as nose-ornaments, javelins, *etc.* The chief rays with little snake heads, and two demons, who are sacrificing two naked prisoners of war. On the back of the double-headed monster, a number of demons approach the god, who again is surrounded by many rays (FIGURE 8). This vase painting leaves no doubt that the god is a mythical being of supreme importance, whose dwelling is to be looked for in the heavenly regions. Doering has therefore not hesitated to identify this god with the moon god "Si," of whom Antonio de la Calancha has left us some information. This identification is supported further by a number of other representations, which show the god in a crescent or in a crescent-shaped "balsa"

FIGURE 8.

of the animal demons may be considered a god who is surrounded by an aureole, whose rays end in little snake heads. The battle ends with the victory of the animal demons, who bring the chief of the object demons as a prisoner of war to the deity with the aureole.

The same god is represented in another vase painting, accompanied by a number of animal and plant demons, his high rank being demonstrated by the fact that he is carried in a beautiful litter, while the two litter bearers hold, again, the little bags full of beans (Figure 37³).

We encounter this god with the aureole again in a vase painting which is divided into two zones by the horizontal body of the big serpent of the heavens. In the lower zone we see the litter of the god, surrounded by crossing the heavenly ocean (Figures 72 and 69³).

Taken as a whole, the effigy vessels and the vase paintings of the Early Chimu may be compared to an enormous atlas of pictures of which the accompanying explanations are lost. No text gives us, as in the Greek vases or in the Egyptian tomb reliefs, the names of the gods or heroes represented. The deeper sense of these representations seems to be lost forever, except as their meaning may be recovered from the representations themselves. The key to an understanding, if there is any at all, lies in the meticulous combination and comparative analysis of the effigy vessels and the vase paintings.

If at some time it becomes possible to reconstruct partly the highly interesting civilization of the Early Chimu, and so to understand the basic principles of this culture, it will be thanks to those unknown and nameless artists who created these ceramics more than a thousand years ago. The monument which they have erected for themselves and for their people is not *"aere perennius"* but was created with the simple tools of potters, who were artists and, in some way, anthropologists at the same time.

## References

1. ROWE, J. H. 1948. The kingdom of Chimor. Acta Americana **VI** (1–2): 26–59.
2. LARCO HOYLE, R. 1939. Los Mochicas **I–II**. Lima.
3. KUTSCHER, G. 1950. Chimu, Eine Altindianische Hochkultur. Mann. Berlin.
4. WISSLER, C. 1947. The cereals and civilization. Science (Am. Mus. Nat. Hist.) 129: 36.

# THE ADVENTURES OF TWO PUCARA STATUES

By JOHN HOWLAND ROWE

The plain of Pucara, looking south. At the lower right is the temple terrace, with Kidder's 1939 excavations visible in the center of it; almost in the center of the picture, in the edge of the cloud shadow, is the area of houses illustrated on page 257. The high hill on the horizon at the left is Llallawa, which has an ancient fort and an Inca garrison house on the summit.

STONE SCULPTURE was never so abundant in the Andean area in antiquity as it was in Mexico and Central America, and historical circumstances have not been favorable to the survival of what there was. Many of the finest ancient sculptures went the way of the statue of the god Qatikilla, made for his shrine at Porcon near Huamachuco in northern Peru. This statue, said to have been an exceptionally fine one, was broken in pieces by an officer of the rebel Inca prince 'Atawallpa in 1532 because the oracle of Qatikilla had predicted victory for the legitimate ruler. Qatikilla's priests rescued the head of the statue and three pieces of the body, and restored them to the shrine. When, a few years later, Augustinian missionaries arrived to convert the people of Huamachuco to Christianity, the friars seized the fragments of Qatikilla's statue, ground them to powder, and cast the powder in the river, "so that there should be no memory of it," says the pious chronicler with approval. In more

Reprinted from ARCHAEOLOGY, Vol. 11, No. 4, 1958.  pp. 255-261.

A corner of the temple at Pucara excavated by Kidder. The building consists of rooms arranged in a horseshoe around three sides of a square sunken court. Only the stone foundations of the walls are preserved; the upper walls were of adobe.

# TWO
# PUCARA
# STATUES

**continued**

recent times we have the case of the sculptures at Tiahuanaco in Bolivia, which were used as targets for rifle practice by the Bolivian army in 1894. With all the circumstances which have favored destruction, it is a miracle that any ancient statues at all have survived in the Andes. Those that still exist have been through many adventures. Usually the adventures of statues are not recorded, but I have succeeded in finding the stories of two exceptionally fine ones in the Pucara style. Apart from the interest of the stories, the statues themselves deserve notice because of their archaeological importance.

Before introducing the statues it may be well to say a word about the Pucara style. Pucara is, first of all, the name of a great archaeological site in the Department of

THE AUTHOR is Professor of Anthropology and Curator of South American Archaeology at the University of California, Berkeley. In 1954 he was awarded an honorary Litt.D. by the National University of Cuzco, Peru, for his contributions to the archaeology of the Cuzco area. Dr. Rowe first visited Pucara in the summer of 1939, immediately following the end of the Harvard excavations there, and the first five illustrations accompanying this article were taken at that time. Dr. Alfred Kidder II has kindly authorized the publication of photographs showing his excavations.

Puno, Peru. It is located on the edge of the flat basin of Lake Titicaca, about thirty miles northwest of the north end of the lake and at an altitude of 12,734 feet. The site consists of a large area of house foundations, now buried under fields of potatoes, and a series of temples at the base of an impressive cliff. The first systematic excavations there were carried out in 1939 by Dr. Alfred Kidder II for the Peabody Museum of Harvard University. Kidder found the remains of only a single culture, although the site was evidently occupied for a considerable time. From indirect evidence it appears that the Pucara culture flourished sometime between A.D. 500 and 1000. In 1941 Kidder explored a large part of the Department of Puno and traced the Pucara culture nearly to Chucuito on the lake shore to the south. To the north he did not succeed in tracing it beyond Qaluyu, a site only two or three miles from Pucara itself.

The artistic style of Pucara is known from pottery and stone sculpture. The decorated pottery is a handsome polychrome ware with painted designs in black, yellow and red. The areas of color are outlined by incised lines, and many of the bowls have modeled puma heads as part of the decoration. The stone sculpture includes both low

Foundations of the houses excavated by Kidder in the plain below the temple at Pucara.

How to study ancient sculpture in the Pucara area: the crew is digging out a carved slab at Qaluyu, near Pucara, so that it can be photographed. The Peruvian authorities have wisely ordered that large pieces of ancient sculpture in this area should be kept buried to prevent both vandalism and the ill effects of weathering.

## TWO
## PUCARA
## STATUES

**continued**

The **results** of the effort: a slab of fine-grained white stone with Pucara-style carving in relief, dug out for photographing at Qaluyu. This slab is not the one being excavated in the photograph on the preceding page, but it had to be disinterred in the same way.

relief work and statues in the round. The surface detail on both kinds of sculpture is often indicated by incised lines, and the style of the incised work is identical to that on the pottery. Since this incised decoration shows many detailed resemblances to the Classic style of Tia-huanaco on the Bolivian end of the lake, it seems clear that Pucara and Classic Tiahuanaco cannot be very far apart in time. In spite of these resemblances, however, the Pucara style is not just a provincial imitation of Tiahuanaco but an original and vigorous style in its own right. The originality of the Pucara style shows most clearly in stone carving. While Tiahuanaco sculptors were generally content to represent human figures by carving the four sides of a square pillar in low relief, Pucara sculptors attempted to show the human figure in the round, in a fairly realistic manner. Stone sculpture is relatively abundant at Pucara type sites. Kidder found

forty-eight pieces of stone sculpture at Pucara itself, including fragments of twenty-one human figure statues.

THE FIRST of the two statues with which we are now concerned, although badly battered, is the finest representation of the human figure which has survived from the Pucara culture. This torso is now in the Instituto Arqueológico at Cuzco. The material is a hard greenish stone which was given a smooth finish by the ancient sculptor. It represents a man wearing a breech-cloth with side flaps. Two snakes descend from his head and rest their heads on his shoulders. The body is conceived in the round and has many naturalistic details such as the slightly stooped posture, the rib lines on the chest and the slightly bent arms, a good approximation to a normal resting position. On the other hand, the arms are unnaturally short, and no distinction is made between

**Torso in the Pucara style** found in the Province of Chumbivilcas and now in the Instituto Arqueológico, Cuzco. To support the piece for photographing, a fragment of an ancient mortar was wedged under the right leg. Note the two snakes, one on each shoulder. *Right:* rear view of the torso. Height 52 cm. Photographs by Martín Chambi.

chest, waist and hips. The snakes and the breech-cloth are shown in low relief, while other details, such as the rib lines and the design or fringe on the breech-cloth flaps, are indicated by incision.

When my attention was first attracted to this statue, in 1946, I inquired for the accession record and found that there was none; the specimen had never been catalogued. The janitor of the Institute, however, remembered that the statue had been brought from Livitaca in 1940, on the occasion of a visit to Cuzco by President Prado. This information was very exciting, for Livitaca is located in the Province of Chumbivilcas in the southern part of the Department of Cuzco, about a hundred miles northwest of Pucara. The statue, therefore, suggested a great extension northward of the known range of Pucara-style antiquities, and determination of its exact provenience became of the greatest importance. Since

there was no more information to be had at the Institute, I began to make inquiries among Peruvian friends who knew the Chumbivilcas area. Fortunately, Dr. Oscar Nuñez del Prado, now Professor of Anthropology at the University of Cuzco but then still a student, had a brother, Alberto Nuñez del Prado, who had worked for two years as telegrapher in Livitaca. Don Alberto knew the whole story.

The statue came from a place called Waraqoyoq Q'asa ("Pitahaya Pass") on the lands of the Indian community of Choqepillku near the town of Totora, northeast of Livitaca. Originally, there were at least six statues at Waraqoyoq Q'asa and two of them were still standing at the time Don Alberto collected his information. The heads had all been knocked off because of a local belief that they caused illness by "eating the heart." The torso which is now in Cuzco was first taken to

# TWO PUCARA STATUES

continued

Totora, to the house of the priest. Then, when President Prado made his visit to Cuzco in 1940, the governor of Totora, Nicanor Molero, took the torso to Cuzco with the idea of presenting it to the president in the name of the Liwi Sport Club. Prado and his party, however, took no interest in the battered relic and left it lying in the yard of a private house in Cuzco. Molero thereupon arranged to give the statue to the Instituto Arqueológico, the staff of which was not much more interested than the president had been but at least has kept the torso from further damage.

According to Don Alberto's report, the head of the Cuzco statue is in the private collection of Francisco Estrada in the village of Pongoña, near Yanaoca. Estrada is supposed to have three other pieces of sculpture from Waraqoyoq Q'asa as well. Don Alberto heard of other examples of ancient sculpture in the province of Chumbivilcas, including a statue reported at Charquío and another in the village jail at Velille. Evidently this virtually unknown area was a major center of ancient stone carving.

The statue in Cuzco has never previously been published. A second piece of Pucara sculpture, which also has a story, has been published twice, but in places where it has not attracted attention. It is a very well preserved statuette now in the Ethnographic Section of the Bernisches Historisches Museum in Bern, Switzerland. Bern is not one of the most obvious places to look for ancient Peruvian sculpture.

The Bern statuette is only about 6¼ inches high. It is made of a dark greenish stone with a white streak in it which was utilized by the sculptor to mark the junction between the head and the neck. The eyes and earplugs are hollowed out, probably for inlays which have now disappeared. There appears to be a hollow in the topknot, barely visible in the back view. Only the head is carved in the round; the body is simply a block of stone with details indicated in low relief and by incision. The figure is evidently supposed to suggest a hunch-backed man sitting on his heels with his knees drawn up under his shirt.

The Bern Museum acquired this statuette in 1929 as part of a small collection of Peruvian antiquities purchased from Mr. Gilg von Tschudi of Bern. The collection had been made by his grandfather, the distinguished naturalist, diplomat and antiquarian, Johann Jakob von Tschudi, on a journey to Bolivia and Peru in 1858. The museum records give no further information beyond the erroneous suggestion that the collector acquired the statuette in Arequipa.

I first ran across the Bern statuette while reading the excellent biography of Tschudi by Paul-Emile Schazmann (*Jean-Jacques de Tschudi, explorateur, médecin, diplomate* [Zurich 1956]). Schazmann's book contains a photograph of the piece (plate 12), and the text gives a summary of the story of how Tschudi acquired it, taken from his account of his travels (*Reisen durch Südamerika* [Leipzig 1866-69] vol. 5, 295-297). Tschudi did not get the statuette at Arequipa but at Tiahuanaco, in Bolivia, where he spent a few days studying the ruins in 1858. Here is Tschudi's own version of the story:

". . . Ponce de León [Tschudi's local guide], accompanied by a crowd of Indians, had brought back to the tambo [inn] an idol about which he had told me a great deal during the excursion. . . . This idol was highly respected by the Indians of Tiahuanaco and was widely known in the area under the name of "the god of thieves" *(el santo de los ladrones)*. The Indians showed to it the same reverence they did to any of the saints of the church. Its owner lit a wax candle to it every Friday; any time a theft took place, the victim of the theft brought a special candle and offered it in the firm belief that he would trace the thief with the help of the saint.

"I jestingly asked the owner whether he did not wish to sell his saint, but he refused the offer indignantly. My two fellow travelers understood the hint, and, while I made a drawing of the idol, they persuaded Ponce de

"**The god of thieves**"—a Pucara-style statuette purchased at Tiahuanaco in Bolivia by J. J. von Tschudi in 1858, and now in the Bernisches Historisches Museum, Bern, Switzerland. Front, profile and rear views. A fine incised frog design may be seen on the back. Height 15.5 cm.; width at shoulders 9.7 cm. Photographs courtesy Dr. Karl H. Henking.

León that he should try to prevail on the owner to let me have it. A flask of cognac made the people more complacent. After much give and take they finally seemed to be in agreement to strike a bargain, and Ponce de León came forward with a quite outrageous demand. I simply rejected it and made a counter offer which in its turn was indicated as unacceptable. I finished the drawing without appearing to be further concerned about the matter. Pempel had meantime given orders to hold the animals in readiness and distributed the rest of the flask among the Indians. They, now entirely drunk, took the initiative, and when we were already sitting in the saddle the affair came to a conclusion. I paid quickly, put the idol in the saddle bag, and, with my companions, rode hastily after the baggage which was already far ahead. The Indians probably regretted the bargain immediately, for scarcely had we reached the open plain when we heard an infernal uproar behind us and saw some Indians pursuing us; their heads, however, were heavy and their feet unsteady. They were unable to overtake us. . . . How must the thieves of Tiahuanaco have rejoiced when they got word of the abduction of the curious saint!"

So the "god of thieves" went to Europe, the first piece of sculpture in the Pucara style to find its way outside of the Andean area and the first to be illustrated in a drawing in which the characteristic features of the style could be distinguished. It was not Tschudi's fault that later archaeologists overlooked his travel account.

As FOR THE crucial problem of provenience, Tschudi's account assures us that the statuette now in Bern was in use as a cult object at Tiahuanaco in 1858. The fact that it had such a modern use is fascinating and tells us something useful about the persistence of native religious traditions in this area. It also means, however, that we have no worthwhile archaeological associations for the statuette. The piece could have been dug up at Tiahuanaco a few years earlier, or it could have been brought across the lake by a traveler at any time in the preceding thousand years. The first of these possibilities is rendered more likely by the fact that a few other specimens of Pucara-style sculpture have been found at and near Tiahuanaco, including the big red sandstone figures which flank the entrance to the church in Tiahuanaco village. Provenience aside, however, the Bern statuette is important because it is one of the finest and best preserved examples of Pucara-style sculpture.

When the definitive monograph on Pucara sculpture is written, the detective work that has gone into this article will be useful chiefly because it establishes the facts of provenience or lack of it for two fine statues. It would be a pity, however, for their amazing adventures to have been hidden away in a footnote.

Fig. 8. Sr. Cordero directing Indian workmen in Pit A at Tiahuanaco.

# DIGGING IN THE TITICACA BASIN

## Alfred Kidder, II

The University Museum undertook its first project in American archaeology in mid-1895 when Max Uhle was engaged by mail to continue his work in the Titicaca Basin. Uhle, who laid the foundations of scientific archaeology in the Central Andes, had been working for the Museum für Völkerkunde in Berlin and was in La Paz, Bolivia, when he became the Museum's first field worker in this hemisphere. Unfortunately, he was unable to secure permission to excavate in Bolivia, and after several exploratory trips in the high country around Lake Titicaca he went to Lima to begin his historic excavation at Pachacamac. At that large and important site, not far from Lima on the Peruvian coast, he discovered the evidence that gave us the first clear ideas of the long history of Andean civilization. It was not until the early 1920's that the Museum was again represented in the relatively neglected Andean field. Dr. William Curtis Farabee, who had spent several years in the forests of British Guiana and the Amazon, making valuable ethnological and archaeological collections for the Museum, went to dig and explore on the coast south of Lima. It was his last trip to the field, however, for he had contracted severe malaria in the service of the Museum and died without being able to publish the full results of his work in Peru.

In the spring of 1955 the Museum's early interest in Andean archaeology was revived when I was able to renew actively my abiding interest in the archaeology of the mountainous part of southern Peru and Bolivia. The heart of this area is Lake Titicaca, 12,500 feet above sea level, the highest body of water navigable by large vessels in the world, and the center of a large interior drainage basin of great archaeological importance.

Our expedition, supported in part by the American Philosophical Society, was not a large one as such projects go. Mrs. Kidder, and

Reprinted from UNIVERSITY MUSEUM BULLETIN (University of Pennsylvania),
Vol. 20, No. 3, 1956. pp. 16-29.

Mr. William Coe, now Assistant in the American Section, accompanied me and Mr. Alan R. Sawyer, Assistant Curator of Decorative Arts in the Art Institute of Chicago, worked with us for two months. We had originally hoped to divide our time about equally between the Bolivian and Peruvian sides of Lake Titicaca (the international boundary cuts the Lake roughly in two). As it turned out we had only a few weeks to devote to the Peruvian side; fortunately they were most productive.

Why did we choose the Titicaca Basin when there are so many other interesting, unworked, and undoubtedly rich sites in less remote, and certainly lower and warmer places? The answer requires a brief review of what has been done in Peru and Bolivia and what needs to be done, and brings us again to Max Uhle and his early work in the highlands and his much more extensive digging on the coast, both for the Museum and later for the University of California. Uhle had spent a good deal of time at the great site of Tiahuanaco, in Bolivia on the treeless high plain that surrounds much of the Lake. He knew that the great ruins of large stone enclosures and of artificial mounds, once faced with cut stone, the stone statues and the distinctive pottery style of the site were not the work of the Incas who conquered the entire area only shortly before the advent of the Spaniards. Tiahuanaco, therefore, had to be earlier than the Inca Empire.

His knowledge of Tiahuanaco style enabled him to recognize its presence in somewhat altered but unmistakable form, again in pre-Inca position, in his excavations at Pachacamac and elsewhere along the Peruvian coast. He thus established the presence of two widespread and easily identifiable styles, chiefly represented in ceramics—one that of the late Inca, spread as they conquered from their capital at Cuzco, the other, earlier, presumably having spread from Tiahuanaco. He also identified a number of local styles separating the two widespread horizons. Starting in the twenties other archaeologists, notably Professor A. L. Kroeber, of the University of California, further analyzed Uhle's unpublished collections and began to do serious field work on the coast to extend the Uhle chronology and learn more about the coastal aspect of Andean civilization. This work is still going on, and has resulted in a chronology that goes back to about 2500 B.C. (on the basis of radiocarbon dating) on the north coast of Peru. It reaches a time before pottery was being made or maize

Fig. 9. *(Left)* The high, treeless plain at Tiahuanaco from Pit A, now so deep that a ladder was needed.

Fig. 10. *(Below)* Lake Titicaca and the snow capped Andes from the mound at Chiripa. The trees are carefully nurtured imported eucalyptus and pine.

was being cultivated. Another major, widespread "horizon" marked by a spectacular art style with strong feline motifs, has been discovered. This is called "Chavin," after a site in the northern highlands. It does not reach the Titicaca area, and it precedes the coastal Tiahuanaco style by many centuries. We have, therefore, as a result of work that has been relatively small in comparison to that devoted to other parts of the world, a very satisfactory outline of the cultural history of the north coast of Peru; other parts of the coast are now being comparably worked and will soon be as well understood.

During the last thirty years, however, while great strides were being made on the coast, very little was done in the highland basins that we know provided the only arable land for the Inca, their conquered neighbors and their predecessors, including the builders of Tiahuanaco and Chavin. From the single fact that the three widespread "horizon styles," Inca, Tiahuanaco, and Chavin, have, or in the case of the two latter, seem to have, highland origins, it is obvious that Andean civilization as a whole cannot be understood by limiting our knowledge to the coast. There is a great deal of evidence that there was trade and contact across the mountains as far as the forests of the eastern slopes. In the highlands the llama and alpaca were domesticated, thus providing the source of wool for the extraordinary textiles of the coast. Highland potatoes and other root crops were traded to the coast, and the highlands were the source of gold, copper, silver, and tin . It is apparent that Andean civilization could not have developed as it did without the highlands and without constant interaction between coast and highland.

In spite of many good opportunities to do so, only a few archaeologists have worked in the highlands; the area has been sadly neglected. The reason for this imbalance in attention to the two geographically contrasting zones is that conditions on the coast favor excellent preservation of perishable materials such as textiles and that vast cemeteries are easy to find and dig. Furthermore, Uhle's early work challenged his colleagues and successors to carry it on. There has not been so great a stimulus to concentrate on highland problems. To give but a single example of how little interest they have aroused, it was not until 1941 that Dr. John H. Rowe, then a student of mine, began the first seriously scientific attempt to find out what lay below the remains of Inca occupation in the Cuzco district. This is as though Rome or any other great seat of empire had failed to arouse any interest in its early history.

The foregoing explains why we wished to do something to correct the disparity between our knowledge of coast and highland by going to the Titicaca Basin. We were not going to an altogether unknown area, for after Uhle left Bolivia, the late Wendell C. Bennett, working for the American Museum of Natural History, excavated at Tiahuanaco and at several other sites on the Bolivian side of the Lake, including one called Chiripa that seemed surely to be even earlier than Tiahuanaco. I had also worked on the Peruvian side of the Lake, so that we were in a position to start an attempt to build a regional chronology and to add to the still very scanty knowledge of several periods of the history of the lake basin.

When we arrived in La Paz in early June, we hoped to concentrate on the earlier phases of Tiahuanaco culture and to learn more about Chiripa. We had not anticipated that we would be permitted to dig at Tiahuanaco, and we were therefore very pleased, and most grateful to the Ministry of Education, when it was suggested that we do so. Bennett, in 1932, had dug a number of pits at the site, finding three sequent pottery styles that he called Early, Classic, and Decadent. The Classic is quite surely associated with the monumental stone architecture and sculpture, the Decadent with the reuse of much Classic building stone, but the Early style was represented by potsherds in only a few of the pits and by some vessels taken from graves many years ago.

We were, therefore, anxious to obtain more information about Early Tiahuanaco, and made arrangements to dig at the site.

Tiahuanaco is on the railroad between La Paz and Guaqui, Bolivia's lake port, but it is an Indian town with rather primitive accommodations. We were most kindly invited to stay with Mr. and Mrs. Fritz Buck, of La Paz, who have been interested in the ruins for many years and had built a house near them. We were also most fortunate in having with us the Assistant Director of the National Museum, Sr. Gregorio Cordero, M., who later went with us to Chiripa. Sr. Cordero speaks fluent Aymara, the Indian language of that part of Bolivia. Without his help we should not have been able to communicate with the Indian workmen, and since he is a very able archaeologist, he could direct the men far more efficiently than an untrained interpreter.

We dug two pits at Tiahuanaco, each as close as possible to the two pits in the bottom levels of which Bennett had found Early Tiahuanaco pottery. This kind of digging is unspectacular. We proceeded by levels of 25 cm. (about 10 inches) each, keeping all potsherds and other objects, including bones, separate from the contents of other levels. We also saved all charcoal and burned bone from each level, placing it in polyethylene bags, for radiocarbon dating. If these samples are not contaminated by grass roots or badly affected by ground water, they should provide us with the first radiocarbon dates from the Andean highlands and allow us to compare them with dates from the coast. The age of Tiahuanaco has always been a question of guess-estimating, and many fantastic theories of great age have been proposed. These are taken very seriously by some Bolivians; it will not surprise us if our radiocarbon dates are not accepted by many people.

We found what we considered to be Early Tiahuanaco remains in both our pits, and have been able to add some bits of information about the period. For example, we are sure that arrowheads were in use at that time; there are thousands of arrowheads at Tiahuanaco, but hitherto they have been considered to be from the Decadent or later, post-Tiahuanaco periods.

Tiahuanaco, we now believe, is probably not the best place at which to study Early Tiahuanaco culture. To reach it, pits have to be too deep to allow lateral expansion without an enormous amount of digging, and in our best pit we reached ground water and finally had to stop digging before we reached sterile soil. The only other place at which Early Tiahuanaco is known to occur is on the Island of the Sun, in the Lake. We hope that some day we shall be able to dig there and that the Early Tiahuanaco phase will not be so deeply buried as to make it difficult to expose a larger area, perhaps sufficiently extensive to give us some idea of the kinds of houses in use at the time and even of village plan.

Since Bolivian law prohibits the permanent export of antiquities, we returned to La Paz to spend several weeks "working up" our Tiahuanaco finds. This is the aspect of archaeology that is so often overlooked by those romantic souls who forget that the work of the archaeologist is only just beginning when he digs up *anything* from the past. Thousands of potsherds must be examined, classified, and counted;

Fig. 11. Mrs. Kidder, Mr. Sawyer and Sr. Cordero watch the beginning of work on the Chiripa mound. The upright stone is part of the Decadent Tiahuanaco temple.

Fig. 12. Part of a Chiripa house, showing the doorway with its still partially covered slot and double walls. Stonework at upper right is of much later date.

Fig. 13. Outer corner of partially excavated Chiripa house. The later wall appears above the doorway in the center of the picture.

Fig. 14. *(Lower left)* Exposed north face of the Chiripa mound. The remains of a house excavated by Bennett may be seen at Mr. Coe's right; another house wall is behind him. Exposed wall below marks a lower level house.

Fig. 15. *(Below)* Mr. Coe cleaning the wall of the upper level house seen in background of Fig. 14. A bin formed by double walls lies below the shovel handle. Arrows point to bin cover slabs still in place.

specimens to be illustrated must be set aside and drawn and photographed. Faced with this problem in La Paz, we experienced the kind of international cooperation and good will that would make short work of "global tension" could it but be transferred to economic and political spheres. Dr. Manuel Liendo Lazarte, Director of the National Museum, Sr. Cordero's chief, closed an exhibition gallery for our use, made available ample table space, and, in short, provided us with every possible facility for the analysis of our Tiahuanaco collections. Sr. Cordero's hard work with us in the field and Dr. Liendo's unfailing help in La Paz made our work a truly joint enterprise.

After finishing the analysis and recording of the Tiahuanaco material, we loaded our equipment on a truck and went to Chiripa. The site is a village mound that must have been occupied for a long time, overlooking the lake shore northwest of Tiahuanaco. We were most kindly offered the *hacienda* house by Sra. Hortensia Pena v. de Ituralde and her sister, Srta. Sara Pena, the owners of the farm on which the ruins are situated. This made life at Chiripa quite easy, since the house was only a few steps from the mound. We had some difficulty in getting supplies; except for potatoes, eggs, mutton, and occasional vegetables, there is little to

Fig. 16. After cutting away most of the upper level houses, Mr. Coe prepares to carry the excavation down to expose the lower level house before which he is standing.

be had in rural Bolivia. Fortunately Srta. Elena del Carpio came to our rescue with her Willys station wagon, and made regular trips from La Paz with beef, bread, butter, evaporated milk, and fruit, as well as our mail. We had found it impossible to persuade anyone else in La Paz to risk a vehicle on the rough road to Chiripa, so Srta. del Carpio's willingness to risk her little car made the difference between comfort and relative hardship. Such a difference is important when you are working as hard as we did at Chiripa. At high altitude with freezing temperatures at night and occasional sleet and snow, good hot food and a comfortable bed in a real house help enormously to get the work done.

Chiripa was quite different from Tiahuanaco archaeologically. Instead of pits dug into flat ground, we were exposing buildings in a rather complex situation that Bennett had first exposed in 1934. He had found what appeared to be a circle of houses, about fifty meters in diameter, around the top of the mound. Inside the circle there was a sunken temple court, made in Decadent Tiahuanaco times, much later than the houses of the Chiripa village. Bennett made a deep trench to the center of the mound and exposed two Chiripa houses. He was unable to analyze his collections fully, so our intention was to add to his data on the houses,

Fig. 17. Mr. Sawyer sitting in the doorway of a house in the east face of the Chiripa mound. All but the inner walls of these houses had been removed in farm operations. Remains of a looted rock-walled grave appear at the right of Mr. Sawyer's feet.

collect charcoal for radiocarbon dating and secure a collection of pottery and other objects for complete study. When we examined the mound we found that it had been cut away at right angles to Bennett's trench, exposing a long, high face that needed only to be cleaned to provide a stratigraphic picture that tied in perfectly with Bennett's and made it possible to interpret the history of the village far better than was possible by means of a single trench.

In brief, we verified the full circle of houses at the top of the mound that Bennett had suspected; Mr. Sawyer made a new map, based on our work and other exposures made since Bennett's day. We then dug down in the newly exposed face, under one of Bennett's houses that had been nearly altogether cut away. Near the bottom of the mound in this excavation remains of two earlier houses appeared—we suspect that they are part of an earlier circle underlying the upper one.

Chiripa houses of the upper level were made of smooth, water-worn stones, set in large amounts of mud. Each is a single room, from about thirteen to eighteen feet long by eight to nine feet wide, inside measurement. The walls were made double to about chest height; the space between was slabbed over, forming a shelf over a series of bins between the double walls. Openings like small windows gave access to the bins. Doorways were provided with covered slots into which sliding doors could be run. What the sliding doors were made of is speculative; planks in this treeless area seem unlikely. Heavy reed matting framed with sticks is a better guess.

Some of the houses, at least, were burned; we suspect that they had roofs of reed thatch, and that they were burned by enemies, since it is almost impossible to fire a roof accidentally at the altitude of Chiripa.

The lower houses were in much poorer condition, having been leveled off to facilitate later construction. They had niches in the walls, but no doublewall bins. There is still a great deal to be done at this level, and there are still a number of intact tombs under the upper level of houses. We opened several rock-walled graves that contained pottery, green stone beads and sometimes beads of rolled gold leaf.

We are now convinced, for a variety of technical reasons, that Chiripa is considerably older than Tiahuanaco. We have excellent samples of charcoal, much of it without any possible contamination, that should provide dates for this most interesting early culture.

Fig. 18. Dr. Liendo and Sr. Cordero examine a Chiripa vessel in the Museo Nacional Tiahuanacu. Restored jar at right is also from Chiripa.

After leaving Chiripa in mid-September, we worked on the collection in La Paz and arranged to borrow for study the large quantity of unpainted ware for which more time was needed than we could spare. Mrs. Kidder and I then crossed the Lake by steamer to Puno, the Peruvian port, where we were met by Dr. M. Chavéz Ballón, an old friend now a professor at the University of Cuzco. Together we made two small excavations near Pucara, in the northern part of the lake basin. These produced charcoal for use in dating the Pucara culture, related to Tiahuanaco but not as yet accurately placed in time, and pottery from a new and earlier culture. We call it Qaluyu; it is represented by only a small collection of potsherds some of which are painted in brown or red on a cream slip. Others of plain brown or gray are decorated with wide groovings. We do not yet know how this phase is related to others in the area.

In retrospect we seem to have raised far more problems than we have even begun to solve, and I venture to predict that this will continue to be the case for a long time unless a great many more archaeologists become interested in this hard, often difficult, but rewarding region.

## STYLE AND TIME IN THE MIDDLE HORIZON
### Dorothy Menzel

#### Conclusions

> If we want to know the real motivation and rationale
> of cultural events, we cannot do better than to find out <u>what</u>
> the events really are and <u>how</u> they actually succeeded one an-
> other.  -  Robert H. Lowie.[406]

The establishment of a detailed ceramic chronology for the earlier
part of the Middle Horizon in a number of areas in Peru makes possible some
preliminary inferences as to what happened in this complex period.  The evidence
is still fragmentary, and it is obvious that new information may make necessary
drastic changes in the reconstruction attempted here, but a statement of the
apparent implications of what is now known may at least call attention to important problems for further investigations.

As many earlier students of the Middle Horizon have recognized, the key
area for understanding developments in this period is the region around Ayacucho
and Huari in the southern sierra.  A local tradition of large urban settlements
developed in this area in the latter part of the Early Intermediate Period, associated with pottery which reflects strong influences from Nasca.  In Epoch 1A of
the Middle Horizon a new style of ceremonial pottery without local antecedents
appeared in the Ayacucho area.  This new kind of ceremonial pottery is known so
far only from a single offering deposit at Conchopata.  It comprises oversize
vessels ornamented with painted depictions of mythical themes.  The native
pottery style in ordinary use at this time in the area of Ayacucho and Huari was
the Chakipampa A style, which continued to reflect influences from Nasca.  Only
a few influences of the new ceremonial style can be detected in Chakipampa A
pottery, an example being the occasional representation of crossed canine teeth
in the heads of mythical animals derived from the Nasca tradition.  The association of the Conchopata A style with a special repertory of new mythical themes
and its isolation in a ceremonial context suggest that it implies the introduction of a new set of religious ideas and practices.

The mythical themes depicted on the new ceremonial pottery, and the
style in which they are executed, resemble so closely mythical representations
at Tiahuanaco in Bolivia, particularly those carved in relief on the Monolithic

Reprinted from ÑAWPA PACHA 2, 1964. pp. 66-73, 104-105.

Gateway or incised on some of the larger statues, that a close connection is obvious. Furthermore, sherds of very large vessels ornamented with mythical themes are said to have been found at Tiahuanaco, although none has been illustrated.[407] The new religion must have come to the area of Ayacucho and Huari from the south, either from Tiahuanaco itself or from some other undiscovered center like it.

No specimens, either whole vessels or sherds, of Tiahuanaco pottery of ordinary size have ever been found in Peru north or west of the Departments of Arequipa and Puno, and no Peruvian specimens have been found in Bolivia. It therefore seems most unlikely that any military conquest was involved in the introduction of the new religious ideas into Peru. Military conquest could be expected to leave some secular traces which might be identified at least in the major habitation sites, and nothing of the sort has been found. The data suggest rather that we are dealing with a purely religious movement in which a very small number of individuals actually traveled between the area of Ayacucho and Huari and the source of the new ideas. Such traveling as did occur may have been done either by missionaries from the Tiahuanaco center or by men from the area of Ayacucho and Huari who learned the new religion abroad and brought it home. In view of the distinctive character of the ceremonial pottery in the Conchopata offering deposit, the second of these possibilities seems the more likely.

In Epoch 1B of the Middle Horizon the new religion was more firmly established in the region of Ayacucho and Huari, and this area became the center of an expansion movement the effects of which can be traced along the coast from Acarí to Chancay and in the sierra as far north as Huaraz in the Department of Ancash. Three kinds of pottery were involved in the expansion, and their associations provide evidence of the nature of the movement. The three kinds of pottery are oversize vessels in the Robles Moqo style, regular size Robles Moqo vessels, and Chakipampa B ware.

Oversize Robles Moqo pottery includes urns, tumbler shaped vessels, and modeled pieces, the urns and tumblers being ornamented with mythological designs. This pottery continues the tradition of oversize ceremonial pottery represented by the Conchopata style in Epoch 1A. Robles Moqo oversize pottery is represented by three fragments from Bennett's excavations on the knoll of Robles Moqo at Huari, five fragments collected from the surface at the southern end of the site of Chakipampa, near Ayacucho, and the contents of a great offering deposit at Pacheco in Nasca. The restricted distribution of oversize ceremonial pottery at Huari and Chakipampa suggests that, at these sites as at Pacheco, it is not a normal constituent of habitation refuse but occurs in special ceremonial contexts. There are slight differences in the Robles Moqo style at each of the sites where it has been found, but the ceremonial pottery from Pacheco is a little closer to that from Huari than it is to that from Chakipampa.

The second kind of pottery associated with the expansion is Robles Moqo style pottery of ordinary size, mainly modeled pieces without obviously mythical features. It has precedents in the fanciest Tiahuanaco style pottery and hence may reflect new Tiahuanaco influence. Some specimens have painted designs derived from the Chakipampa style. A quantity of ordinary size Robles Moqo modeled pottery was found in or adjacent to the offering deposit at Pacheco, and individual specimens also occur in rich burials in the Nasca and Lima areas. One fragment was found in refuse at Cerro del Oro in Cañete. Bennett found three pieces in different parts of the site of Huari, including one from pure Epoch 1B refuse in his Pit 5, but none have turned up at Chaki-pampa. The nature and associations of the regular size Robles Moqo pottery suggest that it was a high prestige ware associated in some way with the new religion but less exclusively ceremonial than the oversize vessels. It could be owned by private individuals and perhaps put to secular use. The fact that it occurs on the coast and at Huari but not at Chakipampa suggests that the center of the Middle Horizon 1B expansion was Huari, rather than Chakipampa or some other site in the Ayacucho area.

The third kind of pottery involved in the expansion is the Chaki-pampa B style, which was the native style of pottery in ordinary secular use in the area of Ayacucho and Huari in Epoch 1B. It is nearly enough homogene-ous throughout this area so that we cannot distinguish Huari examples from ones found at Chakipampa. The Chakipampa B style continued the old local tradition and, as before, reflected influences from Nasca, including new ones of the Nasca 9 style. It also incorporated more details of design from the ceremonial style than had appeared in Chakipampa A pottery, for example, the fret band and small eagle heads, but full mythical figures of the ceremonial style were not reproduced. The Chakipampa B style is the most widely distrib-uted of the three kinds of pottery we have discussed, being represented by trade pieces, imitations, and influence throughout the area of Ayacucho expan-sion, at Acarí, Nasca, Cañete, Lima, Ancón, Chancay, Huancayo, and Huaraz. The fact that it is secular pottery which is the commonest marker of the Ayacucho expansion is a strong indication that military conquest was involved as well as religious propaganda. There are thus grounds for inferring the existence in Epoch 1B of an imperial state with its capital at Huari and ruling the whole central part of Peru.

Nasca influence accompanies influence from the Ayacucho area at Lima and Huancayo as well as being reflected in Chakipampa B pottery in the Ayacucho area itself. Nasca thus seems to have enjoyed a special privileged position in the new empire, sharing its prestige in the provinces, perhaps somewhat in the way in which Greece shared in the prestige of the Roman Empire.

In connection with the occupation of Nasca there was evidently a substantial colony of people from the sierra established at Pacheco in Epoch 1B. There is habitation refuse at this site as well as the offering deposit, and the refuse contains a mixture of sherds of the local Nasca 9 style with pieces in the Chakipampa B style and ones showing Chakipampa B influence. An examination of the paste indicates that the Chakipampa B style pieces were locally made. Paste characteristics also suggest that the large ceremonial pottery from the offering deposit was locally made, although its style shows no Nasca influence and some of the vessels are decorated with representations of sierra plants which do not grow on the coast.

Monumental architecture, represented by the remains of large structures built of fieldstone, is found in the Ayacucho area for the first time in Epoch 1B. Ruined fieldstone buildings are a prominent feature at the sites of Chakipampa and Ñawim Pukyu, both of which were abandoned at the end of Epoch 1B, but they do not occur at Acuchimay, which, as we have noted, was abandoned at the end of Epoch 1A. The appearance of monumental architecture in the Ayacucho area is no doubt in part a response to the need for more imposing public buildings in a new center of power, but it may also reflect the inspiration of Tiahuanaco.

In Epoch 2 of the Middle Horizon the empire of Huari went through a severe crisis and then expanded further to reach its greatest extent. As in Epoch 1, much of the evidence for the events of the time comes from the character and distribution of pottery styles.

There were three closely related pottery styles in Epoch 2 which incorporated Tiahuanaco-related features: the Viñaque style, which was the native pottery style of the Ayacucho area, the Atarco style, proper to Nasca, and the Pachacamac style, the home of which was on the central coast. These three styles together constitute the Huari group. All three represent combinations of features derived from the ceremonial pottery of Epoch 1 with features belonging to the secular traditions of their respective home areas. There was no longer a separate oversize ceremonial style except in the Ocoña Valley in the far south. In the styles of the Huari group the mythical themes of the Robles Moqo tradition were applied, in more or less abbreviated form, to the ordinary secular pottery found in burials and refuse. On fancy specimens the abbreviation is less extreme, while on less fancy pieces elements of mythical figures are used out of context as parts of abstract designs. The application of abbreviated mythical designs to secular pottery took place at the expense of designs of the older local traditions, and the latter became much less common in consequence. Apparently the new religion had permeated Huari society and become popularized.

Epoch 2 can be divided into two sub-epochs, A and B, on the basis of changes in pottery, but the distinctions cannot be fully worked out until more associations are available. Relatively few associations have been reported for Epoch 2A, while for 2B the evidence is considerably better.

At the end of Epoch 1B the great urban site of Chakipampa and the smaller settlement of Ñawim Pukyu, both in the valley of Ayacucho, were abandoned and never reoccupied. Not only was there no Epoch 2 occupation at these sites, but none has been found anywhere else in the valley. Huari continued to flourish, however, so the depopulation of the valley of Ayacucho may have been connected with a concentration of population in the capital. The Pacheco site in Nasca and the two known Epoch 1 habitation sites in the Ica Valley were also abandoned at this time.

On the central coast there was no break in the occupation of the major sites which flourished in Epoch 1, but a new center of great prestige was established at Pachacamac in Epoch 2A. There was also a significant change in burial customs on the central coast. It was traditional in this area to bury the dead in extended position, and this method of burial persisted through Epoch 1. In Epoch 1B there were a few burials in seated flexed position at Ancón, along with the commoner extended ones. After the beginning of Epoch 2A all central coast burials were made in seated flexed position, and the new custom persisted down until the time of the Spanish conquest. The seated flexed position was characteristic of both the south coast and the southern sierra. However, the form of it introduced on the central coast is somewhat different from the south coast form and probably represents Huari rather than Nasca influence.

The changes in settlement distribution and burial pattern which took place during Epoch 2A suggest some inferences as to what was happening in the Huari Empire. There was evidently a severe crisis affecting the valley of Ayacucho and the south coast, perhaps a revolt or an epidemic. On the central coast Huari influence was greatly strengthened at the expense of the local tradition.

Pottery characteristic of the Huari group styles of Epoch 2A has been found at Huari, Nasca, Pachacamac, Ancón, Supe, and Casma. The pieces from Supe and Casma may reflect new Huari expansion, but there is only one specimen from each valley, so they can equally well be explained as trade pieces. So little exploration has been undertaken in the areas of Huancayo and Huaraz that the fact that no Huari pottery of Epoch 2A has yet been reported from them is not necessarily significant. On the whole, the evidence available does not suggest any great change in the territory under Huari control in Epoch 2A.

The focus of the new center established at Pachacamac in Epoch 2A was a temple which grew in importance in subsequent periods and, at the time of the Inca conquest, was an oracle of great prestige and considerable political influence. The prestige of Nasca remained high in Epoch 2A and appears to have been associated with religious activities also. Some Atarco mythical designs of Epoch 2A show new resemblances to Tiahuanaco themes, a fact which suggests continued contacts between Nasca and the Tiahuanaco religious center independent of Huari. The evidence for religious initiative at Pachacamac and Nasca, combined with that for differences in the handling of mythical themes in pottery design between these two centers or between either one of them and Huari, suggests that the religious organization of the Huari Empire was not effectively centralized.

In Epoch 2B the empire of Huari expanded very rapidly and reached its maximum extent. Viñaque B pottery and Viñaque influences are found in the sierra as far north as Cajamarca and as far south as Cacha, near Sicuani, and Chuquibamba, in the Department of Arequipa. On the coast the extreme points of its distribution are Chicama in the north and the Ocoña Valley in the south. Great complexes of storage buildings at Wiraqocha Pampa, near Huamachuco, and Pikillaqta, in the lower Cuzco Valley, provide additional evidence of Huari rule and suggest a centralized administration such as the Incas established later, with similar concern for the collection and redistribution of goods and supplies.

The distribution and influence of pottery in the Pachacamac B style indicates that Pachacamac established a great sphere of influence of its own in Epoch 2B, one which extended north to Chicama, south to Nasca, and inland to Huancayo in the sierra. It is possible that Pachacamac was the capital of an independent state, governing part of this area in full sovereignty, but much more likely that it remained subject to Huari and exercised its influence through an oracle, as it did under Inca rule, when its sphere of influence was at least equally large.

The new prestige of Pachacamac involved the eclipse of Nasca. The Ica Valley, which had been for centuries a part of the area of Nasca culture, came under strong Pachacamac influence in Epoch 2B and developed a distinctive pottery style, called Ica-Pachacamac, which reflected its new ties to the north. Some direct influence of the Pachacamac style is also reflected in the Atarco B style at Nasca. Nasca continued to maintain some degree of cultural independence, but it never regained the leading position it had so long enjoyed on the south coast. Ica succeeded it as the center of prestige in this area.

In association with the Ica-Pachacamac style there appears at Ica a comparatively large amount of intrusive Viñaque pottery, much of which is not found on the coast to the north. This intrusive pottery at Ica is confined to the fanciest Viñaque and Viñaque-associated pieces, either in the form of imports or of excellently made local reproductions and variants. This situation suggests that there was a special relationship of some sort between Ica and the capital at Huari.

Viñaque influence was also strong at Nasca, but in a somewhat different form, involving influences of detail in fancy Atarco B vessels as well as imports and imitations. In some respects, Nasca continued to be more closely related to Huari than any other area on the coast.

The situation at Nasca requires no special explanation. Nasca had had close ties with the Ayacucho area for generations, and these ties continued in Epoch 2B in spite of the decline of Nasca prestige on the coast. The rise of Ica does require explanation. Ica's new prestige clearly rested in part on a new relationship to Pachacamac, but a relationship which left Ica some degree of cultural independence. The Ica-Pachacamac style is not just a provincial imita-tion of Pachacamac models. If the prestige of Pachacamac rested on the power and influence of an oracle, as suggested above, the most reasonable explanation for the developments at Ica is that the priests of Pachacamac established a branch oracle there, as they did at Chincha under the Inca Empire. The fancy Viñaque pottery at Ica would then reflect recognition of the new shrine by important people at Huari.

There were two areas in northern Peru which also enjoyed some special status in the Huari Empire, to judge from the distribution of their pottery. One was Cajamarca, where the Cajamarca III style was flourishing, and the other was the unidentified area which was the source of the pottery style which Bennett called Geometric on Light. The Geometric on Light style has so many resemblances to Cajamarca pottery that it seems reasonable to seek its home somewhere in the northern sierra, perhaps in some part of the Department of Ancash. Both the Cajamarca and the Geometric on Light styles occur in substantial quantity in the Epoch 2B refuse at Huari and are the only styles foreign to the Ayacucho area which do so. Their abundance is such as to suggest that there were colonies of northerners established at the imperial capital, perhaps representing military units like the Cañar and Chachapoyas imperial guards units which the Incas established at Cuzco.

Cajamarca III pottery also occurs in burials on the north coast, in the Moche and Chicama valleys, probably as a result of trade or settlement direct from Cajamarca. Miniature vessels in shapes characteristic of the Cajamarca style have also been found in a rich Epoch 2B burial at Curahuasi in the southern sierra. In this case the influence was more likely transmitted through the capital. Geometric on Light pottery and imitations of it occur associated with pieces in the local styles in burials at Nasca and Ica, again no doubt representing influences channeled through Huari.

The Huari Empire evidently fell at the end of Epoch 2B. Huari itself, which had been a large city, was almost abandoned; sherds attributable to Epoch 3 are relatively rare on the surface there. As there are none which need to be later, the abandonment of the site seems to have been complete by Epoch 4. No new influences from Huari later than Epoch 2B have been found in the former provinces of the empire, although local derivatives of the Huari styles of Epoch 2B continued to be made in a number of areas, notably in Nasca, Ica, Pachacamac, Chancay, and Huarmey. There was no interruption in the occupation of Pachacamac, but the major centers in the valley of Lima, namely Cajamarquilla and the old part of Maranga, were apparently abandoned. The abandonment of Cajamarquilla is an inference from the fact that the latest burials reported from the Nievería cemetery, which lies at the edge of Cajamarquilla, date from Epoch 2B.

The decline and abandonment of Huari brought an end to the tradition of urban settlement in the Ayacucho area. There were no large cities in this area again; the later habitation sites are small ones, and they are scarce enough so that they are not easy to find. At the same time, no more fancy pottery was made. These circumstances suggest that the disintegration of political power was accompanied by both depopulation and economic depression in the area around the capital. It is not clear how widespread the depression was in the sierra, because so little archaeological work has been done there.

On the coast the Lima Valley may have been a depressed area, but the depression was not general. Ica and Nasca remained relatively prosperous, although there was some decline in the proportion of fancy pottery produced. The prestige of Nasca declined further, so that it came for the first time under the influence of Ica. The sphere of influence of Pachacamac was much reduced, so that in Epoch 3 it was scarcely more important than Ica. At Pachacamac also the production of fancy pottery declined. A new center of prestige developed on the north-central coast, perhaps with its focus in Huarmey. It is characterized by a distinctive style of press molded pottery with mythical designs derived from the Huari repertory, and it flourished particularly in Epoch 3. Too little is known of the chronology of the north coast in the Middle Horizon to justify further inferences about what was happening in that area.

The local derivatives of the Huari styles on the south and central coasts persisted through Epoch 4 without drifting very far apart. These are the styles which Uhle appropriately named Epigonal. Their unity may reflect a continued connection of some kind between the oracle at Pachacamac and its presumed branch at Ica. With the beginning of the Late Intermediate Period the last traces of Middle Horizon unity vanished on the coast, and each local area went its own way.

NOTES

Abbreviations:

AIC - Art Institute of Chicago
AMNH - American Museum of Natural History, New York
AR - Aldo Rubini collection, Ocucaje, Ica
CNHM - Chicago Natural History Museum
CS - Carlos Soldi collection, Ocucaje, Ica
MAI - Museum of the American Indian, Heye Foundation, New York
MCP - Museo de la Cultura Peruana, Lima
MNAA - Museo Nacional de Antropología y Arqueología, Lima
MPA - Museum of Primitive Art, New York
MRI - Museo Regional de Ica
RHLMA - Robert H. Lowie Museum of Anthropology, Berkeley, California
YULA - Yale University Laboratory of Anthropology, New Haven, Connecticut

[406] Lowie, 1960, p. 479.

[407] Bennett, 1953, p. 99.

# KEY TO ILLUSTRATIONS

## Plates II-IX

Scale. Except as specifically noted, all drawings of pottery designs and sherd profiles are reproduced at 1/2 original size, and all shape outline drawings are reproduced at 1/4 original size. The photographs were taken at different scales, so individual measurements are given for the specimens shown.

## Plate II

Fig. 1.  CS, from Ullujaya, Ica.
Fig. 2.  RHLMA, from the surface of the Pacheco site, Nasca (PV69-41).
Fig. 3.  YULA, no. 213002, Bennett collection, from Acuchimay.
Fig. 4.  Same as fig. 22 on plate VIII.
Fig. 5.  CS, from the Nasca Valley.

## Plate III

Fig. 6.  CS, from somewhere in the Nasca drainage.
Fig. 7.  CS, from somewhere in the Nasca drainage.
Fig. 8.  CS, from somewhere in the Nasca drainage.  The design is from the top of a double spout bottle similar in shape to the one shown in fig. 9.
Fig. 9.  MRI, no. E-276, from Ica or Nasca.

## Plate IV

Fig. 10.  Same as fig. 18 on plate VII.
Fig. 11.  Same as fig. 19 on plate VII.

## Plate V

Fig. 12.  MNAA, design from a sherd excavated at the Conchopata site in 1942.  Actual size.
Fig. 13.  Angel figure reconstructed from fragments at MNAA and YULA. Actual size.

## Plate VI

Fig. 14.  MRI, from Tomb 2, Cahuachi, Nasca Valley; 8.5 cm. high.  Ocros style.
Fig. 15.  MRI, from Tomb 2, Cahuachi, Nasca Valley; 11 cm. high.  Nasca 9 style.
Fig. 16.  MRI, from Tomb 2, Cahuachi, Nasca Valley; 7 cm. high.  Ocros style.
Fig. 17.  AIC, no. 55.2236, central coast of Peru; 17 cm. high.  A Nieveria style vessel decorated with a Chakipampa B ("Ayacucho Serpent") design.

## Plate VII

All figures on this plate CS, from Tomb 1, San José de Ingenio, Nasca. Atarco B style.

Fig. 18.  21.5 cm. high.
Fig. 19.  22 cm. high.
Fig. 20.  15.5 cm. high.
Fig. 21.  25 cm. high.

## Plate VIII

Fig. 22.  CS, from Tomb 1, San José de Ingenio, Nasca; 15 cm. high. Atarco B style.

Figs. 23-25 on this plate AR, Tomb 1, Huaca José Ramos, Pinilla sector of Ocucaje, Ica.

Fig. 23.  10 cm. high.  Ica-Pachacamac style.
Fig. 24.  14 cm. high.  Viñaque style.
Fig. 25.  9.3 cm. high.  Derived Chakipampa style.

## Plate IX

All figures on this plate AR, Tomb 1, Huaca José Ramos, Pinilla sector of Ocucaje, Ica.

Fig. 26.  9 cm. high.  Ica-Pachacamac style.
Fig. 27.  9 cm. high.  Ica-Pachacamac style.
Fig. 28.  8 cm. high.  Ica-Pachacamac style.
Fig. 29.  6.5 cm. high, 14 cm. diameter.  Ica-Pachacamac style.

Plate I. Chronological chart.

| PERIODS | | Nasca Drainage | Ica Valley | South-central Coast | STYLES Central Coast | North Coast | Northern Highlands | Central Highlands |
|---|---|---|---|---|---|---|---|---|
| ca. 1100 a.d. | | | | | | | | |
| MIDDLE HORIZON | Epoch 4 | Nasca Epigonal | Ica Epigonal | | *(hatched)* | *(hatched)* | *(hatched)* | *(hatched)* |
| | Epoch 3 | Soisongo | Pinilla | | *(hatched)* | *(hatched)* | Cajamarca IV ?← | *(hatched)* |
| | Epoch 2B | Atarco B | Ica-Pachacamac | | Pachacamac B | Huari Norteño A | Cajamarca III | Viñaque |
| | Epoch 2A | Atarco A | | | Pachacamac A | | | |
| | Epoch 1B | Robles Moqo Nasca 9 | | Cerro del Oro | Nievería | Moche V | [Cajamarca II?] | Robles Moqo Chakipampa B |
| | Epoch 1A | Nasca 9 | Nasca 9 | Lima (Interlocking) | Lima | Moche V | | Conchopata Chakipampa A |
| ca. 800 a.d. | | | | | | | | |
| EARLY INTERMEDIATE PERIOD | Epoch 8 | Nasca 8 | Nasca 8 | Lima (Interlocking) | Lima (Interlocking) | Moche IV | | Huarpa |
| | Epoch 7 | Nasca 7 | Nasca 7 | | | Moche IV ← | | |

Plate I. Chronological chart. Hatching indicates that evidence is available but is not reviewed in this study. Blank spaces indicate gaps in the evidence.

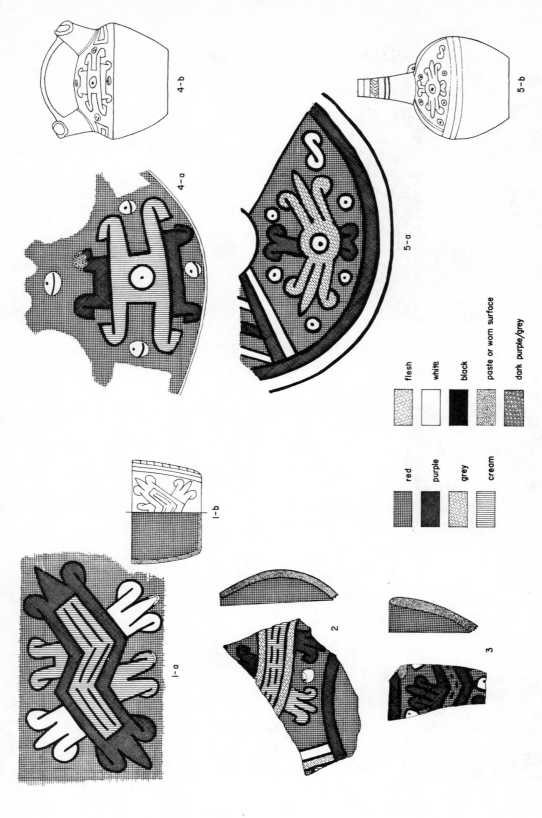

Plate II. Stylistic changes in Nasca-influenced designs of sierra origin: three-fillet band (fig. 1, Viñaque; fig. 2, Chakipampa B; fig. 3, Chakipampa A); "fleur-de-lys" (fig. 4, Atarco B; fig. 5, Atarco A). Fig. 4 shows the same vessel as fig. 22. See key to illustrations.

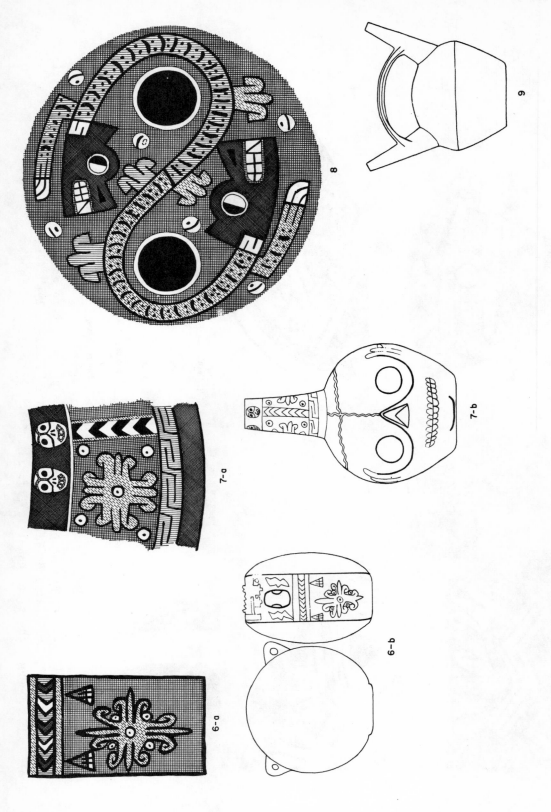

Plate III. Stylistic changes in Nasca ray designs of south coast tradition: radial ray designs (fig. 6, Nasca 9; fig. 7, Atarco A); serpentine figure with ray appendages (fig. 8, Atarco B). See key to illustrations.

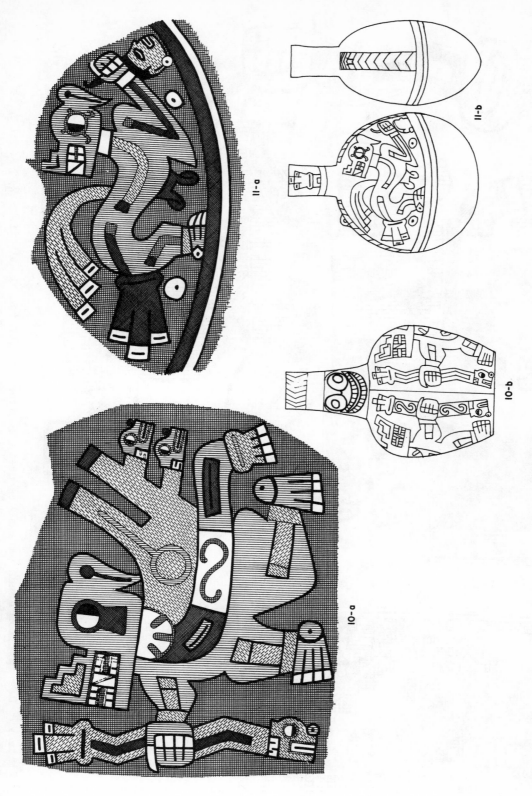

Plate IV. Mythical representations in the Atarco B style: angel (fig. 10); mythical feline (fig. 11). Fig. 1a shows the same vessel as fig. 18, and fig. 11 the same as fig. 19. See key to illustrations.

159

Plate V. Designs from Conchopata style oversize urns: split-face band (fig. 12); Angel A (fig. 13). See key to illustrations.

Plate VI. Grave lot of three vessels of Epoch 1B from Nasca (figs. 14-16); Nievería style bottle with a design borrowed from the Chakipampa B style (fig. 17). See key to illustrations.

18                                    19

20                                    21

Plate VII. Four vessels from a grave lot of five vessels of Epoch 2B
from Nasca (figs. 18-21); the fifth is shown in fig. 22 on plate VIII.
Fig. 18 shows the same vessel as fig. 10, and fig. 19 the same as fig.
11. See key to illustrations.

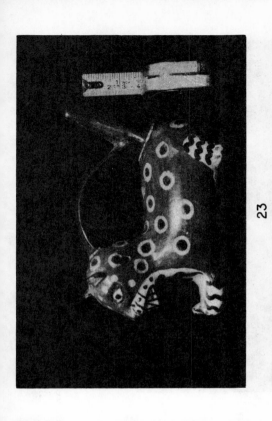

23

25

22

24

Plate VIII. Vessel from a grave lot of five vessels of Epoch 2B from Nasca (fig. 22); the other four vessels in this lot are shown in figs. 18-21, plate VII. Fig. 22 shows the same vessel as fig. 4. Three vessels from a grave lot of seven vessels of Epoch 2B from Ica (figs. 23-25); the other four are shown in figs. 26-29, plate IX. See key to illustrations.

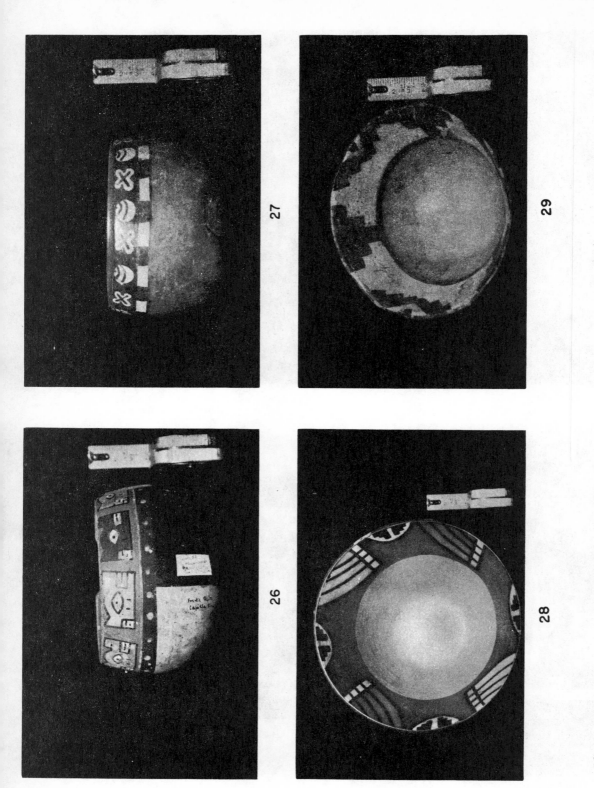

27

29

26

28

Plate IX. Four vessels from a grave lot of seven vessels of Epoch 2B from Ica (figs. 26-29); the other three are shown in figs. 23-25, plate VIII. See key to illustrations.

# TIAHUANACO TAPESTRY DESIGN

Alan R. Sawyer

## INTRODUCTION

The people in ancient Peru excelled in the textile arts for over four thousand years before the arrival of their Spanish conquerors. From the infinite variety of weaving techniques and art styles to be seen in fabrics surviving in desert cemeteries from this time no group is more outstanding for its consistent high quality than the finely woven interlocking tapestry shirts from the period of the Tiahuanaco Empire (about A.D. 600 to 1100). The dramatic designs and striking color harmonies of these tapestries have made them one of the most universally admired and sought after types of hand woven textiles.

It is unfortunate that the popularity enjoyed by these fine weavings is not matched by our archaeological knowledge of the period which produced them. Partly for this reason there has been little written that contributes to our better understanding of the fabrics themselves. It is hoped that, in the not too distant future, the Textile Museum staff may be able to help fill this gap with a definitive stylistic and technical study based on the museum's extensive and important Tiahuanaco collection together with examples in other institutions. In this short paper I will attempt to sketch some of the broader aspects of the subject with special attention to the problems of establishing a relative chronology based on a theoretical reconstruction of stylistic evolution.

## Provenience

Of the several hundred Tiahuanaco tapestry shirts in public and private collections, the number which has been scientifically excavated or which come to us with reliable provenience and associated data is pitifully small. Nearly all of these derive from the Coastal cemeteries of Peru, especially from the South Coast Nazca area where conditions for textile preservation are most favorable. It is not unreasonable to speculate that at least a few of the many remaining undocumented pieces were found elsewhere in the wide area once covered by the Tiahuanaco empire, which includes most of Peru, Bolivia and Northern Chile.

Taken as a group, what is most remarkable about these weavings is that in spite of an apparently wide distribution they evince surprisingly little variation in technique or design content. Some slight regional differences may be indicated, but the principal variations would seem to be temporal, reflecting stages in several centuries of an evolving art tradition.

## Construction

Tiahuanaco tapestry shirts consist of two matching pieces woven in alpaca wool on looms averaging around 80 inches in width with a warp, usually cotton, about 22 inches long. One warp selvage of the finished piece almost always consists of chained warp loops, while on the other end, presumably the last woven, the warps were cut and diagonally interworked. In assembling the garment the two pieces were doubled in the weft direction and the chained selvages bound together to form a center seam leaving a gap for the neck slit. The interworked selvages were similarly joined at the outer edges except for arm holes left at the shoulder. The result was a simple garment roughly 40 inches square with the wefts running the length of the garment and the warps, the width (see Figure 7). When worn, it covered the entire torso and upper arms and hung down to below the knees.

## Tradition

The unusual weaving tradition manifested in the structure of these shirts is not one found on the Coast of Peru prior to the Tiahuanaco occupation. It contrasts markedly with the regional techniques used in weaving "Coastal Tiahuanaco" textiles found in the same cemeteries and often in the same graves. It appears logical to conclude that the Tiahuanaco tapestry shirt reflects a distinctive and long established Highland weaving tradition. It is quite possible that it was a garment worn only by officials of the Tiahuanaco Empire and made only in highland centers or by weavers imported from those areas. It is interesting to note that the official garments of the later Inca Empire, which borrowed much from the Tiahuanaco culture, were woven on similar wide looms, the chief difference being that Inca shirts were woven in one piece with the neck slit accomplished by means of scaffolding wefts.

## Iconography

The iconography of Tiahuanaco tapestries is surprisingly limited. Repetitions of a single motif usually form the entire ornamentation of an individual garment. The range of motifs may be broken down into three main types, each consisting of two or more categories. They are outlined below in the order of the frequency of their occurrence with illustrations of typical examples of each major variation, except for Type III-A adequately demonstrated elsewhere in this paper.

It seems probable in view of known Inca practice that each distinctive design in the rigid Tiahuanaco

---

Reprinted from TEXTILE MUSEUM JOURNAL, Vol. 1, No. 2, 1963. pp. 27-38.

**TYPE I   PAIRED ELEMENTS.** *(A) Stepped spirals of opposing orientation are paired within a rectangle and divided by a diagonal. Alternate registers reverse direction. (B) Stepped spirals are paired with stylized profile human or feline heads. Orientation is alternated as in A. (See also Figure 7-a). (C) Two different paired elements are alternated in checkerboard fashion. One is often Type A or B, while the other is usually made up of vertical bars terminating in stylized heads (as in example shown) or a stepped diamond.*

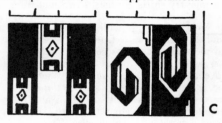

**TYPE II   COMPOSITE MOTIFS.** *These appear to be figure motifs altered by the substitution of symbolic elements such as spirals and stylized heads for some of their natural components. The resulting composites (shaded in our illustrations) are repeated in four orientations around a central point. (A) Profile Feline (puma?) heads facing each other along the central axis suggest a frontal human face. The motif may be a feline figure much altered by substitution. (See also Figure 7-b) (B) Profile Bird (falcon?) and sometimes human heads oppose each other along the vertical and, often, the horizontal axis. The motif appears to be a substitution-altered bird figure which may be related to the eye patterns found on Type III figures.*

**TYPE III   STAFF BEARING FIGURES.** *These are closely related to those found in low relief on the stone "Gateway of the Sun" at Tiahuanaco, Bolivia, and other Highland Tiahuanaco monuments. (A) Winged anthropomorphic figures with puma, falcon, human and, rarely, other type heads. The profile figures hold a staff to the front and the legs are shown in a running position. (See Figures 1 through 4 and 7-c) (B) Similar anthropomorphic figures without wings which hold staffs in each hand. They are usually shown in a standing position.*

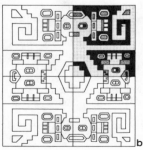

iconography outlined above was the property of a specific rank of governmental or religious functionary. The simpler and more common of these motifs would appear to have been the emblems of the more numerous officials of lower rank, while the elaborate and the more rarely encountered designs signified officials of high status. Space does not permit our detailed discussion of this iconography though we will presently examine in more detail some characteristic motifs of Type III. First we should examine briefly the design organization of Tiahuanaco shirts, which is even more rigidly limited than their iconography.

## Design Organization

Tiahuanaco shirts are always of extremely formal centrally balanced design (see Figure 7). Motifs are organized in vertical columns which are aligned horizontally by register. In the majority of cases we find one or two or three vertical bands of motifs (which in Type I may be up to three columns wide) separated by plain weft stripes on each half of the shirt front. A partial band of motifs is found along the side seam in addition to the one or more full bands. In a variant of this scheme, found in Types I and II, the registers in the upper half to two-fifths of the shirt are filled solidly with motifs, eliminating the plain stripes in that portion. A few shirts of Type III are entirely covered with columns of motifs with two different figures alternated. Exceptions to these limited ranges of iconography and design scheme are extremely rare. When found, they usually exhibit other departures from the strict conventions which govern the main group. These cases may represent rare survivals of weaving centers not fully subject to centralized Tiahuanaco control. On the other hand, they may represent a late period during which central Tiahuanaco authority was breaking down.

## Chronology

While it is impossible at this time to establish a stylistic chronology for Tiahuanaco tapestery substantiated by archaeological data, it may prove useful to propose a relative one based on stylistic analysis. This assumes that stylization of figures evolved from easily identifiable motifs bearing close resemblance to their Highland Tiahuanaco prototypes through successive stages of simplification and geometricization of component elements, and a growing application of a distortion convention peculiar to Tiahuanaco tapestry. I propose to demonstrate the application of this hypothesis through a discussion of a selected group of tapestry designs representative of Type III-A, the important staff bearing figure category of motif.

## Conventionalization and Distortion

Most Tiahuanaco tapestry designs display, to a greater or lesser degree, distortion effected by the device of lateral expansion of those elements of the motif which lie towards the center of the garment and compression of those nearest the side hem. In addition, both bands and stripes become progressively narrower as they approach the side seams. The degree to which this distortion is carried usually becomes more pronounced in direct relationship to the extent to which the motif is stylized. Let us examine a series of related Type III-A motifs which demonstrate this principle. In Figure 1-a, we see a falcon-headed staff bearing figure as it appears in low relief on the "Gateway of the Sun." (The falcon identification is based on its beak shape and eye markings.) In the tapestry version 1-b, a somewhat simplified rendering of the same motif is depicted with little change in the relationship of its component elements other than that necessary to make the figure conform easily to the warp and weft of the fabric. It has been drawn from a vertical band in which the figures alternately face left and right (Figure 2) as is often the case in tapestries employing this class of motifs. A comparison reveals that the figures above and below the one illustrated display a little expansion of the wing, tail and foot appendage elements which lie closest to the center of the garment, while the staff, appearing now on the left towards the outer edge of the garment, is slightly more compressed than when the motif faces inward. Since the amount of compression and expansion is small, there is little distortion of motif in relation to its prototype on the "Gateway of the Sun." While our convention can be seen to have already been established, this version would appear to show an early stage of its development.

In Figure 1-c the same figure is shown as it appears in two different vertical bands on adjacent sides of the central seam of another Tiahuanaco tapestry shirt. This garment, like the one from which 1-b was drawn, has two full bands of motifs on each side of the shirt front. Note that elements are greatly expanded on the side towards the central seam, whereas the portions towards the outer edges of the garment are compressed. In addition, the motif itself is much more geometricized and simplified than 1-b. Four distinct vertical zones are now apparent which may be identified by their uppermost elements as the staff, head, headdress and wing. We should keep in mind that these zones correspond to the weft direction of the fabric. The expansion and compression therefore was accomplished by the simple expedient of adding or subtracting from the number of weft threads used to form the elements in a given zone. In each figure the two zones towards the central seam, which would normally form half the width of the figure, here account for two-thirds. A secondary application of the expansion-compression device, which elsewhere achieves a high degree of refinement, is noticeable in this rendering in its rudimentary form. I refer to the expansion and compression of motif elements within each zone reflecting the overall lateral distortion scheme of the complete motif. This becomes evident, for example, when the eye ornaments of the two figures are compared. This and other details convey the impression of a gradual increase in expansion or compression as we move horizontally across the figure. Further analysis

**Figure 1**  *Representation of falcon-headed, staff bearing figure motifs (Type III-A)*

a. From the "Gateway of the Sun" at Tiahuanaco, Bolivia

b. T.M. 1959.5.6.  Gift of Raymond
Wielgus

c. T.M. 1961.24.1  Gift of John Wise

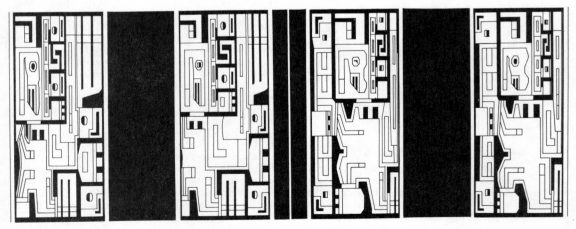

d. T.M. 1962.51.1  Gift of Junius B. Bird

proves, however, that this is not the case here but that the major distortion is effected through a more or less uniform widening or narrowing of each zone. There is a tendency to treat upper portions of the headdress and wing zone independently from the rear leg, foot and foot appendage elements below. Note that vertical relationships shift in the expanded and compressed versions, due no doubt to the greater complexity of the upper group.

Our third example, shown in Figure 1-d, is taken from a shirt having three bands of motifs to each side as well as the usual narrow band on the edge. Our drawing includes a central portion of a single register similar to that shown in 1-b, but in this case including two figures on each side of the central seam. In comparison to our previous example, the present motifs appear elongated. Actually, they are approximately the same height but have been subjected to an overall lateral compression to fit within narrow bands half the width of those in 1-c. The falcon-headed figures are now much more simplified and highly stylized than before.

In the figures on the right of 1-d which face the central seam, the first zone, that of the staff, is of about normal proportion. The second, including the head and body, is somewhat compressed, yet together with the staff accounts for nearly two-thirds of the width of the figure. The third, the headdress zone, is still further compressed especially on the right where the wing band and hind foot have been greatly simplified. The fourth zone of wing, tail and foot appendage has been entirely omitted. Moving to the left of the center seam we note that in the other two figures the opposite is true. The wing zone now nearest the center is present and in normal proportion. The headdress zone is compressed but complete, with the usual third toe restored to the hind foot. Finally, the head zone is even more compressed and on its extreme left the arm, knee and foot have been greatly simplified. As before, the final zone towards the outer seam, in this case the staff, is missing.

A comparison with our previous examples shows an advancement in stylization and distortion trends in this motif. There is an increasing reflection within zones of the expansion-compression convention affecting the entire figure and a greater tendency to treat the lower half of the figure independently from the upper. The weaver, faced with the problem of fitting the figure within a narrow band, has in this case eliminated the final most compressed zone in order to reduce the crowding of his motif. The slightly wider motifs which may be seen in Figure 7-c demonstrate that this device of omitting zones was not always used in three-band schemes. The manner in which a similar motif was treated within the broader bands of a two-band scheme is illustrated by our next example.

Two opposite facing versions of a puma-headed Type III-A motif are shown in Figure 3, as they appear in adjoining registers of the two bands on each half of another Tiahuanaco shirt. When measured by our stylization yardstick they prove to be roughly contemporary with those of Figure 1-d.

**Figure 2** *Fragment of Tiahuanaco tapestry shirt, T.M. 1959.5.6. Gift of Raymond Wielgus*

**Figure 3**  *Two puma-headed, staff bearing figure motifs from adjoining registers in Tiahuanaco shirt, T.M. 1962.30.2*

Unlike the latter, they do not lack their most compressed zones since the wider bands made their omission unnecessary. Each example, however, evinces a complex application of lateral distortion conventions in which expansion and compression of the staff and wing zones is less pronounced than in those of the head and headdress. This trait becomes most obvious in the wide motif of Figure 3. The independent lateral distortion treatment of the upper and lower portion of these central zones also becomes increasingly apparent in the wide band. Note for example that in Figure 3 both legs are found within the head zone where it is compressed, while the foreleg occupies the entire width of the same zone in the expanded version. The vertical alignments of the rear foot and its appendage are similarly dislocated. The secondary expansion and compression of elements within zones is also most evident in the wider motif. Comparison of these similar and more or less contemporary motifs serves to demonstrate the flexibility of conventions in adapting motifs to bands of different widths. To illustrate the full extent to which the trends we have observed ultimately developed we now turn to the last example in our selected series of motifs.

Alfredo Taullard illustrates a Tiahuanaco tapestry shirt in Plate 19 of his book *Tejidos y Ponchos Indigenas de Sudamerica* (Buenos Aires, 1949) which is said to have been found in Ayacucho (in the Southern Highlands of Peru) and is listed as the property of "Museo de Lima" (the National Museum of Archaeology and Anthropology?). The shirt has a characteristic Tiahuanaco design layout of single broad bands of alternating motifs on each half of the front with narrower partial bands along the side seams. The motifs themselves are made up

of simplified geometric elements which become compressed within a narrow zone nearest the side seam. At this point resemblance to the Tiahuanaco motifs we have been discussing becomes difficult to see. A close analysis reveals that each alternate register includes a little less than half of a complete figure. In both versions, two zones, each with a secondary compression and expansion, are found with elements on the compressed side of the left hand zone omitted. In Figure 4 I will attempt to show visually how this motif may be reconstituted and resolved to its normal proportions in order to make it more readily identifiable and to demonstrate how the conventions have been applied.

At the top of Figure 4 I have placed the two versions of the Lima tapestry motif as they appear in adjacent registers of the broad band on the left half of the shirt front. For our convenience I have designated them A and B. Below these, I have reversed A and placed it next to B. We should now be able to recognize a highly abstract version of the same winged, puma-headed staff bearing figure which we encountered in Figure 3. The composite we have just created shows an exaggerated expansion of elements towards the sides and a compression in the center which has crowded out some components which normally appear there. To make our motif more recognizable I have next attempted to eliminate distortion caused by expansion and compression and supply the missing elements (indicated by shading). The space required by these omitted elements makes our result wider than the original band. While I have made some readjustments to compensate for horizontal shifts of components, I have not changed their vertical dimensions.

170

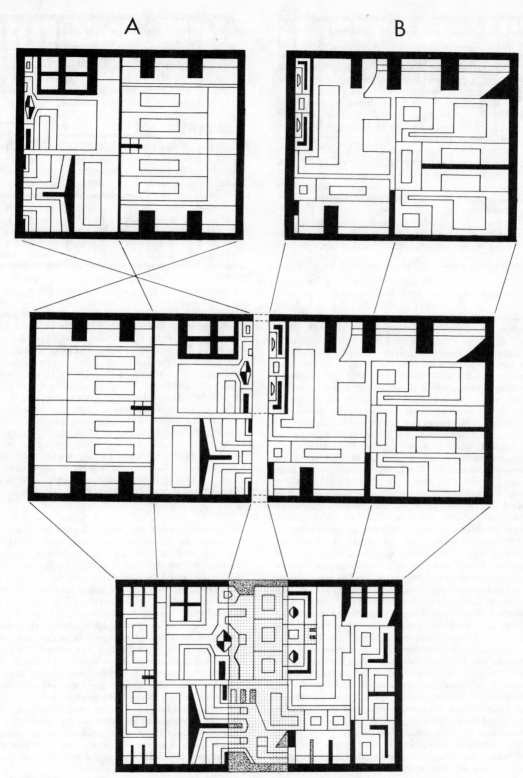

**Figure 4** *Resolution of the puma-headed, staff bearing figure motif of the Lima tapestry*

In this tapestry both omission of zones and advanced stylization have been exploited for their own sake, creating two highly abstract patterns of geometric elements. A comparison with its less stylized equivalent in Figure 3 and with the motifs of Figure 1, gives us some understanding of the manner in which the abstraction was achieved.

The staff of the Lima motif occupying half the width of A possesses simplified equivalents of all the usual component elements, distorted by exaggerated expansion and secondary compression within the zone. The three feather elements at each end have all been made of equal length. The thumb and heel of the hand have been eliminated and only two fingers are shown, as in our comparative example, although as may be seen in Figure 1 there are usually three.

The head in A again retains all of its components in simplified form. The lower half of this zone, however, shows greater simplification and a pronounced dislocation of elements in relation to their normal vertical alignment with features of the head. Emphasis is placed on the T-shaped negative space silhouetting the arm and the leg, which is also prominent in the Figure 3 version. The arm, however, is no longer under the jaw or connected with the hand, and the forefoot is missing from its usual position. It now appears as a rectangle deliberately displaced to a position in front of the arm and leg. On the compressed side, a small L-shaped element is all that is left of the neck ornament characteristic of these figures, while the inverted L below delineates the back of the knee.

In B the zone at the left, representing the headdress zone, has undergone considerable transformation. The headdress band which should be found on the left side has been omitted but three of its ornaments are present. The upper and lower of these, identifiable by the L-shaped beak lines, may be seen to be bird heads when compared to other more detailed and less compressed renderings. The hollow square in the center represents a bird-tail headdress element with the feathers omitted. A fourth headdress ornament, present in most versions of the motif, has not been included. To the right of the headdress ornaments we find a broad vertical wing band with two projecting elements leading to components of the wing zone, a feature usually found only in earlier versions as in Figure 1-b. The two rectangular elements immediately below represent the tail band, in this case dislocated downward so that it does not coincide with the center of the tail as in less stylized renderings. It reflects a vertical dislocation tendency already present in the semi-abstract Figure 3 version. Like the headdress band, the portion of the tail band usually shown sweeping up toward it is missing. The simple elements in the bottom section of the zone represent a two-toed rear foot and its ankle band. The rear leg, along with the other elements on the compressed side of this zone, is missing.

The wing zone of the Lima motif compares easily with our more recognizable version. The three wing feathers can be seen at the top with one extending over the wing band projection already mentioned, which leads directly to the next component, a simplified bird head. The second projection of the wing band leads to a greatly simplified tail element with two, rather than the usual three, feathers. At the bottom of the zone we find a bird head foot appendage element as in all previous examples cited.

## SUMMARY

The series of five tapestry motifs belonging to Type III-A which we have discussed suggest that a relative chronology may be manifested in a gradual evolution of stylization and abstraction coupled with an increasing application and growing complexity of lateral distortion conventions. It should be pointed out, however, that in attempting to make our demonstration of evolutionary trends understandable, we have been of necessity guilty of great oversimplification. We have bypassed many refinements and variations of iconography, stylization and distortion, which are present in the sequence, and we have completely ignored major factors such as the use of color and evolutionary trends in overall design, both of which become every bit as intricate as the ones we have discussed. Further and more detailed comparative analysis of all available examples of Tiahuanaco tapestry must be made before any but the broadest of trends can be proposed. Such a study may reveal that each of the different design categories we have cited has its own distinctive evolutionary trends. We may also find it possible to divide Tiahuanaco tapestries into groups representing different weaving centers, each with its own regional traits while conforming to the general evolutionary pattern. We must be prepared to recognize that considerable variation of motif treatment could exist at any given stage of style development, especially as conventions and their interrelationships became more highly complex.

## Application

To demonstrate the kind of problems we will encounter in attempting to establish a relative chronological position for an individual tapestry, let us now consider the striking example shown in Figure 5 from the collection of the Museum of Primitive Art. It is a fragment representing most of the left half of a shirt front on which a single broad band of stylized motifs occupies nearly half of the warp and the partial band at the side seam is extremely narrow. The elements within the main motifs are broadly delineated in an expanded form, except for the extreme left where they become drastically compressed. The four complete motifs contained within the band alternate between what appear to be two distinct designs; actually, as in the Lima tapestry, there is but one motif involved which reverses direction by register. Again the degree of expansion and compression has been carried to such an extreme that the original motif is rendered almost unrecognizable to any one not familiar with the unusual conventions involved.

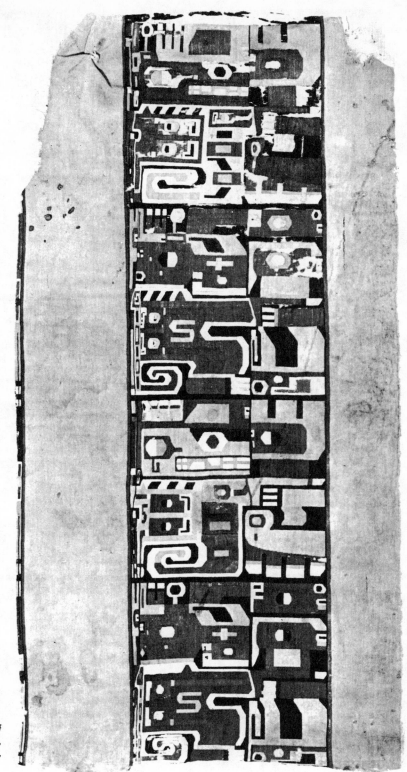

**Figure 5** *Fragment of Tiahuanaco tapestry shirt, Museum of Primitive Art, 56.195*

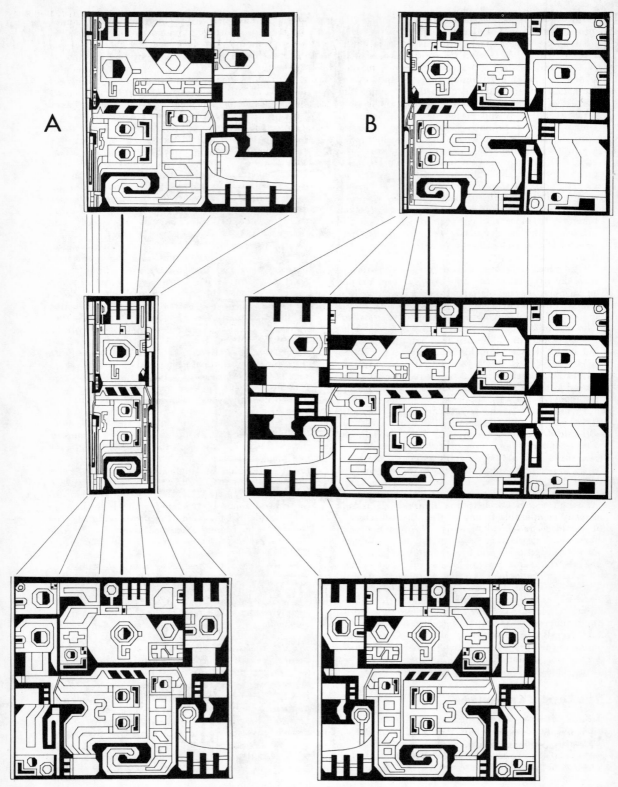

**Figure 6** *A resolution of the motif of the Museum of Primitive Art tapestry, 56.195*

In Figure 6 I have attempted to resolve the distorted motif into recognizable form using variations of the same techniques as in the case of the Lima tapestry. At the top we see the two versions of the motif as they appear on the textile, marked A and B. After determining that the split eye is the actual center, I have combined the compressed portion of A with a reversed rendering of the compressed part of B and placed the result below A. Under B I have similarly combined the expanded portions of the two versions. The composite figures are now identifiable as greatly compressed and expanded renderings of an unusual Type III-B anthropomorphic feline figure, seemingly seated on its tail, its head turned backwards and arms outstretched holding staffs in each hand. By readjusting the expanded and compressed versions thus obtained to more normal proportions within the original width of the band, we achieve the theoretical undistorted motifs shown at the bottom of the figure.

Our reconstructions, though more recognizable than the original motifs appearing at top, exhibit an advanced degree of stylization. I have not been able to find equivalent examples of this motif, though a few related motifs showing similar stylization are to be found. None of the latter exhibits the same extreme application of lateral distortion but it would seem probable that they belong to the same period. If this is correct, it again demonstrates that considerable latitude existed in a given period as to the manner and degree to which distortion conventions were applied.

In our analysis and reconstruction of the motif it has become apparent that we are dealing with an ultimate degree of refinement in both the primary and secondary application of the lateral distortion convention. We also find fully developed the tendency to simplify elements greatly in compressed zones but without their omission as in the Lima tapestry and the narrow motif of Figure 1-d. Although the elaborate puma figure itself is not directly comparable to any of the others discussed, it would seem logical to assign the weaving to a chronological position between the two examples shown in Figure 1-d and Figure 3 on one hand, and the abstract Lima piece. If our proposed system of relative chronology is valid, this would place it rather late in the Tiahuanaco Empire period. The technical excellence, and the mastery of the subtle inter-relationships of intricate conventions governing iconography, stylization, lateral distortion, color and overall design organization, give eloquent testimony of the high level of artistic achievement which had been maintained by Tiahuanaco weavers throughout the long Tiahuanaco Empire period.

## The Logic of Conventions

In this paper we have been concentrating our attention on the developmental trends of Tiahuanaco stylization and distortion without taking time to consider the obvious question of what logical purpose these and other conventions served. They appear to have been deliberately applied to counteract the twin dangers of monotony inherent in the severe simplicity of the garments themselves and the strict limits of the iconography they carried.

The flat sandwich board effect of the somewhat stiff finely woven shirt was overcome mainly by illusions of false perspective created by refinements in the design layouts and a related use of lateral distortion. In Figure 7-b we see the simplest of Tiahuanaco design schemes with one broad band of motifs to each half of the shirt front and a narrower band of partial motifs at each side seam. The plain weft stripe at the center is somewhat wider than those at the sides. The motifs in this case show no lateral distortion, although elements in the partial side bands are somewhat narrower. The total effect is to create the illusion of a cylindrical volume with the narrow side bands seen obliquely as they pass around the sides.

Illusions became more complex with the introduction of additional bands and the application of expansion and compression conventions. The shirt in Figure 7-a has a two-band scheme in which there is considerable application of lateral distortion. Again, we will note a progressive reduction in the widths of the plain weft stripes as they approach the sides, creating an illusion of volume. Lateral distortion tends to create an additional effect; that of a curved surface within bands, with the compressed zones of each motif occupying planes receding from the viewer. The overall illusion now is almost one of folds as they would appear on a draped column.

In Figure 7-c we see a shirt of three bands per side with stylization and lateral distortion more advanced than that of the previous two examples. A progressive narrowing in the width of both bands and plain stripes accentuates the volume effect. We noted earlier that the application of expansion and compression to the motifs at this stage of stylistic development (Figures 1-c and 3) gave emphasis to the central zones of the band while following the general rule of expansion of elements lying towards the center and compression of those on the side towards the edge of the garment. The draped fold illusion is heightened by this device.

It would be interesting if space permitted to attempt to plot diagramatically the solid form illusion created in each of the motifs we have studied. To do this with the motif of The Museum of Primitive Art shirt would require our imagining a figure somewhat wider than our composite expanded version with uniform expansion throughout its entire width. We would then need to visualize the solid form this motif would have to be applied to in order to recreate the effects present in the two actual versions on the tapestry which we designated A and B. In each case the expanded portions would be applied to two slight vertical folds to duplicate the illusion brought about by the secondary expansion and compression within each zone. In the central zone of the motif, the surface would bend away from us until we saw only the near sides of the two undulations occupied by the last two zones. In the

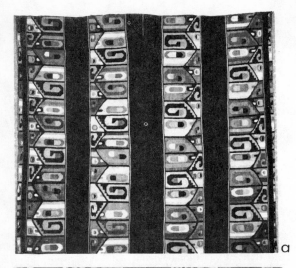

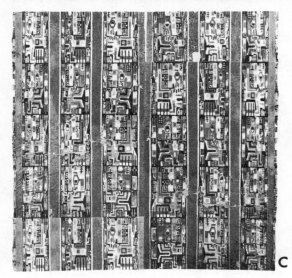

**Figure 7** *Three Tiahuanaco tapestry shirts in the Textile Museum Collection:*

*a. 91.343      Two band shirt, Type I-B*
*b. 1962.5.1    Single band shirt, Type II-A*
*c. 91.386      Three band shirt, Type III-A*
*(Photographic reconstruction from a large fragment)*

Lima tapestry, and others in which zones have been eliminated, the illusory folds in the fabric are deeper with a portion of the motif disappearing from view.

Among the conventions used to counter the monotony threatened by the limitation of motifs on a garment to a single one or a related pair, lateral distortion played an important role. With the alteration of the direction of motifs by register, expansion and compression tended to accentuate their different appearance to the point that towards the end of the sequence they bore little resemblance to each other. The overall design of the shirt would still have suffered from geometric repetition if it were not for a skillful application of color variation. The simple sequence of color harmonies found in early shirts such as that shown in Figure 2 grew increasingly intricate with a tendency of the color juxtapositions to de-emphasize the motif, creating a kaleidoscopic pattern on the surface of the bands. Unfortunately, space prohibits our detailed examination here of this important aspect of Tiahuanaco design. Tiahuanaco weavers were great masters of color harmony who deftly exploited the sumptuous palette available to them in the wide range of natural golden yellows and browns of alpaca wool, amplified by use of a few dyes such as cochineal red and indigo blue. The infinite variety of effect conveyed by their tapestry shirts, in spite of the rigid limits imposed by conventions, gives eloquent proof of their creative genius.

## CONCLUSION

Our preliminary study reveals that a relative chronology may be derived from a study of the gradual evolution and growth in complexity of Tiahuanaco tapestry design conventions. These conventions appear to have formed a logical system which allowed the weaver considerable flexibility in their combination and emphasis, enabling him to achieve a rich variety of effect while maintaining the distinctive appearance and symbolic meaning required of garments worn by the Tiahuanaco official class.

# INNOVATION THROUGH ARCHAISM; THE ORIGINS OF THE ICA POTTERY STYLE

Patricia J. Lyon

Interesting problems are posed when a tradition of decorative style abruptly changes character and direction, since change in style is usually gradual and consistent.  How and why do abrupt changes come about?

The pottery tradition of the Ica Valley of the south coast of Peru provides a number of examples of such changes, most of which can be explained by the impact of foreign influences.  One of the changes which cannot be explained by foreign influence is the one which originated the Ica style, the decorative style characteristic of the Late Intermediate Period at Ica.  This style is not a simple and consistent development out of the Middle Horizon styles which directly preceded it. I propose to present evidence that the new style was based on archaism; that its peculiar features represent a revival in modified form of motifs characteristic of the first three epochs of the Middle Horizon.

During the Middle Horizon most of Peru, including Ica, was affected by an expansion movement having its center at Huari, near Ayacucho in the sierra.  As Dorothy Menzel has demonstrated, the expansion was both military and religious.[1]  The religion emanating from Huari is reflected in decorative art in a variety of mythical themes which are easily recognizable, even in provincial imitations.

In following subsequent stylistic developments it is important to keep in mind their chronological order.  The initial expansion of Huari was a phenomenon of the beginning of the Middle Horizon.  This expansion, evidently the establishment of an empire in historical terms, affected Ica as it did other valleys on the coast.  The Huari empire seems to have fallen at the end of Epcoh 2 of the Middle Horizon, when the site of Huari was virtually abandoned.  In Ica the local variant of the Huari style of Middle Horizon 2 was affected by influences radiating from the great shrine of Pachacamac on the central coast; for this reason it is called Ica-Pachacamac.  Local styles derived from Ica-Pachacamac persisted at Ica for two more epochs, and then gave place to the new Ica tradition at close of Middle Horizon 4.

The sequence of stylistic phases at Ica established by Menzel is as follows:

| Time | Style |
|------|-------|
| Middle Horizon 2 | Ica-Pachacamac |
| Middle Horizon 3 | Pinilla |
| Middle Horizon 4 | Ica Epigonal |
| Late Intermediate Period 1 | Ica 1 |

Reprinted from ÑAWPA PACHA 4, 1966. pp. 31-47. 51-61.

The chronological order of the major styles between the beginning of the Middle Horizon and the Late Horizon was established by Max Uhle on the basis of seriation and some stratigraphic evidence and has remained unchanged except for the addition or subdivision of some styles.[2] Uhle, however, defined his stylistic units only in the most general terms. My interpretation is based upon a new and more detailed seriation of the materials, and it will be necessary to begin by presenting the evidence for the phase divisions and indicating the most salient features of each phase.

Menzel has described both the general background of the Middle Horizon and the specific characteristics of Middle Horizon 2B at Ica.[3] She has also summarized some characteristics of the Pinilla phase of Middle Horizon 3. Using her data as a base, I propose to expand the description of the Pinilla phase by the use of additional materials. Then I shall distinguish two sub-phases, A and B, in the Ica Epigonal phase and offer a definition of the Ica 1 phase.

Several problems are presented by the materials on which this sample is based. The total sample is small, and only part of it has archaeological associations. The present study was carried out at the Robert H. Lowie Museum of Anthropology in Berkeley, and this museum has very few specimens from Ica dating to Middle Horizon 2 and 3; in consequence, the study of the pottery of these epochs had to be done primarily from color slides.[4] Most of the Epigonal grave lots were excavated by Uhle and are in the Lowie Museum; otherwise, the majority of the specimens utilized is from private collections. This fact is reflected in a selection for fancy decorated pieces as opposed to such vessel types as cumbrous bowls. My seriation is primarily based on associated materials from burials, but it was necessary to utilize also many isolated specimens which were seriated on the basis of associations of stylistic features on individual vessels.

The sample upon which this study is based consists entirely of vessels with painted decoration. Although some of the burials include undecorated utilitarian ware, the number of utilitarian specimens was too small to permit any useful generalizations. It is obvious, however, that the utilitarian ware throughout the period under consideration is significantly different in form from the decorated ware.

## The Pinilla phase

Some further specimens of the Pinilla phase have been identified, in addition to the materials used by Menzel.[5] The additional materials consist of the contents of three burials. Two of these burials were excavated by Max Uhle at Site E, Ocucaje, and have previously been assigned to the Epigonal phase on the assumption that the pottery from Site E constituted a single stylistic unit.[6] Upon closer examination of the material I have been able to divide the burials from this cemetery into three units corresponding to the Pinilla, Ica Epigonal A, and Ica Epigonal B phases. The third grave lot newly assigned to the Pinilla phase belongs to Duncan M. Masson in Ica and was reported excavated by E. Uchuya at Cruz Grande, Ocucaje.

Burial E-10 contained two vessels, a flat based flaring-sided bowl with a conservative rim decoration of a pattern common in Ica-Pachacamac (fig. 12) and a small spheroid incurving bowl (fig. 13).[7] Burial E-7 contained a single vessel, a small spheroid incurving bowl (fig. 14). This burial had been disturbed.[8] The third burial, Masson Grave Lot 7, contained one face-neck jar (DM 260) which is decorated with the only completely abstract feline head found in this phase (fig. 29) and two small spheroid incurving bowls. One of these bowls (DM 262) is decorated with a white band within which are interlocking small L-shaped elements, a derivative of the meander band of Middle Horizon 2.

A few additions can be made to the features diagnostic of the Pinilla phase mentioned by Menzel.[9] On the small spheroid incurving bowls there is frequent use of a fine-line red or black element associated with the principal design (figs. 13a and 14a). A solid step fret is extensively used (fig. 7).[10] There is a tendency to divide design bands into small rectangular units, either by the use of vertical lines or by extending step frets to the top and bottom of the design panel.[11] The disembodied feline heads which occur in the Pinilla phase are bilaterally symmetrical but have some recognizable features, such as a mouth, neck marking, eye, etc., with the single exception noted above (figs. 28, 32, 34, 35).[12] Menzel mentions the lipped cup as a new vessel type in this phase.[13] It is possible, however, that this vessel type has antecedents in the Ica-Pachacamac phase.[14]

## The Ica Epigonal A Sub-phase

The Ica Epigonal A sub-phase is the culmination of a trend toward simplification which will be described below. The style is characterized by matte surfaces, careless painting and surface finish, and lack of variety in shape, color and design.

This sub-phase is represented by a sample of twenty-one decorated vessels. Sixteen of these vessels are from eight burials (E-3, E-5, E-6, E-8, E-9, E-11, E-13 and E-15) excavated by Uhle at Site E, Ocucaje. Uhle mentions that graves E-3, E-6, E-8 and E-9 were disturbed.[15] Eleven vessels from these burials have been illustrated.[16] One additional burial including three decorated vessels was excavated by Alejandro Pezzia at Rinconada de Pinilla, Ocucaje, and is in the Regional Museum of Ica.[17] Two unassociated specimens in the collection of Aldo Rubini, Ocucaje, are from the Huaca José Ramos, and another specimen in the same collection is from the Pinilla sector of Ocucaje. The total sample consists of five small spheroid incurving bowls, two larger sharply incurving bowls, four jars, one face-neck jar, seven cumbrous bowls, one lipped cup, and one modeled bowl.

In characterizing this style unit one must consider both elements of continuity with the preceding phase and evidence of change which will serve to distinguish Ica Epigonal A from the units which precede and follow it.  The evidence of change is found in the introduction of new elements, modification of old elements and the absence of elements found in the preceding phase, although negative evidence is weak in this case because of the small size of the sample.

There is abundant evidence of continuity with the Pinilla phase. All vessel types which are found in Ica Epigonal A were also present in the preceding phase, with the possible exception of the modeled bowl.  The use of short wavy lines and unoutlined white crosses with black centers as decorative elements, and the division of design bands into rectangular panels, are also continuous.  The highly abstract feline head found in the Pinilla phase (fig. 29) is the only type represented in Ica Epigonal A.  The tendency to reduce colors from the Middle Horizon 2 maximum of six culminates in this phase, and only three colors, black, white and red, are used.

Important elements found in the Pinilla phase which do not occur in Ica Epigonal A are fine-line red or black decoration, step frets, and some vessel shapes, such as bottles and dishes.  The bodiless profile eagle head design is also absent.

In Ica Epigonal A the small spheroid incurving bowls are essentially identical in size and shape with those of the preceding phase, but the decoration is somewhat different.  Only geometric elements are used, and there is less tendency to divide the design band into panels.  Decorative elements used on this vessel type are unoutlined white crosses with black center crosses, pyramidal step blocks and chevrons.  In the Pinilla phase the bowls with a chevron design are black slipped all over, with the exception of the design band and, sometimes, a small portion of the base.[18]  In Ica Epigonal A these bowls have only a black band below the chevron band, and the remainder of the vessel is unslipped.  The principal design band on all small bowls continues to be located just below the rim, as in the preceding phase.  This vessel type is relatively rarer than in Pinilla.

The larger, more sharply incurving bowls are decorated at the rim with a highly abstract version of the bodiless feline head design (figs. 36 and 38).[19]  These bowls are considerably larger than in the preceding phase.

Jars and face-neck jars show modifications in shape.  The base is markedly smaller, and there is a noticeable flare to the lip.  Necks may be decorated around the rim.  Designs on the body are varied, consisting of abstract feline heads (fig. 37),[20] "hand" designs,[21] and inverted pendent crescents.[22]  Simple jars are considerably more common in this phase than in the preceding one.  A jar in the Rubini collection (AR 15) may represent a degenerate version of a face-neck jar.  On the neck of the jar there is a small, smoothly rounded protuberance, and, parallel to each other on each side of this protuberance, are two elongated rectangular spots slanting diagonally down and inward toward the raised area, perhaps representing facial features.

Cumbrous bowls, with a single exception, are decorated with some variant of the pendent crescent, simple, concentric, or with a pyramidal step block.[23] The pendent crescents are generally separated by a new design element, a smaller solid black pendent crescent.[24] A single example (AR 31) is decorated with a wing design which alternates with the solid black pendent crescent. The placement of the designs is the same as in the preceding phase, with the difference that, on many of the Pinilla phase cumbrous bowls, there is a solid color band inside the rim within which the other decorative elements are contained. This band is absent in Ica Epigonal A. Although the shape of cumbrous bowls is somewhat variable, there is none in this sub-phase with a completely flat base.

The lipped cup (AR 66) is the same shape as examples in the Pinilla phase, but the lip is decorated with a pendent crescent design similar to that on cumbrous bowls.

In general, there is much less care, both in painting and in general surface treatment, in this style unit than in the preceding one. There is a tendency to uniformity of line width, in contrast to the juxtaposition of broad and narrow lines in the Pinilla phase. The red pigment in Ica Epigonal A is almost orange, in contrast with the more purple red pigment used in the preceding phase.

## The Ica Epigonal B Sub-phase

The Ica Epigonal B sub-phase is represented by a sample of thirteen decorated vessels. Eleven of these vessels have burial provenience data, and two are isolated specimens. Uhle excavated four burials, containing a total of eight vessels of this sub-phase, at Site E, Ocucaje (E-1, E-2, E-12 and E-14) and reported that Grave E-2 was disturbed.[25] Six of the vessels excavated by Uhle have been illustrated.[26] One burial of this sub-phase in the Duncan Masson collection at Ica (Masson Grave Lot 2) is reported to be from the Rinconada de Pinilla, Ocucaje; it includes three decorated vessels. The unassociated specimens are a jar (16-10071) in the Wattis collection, Lowie Museum of Anthropology, and a lipped cup (AR 67) in the Rubini collection, reported to be from the Huaca José Ramos, Ocucaje. The total sample includes two small spheroid incurving bowls, three cumbrous bowls, one lipped cup, four jars and two face-neck jars, plus one lipped bowl (E-14, 4-4549) which is probably a trade piece from Nasca.

This style unit is quite distinct from Ica Epigonal A in a number of features, primarily decorative motifs and the relative frequency of certain elements. There are still only three colors used, and only five vessel types are represented. However, it is in this sub-phase that we see the first foreshadowing of the Ica style.

The two most important design elements in this sub-phase are the disembodied feline head in various guises and a version of the Pinilla step fret. Succeeding the highly abstract representations of the feline head found in Ica Epigonal A, we find in the present sub-phase a number of variations of this motif, some quite representational (figs. 39, 42 and 43) and others so abstract as to appear purely geometric (figs.40 and 41). The significance of these representations will be discussed below. The step fret used in this sub-phase, although similar in shape to that in the Pinilla phase, is significantly different in having a "hollow" base and added squares containing dots or dashes (figs. 8 and 9). The dotted square is also found on the feline head design of a face-neck jar (fig. 42) and on the wing design of a cumbrous bowl.[27]

A lipped bowl from burial E-14 (4-4549) is apparently a trade piece, probably from the Nasca Valley.[28] Not only is the shape one which is not otherwise found in Ica, but the representation of the feline head which decorates it is identical to those found on two vessels in the Wattis collection which come from Poroma in the Nasca drainage (Lowie Museum of Anthropology 16-10945 and 16-11035). The treatment of this design element is totally different from that used in Ica, especially as regards ear form and the treatment of nose and mouth, but it shows definite affinity with the feline head of the Atarco style of Middle Horizon 2.[29]

Small spheroid incurving bowls are represented by only two examples in this sub-phase. One of these bowls (E-1, 4-4465) is decorated with a geometric version of the feline head (fig. 41) on a white band around the rim with a plain purple band immediately below. The other bowl (Masson Grave Lot 2, DM 78-2) has three hollow-base step frets placed rather asymmetrically around the equator of the vessel. This is a new design placement for the small bowls, which were previously decorated from the rim downward in bands.

Of the four simple jars in the sample, two (E-12, 4-4544 and 16-10071) are decorated with alternating feline heads and hollow-base step frets, one (E-1, 4-4464) has only feline heads, and the fourth (E-14, 4-4550) has only step frets. Three of the jars have decorated necks. The bases of the jars are even smaller than in the preceding sub-phase, and the necks continue to flare out at the lip. The placement of decoration is the same as in the preceding sub-phase; that is, the decoration starts at the base of the neck and extends to just above the equator. In all cases, however, there are one or more somewhat narrower, plain painted bands immediately below the decorated principal band.[30]

The two face-neck jars are considerably simplified in form. One face-neck jar (Masson Grave Lot 2, DM 78-1) has no modeling whatever on the neck, the face being painted instead and consisting of two eyes and a nose. No arms are indicated, and the hair treatment is very simple. There is no decorated band around the top of the neck. The neck of the jar is only slightly flared and quite small in diameter, while the body is flattened front to back, giving the vessel a somewhat flask-shaped contour. The other face-neck jar (E-2, 4-4471) has a modeled nose, but the eyes and mouth are merely painted, no arms are indicated, hair treatment is simple, and there is only a thin black line around the lip of the neck.[31] A decorated band extends from one side of the handle to the other side. The decoration of this band consists of bilaterally symmetrical bird heads with an eye in the center and a beak on each end. The shape of this jar is essentially the same as that of the simple jars, although there is less flare at the lip. These are the last face-neck jars to appear until much later in the Late Intermediate Period.

Cumbrous bowls continue to be decorated with pendent crescents, wing designs,[32] and pyramidal step blocks.[33] The use of the solid black pendent crescent as a separator continues, and the bowl with a pyramidal step block inside a pendent crescent (E-12, 4-4545) has a solid white band inside the rim within which the main design is contained.[33] The bowl with the wing design (E-2, 4-4470) also has, in the center of the bottom of the bowl on the inside, a design consisting of two traingles joined at the apex with a dot inside each triangle. The wings have the tips of the feathers divided into squares, some of which contain dots. Placement of decoration is the same as in the preceding sub-phase.

The single lipped cup belonging to this sub-phase (AR 67) is the same shape as that in the preceding style unit. The top of the lip is decorated with hollow-base step frets alternating with small unoutlined red triangles.

In summary, Ica Epigonal B shows continuity with the preceding sub-phase in the exclusive use of three color decoration, the presence of the same vessel types, the use of certain design themes (feline head, pendent crescent and small solid black pendent crescent, wing and pyramidal step block) and the placement of decorative elements on the vessels. However, a number of characteristics may be used to contrast this style unit with Ica Epigonal A. There is an increase in the proportion of jars to other vessel types in the total sample and a decrease in the number of small bowls and cumbrous bowls. The larger, sharply incurving bowls are gone from the shape inventory. Surface finish is more even and includes some polishing. Design bands are continuous rather than divided into small rectangular panels, and a number of new or greatly altered design themes (hollow-based step fret, realistic and purely geometric feline head, and square with dot or dash) are in common use. Most simple jar necks are decorated. Lines tend to be narrower, and the red pigment now tends to purple rather than orange.

## The Ica 1 Phase

Ica 1 represents the first phase of a new tradition in Ica and marks the beginning of the Late Intermediate Period. In spite of the fact that there is a marked change in pottery style at this time, it is possible to demonstrate a clear development from Ica Epigonal B to Ica 1 through the continuation of trends and certain design elements.

The sample for this phase consists of fifty-seven decorated vessels. Two burials excavated by Uhle at Site C, Ocucaje (C-2 and C-8) include six decorated vessels. One burial excavated by Pezzia in the Pinilla sector of Ocucaje contains five decorated vessels.[34] Two grave lots in the collection of Duncan Masson also belong to this phase.

One of these lots (Masson Grave Lot 1) is from the Rinconada de Pinilla, Ocucaje, and includes two decorated vessels. The other lot (Masson Grave Lot 3), reported to be from the Córdova area of Ocucaje, also contains two decorated vessels. There are also a number of unassociated specimens which were used in the analysis; six vessels in the Regional Museum of Ica, one in the collection of Ernesto Tabío, fourteen in the collection of Duncan Masson, and eighteen in the Wattis collection. In addition, there is one vessel in the Lowie Museum of Anthropology purchased by Uhle (4-4623).[35] Three Ica 1 jars in the Gretzer collection in Berlin are illustrated by Schmidt.[36] A total of twelve of the vessels listed have been illustrated.[37]

Forty-three jars constitute 75% of the total sample. In addition to the jars there are two small spheroid incurving bowls, one cumbrous bowl, one lipped cup, one cambered rim bowl and ten dishes distributed among three dish types.

Decoration in this phase is often in five colors: purple, red, cream, white, and black. Surfaces are more highly polished than in Ica Epigonal B but not as highly polished as in Ica-Pachacamac. There is a great variety in design themes, both representational and geometric. There is also considerable variability in size within some vessel types. Some vessels were entirely slipped before decoration. Many of the designs used appear to be derived by archaistic imitation from ones used in earlier phases. The problem of archaizing will be discussed in detail below.

Small spheroid bowls are rare in this phase. Both the decorated examples (Masson Grave Lot 1, DM 77-3; Masson Grave Lot 3, DM 223) have geometric designs, and the design arrangement is the same as the most common one in the preceding sub-phase. All of the incurving bowls, including two undecorated specimens, are poorly finished in comparison with the other vessels with which they are associated.

Jars are clearly the most important vessel type in Ica 1. Their importance is indicated both by the high ratio of jars to other vessels in burials and by the elaboration and variation in the form and decoration of jars as compared to vessels of other shapes. The size of the jars is highly variable. Bases are smaller than in the preceding sub-phase and are often rounded. In several cases there is no clear break between the base and the body of the jar (figs. 1b, 18, 19b, 20b). The maximum diameter is greater in proportion to total height than in Ica Epigonal B. Neck bases are proportionately narrower and mouths wider than in the preceding phases, resulting in a marked flare of the neck. Most jar necks are decorated, the two most common designs being a solid scallop design pendent from the rim,[38] and a hook and dot design which may represent the remnants of the earlier face-neck decoration.[39] The rim of one of the jars (C-2, 4-4596A) is decorated with a broken line like those used in Ica-Pachacamac and Pinilla. Although the design area on the body of the jars usually terminates at or above the point of maximum diameter, it sometimes extends over the greater portion of the body and even onto the lower portion of the neck.

As in the preceding sub-phase, the design is usually arranged in a principal design band starting at the base of the jar neck, with subordinate bands below it. As mentioned above, however, the principal design may extend onto the neck itself, and in other cases there may be one or more subordinate bands between the base of the neck and the principal design.[40] In this phase there is a proliferation of subordinate bands which may occur above the principal band, below the principal band, or both. One or more of the subordinate bands may constitute a field for decoration. Common designs on subordinate bands are unoutlined white or black dots, white crosses with black centers, step designs formed of solid black squares (figs. 20a and 22a), a linked dot design (fig. 19a),[41] Z-shaped elements (fig. 15a), and a solid black bird head which occurs only on subordinate bands.[42] Generally there is considerable difference in width between the principal design band and the subordinate ones, but in some cases the principal design band is only slightly wider.[43]

Small filler elements are common in association with the principal design. More than one filler element may be used within a single principal design band. Common fillers are outlined white dots with black centers (fig. 19a), white and black crosses in various forms (figs. 3-6), "hand" designs, outlined white squares with dots (fig. 22a), and a triangle with a dot in the center. On some of the jars the entire base of the vessel below the lowest subordinate design band is quartered in black and white.

Most commonly the principal design band is continuous, with the principal design element placed horizontally. However, the band may be divided into rectangular panels, the principal design element may be placed vertically, or there may be no outlined band whatever.[44] The most commonly used principal design elements on jars are full-bodied birds (figs. 57-64), disembodied feline heads and their geometric derivatives (figs. 44-54), seated anthropomorphic figures with feline heads (fig. 2a), and a variety of geometric figures. There are two jars[45] which have designs that appear to depict a feline head attached to a segmented bar body.[46] The body of the figure on the Masson specimen (fig. 1a) terminates in an arm with a wing at one extremity and a hand, similar to those used in Atarco B, at the other.[47]

The only decorated cumbrous bowl occurring in this phase is from the burial excavated by Pezzia.[48] The decoration consists of concentric pendent crescents with adjacent step blocks on each side, alternating with large black dots arranged in a triangular pattern. The decoration is within an outlined band.

The single lipped cup present in the sample (DM 271) has the same form as those of the preceding phases, but the placement of the decoration is different. The surface of the lip is decorated with disembodied feline heads (fig. 50), "hand" designs and step blocks. On the body of the vessel, starting just below the lip, is a principal design band consisting of disembodied feline heads with feather tufts (fig. 46), alternating with a design which appears to represent feathers. Below this band there are two subordinate bands decorated with unoutlined white dots. The remainder of the base of the vessel is quartered in black and white.

The cambered rim bowl appears in this phase but is represented by only one example (DM 247). This form may derive from the lipped cup. The rim of the Ica 1 specimen is decorated with geometric elements, and the body is decorated with a bird similar to fig. 64. There is a large number of filler elements associated with the principal design. These fillers consist of outlined white and black crosses, outlined white dots with black centers, and an abstract version of the feline head (fig. 51) which is placed vertically, apparently as a sort of panel divider.

The first of the three new dish types may derive from the small spheroid incurving bowls. The dishes of the first type, represented by five specimens (DM 207, DM 268, DM 269, DM 306, and 16-10086), have the form of a slightly flattened sphere with a more or less pronounced, but smoothly rounded, shoulder at the equator. They are somewhat more constricted at the mouth than the small spheroid incurving bowls. The maximum diameter is approximately midway of the total height or slightly below that point. Three of these dishes (DM 269, DM 306, and 16-10086) are decorated with geometric versions of the feline head (figs. 45, 49, and 52). Of the other two dishes, one (DM 268) is decorated with pyramidal step blocks lying horizontally. In the middle of the base of each block is a white dot with a black center. The other dish (DM 207) is decorated with a band containing unoutlined white dots with black centers, and pendent from the band at regular intervals are L-shaped elements with two white dots with black centers in the horizontal portion of each L. Decoration on all of the above dishes is placed entirely above the line of maximum diameter, generally just below the rim.

A second dish type is represented by one example from the Masson collection (DM 267) and two from the burial excavated by Pezzia.[49] This dish type has slightly concave sides terminating in a fairly sharp shoulder which separates the sides from a smoothly rounded base. The mouth diameter is only slightly less than the maximum diameter which occurs at the shoulder; alternatively, these diameters may be equal. The overall size of dishes of this type is variable. One of these dishes (MRI-2791) is decorated around the rim with a band containing unoutlined white dots. The second dish from the same burial (MRI-2795) has a decoration consisting of interlocking step frets with dotted hollow bases. The Masson dish is decorated with a design consisting of a cream colored snake with outlined white dots on his body.

The third new dish type is represented by two specimens, both from burials. These dishes are low and open with sides which slant outward from the rim to a sharply defined shoulder at the point of maximum diameter. From the shoulder is a smooth curve forming the base. Height from shoulder to rim and base to shoulder is approximately equal.[50] A specimen in the Masson collection (Masson Grave Lot 3, DM 222) is covered with a bright orange-red slip and has no further decoration. The other dish (C-2, 4-4595) is more elaborately decorated, with step frets with dotted hollow bases in alternating purple and white. The rim is also decorated in a fashion similar to that used in Ica-Pachacamac and Pinilla (fig. 21a).  Both vessels are highly polished.

In summary, Ica 1 shows continuity with Ica Epigonal B in the persistence of some vessel types, the general placement of decorative elements on the vessels, and certain design themes, such as realistic and totally geometric feline heads, hollow base step frets, and dotted squares.  There are, however, many elements found in the Ica 1 style which occur in neither Ica Epigonal A nor B.  Examples of these features are the use of five color decoration, black and white quartering of vessel bases, rim decoration, the use of filler elements, vessel types such as dishes and cambered rim bowls, and design themes such as full-bodied birds, feline-headed anthropomorphic figures, feline heads with segmented bar bodies, solid black bird heads, Z- and L-shaped elements with a broad wavy black line which is used as a subordinate band (fig. 22a).  In addition there are several features which are modifications of elements found in the preceding sub-phase, such as the use of decoration on subordinate design bands, an increase in the number of design bands per vessel, the use of dots within the hollow base of step frets (figs. 10 and 11), a sharp increase in the proportion of jars to other vessels, modifications in jar shape, and a red pigment which tends more to orange than to purple.  Although the Ica 1 style is based primarily on the addition of elements to the preceding Ica Epigonal B style, there are some elements present in Ica Epigonal B which do not occur in Ica 1.  Face-neck jars are no longer found, and both small spheroid incurving bowls and cumbrous bowls are negligible as categories of decorated vessels.

It is highly probable that, with further research, Ica 1 can be subdivided into at least two subphases.  That problem lies outside the scope of this study, however,

It is of some interest to note that in the next phase, Ica 2, a number of features present in Ica 1 do not occur.  Small spheroid incurving bowls are absent from the vessel inventory, and some design features, such as feline heads, feline-headed anthropomorphic figures, feline heads with segmented bar bodies, solid black bird heads, "hand" designs, black and white quartering of vessel bases, broad wavy black lines as subordinate design bands, and neck decoration on jars are also absent.

General trends

There are two trends to be discussed.  One of these trends begins in the Pinilla phase of Middle Horizon 3 and extends through Ica Epigonal B.  The other trend continues through Ica 1 and perhaps beyond.

The key word which describes the trend from Pinilla through Ica Epigonal is "simplification."  All aspects of the pottery are simplified through Ica Epigonal A, and some through Ica Epigonal B.  The only unchanging element seems to be the paste, which is surprisingly uniform throughout the entire period under consideration.

In the Ica-Pachacamac phase, surfaces are generally highly polished. In the Pinilla phase there are a number of vessels which are entirely matte or are polished only on the design area, leaving the remainder matte. In Ica Epigonal A all vessels have matte surfaces. There is a reversal of this trend in Ica Epigonal B; in this sub-phase there are some vessels with an entirely polished surface, although only a low gloss is achieved. In Ica 1 many vessels are quite highly polished.

Six color decoration is used in both Ica-Pachacamac and Pinilla, although in the Pinilla phase there is a marked increase in the proportion of vessels decorated in only three colors. In Ica Epigonal only three colors are used.

The great variety of vessel types found in Ica-Pachacamac is considerably reduced in Pinilla. In Ica Epigonal A there are only seven basic shapes, and the sample for Ica Epigonal B includes only five vessel types, not counting the Nasca trade piece. It is possible that some types which actually occurred are not represented, due to the small size of the sample for Ica Epigonal, but the tendency to reduction in number of vessel types seems well documented.

The process of simplification also operates in the field of design. In Ica-Pachacamac there are numerous designs, each one of which may be used on almost any vessel form. In the Pinilla phase, although some new elements are introduced, the number that may be used on any given vessel form is limited. Cumbrous bowls and lipped cups may now be decorated only with geometric designs, and by the end of the phase the same is true for the small incurving bowls. The larger, more incurving bowls, with one exception, are decorated with disembodied feline heads. Only jars seem to escape this tendency to limit the type of design which may be used on each vessel shape. In Ica Epigonal A the convention is firmly established, so that only jars have any freedom of design. Accompanying this rigidity of design use there is a considerable reduction in design vocabulary. The only design elements that persist continuously from Middle Horizon 2 through late Intermediate Period 1 are the disembodied feline head, the pendent crescent, and, perhaps, the white cross with a black center.

The second trend, running from Ica-Pachacamac through Ica 1, is a trend in vessel shape. There is a tendency toward rounding of bases in all vessel types. Any form which had a flat base in Ica-Pachacamac has a round, or at least somewhat rounded, base in Ica 1. This tendency is most easily noted in the case of the small incurving bowls, cumbrous bowls and jars. Jars in Ica-Pachacamac have a rather broad flat base with sharply defined edges. This base becomes gradually smaller and smaller with less well defined edges until, in Ica 1, there are some jars with no division between sides and base. Jars are also subject to other changes. Jar necks in Ica-Pachacamac are either cylindrical or slightly tapered. In Ica Epigonal A the necks develop a slightly flared lip, and in Ica 1 there is often a sharp flare to the neck. Also in Ica 1, the necks of jars become narrower at the base and wider at the mouth, and the maximum diameter of the body is greater in proportion to the total height of the vessel than is the case in the preceding phases (figs. 16-18).

## Archaism

The principal problem to which this study is directed is to determine the basis for the development of the Ica style of the Late Intermediate Period. It has been demonstrated that there is a basic continuity in vessel shapes, although the origin of the Ica 1 dishes remains a problem. The jar shape is a logical outgrowth of developments in previous phases, and the popularity of this vessel type in Ica 1 may have been due to the fact that it was the only form which was not restricted as to design. The real problem, then, in considering Ica 1 is not the shapes, but all the other features -- surface finish, colors used in decoration, and design elements. I suggest that many of the changes in these features that appear in Ica 1 may be attributed to a strong archaizing tendency which began in Ica Epigonal B but became fully manifest only in Ica 1.

The evidence for archaism is overwhelming. The sources from which the archaistic elements were drawn are primarily the Ica-Pachacamac and Pinilla phases, although some elements may derive from the Nasca 9 phase of Middle Horizon 1 or even earlier phases of the Nasca tradition.

Numerous representational themes are found on the pottery of the Ica-Pachacamac phase. Some of the more important of these themes are a griffin which consists of a winged body with a mythical eagle head and human hand and foot (fig. 56), a profile eagle figure with bird feet and a circular star symbol hanging from its beak (fig. 55), a bodiless eagle head, a full-face human head, a full-bodied Male Deity figure, and disembodied feline heads.

After Ica-Pachacamac both types of full-bodied birds disappeared from the design repertoire and did not recur until they were copied in Ica 1. I shall return to them later. The bodiless eagle head and the bodiless full-face human head continued through the Pinilla phase and then disappeared. The single major theme which maintained continuity throughout the Middle Horizon is the disembodied feline head.

It may easily be seen, by reference to Plate VI, that after the Ica-Pachacamac phase there was a gradual simplification and stylization of the feline heads which continued through the Ica Epigonal A phase. In Ica-Pachacamac the head was generally represented quite realistically, with a distinct nose and mouth on one end and an ear and neck attachment on the other. Eyes have pupils, and frequently tear lines and eyebrows were added.

In the Pinilla phase there is a strong tendency to bilateral symmetry in the feline heads, leading to forms with no clear cut nose or ear and two neck attachments instead of a neck and a mouth. Eyes frequently have no pupil, and eyebrows and tear lines are absent. There is one example of a totally abstract feline head in this phase (fig. 29).

In Ica Epigonal A the feline head became a geometric abstraction with virtually no realistic characteristics. It was reduced to a meaningless figure. That the meaning of the design was really lost to the artists is indicated by what happens to the design in the following sub-phase.

In Ica Epigonal B the feline head representations took two paths. Continuing the previous trend, there are totally abstract designs which, in Ica 1, became geometric figures impossible to relate to the feline head without the intervening forms as guides. On the other hand, quite realistic representations reappeared, representations which could not be derived from the abstract heads of the preceding sub-phase. However, these realistic designs could well have derived from the representational heads of Ica-Pachacamac and Pinilla. One of these forms (fig. 39), although absent in Ica 1, reappeared attached to a body in Ica 2 to become the principal form of feline in the Ica style.

The variations in feline head designs in Ica 1 are very similar to the variations found in the earlier phases. Some of the heads are almost as realistic as those in Ica-Pachacamac, although the majority is more similar to those found in the Pinilla phase. At the end of Ica 1 all versions of the disembodied feline head disappeared.

The first phase of the Ica style is characterized by extreme variation in design detail. Full-bodied birds were reintroduced in quantity, obviously copied from representations in the Ica-Pachacamac style. Although the primary model for the Ica 1 birds is the Ica-Pachacamac griffin, some elements appear to be drawn from the star bird of the same phase (figs. 56 and 55). The elements of the Ica 1 bird (figs. 57 and 58) which are drawn from the Ica-Pachacamac griffin are the arm, the lower wing, which is a reinterpretation of the griffin's leg, and the small squares on the body, which are taken from the rectangles on the segmented bar body of the griffin. The tail, on the other hand, is apparently drawn from the star bird, as may be the wing treatment, and some Ica 1 birds have dotted circles on their bodies instead of squares (fig. 61), a feature which is found only on the star birds in Ica-Pachacamac. The feather tuft or headdress could have come from either of the two models. There is a definite developmental sequence in the Ica 1 birds, the earlier ones being more obviously related to the Ica-Pachacamac figures than are the later ones. Figs. 57-64 illustrate the sequence, and figs. 62 and 64 are the types of birds that continue into Ica 2.

It is clear that the Ica 1 birds represent a misunderstanding of the representations that inspired them. The bird elements of the Ica-Pachacamac griffin are those of an eagle or hawk. In beak, head, and tail form the Ica 1 birds resemble not eagles but parrots. If the representational meaning of the older figures could be so far misunderstood it is probable that their mythical significance had also been lost.

The attachment of an anthropomorphic body to the disembodied feline head (fig. 2a) is another indication of archaism. The figure appears to be a distorted version of an Atarco style running angel without the iconographically vital wing and staff.[51]  Fig. 1a illustrates a still more bizarre treatment of the feline theme, perhaps an attempt to imitate a feline-headed angel such as that illustrated by Menzel.[52]

The revival of colors used in Ica-Pachacamac and Pinilla is also an indication of archaism.  Of the six colors used in Ica-Pachacamac, only gray did not reappear.  The failure to revive gray may be due to the fact that this pigment is extremely difficult to make from the materials available in the Ica Valley.[53]  In addition to the revival of colors there was also a return, in Ica 1, to overall slipping and well polished surfaces, both features which were absent in the Ica Epigonal phase.

A further archaistic character is the black and white quartering of vessel bases, a treatment which is probably derived from the black and white halving on some of the small incurving bowls in Ica-Pachacamac and Pinilla.[54]  Alternatively, it may go back to Nasca 5-7 antecedents. If I am correct in supposing that there was a connection between the lipped cups and the Ica-Pachacamac collared jars, then the placement of the decoration on the body of the Ica 1 lipped cup may also be an archaistic treatment.  The broken line patterning of vessel rims which is common in Ica Pachacamac and occurs occasionally in Pinilla was also revived on a few Ica 1 vessels, as was the use of filler elements. Both the pendent L-shaped elements and the step designs formed of solid black squares appear to derive from the Pinilla phase.  The pendent L-shaped elements probably represent a misinterpretation of the interlocking L band of the Pinilla phase, reproducing the upper row of elements only.  Since step frets do not occur in Ica Epigonal A, it is likely that those found in Ica Epigonal B are also derived from the Pinilla style.


## Conclusions

It has been demonstrated that the Ica style is in many ways the result of a gradual development of the usual kind out of Ica-Pachacamac. The development changed its direction rather suddenly at the beginning of the Late Intermediate Period, through attempts to imitate the fancy pottery of earlier phases, principally Ica-Pachacamac and Pinilla.  It is possible, on the basis of these changes in pottery style, to discuss certain aspects of the broader context of Ica culture.

Under the Huari empire, the pottery of Ica showed heavy influence from Pachacamac, a fact reflected in the name of the Ica-Pachacamac phase.  Pachacamac was a major religious center, and its art is a variation on the religious art of Huari.  The pottery designs of Ica-Pachacamac reflect the same mythical and religious base as the designs found at Pachacamac and Huari.  Evidently the imperial religion was well established at Ica.

The Huari empire fell at the end of Middle Horizon 2, and, with its fall, communication between distant regions was reduced.  Each local area went its own way, and local pottery styles developed.  It is reasonable to suppose that local religions developed also, once religion was freed from the unifying force of central direction. It is also likely that the official religion of the empire suffered a decline in prestige with the collapse of the central government, and surviving local religions may have recovered their importance.

At Ica the fall of the empire was followed by a simplification of the pottery style which involved a reduction in the number of colors and vessel shapes used and a loss of complex mythical designs. The rules of ornamentation became more rigid, and fewer choices were allowed. At the same time, there was a gradual loss of meaning in the old designs, the beginnings of which can be traced as early as the Pinilla phase.

After two phases the changes had reached a point where there was little resemblance between the pottery of the imperial period and the contemporary ware, either in design motifs or technique. At this point, beginning in Ica Epigonal B and reaching its climax in Ica 1, there occurred an archaizing movement in which the Ica potters attempted to imitate the colors, finish and designs of the Ica-Pachacamac and Pinilla style units.

In spite of the fact that the designs which were revived were originally mythical and connected with the official religion, it was apparently not a religious revival which led to the archaism in pottery design. This statement is based primarily on the misinterpretation of the bird and full-bodied feline designs and the failure to revive other mythical motifs found in Ica-Pachacamac. The bodiless eagle head, the full-face human head and the Male Deity figure, which were apparently important elements in Ica-Pachacamac religion, were not revived at all in Ica 1. We cannot, on the basis of this evidence, state that the religion present in Late Intermediate Period 1 was totally different from that found in Middle Horizon 2, but we can suggest that if there was continuity in the oral tradition, the continuity was not sufficient to permit a recognition and correct interpretation of the earlier religious art.

If it was not a revival of religion that sparked the archaism, however, what was it that inspired the imitation of the past? The time elapsed between the fall of Huari and the archaistic movement was of the order of 150 to 175 years, according to available radiocarbon evidence.[55] With so short a time interval, it is reasonable to suspect that reminiscences of the Huari empire still existed in oral tradition. It is even possible that there might have been a few old people still alive who had, as children, met elders who had seen the last days of the empire. Specific sites might still have been associated with the empire and, at these sites, it would have been possible to obtain pottery from which the Ica 1 motifs were drawn. Stylistic change had gone so far that the difference between imperial and modern pottery would have been obvious. Anyone finding an older pottery vessel and comparing it to those of his own time would no doubt have been impressed with the designs and the greater technical skill reflected in the earlier pieces.

Whatever the source material from which the archaistic elements were drawn, the result of their utilization was far more than a copy of the older styles. The potters of Ica succeeded in creating an important and original new style as the result of their attempt to imitate an antiquity which they no longer understood.

## Acknowledgements

The study upon which this paper is based was originally undertaken in a seminar at the University of California, Berkeley, under the direction of John H. Rowe and Dorothy Menzel. Dr. Menzel's knowledge of the Middle Horizon in Peru was an invaluable aid to me during the study as were her unfailing enthusiasm and encouragement. Dr. Rowe contributed greatly to the final conclusions and to the general form of the manuscript through his careful editing. Lawrence E. Dawson and Marianne Y. Winton also offered valuable comments on the manuscript.

Special thanks are due to Duncan M. Masson for his constant cooperation with students of Peruvian archaeology in making available his collection both for study and publication. Several specimens from the Masson collection were crucial in this study.

The illustrations of figures 12a, 13a, 14a, 15a, 17, 18, 19a, 20, 21, 22a, 23 and 25 were drawn by Jane Bendix and the remainder by Robert Berner.

## NOTES

[1] Menzel, 1964.

[2] Uhle, 1913.

[3] Menzel, 1964.

[4] Most of the color slides used in this study were supplied to me by Dr. Dorothy Menzel. I have catalogued these slides and reference is made to them by my catalog numbers. The key to the catalog number prefixes is as follows: AR, Aldo Rubini collection; CS, Carlos Soldi collection; DM, Duncan Masson collection. Slides of specimens in the Ica Regional Museum are referred to by museum number, and all have the prefix MRI. One slide of a specimen in the collection of Ernesto Tabío was supplied to me by Lawrence E. Dawson. Neither this slide nor the specimen is numbered.

[5] Menzel, 1964, pp. 64-65.

[6]Kroeber and Strong, 1924, p. 101.

[7]Kroeber and Strong, 1924, pl. 30b.

[8]Kroeber and Strong, 1924, p. 124.

[9]Menzel, 1964, pp. 64-65.

[10]Strong, 1957, Fig. 18F, M.

[11]Strong, 1957, Fig. 18C, F, M. O.

[12]The disembodied feline heads which occur as design motifs in Ica from Middle Horizon 2B through Late Intermediate Period 1, are derived from appendage heads which first appear in Middle Horizon 1 in the Conchopata and Robles Moqo styles. These feline appendage heads are found as terminators on ray appendages, headdress appendages and staffs (e.g., Menzel, 1964, pl. IV fig. 10-a and pl. V fig. 13). Appendage heads are easily distinguished from other disembodied feline heads (e.g., Menzel, 1964, pl. VII fig. 20) by the presence of a rectangular neck attachment which is placed below the ear on the end of the head opposite the mouth (figs. 26, 27, 31, 33). In Middle Horizon 2B most disembodied feline heads distinguish between neck attachment and mouth, a distinction which is lost in Middle Horizon 3 and 4A when the heads are bilaterally symmetrical. At present it is not possible to distinguish with absolute certainty between all isolated specimens of Middle Horizon 2 and 3 vessels decorated with feline heads. I have included illustrations of feline heads in this uncertain category in order to show the range of variation in this design theme at that time. One of the feline heads revived in Middle Horizon 4B (fig. 39) may not derive from an appendage head, since it has no neck attachment. All the feline heads found in Late Intermediate Period 1 do have the neck attachment, either as such or moved upward into mouth position to form a second mouth on a bilaterally symmetrical head.

[13]Menzel, 1964, p. 64.

[14]A possible forerunner of the lipped cup is represented by a collared jar in the Carlos Soldi collection (CS 5) which is decorated on the body with a Pachacamac B griffin while the interior of the collar, which is quite broad and flaring, is decorated with white lines.

[15]Kroeber and Strong, 1924, p. 124.

[16]All previous illustrations of specimens of this style are noted in the list of specimens studied at the end of this paper. Note that Kroeber and Strong have listed incorrectly the museum number of the specimen illustrated in pl. 30i (Kroeber and Strong, 1924, p. 132).

[17]Pezzia, 1959, pp. 291-295 and lám. LXXXVI. It should be noted that the drawings in this article are innaccurate as regards both the form and the decoration of the specimens. My treatment of them is based on Menzel's unpublished slides and notes.

[18] Strong, 1957, Fig. 18K, L.

[19] Pezzia, 1959, lám. LXXXVI, TE-3; Kroeber and Strong, 1924, pl. 30k.

[20] Pezzia, 1959, lám. LXXXVI, TE-1.

[21] Kroeber and Strong, 1924, pl. 30p; Uhle, 1913, fig. 5, no. 4.

[22] Kroeber and Strong, 1924, pl. 30n.

[23] Kroeber and Strong, 1924, pl. 30h, m and fig. 11; Pezzia, 1959, lám. LXXXVI, TE-4.

[24] Kroeber and Strong, 1924, pl. 30m and fig. 11.

[25] Kroeber and Strong, 1924, p. 124.

[26] All previous illustrations of specimens of this style are noted in the list of specimens studied at the end of this paper.

[27] Kroeber and Strong, 1924, pl. 30g; Uhle, 1913, fig. 5, no. 8.

[28] Kroeber and Strong, 1924, pl. 30j and fig. 8.

[29] Menzel, 1964, pl. VII, fig. 20.

[30] Kroeber and Strong, 1924, pl. 30c, o.

[31] Kroeber and Strong, 1924, pl. 30d and fig. 6.

[32] Kroeber and Strong, 1924, pl. 30g; Uhle, 1913, fig. 5, no. 8.

[33] Kroeber and Strong, 1924, pl. 30 l.

[34] Pezzia, 1959, pp. 295-297 and lám. LXXXVII. See note 17 for drawings.

[35] Uhle, 1913, pl. XI, B5.

[36] Schmidt, 1929, fig. 305-1, -2 and 324-2.

[37] All previous illustrations of specimens of this style are noted in the list of specimens studied at the end of this paper.

[38] Pezzia, 1959, lám. LXXXVII, TI-2, -4.

[39] Schmidt, 1929, fig. 305-2.

[40] Schmidt, 1929, fig. 305-1, 324-2.

[41] Pezzia, 1959, lám. LXXXVII, TI-2.

[42]Schmidt, 1929, fig. 324-2.

[43]Kroeber and Strong, 1924, pl. 31d; Schmidt, 1929, fig. 305-1.

[44]Uhle, 1913, pl. XI, B5.

[45]Schmidt, 1929, fig. 305-2 and specimen DM 452 from Avispas near Ica.

[46]Menzel, 1964, p. 61.

[47]Compare Menzel, 1964, pl. IV, fig. 10-a.

[48]Pezzia, 1959, lám. LXXXVII, TI-3.

[49]Pezzia, 1959, lám. LXXXVII, TI-1, -5.

[50]Kroeber and Strong, 1924, pl. 31b.

[51]Menzel, 1964, pp. 50-51.

[52]Menzel, 1964, pl. IV, fig. 10.

[53]Personal communication from Lawrence E. Dawson.

[54]Menzel, 1964, pl. IX, fig. 26.

[55]Rowe, 1966, Table 3.


BIBLIOGRAPHY

Baessler, Arthur
   1902-03    Ancient Peruvian art; contributions to the archaeology of
              the empire of the Incas. A. Asher & Co., Berlin; Dodd,
              Mead & Co., New York. 4 vols.

Kroeber, Alfred Louis, and Strong, William Duncan
   1924       The Uhle pottery collections from Ica. With three append-
              ices by Max Uhle. University of California Publications in
              American Archaeology and Ethnology, vol. 21, no. 3, pp.
              [i-ii], 95-134. Berkeley.

Menzel, Dorothy
   1964       Style and time in the Middle Horizon. Ñawpa Pacha 2,
              pp. 1-106. Berkeley.

Pezzia A., Alejandro
 1959        Dos tumbas precolombinas en el valle de Ica correspondientes
             a los estilos culturales Epigonal e Ica.  Actas y Trabajos
             del II Congreso Nacional de Historia del Perú (Epoca Pre-
             hispánica), vol. 1, pp. 291-297.  Lima.

Rowe, John Howland
 1966        An interpretation of radiocarbon measurements on
             archaeological samples from Peru.  Proceedings of the
             Sixth International Conference, Radiocarbon and Tritium
             Dating, held at Washington State University, Pullman,
             Washington, June 7-11, 1965, pp. 187-198.  U.S. Atomic
             Energy Commission, Division of Technical Information,
             CONF-650652 Chemistry (TID-4500).  Springfield, Va.

Schmidt, Max
 1929        Kunst und Kultur von Peru.  Propyläen-Verlag, Berlin.

Strong, William Duncan
 1957        Paracas, Nazca, and Tiahuanacoid cultural relationships
             in south coastal Peru.  Memoirs of the Society for American
             Archaeology, no. 13.  Salt Lake City.

Uhle, Max
 1913        Zur Chronologie der alten Culturen von Ica.  Journal de
             la Société des Américanistes de Paris, n.s., T. X., fasc.
             II, pp. 341-367.  Paris.

## KEY TO ILLUSTRATIONS

All drawings of pottery designs are reproduced at one half
original size with the exception of those on Plates II, VI and VII
which are idealized drawings and not to scale.  All shape outline
drawings are reproduced at one fourth original size with the exception
of Figs. 1b, 2b, 15b, 19b and 22b which are at one sixth original size.
Burial numbers with the prefix E- are from site E, Ocucaje, Ica, and
those with prefix C- are from site C, Ocucaje, Ica.  Specimen numbers
with the prefix 4- are from the Uhle collection; numbers with the
prefix 16- are from the Wattis collection.  Both of these collections
are in the Robert H. Lowie Museum of Anthropology, University of
California, Berkeley.  For key to other number prefixes see Note 4.

## Plate II

Fig. 1.  Feline head with attached segmented bar body, wing and
hand.  Specimen DM 452 from Avispas, Ica.  Ica 1.

Fig. 2.  Feline head with seated anthropomorphic body.  Specimen 16-10063 from Ica.  Ica 1.

Figs. 3-6.  Black and white crosses showing the variety of treatment of this design theme in the Ica 1 phase.

Fig. 3.  Unoutlined black and white cross.  This is the only type of cross which occurs in the Middle Horizon, and it is found in all phases in Ica.  Specimen 4-4594, Burial C-2.  Ica 1.

Fig. 4.  Semi-outlined black and white cross.  This may be a transitional form between the unoutlined and wholly outlined crosses.  Specimen 16-10069 from Ica.  Ica 1.

Fig. 5.  Outlined black and white cross.  Used as filler element on the same vessel as Fig. 6.  Specimen 16-10074 from Ica. Ica 1.

Fig. 6.  Outlined cross with dotted arms.  This form first appears in Ica 1 and becomes very common in later phases of the Ica style.  Used as filler element on the same vessel as Fig. 5.  Specimen 16-10074 from Ica.  Ica 1.

Figs. 7-11.  Step frets showing the different forms in the Pinilla phase (Fig. 7), Ica Epigonal B (Figs. 8-9) and Ica 1 (Figs. 10-11).

Fig. 7.  Solid black step fret.  After Strong, 1957, Fig. 18F. Pinilla phase.

Fig. 8.  Hollow base step fret.  The added squares with dashes or dots are new in this sub-phase.  Specimen 4-4450, Burial E-14. Ica Epigonal B.

Fig. 9.  Hollow base step fret.  Specimen 16-10071 from Ica. Ica Epigonal B.

Fig. 10.  Step fret with dotted hollow base.  Specimen 4-4595, Burial C-2.  Ica 1.

Fig. 11.  Step fret with dotted hollow base.  The use of added squares with dots or dashes is continued in this phase.  Specimen DM 223, Masson Grave lot 3 from the Córdova area of Ocucaje, Ica. Ica 1.


Plate III

Fig. 12.  Specimen 4-4534, Burial E-10.  Pinilla phase.

Fig. 13.  Specimen 4-4535, Burial E-10.  Pinilla phase.

Fig. 14.  Specimen 4-4481, Burial E-7.  Pinilla phase.

Fig. 15.  Specimen 4-4593, Burial C-2.  Ica 1.  (For remainder of Burial see Plates IV and V.)

Figs. 16-18.  Change in jar shapes, Ica Epigonal A-Ica 1.

Fig. 16.  Specimen 4-4555, Burial E-15.  Ica Epigonal A.

Fig. 17.  Specimen 4-4464, Burial E-1.  Ica Epigonal B.

Fig. 18.  Specimen 4-4623 from Ica.  Ica 1.  (See also Figs. 1b, 2b, 15b, 19b, 20b and 22b.)


Plate IV

All vessels on this plate are from Burial C-2, Ocucaje, Ica, and belong to the Ica 1 phase.  For remainder of the burial see Fig. 15 and Plate V.

Fig. 19.  Specimen 4-4592.

Fig. 20.  Specimen 4-4594.

Fig. 21.  Specimen 4-4595.


Plate V

All vessels on this plate are from Burial C-2, Ocucaje, Ica, and belong to the Ica 1 phase.  For remainder of the burial see Fig. 15 and Plate IV.

Fig. 22.  Specimen 4-4596A.  The drawing of Fig. 22a was done for a previous study of this collection.  Upon closer examination of the specimen it was noted that the portions of the figure which are coded as cream-colored are, in fact, the same red as the base slip.

Fig. 23.  Specimen 4-4596B.  Undecorated jar, not studied.

Fig. 24.  Specimen 4-4596C.  Undecorated jar, not studied.

Fig. 25.  Specimen 4-4596E.  Undecorated small spheroid incurving bowl, not studied.


Plate VI

Changes in the form of disembodied feline heads from Ica-Pachacamac through Ica 1.

Figs. 26-27.  Disembodied feline heads, Ica-Pachacamac phase.  The feline head in this phase is generally quite realistic with well defined ear and nose, mouth and neck marking, and often eyebrow and tear lines.

Fig. 26.   Specimen AR 2, Tomb 1, Huaca José Ramos, Pinilla sector of Ocucaje, Ica.   Ica-Pachacamac.

Fig. 27.   Specimen CS 3 from Ulluhaya, Ica.   Ica-Pachacamac.

Figs. 28-29.   Disembodied feline heads, Pinilla phase.   In this phase there is a strong tendency toward bilateral symmetry in the feline heads, but there is still a realistic eye, and sometimes eyebrow or tear-line are indicated.   Neck markings are generally clear.

Fig. 28.   After Strong, 1957, Fig. 18J.   Pinilla phase.

Fig. 29.   Specimen DM 260, Masson Grave lot 7, Cruz Grande, Ocucaje, Ica.   Pinilla phase.

Figs. 30-35.   These figures represent specimens which belong to either the Ica-Pachacamac or the Pinilla phase, but cannot be attributed with certainty to one or the other.   They are included here to show the variety of treatment of this design theme.   (See Note 12)

Fig. 30.   Specimen AR 19 from Huaca José Ramos, Pinilla sector of Ocucaje, Ica.   Probably Ica-Pachacamac.

Fig. 31.   Specimen AR 61 from Huaca José Ramos, Pinilla sector of Ocucaje, Ica.   Probably Ica-Pachacamac.

Fig. 32.   Specimen AR 21 from Huaca José Ramos, Pinilla sector of Ocucaje, Ica.   Either Ica-Pachacamac or Pinilla phase.

Fig. 33.   Specimen DM 231 from Ica.   Either Ica-Pachacamac or Pinilla phase.

Fig. 34.   Specimen AR 62 from Huaca José Ramos, Pinilla sector of Ocucaje, Ica.   Either Ica-Pachacamac or Pinilla phase.

Fig. 35.   Specimen AR 34 from Huaca José Ramos, Pinilla sector of Ocucaje, Ica.   Probably Pinilla phase.

Figs. 36-38.   Disembodied feline heads, Ica Epigonal A sub-phase. In this sub-phase the feline heads are bilaterally symmetrical and have almost no representational elements.   It appears that the meaning of the design was lost at this time.

Fig. 36.   Specimen 4-4474, Burial E-5.   Ica Epigonal A.

Fig. 37.   Specimen MRI-3209, Epigonal burial, Rinconada de Pinilla, Ocucaje, Ica.   Ica Epigonal A.

Fig. 38.   Specimen MRI-2789, Epigonal burial, Rinconada de Pinilla, Ocucaje, Ica.   Ica Epigonal A.

Figs. 39-43.   Disembodied feline heads, Ica Epigonal B sub-phase. The first indications of archaism appear in this sub-phase, as reflected in Figs. 39, 42 and 43 which have no antecedents in the preceding sub-phase. Figs. 40 and 41 continue in a straight line development from the abstract forms of the preceding sub-phase, becoming even more abstract and geometric in form.

Fig. 39. Specimen 4-4544, Burial E-12. Ica Epigonal B.

Fig. 40. Specimen 16-10071 from Ica. Ica Epigonal B.

Fig. 41. Specimen 4-4465, Burial E-1. Ica Epigonal B.

Fig. 42. Specimen DM 78-1, Masson Grave lot 2, Rinconada de Pinilla, Ocucaje, Ica. Ica Epigonal B.

Fig. 43. Specimen 4-4464, Burial E-1. Ica Epigonal B.

Figs. 44-54. Disembodied feline heads, Ica 1 phase. In this phase there is a great amount of variation shown in the treatment of this design theme, but the basic dichotomy seen in the preceding sub-phase continues--realistic treatment based on archaism and abstract and geometric forms arising from immediate antecedents. Figs. 46, 50, 53 and 54 show some of the variation in the realistic treatment and elaboration, including eyebrows, tear lines and a feather tuft. The remainder of the figures in this group show the three types of geometric treatment common in this phase.

Fig. 44. Specimen 16-10072 from Ica. Ica 1.

Fig. 45. Specimen DM 306 from the Pinilla sector of Ocucaje, Ica. Ica 1.

Fig. 46. Specimen DM 271 from the Pinilla sector of Ocucaje, Ica. Ica 1. (See also Fig. 50.)

Fig. 47. Specimen 16-10078 from Ica. Ica 1.

Fig. 48. Specimen 16-10068 from Ica. Ica 1.

Fig. 49. Specimen DM 269 from the Pinilla sector of Ocucaje, Ica. Ica 1.

Fig. 50. Specimen DM 271 from the Pinilla sector of Ocucaje, Ica. Ica 1. (See also Fig. 46.)

Fig. 51. Specimen DM 247 from near La Capilla, Pinilla sector, Ocucaje, Ica. Ica 1.

Fig. 52. Specimen 16-10086 from Ica. Ica 1.

Fig. 53. Specimen MRI-DA-3779, Rinconada de Pinilla, Ocucaje, Ica. Ica 1.

Fig. 54. Specimen DM 77-1, Masson Grave lot 1, Rinconada de Pinilla, Ocucaje, Ica. Ica 1.

Plate VII

Changes in bird figures between Pachacamac (Middle Horizon 2) and Ica-Pachacamac, and Ica 1. There are no full-bodied bird figures in the intervening phases from which the Ica 1 birds could be drawn. It is therefore assumed that the models for the Ica 1 birds are those shown in Figs. 55 and 56.

Fig. 55. After Baessler, 1902-03, vol. 4, Pl. 133, Fig. 368. Pachacamac style star bird (Middle Horizon 2) from Pachacamac. Although birds of this type do occur in Ica-Pachacamac, there are no good examples from which an illustration could be made; therefore, this specimen from Pachacamac was used.

Fig. 56. Griffin, specimen AR 11, Rinconada de Pinilla, Ocucaje, Ica. Ica-Pachacamac.

Fig. 57. Note how hind leg of griffin has become lower wing, and the form of the beak has changed. Squares on body probably represent segmented bar body of griffin, and tail form is probably taken from star bird. Specimen 16-10075 from Ica. Ica 1.

Fig. 58. Lower wing is attached to arm, and hand has a wing shape. For similar hand treatment see Fig. 59. Specimen 16-10074 from Ica. Ica 1.

Fig. 59. In this figure only the head, chest and arm remain of the full-bodied bird, and the wing is attached directly to the back of the chest. The form of the hand seems to be due to crowding on the design panel. See Fig. 60 from the same vessel and also Fig. 61 from the same burial. Specimen MRI-2794, Ica burial, Pinilla sector, Ocucaje, Ica. Ica 1.

Fig. 60. See remarks for Fig. 59 above. Note occurrence of feather tuft. Specimen MRI-2794, Ica burial, Pinilla sector, Ocucaje, Ica. Ica 1.

Fig. 61. This figure is most closely related to Figs. 57 and 58, but the lower wing is absent. Note the use of outlined circles with black dots instead of dotted squares on the body. This figure is on a vessel from the same burial as the vessel decorated with Figs. 59 and 60. Specimen MRI-2792, Ica burial, Pinilla sector, Ocucaje, Ica. Ica 1.

Fig. 62. This is an even more stylized version of the type of bird represented in Figs 59, 60 and 63. The dotted squares on the "arm" may be from the dotted squares on the body of the full-bodied birds (Figs. 57-58) and thus, the "arm" may really represent the body of the bird. This type of bird is commonly found in Ica 2 and later phases. Specimen 4-4592, Burial C-2. Ica 1.

Fig. 63. This bird is an obvious outgrowth of forms such as Figs. 59 and 60. Note feather tuft. Specimen 4-4596A, Burial C-2. Ica 1.

Fig. 64.  This bird could easily derive from the type of bird represented by Fig. 63, by simply cutting off the figure just below the wing and changing the beak form.  There are no other antecedents for this type of bird, but it becomes exceedingly common in later phases.  Specimen 4-4596A, Burial C-2.  Ica 1.

Grave lots which are illustrated in their entirety in this report are as follows:  E-7, Ocucaje, Ica, Fig. 14; E-10, Ocucaje, Ica, Figs. 12-13; C-2, Ocucaje, Ica, Figs. 15 and 19-25.

## Acknowledgment of support.

The seminar research on which this study is based was undertaken while the author was supported by the National Institutes of Health (National Institute of General Medical Sciences), Training Grant No. GM-1224.

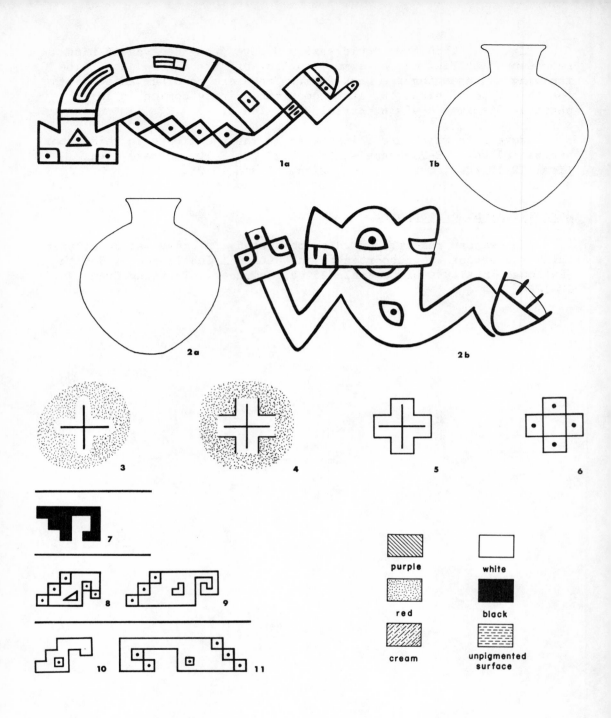

Plate II. Ica 1 felines (figs. 1, 2); Ica 1 black and white cross
variants (figs. 3-6); step frets (figs. 7-11): Pinilla (fig. 7);
Ica Epigonal B (figs. 8, 9); Ica 1 (figs. 10, 11).

Plate III. Pinilla phase vessels (figs. 12-14): Burial E-10, Ocucaje
(figs. 12, 13); Burial E-7, Ocucaje (fig. 14). Ica 1 vessel from Burial
C-2, Ocucaje (fig. 15; see plates IV and V for remainder of grave lot).
Changes in jar shapes, Ica Epigonal A to Ica 1 (figs. 16-18): Ica
Epigonal A (fig. 16); Ica Epigonal B (fig. 17); Ica 1 (fig. 18).

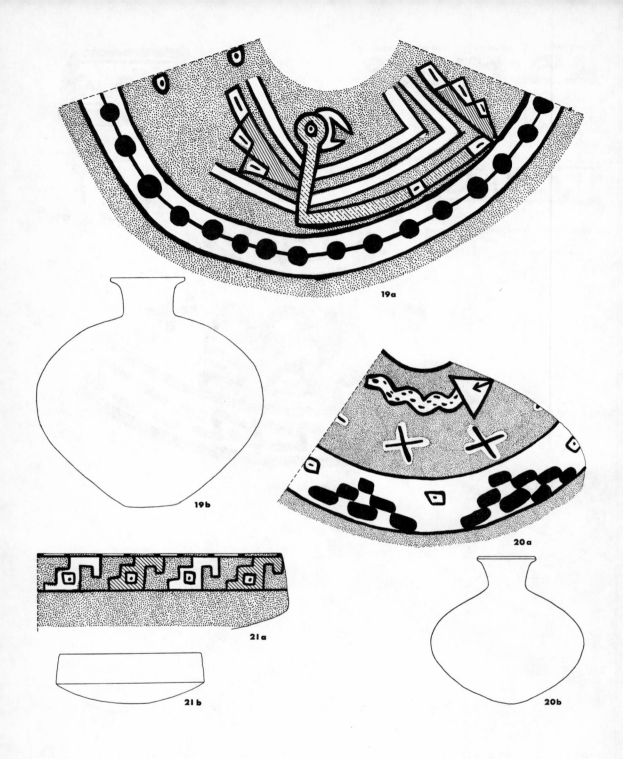

Plate IV.  Ica 1 vessels from Burial C-2, Ocucaje (see plate III, fig. 15, and plate V for remainder of grave lot).

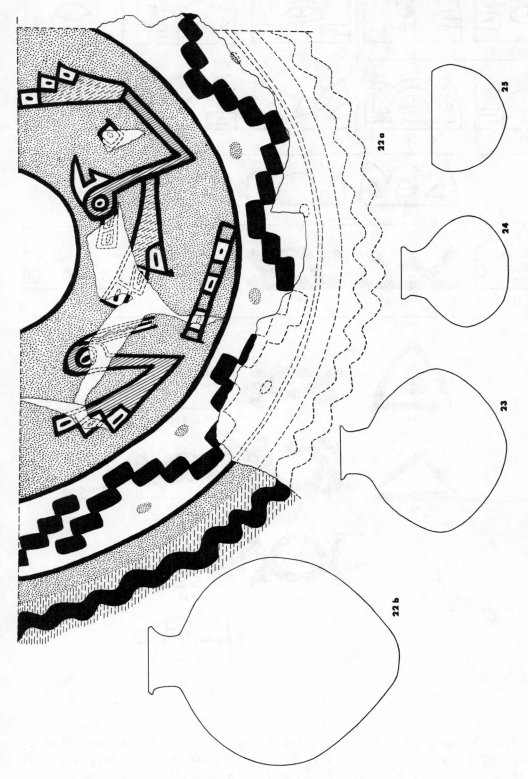

Plate V. Ica 1 vessels from Burial C-2, Ocucaje (see plate III, fig. 15, and plate IV for remainder of grave lot).

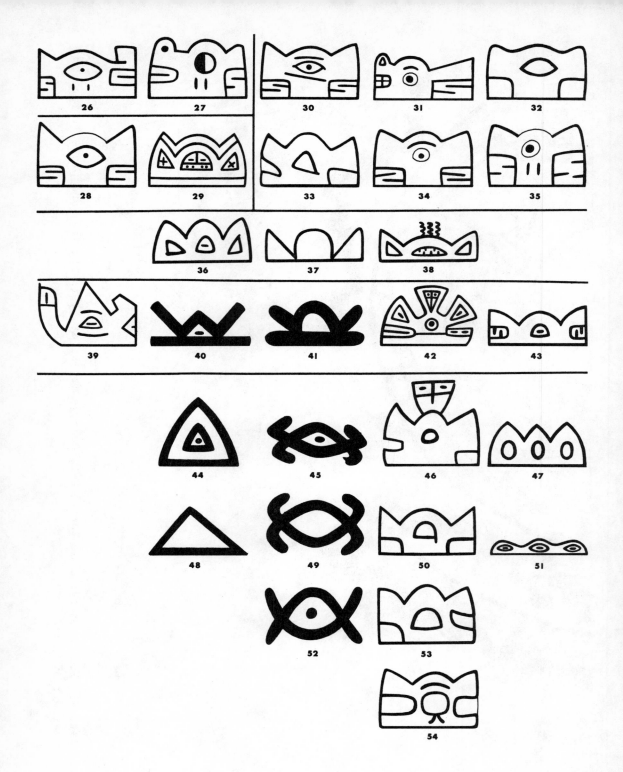

Plate VI. Changes in disembodied feline heads: Ica-Pachacamac (figs. 26, 27); Pinilla phase (figs. 28, 29); Ica-Pachacamac or Pinilla (figs. 30-35); Ica Epigonal A (figs. 36-38); Ica Epigonal B (figs. 39-43); Ica 1 (figs. 44-54).

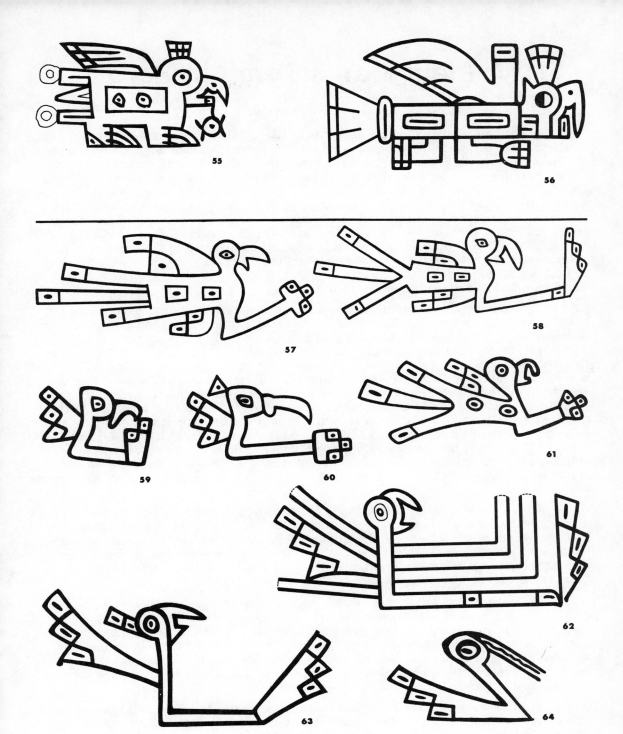

Plate VII. Changes in birds: Pachacamac style (Middle Horizon 2) from Pachacamac (fig. 55); Ica-Pachacamac (fig. 56); Ica 1 (figs. 57-64).

# A Plain Man's Tomb in Peru

Ephraim George Squier

Among the vast remains of antiquity scattered along the coast of Peru, which antedate the civilization of the Incas, and were old when the Inca empire was founded, the most celebrated, if not the grandest, are those of Pachacamac, twenty miles to the south of Lima. They take their name from the divinity Pacha-camac, signifying Creator of the World, who had here a vast temple or shrine, of such sanctity that it was resorted to by pilgrims from the most distant tribes, who were permitted to pass unmolested through the countries or tribes with whom they might be at war, to perform this act of devotion. In fact, this spot was the Mecca of South America; and the worship of Pacha-camac had such a hold on all the peoples of the coast that the politic Incas did not undertake to overthrow it, but cautiously sought to undermine it by building close to the chief temple of Pachacamac a "sumptuous structure," as the early Spaniards describe it, dedicated to the Sun.

Both structures are still distinct and impressive, although in great decay. I shall not attempt to describe them here. Of course, around both, the ancient and the modern temple, there gradually sprung up a large town, occupied by priests and servitors, and containing tambos or inns for the pilgrims that flocked thither. This town was built on a high, arid plain overlooking the river and valley of Lurin, and was several miles in circumference, enclosed by a heavy wall of indurated clay and sun-dried bricks. The desert intervening between the valley of Lurin and that of Rimac, in which the city of Lima stands, has encroached on the old city, and buried a large part of it, with a portion of its walls, under the drifting sands. Nothing can exceed the bare and desolate aspect of the ruins, which are as still and lifeless as those of Palymra of the Desert. No living thing is to be seen, except, perhaps, a solitary condor circling above the crumbling temple, nor sound heard, except the pulsations of the great Pacific breaking at the foot of the eminence on which the temple stood.

It is a place of death, not alone in its silence and sterility, but as the burial-place of tens of thousands of the ancient dead. Of old, as now, the devotees of religion sought to draw their last breath in places sanctified by the shrines of their divinities, and to be buried near them. In all time the tomb and temple have been inseparable, and it is only in great cities that the shadow of the church no longer falls on the graves of the departed.

In Pachacamac the ground around the temple seems to have been a vast cemetery. Dig almost anywhere in the dry, nitrous sand, and you will come upon what are loosely called mummies, but what are really the desiccated bodies of the ancient dead. Dig deeper, and you will probably find a second stratum of ghastly relics of poor humanity, and deeper still, a third, showing how great was the concourse of people in Pachacamac, and how eager the desire to find a resting-place in consecrated ground.

Most of the mummies are found in little vaults or chambers of adobes, roofed with sticks or canes and a layer of rushes, and of a size to contain from one to four and five bodies. These are invariably placed in a sitting posture, with the head resting on the knees around which the arms are clasped, or with the head resting on the outspread palms, and the elbows on the knees, enveloped in wrappings of various kinds, according to the rank or wealth of the defunct. Sometimes they are enveloped in inner wrappings of fine cotton cloth, and then in blankets of various colors

Reproduced from FRANK LESLIE'S ILLUSTRATED NEWSPAPER, Vol. XXVIII, No. 704, March 27, 1869. pp. 21-22.

and designs, made from the wool of the v̄icuna and the alpaca, with ornaments of gold and silver on the corpse, and vases of elegant design by its side. But oftener the cerements are coarse, the ornaments scant and mean, indicating that of old, as now, the mass of mankind was as poor in death as impoverished in life.

Fortunately, as I have already said, for our knowledge of the people of the past ages, who lived before the discovery of written language or who never attained to it, they were accustomed to bury with their dead the things they regarded in life as most useful or beautiful, and from these we may deduce something of their modes of life, their habits, fancies, and follies, as will obtain some idea of their arts, and sometimes a clue to their religious notions and beliefs. In fact, the interment of articles of any kind with the dead is a clear proof of a belief in the doctrine of a future state, the theory being that the articles thus buried would be useful to their possessor in another world.

To ascertain something more about the old inhabitants of Pachacamac than could be inferred from their monuments, I explored a number of their graves, during my ten days' visit there in 1864. I will not undertake to give all, nor even the general results of my inquiries, but record what I found in a single tomb, which will illustrate how a family, not rich nor yet of the poorest, lived in Pachacamac — who can tell how many hundreds of years ago?

I will take it for granted that the family occupying the tomb, lived beyond the Bowery of the ancient city, and inhabited a tenement house, or rather, what might be called "an apartment." Now, the tenement houses of Pachacamac were in some respects better than ours. In the first place, they were never of more than one story, and consequently had no need of fire-escapes, nor could babies tumble out of third-story windows, or drunken husbands topple down stairs. In the second place, there were no narrow, dark, common passages, always filthy because it was nobody's special business to keep them clean. On the contrary, all the apartments opened, not on the street, but around a spacious central court, on one side of which, raised on a platform, was the house of the special officer who kept order in the establishment. Sometimes but a single room was allowed to the tenant, yet our family probably had three rooms — a large room, it may be fifteen feet square, a small sleeping-room, with a raised bunk of earth at one end whereon to spread the skins or blankets that constituted the bed, and another smaller room, with niches in the walls to receive utensils, and with a series of vases sunk in the earth to supply the place of closets and secure the maize and beans that seem to have been leading articles of food. The plan, on p. 22, (cf. p. 216), is of such a dwelling as I have described.

The blankets, the implements, the utensils, the ornaments, and the stores in the frugal granaries of the inhabitants of the tenement apartments have disappeared, but we shall find most if not all of them in their family tomb, in the neighborhood of the temple. This particular tomb was one of the second stratum of graves, and therefore neither oldest nor latest. Like the others I have described in general terms, it was walled with adobes, was about four feet square by three feet high, and contained five bodies; one of a man of middle age, another of a full grown woman, a third of a girl of about fourteen years old, a fourth of a boy some years younger, and the fifth of an infant. I assume that here was grouped an entire family, in life united, in death not divided. Whether they all succumbed at once under the attacks of some pestilence, or were the simultaneous victims of some catastrophe, or were deposited here, one by one, as they successively paid the common debt of nature, there was no evidence to show. The latter suggestion is probably the correct one. At any rate there they were, the little one placed between the father and mother, the boy by the side of the first, the girl by the side of the latter. All were enveloped in a braided network or sack of rushes or coarse grass, bound closely around the bodies by cords of the same material.

I unwrapped the body of the presumed husband and father first. Under the outer wrapper of braided reeds, was another of stout, plain cotton-cloth, fastened with a variegated cord of llama wool. Next came an envelope of cotton-cloth, of finer texture, which, when removed, disclosed the body shrunken and dried hard, of the color of mahogany, but well preserved. The hair was long, slightly reddish from the effects, perhaps, of the nitre that almost saturated the soil. Passing around the neck, and carefully folded on the knees, on which the head rested, was a net, of the twisted fibre of the agave (a plant not found on the coast), the threads as fine as the finest used by our fishermen, and the meshes formed and neatly knotted precisely after the fashion of today. This indicated that the father had been a fisherman in his time, a conclusion further sustained by finding, wrapped up in a cloth between his feet, some fishing-lines, of various sizes, some copper hooks, barbed like ours, and some copper sinkers. Under each armpit was a roll of white alpaca wool, and behind the calf of each leg a few thick, short ears of variegated maize or Indian corn. A small thin piece of copper had been placed in his mouth, corresponding, perhaps, with the obolos which the ancient Greeks put in the mouths of their dead, as a fee for Charon, the ferryman of the Styx. This was all discovered belonging exclusively to the fisherman, except that suspended by a thread around his neck was a bronze tweezers, for plucking out the beard, of which I give an engraving. It seems it was a custom in Pachacamac, as in many other parts of aboriginal America, to extirpate the beard in this way.

His wife, beneath the same coarse outer wrapping of braided reeds, was enveloped in a blanket of alpaca wool, finely spun, woven in the style technically known as "three-ply," in two colors, a soft chestnut brown and a pure white. The figure, somewhat intricate, is reproduced on a reduced scale in the above engraving. (cf. 215, upper right)

Below this was a sheet of fine cotton-cloth, with sixty-two threads of warp and woof to the inch. I have what is regarded as a very fine specimen of Egyptian linen mummy cloth, from the wrappings of a body unrolled in the Paris Universal Exposition, which has only forty-four threads to the inch. This Pachacamac cloth has a diamond-shaped pattern formed by very elaborate lines of ornament, inside of which, or in the spaces themselves, were conventional, but unmistakable representatives of monkeys, which seemed to be following each other as up and down-stairs.

Beneath this was a rather coarsely-woven, but yet very soft and flexible cotton-cloth, twenty yards or more in length, wrapped in many folds around the body of the woman, which was in a similar condition, as regards preservation, with that of her husband. Her long hair, perhaps in consequence of having been braided and wound in heavy plaits around her head, was less changed by the salts of the soil than that of her husband, and was black, and in some places lustrous. She had evidently been proud of her hair, for in one hand she held a comb, rude as compared with some modern contrivances of the same sort, made by setting what I took to be the bony parts, the rays, of fishes' fins in a slip of the hard, woody part of the dwarf palm tree, into which they were not only tightly cemented but firmly bound. In her other hand were the remains of a fan, with a cane handle, from the upper points of which radiated the gayest, but not much faded feathers of parrots and humming-birds.

Around her neck, as befitting the wife of a fisherman, was a triple necklace of shells, bright once, perhaps, but dim in color, and exfoliating layer after layer when exposed to light and air. Resting between her body and bent-up knees were several small domestic implements, among them an ancient spindle for spinning cotton, half covered with spun thread, which connected with a mass of the raw cotton, as if death had overtaken the matron with her last task of industry in life but half finished. I give a cut of the primitive spinning apparatus, which consisted of a section of the stalk of the quinua, half as large as the little finger, and eight inches long, its lower end fitted through a whirl-bob of stone, to give it momentum when set in motion by a twirl of the forefinger and thumb grasping a point of hard wood stuck in the upper end of the spindle. The contrivance is precisely the same with that in universal use by the Indian women of the present day. Only I have seen a small lime, lemon, or potato with a quinua stalk stuck through it, and instead of the ancient stone or earthen whirl-bob.

But one of the most interesting articles found with the matron of Pachacamac, was a kind of wallet, if I can so describe it, composed of two distinct pieces of thick cotton cloth of different colors, ten inches long, by five broad, the lower end of each terminating in a fringe, and the upper end at each corner in a long braid, the braids of both being again braided together. These cloths, placed together, were carefully folded up and tied by the braids. I have this moment opened the packet, and find it to contain some kernels of the large lupin, sometimes called "Lima beans" a few pods of cotton, gathered evidently before maturity, the husks being still on, some fragments of an ornament of thin silver, and two little thin disks of the same material, three-tenths of an inch in diameter, each pierced with a small hole near the edge, too minute for ornament apparently, and possibly used as a coin. Also some tiny beads of chalcedony, scarcely an eighth of an inch in diameter. Placed under the chin of the matron were the beans to feed her on the way to the realms of the god Pachacamac, and the silver disks to propitiate the fiends and monsters which the Indian imagination pictures as obstructing the passage of the dead from earth to heaven. Who knows?

But I cannot stop to describe all the various articles of feminine use or adornment found with the mother of the family which disappeared, it may be, a thousand years before Pizzaro put his foot on the soil we are now turning up, and possibly while Our Saviour trod the shores of Galilee!

The body of the daughter, as I assume her to have been, was peculiar in position, having been seated on a kind of workbox of braided reeds, with a cover hinged on one side and shutting down and fastening on the other, exactly as similar boxes do today. It was about eighteen inches long, fourteen wide, and eight deep, and contained a greater and more interesting variety of articles than I ever found together in any grave of the Aborigines. I suspect the girl had died before the mother, for there were grouped together in her workbox (if I may so call it) things childish, and things showing approach to maturity, but nothing womanly. There were rude specimens of knitting — little strips, coarse and awkward, with places showing where stitches had been "dropped," all carefully folded up, as if to mark stages of progress in the mysteries of textile art. There were mites of spindles and implements for weaving, and braids of thread of irregular thickness, kept as if for sake of contrast with others larger and nicely wound, with a finer and more even thread. There were skeins; oh, yes, quite as well done up as those that you, fair reader, buy today in the silk mercer's, and perhaps, one day long ago, as gay in color. There were "spools" too (that's what I believe you call them), only they were not made after the fashion you are accustomed to see. They were not round, and very thick of wood inside as yours are, but composed of two splints placed across each other at right angles, and the thread wound "in and out" between them. There were also woven strips of cloth, some wide, some narrow, and some of two and even three colors. Then there were pouches, plain and variegated, of different sizes, and all woven or knitted (I confess myself unable to say which — like the garment spoken of in the Testament, "without seam." There were also needles of bone and of bronze; I would figure one of the latter, only it would be too like our modern bodkin. A fan, smaller and more delicate, and I should say — for the centuries maltreat colors — gayer in tint than that of the mother, was also stored away in the box. A comb, a little bronze knife, and some other articles, which I will not attempt to enumerate. Only I will say that there were several sections of the hollow bones of the pelican or other large water-birds, each carefully stopped by a wad of cotton, and containing pigments of various colors. I assumed at first that all were intended for dyes of the various cotton textures we had discovered, but I became doubtful as to the roseate or pink when I found a curious contrivance, made of the finest cotton, and represented in the engraving, which my wife's hairdresser says is "A DAB" (if anybody knows what that is), and "intended for the diffusion of bloom over the human countenance." So the little coquette of Pachacamac "painted," perhaps to attract the attention of some of her father's fishermen acquaintances, it may be apprentices! It is not to be supposed he had a coachman!

Yes, she certainly painted, for here, by the side of her novel cosmetic boxes, we find a contrivance for rubbing or grinding the pigments they contain to the requisite fineness for use! It is a small oblong stone, with a cup-shaped hollow on the upper side, in which fits a little, round stone ball, answering the purpose of a pestle or crusher.

They did not have glass mirrors in those ancient days of Pachacamac, but they polished plates of bronze and silver, wherein the women admired themselves. The girl at Pachacamac was perhaps too poor to have one of these; she had, however, a substitute in a piece of iron pyrites, resembling the half of an egg, with the plane side highly polished.

There were many other curious things in the poor, withered girl's work-box, but among them, I dare say, none she prized in life more than a little badly-crushed ornament of gold, evidently intended to represent a butterfly, but so thin and delicate that it comes in pieces and loses form when we attempt to handle it. There was also a netting instrument of hard wood, not unlike those now in use, indicating that, like a good daughter, the girl of Pachacamac helped make nets for her father.

The envelopes of the mummy of the girl were similar to those that enshrouded her mother. There were but few articles around her person. Her hair was braided and plaited around her forehead, around which, also, was a cincture of white cloth, ornamented with little silver spangles; a thin narrow bracelet of the same metal still hung on the shrunken arm, and between her feet was the dried body of a parrot — brought perhaps from the distant Amazonian valleys, and which had been her pet in life. There was nothing of special interest surrounding the body of the boy; but bound tightly around his forehead was his sling, finely braided from cotton threads.

The body of the infant, a girl, had been tenderly imbedded in the fleece of the alpaca, then wrapped in fine cotton cloth and placed in a strangely braided sack of rushes, with handles or loops at each end, as if for carrying it. I cannot resist the impression that the little corpse had been suspended for a time in the house of the fisherman, before being placed in the family tomb. The only article found with this tiny body was a sea-shell containing pebbles, the orifice closed with a hard pitch-like substance. It was the child's rattle.

Beside the bodies, there were a number of utensils, and other articles, in the vault. Among them half a dozen earthen jars, pans, and pots of various sizes and ordinary form. One or two were still encrusted with the soot of the fires over which they had been used. Every one contained something. One was filled with ground nuts, familiar to use as peanuts; another, maize etc., all except the latter in a carbonized condition.

Besides these articles, there were also some others, illustrating the religious notions of the occupants of the ancient tomb, and affording us scant but, as they go, certain ideas of the ancient faith and worship. This article, however, is too long already, and I must reserve their description for another time, if not another place, feeling sure, in the interval, that what we have seen of the implements and arts, and deduced as regards the practices, of the ancient inhabitants of Pachacamac, will furnish another proof of the accuracy of Mr. Lincoln's quaint averment that "there is and always was a good deal of human nature in mankind." It is clear that human wants and vanities are and ever were the same, and were met, more or less rudely, in like manner.

CONTENTS OF THE PERUVIAN GIRL'S WORKBOX.

PATTERN OF BLANKET.

ANCIENT WALLET, FROM PACHACAMAC. UNFOLDED.

FIGURES ON COTTON SHROUD.

POTTERY FROM PACHACAMAC.

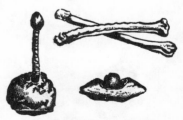

THE PACHACAMAC GIRL'S MYSTERIES.

215

SLING OF THE BOY OF PACHACAMAC.

ANCIENT PERUVIAN SPINDLE.

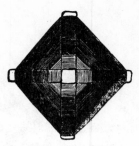

A SPOOL OF THREAD FROM PACHA-CAMAC.

SKEIN OF THREAD FROM PACHACAMAC.

NETTING INSTRUMENT, PACHACAMAC.

PARROT OF THE GIRL OF PA-CHACAMAC.

THE BABY'S COFFIN, PACHA-CAMAC.

THE FISHERMAN'S TWEEZERS.

ANCIENT WALLET, PA-CHACAMAC, FOLDED.

VASE FROM PA-CHACAMAC.

PLAN OF A TENEMENT-HOUSE IN PACHACAMAC.

A PERUVIAN MUMMY.

# THE INCA OCCUPATION OF THE SOUTH COAST OF PERU

## DOROTHY MENZEL

THE OVERWHELMING MAJORITY of historical documents dealing with Inca history and culture refer to events and conditions around Cuzco, the Inca capital. If we are interested in the cultural situation which the Incas found in the provinces they conquered and in the effect which their rule had on it we are lucky to find a few scraps of information on any one area. Archaeological investigations, on the other hand, can throw a flood of light on such problems. The possibilities can be illustrated from recent work on the south coast of Peru.

The part of the south coast with which we are concerned in this paper is the area between Chincha and Yauca; in terms of modern political units, the whole of the Department of Ica and the western extremity of the Department of Arequipa. This area is a desert plain with some low hills, crossed by a series of rivers which make irrigation-farming possible. From northwest to southeast the river valleys are Chincha, Pisco, Ica, Nasca, Acarí, and Yauca. Nasca is not a single valley unit like the others, however; it forks into several nearly parallel ravines of which the largest are Huayurí, Río Grande-Palpa, Ingenio (called Collao in ancient times), Nasca proper (the ancient Caxamarca), Taruga, and Poroma. Due to peculiarities of the local topography, the irrigated areas in Ica and the ravines of Nasca are located inland, at the foot of the mountains, rather than at the mouths of the rivers as is more usual in Peruvian coastal valleys.

No sharp natural or cultural boundary separates the valley of Chincha from the valleys of Cañete (ancient Huarco and Runahuana), Asia, and Mala, the next valleys going up the coast to the northwest. At the other end of the area we are considering, however, there is a sharp break; beyond Yauca the Andean foot-hills reach out to the sea, natural conditions are quite different, and there are important differences in the archaeological picture as well.

The historical sources which mention the south coast are not particularly helpful, except in so far as they provide us with a few dates. To begin with, no chronicler gives an explicit account of the political organization of the south coast at the time it came into contact with the Incas. It can, perhaps, be inferred from Cabello Balboa's statements about common policy toward the Inca invaders that there was some sort of political connection between the valleys of Mala, Cañete, and Chincha, but the connection need have been no more than a temporary military alliance. Cabello makes no mention at all of Pisco. The valleys of Ica, Nasca, and

Reprinted from SOUTHWESTERN JOURNAL OF ANTHROPOLOGY, vol. 15, No. 2, 1959. pp. 125–142.

Acarí are named together, but perhaps only because they offered no serious re-sistance to the Incas.[1] The authors of the *Relación de Chincha* of 1558 state that the valleys of Cañete, Chincha, and Ica each had its own ruler at the time of the Inca conquest, but no further details are given.[2]

The south coast had its first contact with the Incas early in the reign of Pachakuti (1438-1471) when, following the successful outcome of the Chanca War, the Inca ruler dispatched a raiding party under his brother, Qhapaq Yupanki, to visit the south coast valleys. The tradition of this contact was preserved at Chincha.[3] This event probably took place about 1440 according to Cabello Balboa's chronology.[4] No permanent conquests resulted from this raid, however.

The attention of the Inca rulers was distracted by campaigning in the north and around Lake Titicaca, and it was not until after Thupa Inka's expedition to Chile that a serious attempt was made to subjugate the south coast valleys. The conquest is described briefly by Cieza de León, Cabello Balboa, and Castro and Ortega Morejón. These authors agree that Ica, Nasca, and Acarí submitted peace-fully, but there is some disagreement in the native tradition regarding the conquest of Chincha. Cieza says that the people of Chincha and the Incas of Cuzco were in agreement that Chincha also submitted peacefully, but that people from some of the other provinces claimed that the Chincha valley resisted. This latter tradition is reflected by Cabello.[5] According to Cabello Balboa's chronology, the conquest must have taken place about 1476.[6]

Direct Inca rule came to an end on the south coast in 1534, when Pizarro dispatched a party to found a Spanish settlement at Zangalla in the valley of Pisco, a place now known as Lima la Vieja, and granted the natives of the region in encomienda to the settlers of the new town. The town was abandoned when Lima was founded early in the following year, but the encomienda system was not interrupted.

This brief outline includes virtually all of the specific information about Inca rule on the south coast which can be gleaned from the historical sources. Now let us turn to the archaeological record and look for evidence reflecting the impact

---

1 Cabello Balboa, pt. 3, ch. xvii; 1945, p. 320.

2 Castro and Ortega Morejón, 1936, p. 236.

3 Cieza de León, pt. 1, ch. lxxiv; 1922, p. 247; pt. 2, ch. lix; 1943, p. 272; Castro and Ortega Morejón, 1936, p. 237.

4 Rowe, 1945, pp. 270, 279.

5 Cieza de León, pt. 2, ch. lix; 1943, pp. 273-274; Castro and Ortega Morejón, 1936, p. 237; Cabello Balboa, pt. 3, ch. xviii; 1945, p. 320.

6 Rowe, 1945, pp. 271-272, 279.

which Inca culture had on the area and the degree to which native traditions survived the brief period of Inca rule. The data available at present include the results of intensive studies of the Uhle collections from cemeteries in Chincha and Ica, preserved in the University of California Museum of Anthropology, information collected as part of the program of the Fourth University of California Archaeological Expedition to Peru in 1954-55, and subsequent survey work by a number of workers.[7] The information so far assembled refers principally to architecture and pottery. It is far from complete, but there is enough to permit some useful interpretations.

## ARCHITECTURE

Among the occupation sites of the Late Horizon, the period of Inca rule on the south coast, it is possible to distinguish a group of ruins which, because of their peculiarities of plan and construction and their association with Inca pottery, can be identified as centers of imperial administration. Most other Late Horizon habitation sites on the south coast show little or no evidence of Inca influence and belong rather in the native cultural tradition of the valley in which they are found. This contrast suggests a promising line of investigation.

The Inca administrative center in the Chincha valley appears to be a building complex which forms part of the site of La Centinela, near Tambo de Mora.[8] La Centinela is an extensive group of ruins of tapia construction in the native Chincha tradition, and much of it was probably built before the Inca conquest. It is the largest and most imposing site in the valley, and Dwight T. Wallace discovered in 1958 that it was the hub of a system of straight roads radiating across the valley. The pattern of building complexes and roads attributable to the native tradition in Late Intermediate Period and Late Horizon times suggests that Chincha had a highly centralized administration before the Incas came, and that the Incas took over the native capital and administrative machinery when they conquered Chincha.

The situation in Pisco is somewhat different. There are at least two big Inca sites in this valley, Lima la Vieja, below the modern town of Humay, and Tambo

7 My participation in the program of the Fourth University of California Archaeological Expedition to Peru in 1954-55 was financed in part by a grant made by the Wenner-Gren Foundation for Anthropological Research for expedition expenses and in part by Mr Victor W. Von Hagen's Inca Highway Expedition. Another field trip in 1958 was made possible by a grant from the American Philosophical Society. This support is gratefully acknowledged. I want to express my thanks to Francis A. Riddell, David A. Robinson, Dwight T. Wallace, John H. Rowe, and Seth Leacock for unpublished information on south coast archaeology, and to John H. Rowe and Eugene A. Hammel for advice in the preparation of this paper.

8 Uhle, 1924, pp. 70-80, plates 1-4; Lothrop, 1926.

Colorado above it, and neither is associated with buildings in the native tradition comparable to those of La Centinela.[9] The archaeological evidence suggests that the Incas administered this valley in a series of separate units, and the situation may reflect a lack of centralized administration before the Incas came.

In the Ica valley, the center of Inca administration seems to have been the site of Old Ica in the *pago de Tacaraca* about 10 km south of the modern city of Ica. Old Ica is a dispersed cluster of monumental buildings, many built on mounds or raised platforms, with little or no evidence of habitation in the spaces between them. The pottery associated with the buildings of Old Ica suggests that construction of the site started not later than the beginning of the Late Intermediate Period. The site is the most imposing one in the valley, and it was probably the capital of Ica at the time of the Inca conquest. In one section of Old Ica there was apparently an Inca building complex, identifiable by construction details and surface sherds. At Soniche, one of the cemeteries adjacent to the site of Old Ica, Uhle excavated a number of elaborate burials of the Inca period containing a wealth of imported objects. Elsewhere in the Ica valley traces of Inca occupation are very scarce.

In the ravines of Nasca two major Inca centers have been identified. One is the Tambo de Collao, in the ravine of Ingenio, and the other is Paredones, the ancient Caxamarca, on the opposite side of the river from the present town of Nasca. Neither of these sites is associated with a major occupation referable to the native tradition. Further survey work in the Nasca drainage may lead to the identification of other Inca centers.

In Acarí the Inca administrative center was at Tambo Viejo (Old Acarí), 3 km south of the modern town. The Inca building complex at Tambo Viejo was built on top of the ruins of a very extensive walled town dating from the early part of the Early Intermediate Period (Nasca 3). There is no evidence for any really imposing late site of the native tradition anywhere in the valley which might have served as the capital of a centralized government before the Inca conquest.

In Yauca the Inca center was at the Tambo de Jaqui on the Hacienda Lampilla. Again it is not associated with any major construction in the native tradition.

The available archaeological evidence, therefore, suggests that the valleys of Chincha and Ica had some pattern of centralized authority at the time of the Inca invasion and that the other valleys did not. The evidence for centralized government is very strong in Chincha and less so in Ica, where the site of Old Ica could have been a center of religious rather than political authority, because the major

---

9 For plans and photographs of Tambo Colorado see Urteaga, 1939, and Kroeber, 1944, plates 18-20.

structures are on artificial mounds. The Incas took advantage of native centralization where it existed, constructing their own administrative headquarters in the native capital; elsewhere they established a new center, sometimes, as in the case of Acarí, taking advantage of an abandoned site which had dominated the valley in much earlier times.

The building complexes identified as Inca administrative centers share a number of distinctive features of plan and construction, although no two are exactly alike. The most obvious common feature is the arrangement of substantial buildings of rectangular plan around a plaza. It is a formal layout, formal in the sense that it was laid out on a preconceived plan. It is possible that excavations at Chincha would reveal that some of the late sites in the local tradition were also built on a regular plan, but elsewhere on the south coast the plans of sites in the native tradition are far less regular than those of Inca sites.

The central plaza in the Inca centers varies from rectangular to trapezoidal. On one side is a large rectangular building consisting of a complex of small rooms and enclosed courts built with special care and often having special decorative features, such as niches or wall painting. Less elaborate buildings may be found on the other sides of the plaza, but one side is often left open. There is a low platform in front of the principal building unit, and sometimes on other sides of the plaza as well. The principal building is built on a slope on the uphill side of the plaza at Tambo Colorado, Tambo de Collao, and Paredones; at Tambo Viejo and Tambo de Jaqui it is set on the edge of a bluff overlooking the river. At Tambo Viejo another principal building is built on a raised platform, and the Inca highway led directly to it.

A certain type of large rectangular adobe with a smooth surface is used in varying amounts in the construction of all the formal Inca centers. These adobes differ in shape, size, and temper from Inca adobes in the highlands, so it must be supposed that the Incas derived the coastal form from some local tradition. The architecture of Chincha is unlikely to have served the Incas as a model, since the prevailing construction material at Chincha was tapia. If the coast type of Inca adobe was derived from any south coast tradition Ica is the best candidate, for rectangular adobes were used in the construction of Late Intermediate Period sites in Ica which were not occupied in the Late Horizon. The Ica tradition adobes are less regular than the Inca ones, however, and are laid up with more clay between the courses.

The use of adobes in Inca buildings on the south coast did not preclude the use of other construction materials as well, especially field stones from the vicinity of the respective sites, used mainly for foundations. Cobbles from the adjacent river bed were used at Tambo Viejo in Acarí. Dressed stone construction in the Inca style is very rare on the coast, but some dressed stone was used in wall foundations at Paredones. On the whole, the proportion of adobes used is highest in the more elaborately decorated buildings.

Inca architecture on the south coast shows expectable parallels with Inca adobe construction in the Cuzco area, but there are also some interesting differences. The coast buildings share with the highland ones the use of adobes on stone foundations, lintels of wooden beams covered with braided rope, battered supporting walls, trapezoidal niches and doorways, and plastered wall surfaces. The first Spanish invaders reported seeing painted adobe walls at Cuzco, and some paint is preserved on the walls of Inca buildings on the coast. The walls of Tambo Colorado are extensively painted in red and yellow, while one room of the principal Inca building at La Centinela has the remnants of a fine Inca geometric design painted in black and red on white. On the coast, as in the sierra, Inca buildings consist characteristically of groups of connecting rooms which have only a single common access to the outside for each group. On the other hand, gable roofs, which are common in the sierra, do not occur on the south coast, and there is a frieze of adobe reliefs at Tambo Colorado which has no known sierra prototype.

Our best information about the relationship of the Inca administrative centers to contemporary settlements of the native tradition comes from the valley of Acarí, where several native settlements dating to the Late Horizon were explored by the University of California expedition in 1954. Three important foci of native settlement were located in this valley. One of these foci consists of four clusters of houses scattered on the plain within 500 meters of the Inca administrative center at Tambo Viejo. Only low wall foundations of river cobbles remain. These foundations outline small courtyards surrounded by smaller rooms and storage pits in irregular fashion, some of the units being separated by narrow alleys. The upper walls of the houses were probably made of matting or of wattle and daub, the common construction materials used today for dwellings in this area. The arrangement of these four clusters of houses suggests that they were satellite communities of the Inca center, established to provide convenient sources of labor for the representatives of the Inca government. No larger building such as one might expect a native noble to have occupied is found in these clusters. The second major focus of native settlement is the site of Sahuacarí, located on a steep slope on the edge of the valley across the river and slightly above Tambo Viejo. Sahuacarí is built on terraces and consists of compounds of rectangular houses of varying sizes and narrow rectangular storage bins. The compounds are separated at intervals by narrow streets. The walls are built of angular field stones laid in mud, and some of them are preserved to their original height of two to three meters. Some of the houses have small interior niches and pegs protruding from the walls, features which strongly suggest Inca influence. The third major native site is Otaparo, located on a prominent hill about 20 km up-valley from Tambo Viejo. The buildings at Otaparo are poorly preserved, and only the stone foundations can be traced. The pottery, however, indicates that the site belongs to the period of Inca occupation. Both Sahuacarí and Otaparo are more ambitious settlements than the clusters of houses near Tambo Viejo, but neither has any truly monumental buildings.

The settlement pattern situation in Acarí may be summarized as follows. There was no monumental site built in the native tradition comparable to La Centinela in Chincha and Old Ica. Sahuacarí and Otaparo, the largest concentrated native settlements, are no more than good sized villages, without imposing monumental buildings. The Inca administrative center appears to have attracted some local people who were settled in four hamlets around it.

The clustering of informal settlement units around an Inca administrative center is found only at Acarí. In the other valleys, native villages are not directly associated with the Inca centers, and the native tradition of settlement pattern and domestic architecture survived without any traceable Inca influence. In each valley the situation is different in detail, however, as the native traditions differed in type of site preferred, arrangement of buildings, and construction methods. In Chincha, Pisco, and Ica there were also monumental structures of the native tradition, but it is not yet clear whether all of them simply survived from before the Inca conquest, or whether new ones were built in the period of Inca rule. Comparable monumental structures in the native tradition have not been reported from Nasca and Yauca, as they have not been found in Acarí.

## POTTERY

At the time of the Inca conquest there were four native styles of pottery in the south coast area with which we are concerned: Chincha, Ica, Poroma, and Acarí. There were, that is, fewer separate traditions of pottery than there were valleys.

The Chincha style had its home in the valley of Chincha. It seems to have been more closely related to the style of Cañete than to other south coast styles, although it traded some influences with the style of Ica. Occasional imports from Chincha are found in Pisco, and imitations of Chincha vessels occur in Ica.

The Ica style was the most highly decorated style in the south coast area and, at the same time, the one which had the most influence on other styles.[10] It was the

---

10 Menzel, ms.

style not only of the Ica valley but of the valley of Pisco and the ravine of Huayurí as well. In the Late Horizon two regional variants developed in the Ica style. One of the variants is found in the main part of the valley of Ica, down to Ocucaje, and in Pisco; the other is found at Cayango and other parts of the Ica valley below Ocucaje and in Huayurí. Ica pottery was imitated in Inca times as far north as Chincha and as far south as Acarí at least.

Poroma is the name given to the Late Intermediate Period and Late Horizon style found in the ravines of Nasca south of Huayurí. It is best known from collections made in the ravine of Nasca, and it might appropriately be called Nasca except for the fact that this name is already in use for an earlier style.

The Acarí style is found in the valleys of Acarí and Yauca, and occasional trade pieces turn up even farther south. This style is obviously related to the Poroma style, though not identical to it.

Our information is not sufficiently complete to permit an equally thorough analysis of the effect of Inca rule on all four of these local south coast styles. We have the most detailed chronology and the best record of archaeological associations for the Ica tradition, some information of this sort for Acarí and Chincha, and very little for the Poroma tradition. It will be convenient to discuss the four situations in the order of the completeness of the record rather than in their geographical order. We begin, therefore, with Ica.

The Uhle collection from Ica in the University of California Museum of Anthropology includes lots of material from four burials representing the period just before the Inca conquest, thirteen which can be dated to the period of Inca rule, and ten burials of the early Colonial Period, some of which contain Spanish glass trade beads. On the basis of the grave associations in these burials, Ica pottery of the native tradition can be sorted into three stylistic phases, each one corresponding to one of the time periods represented by the graves. The pre-Inca phase is named Soniche, after the principal cemetery at Old Ica which Uhle excavated, the phase corresponding to the Inca occupation is called Tacaraca A, and the early Colonial phase is called Tacaraca B.

In the burials corresponding to the period of Inca rule three additional types of pottery, more or less foreign to the native tradition, may be found alongside of pottery of the Tacaraca A phase. These three additional types are:

1. Inca style, including some examples so characteristic of the Inca tradition that they are probably imports from the Cuzco area and others which are certainly local imitations of vessels of Cuzco type.

2. Ica-Inca style, a peculiar style of local manufacture which includes some Inca features and, rarely, some derived from the Ica tradition. Most of its features,

however, cannot be traced to antecedents in either tradition. There are two common shapes, a barrel shaped jar[11] and a small flat-bottomed bottle with a loop handle.[12] Inca influence can be traced in the handles and spouts of these vessels but is largely absent in the painted designs. The designs have only vague antecedents in the Ica tradition, and thus represent essentially new creations. The Ica-Inca style, more than any other, characterizes the period of Inca rule at Ica, and Ica-Inca design elements are occasionally found on local imitations of Inca vessels and on vessels of the native Tacaraca A style.

In addition to the characteristic jar and bottle, there is a type of plate which, in the Ica valley, has much the same relation to the Ica and Inca traditions of pottery-making that the containers do. This plate has a standardized shape and is usually decorated with a painted bird design, for which reason the name "bird plate" seems appropriate. As far as its associations in Ica are concerned, the bird plate can be treated as simply a third Ica-Inca vessel type. It has a different distribution pattern from that of the Ica-Inca jar and bottle on the rest of the south coast, however.

3. Chimu style, either in the form of specimens imported from the north coast or as local imitations. The commonest Chimu style specimens are double-bodied whistling jars of smoked blackware with modelled bird heads at the top of the spouts. These vessels are usually found in pairs, one pair to a tomb. Blackware stirrup-spout bottles are also found.

There are some interesting differences in construction and contents among the burials of the Inca period excavated by Uhle at Ica. Some of the burials are large and carefully arranged, with an abundance of grave goods, including objects such as gold and silver ornaments and, in one case, a wooden stool, which is known from historical sources to have been a symbol of rank the use of which was restricted by the Incas to the higher nobility. Other burials are smaller and more informal and lack known symbols of rank. Pottery belonging to the Inca, Ica-Inca, and Chimu styles is concentrated in the larger and more elaborate tombs, although these usually also contain some Tacaraca A specimens; the smaller tombs may contain Tacaraca A style vessels only, or sometimes a mixture of Tacaraca A and Ica-Inca pieces. The concentration of exotic pottery in the larger tombs is impressive. As many as half the vessels in a large grave lot may be Inca and another third Ica-Inca style.

Surface collections from habitation sites in the Ica valley give quite a different picture. Inca and Ica-Inca sherds are concentrated in the section of Old Ica which

---

11 Kroeber and Strong, 1924b, pl. 38, d-f; pl. 39, a, e.
12 *Idem,* pl. 40, e, n.

served as the Inca administrative center. Elsewhere they are very rare, and most of the small habitation sites of the period of Inca rule yield pure Tacaraca A sherds.

The burials of the early Colonial Period present a marked contrast to those of the period of Inca occupation. The early Colonial burials are noticeably poorer, both in luxury goods and in numbers of pottery vessels. Inca influences are completely absent from the pottery. No Inca or Ica-Inca vessels occur in these burials, the only pottery found belonging to the Tacaraca B phase of the native Ica tradition. At the same time, the only sign of Spanish influence takes the form of rare trade beads. The Tacaraca B style is in part an expectable development out of Tacaraca A, but it also includes the deliberate revival of many features of the Soniche style which are absent from pottery of the intervening Inca period. In many respects, Tacaraca B pottery looks more like Soniche pottery than Tacaraca A does, a situation which has created understandable difficulties in earlier interpretations of the Ica evidence, including Uhle's.

The evidence of pottery in the Ica valley, then, suggests that direct Inca influence after the Inca conquest was felt most strongly in the upper ranks of the native nobility and in the immediate vicinity of the Inca administrative center. Among the ordinary inhabitants of Ica and in the settlements more remote from the Inca control point there is as little sign of Inca influence in pottery as there is in architecture. The potters working for the nobility, however, not only imitated Inca vessels directly but developed a new and original style of their own which owes remarkably little to the earlier native tradition of Ica. After the Spanish conquest, all elements of decoration associated with Inca rule were swept away, and an attempt was made to return to the "pure" native style. The fact that the Inca dominion had only lasted for about sixty years probably facilitated this striking reaction.

The archaeological associations in which the various styles of pottery are found in the Ica valley permit some inferences regarding prestige differences between the styles. During the period of Inca rule, the Inca style had, as we might expect, the highest prestige at Ica, a prestige inferable from its associations with the nobility and the imitation of Inca decorative features in the locally made styles. The Ica-Inca style was next in prestige, to judge from its abundance in the richer burials. The fact that the Ica-Inca style was eliminated at the time of the Spanish conquest in the same way as the Inca style suggests that the prestige of Ica-Inca pottery was closely related to Inca prestige in spite of the fact that the Ica-Inca style was essentially a local creation. The Chimu style vessels found in the tombs were imports ranking with Ica-Inca pottery in prestige at Ica. The native Ica tradition had the lowest prestige in the society of the capital but maintained its strength in the rural areas.

The pattern of distribution of pottery styles in Inca period Ica fits the normal pattern of distribution of customs in a social hierarchy, that is, that radically new features are taken in at the top of the hierarchy, while more conservative ones persist among people at the bottom, with rural areas associated with the lowest levels of the hierarchy. There is thus clear archaeological evidence for the existence of a fairly elaborate social hierarchy at Ica in the period of Inca rule.

The distribution of Ica valley pottery styles elsewhere on the south coast during the period of Inca occupation also offers some points of interest. Ica-Inca fragments are rare, but they do occur in Chincha and other valleys near Ica. Vessels of Cuzco Inca shape with Ica-Inca designs are not uncommon in museum collections and are said to come from a number of other places besides Ica. Occasional specimens in the Ica-Inca style may have been traded even more widely, for there is a small jar in the Bandelier Collection in the American Museum of Natural History in New York which is supposed to come from the Lake Titicaca area.

While Ica-Inca jars and bottles are not common outside of the Ica valley, bird plates are found in the Nasca region and in the valley of Acarí in about the same proportion as at Ica, and with no apparent stylistic variations. The bird plate has the same abrupt origin and Inca associations in these other valleys that it does in Ica.

Sherds representing vessels of the more traditional Tacaraca A style occur in small but regular percentages in the Chincha, Nasca, and Acarí valleys, and decorative traits derived from the Tacaraca A style are found as far south as the Chala area, although there in a very diluted form and mixed with a larger component of Inca influence. In the Nasca and Acarí valleys, too, traditional Tacaraca A shapes are often associated with Inca or Inca associated traits of paste, shape, and pigmentation.

In contrast to this occasional influence, there is one Tacaraca A vessel, a shallow dish (Dish C shape in the Ica classification), which is found as commonly at Nasca and Acarí as at Ica. It appears to have been incorporated into the respective local styles as a standard type. This dish shape is found in both painted redware and smoked blackware at Ica, while at Nasca and Acarí it occurs predominantly in smoked blackware. The details of its shape in the Late Horizon styles of the Nasca and Acarí valleys are such that it must have been newly diffused from Ica during the period of Inca rule and could not have developed independently in the southern valleys from some variety which diffused earlier. The Dish C shape is not associated with Inca traits, either at Ica or elsewhere.

These distributions and associations convey the impression that, north and south of Ica, all Ica-made pottery, even the native Tacaraca A style which has the lowest prestige associations at Ica, enjoyed some prestige. There is abundant evidence that the previous phase of the Ica pottery tradition had a very influential relation to its neighbors in the period just preceding the Inca conquest, so the Inca period situation is in part simply a continuation of something much older. Except in the case of the adoption of the Dish C shape, the evidence suggests that the prestige of Ica pottery was in some way associated with Inca prestige. There is no historical evidence which might help to explain this situation. We can only speculate that the Incas accorded Ica some sort of preferential treatment in the south coast area, perhaps subordinating their administration of some of the other valleys to a governor at Ica, as the Spanish conquerors did later, or using the Ica nobility as agents in other valleys.

Next to Ica, our fullest evidence for Inca period pottery comes from the valley of Acarí. The evidence is not precisely comparable to that from Ica, because no tombs of the Inca period have been excavated at Acarí. The evidence in the latter valley comes rather from excavations in the midden at the Inca administrative center of Tambo Viejo, conducted by Francis A. Riddell and me, and from surface collections at other sites.[13] In the excavations at Tambo Viejo an attempt was made to distinguish between the pottery of the Inca occupation and that of the early Colonial Period. No distinction could be drawn in the native pottery, in spite of the fact that the occupation of the site was continuous between the two periods and that a few artifacts of Spanish origin were found in the upper levels of the midden. Evidently there was no abrupt reaction to the fall of Inca power at Acarí such as we noted for Ica.

As noted earlier, Acarí had a native pottery tradition of its own, most closely related to Poroma, and this tradition continued into early Colonial times. The pottery in the native tradition is classified in two types, Acarí Polychrome and Otaparo Polychrome, neither of which shows any significant Inca influence.

Pure Cuzco Inca pottery and local imitations of it occur in small proportions in all parts of the Inca period site at Tambo Viejo but are very rare elsewhere in the valley. The local imitations are considerably more common than the actual imports.

Acarí has an original local style corresponding in its relations to other styles to the Ica-Inca pottery of the Ica valley. It can appropriately be called Acarí-Inca. The most common type of Acarí-Inca pottery is Sahuacarí Polychrome, and it includes a jar shape and a plate. The painted designs of Sahuacarí Polychrome

13 Rowe, 1956, pp. 137-138.

include a number of features which have no immediate local antecedents. One is a checkerboard design which resembles a Qoripata Polychrome pattern at Cuzco.[14] Another common feature is a ball band design which is derived from the Poroma tradition.[15] Then there is a dotted horseshoe design identical with a pattern found on Middle Horizon pottery in the Acarí valley but not occurring in other later styles. Another new design is an eight-pointed star which seems to be borrowed from the pottery tradition of the Ocoña and Majes valleys far to the south. Sahuacarí Polychrome is thus a remarkably eclectic style.

As noted earlier, the bird plate is also common at Acarí, where it is associated with the Acarí-Inca style more or less the way it is associated with Ica-Inca in the Ica valley.

There is another peculiar complex of features at Acarí in the period of Inca rule which is closely associated with Inca influence without being a direct imitation of Cuzco models. The complex consists of a peculiar type of white paste with very fine crystalline white temper and occasional fine reddish specks in it, and a series of painted designs, notably a catfish design which seems to be at home in the Titicaca basin. The white paste also suggests a relationship with the Titicaca area, for white paste is a characteristic of the Inca-associated Taraco Polychrome style in Puno.[16] At Acarí and Nasca white paste is very often used for bird plates, and sometimes it is the base for Inca and Acarí-Inca vessels and for Acarí imitations of the Tacaraca A style. The catfish design is found on Ica tradition shapes at Ica as well, but no white paste specimens have yet turned up in the Ica valley.

The distribution of the Acarí styles of the Inca period does not exactly parallel the distribution of the styles of Ica. Acarí Polychrome is the most abundant type and is found all over the Acarí valley and also occasionally in the Nasca drainage and at Chala. Otaparo Polychrome is less abundant but is also found all over Acarí and sometimes in the Nasca drainage. Acarí-Inca pottery, including Sahuacarí Polychrome and bird plates, is not restricted to the Inca administrative center, the way Ica-Inca pottery is in Ica. It is found in small percentages on most of the Inca period sites in the Acarí valley and is not concentrated at any one particular site. However, it has not been found in the Nasca drainage or anywhere south of Yauca.

The distribution of Acarí pottery styles suggests that Acarí had a relatively modest prestige position among the south coast valleys in Inca times, and that it had a less elaborate social hierarchy than Ica. Inca influence was probably no greater than at Ica, but it seems to have been somewhat more evenly distributed through the population.

---

14 Rowe, 1944, p. 48-49.
15 Robinson, ms.                                    16 Tschopik, 1946, pp. 31-32.

The principal evidence for Chincha pottery in the period with which we are concerned is still furnished by the collections made by Max Uhle at the turn of the century as a result of his excavations in Chincha cemeteries.[17] The pottery from Uhle's excavations which belongs to the native tradition of Chincha can be separated into two stylistic units which, for the purposes of this discussion, we can call Chincha and Derived Chincha. The Chincha phase represents the phase of the local tradition which was flourishing at the time of the Inca conquest, while the Derived Chincha phase corresponds to the period of Inca rule and continues into early Colonial times. Derived Chincha pottery is associated in the graves dug by Uhle with imported Inca vessels, local imitations of Inca pieces, a Chincha-Inca style of composite origins, some Chimu style specimens, and a few imitations of Tacaraca A and Ica-Inca vessels.

The Chincha style of our discussion is Kroeber and Strong's Late Chincha I.[18] It is a highly characteristic local style including many well made and elaborately decorated pieces. The succeeding Derived Chincha pottery—no illustrations of which have been published—is an impoverished version of the Chincha style rather than a further development at about the same level of quality such as we noted at Ica. Derived Chincha vessels are relatively poorly made, and very few of them have painted designs. In the burials containing Derived Chincha vessels the more elaborate pieces are in other styles.

Chincha-Inca pottery is composed of a mixture of elements, including Inca influences and elements borrowed from other regional pottery styles, most notably, perhaps, from Pachacamac on the central coast. It may also include some older features from the Chincha tradition. The most common shapes are a small bottle[19] and a jar.[20] The Chincha-Inca style is a mixture of very much the same type as the Ica-Inca and Acarí-Inca styles which we have described.

Inca style pieces imported from Cuzco and local imitations of Inca pottery are so abundant in the graves dug by Uhle that Kroeber and Strong undertook to describe the Inca style on the basis of this collection.[21]

The Inca period cemeteries excavated by Uhle are all located in the immediate vicinity of La Centinela, the Inca administrative center, so they probably reflect the situation at the local capital. I have not had an opportunity to make the type of study of surface collections from other parts of Chincha on which reliable statements about distributions might be made. In spite of the area limitation, however, some interpretive observations may be made.

17 Kroeber and Strong, 1924a; Uhle, 1924.
18 Kroeber and Strong, 1924a, plates 11-12, fig. 6.
19 *Idem*, fig. 3a,b.
20 *Idem*, fig. 4c,d; fig. 9a,c,d.
21 *Idem*, pp. 9-16.

None of Uhle's tombs in the Chincha valley were as rich as the richest he dug in Ica. This fact does not mean that there were no very rich tombs in Chincha, of course; what it does mean is that our evidence probably relates to statuses farther down the social hierarchy than those at the top represented at Ica. In view of this fact the proportions of the styles in the Inca period graves is very remarkable. The Derived Chincha style represents only twenty percent of the total pottery found, while most of the rest consists of imitation Inca and Chincha-Inca specimens. Evidently the impact of the Inca conquest was more far reaching at La Centinela than at Old Ica. Inca influences penetrated down the hierarchy in greater strength, and the local pottery tradition lost more of its prestige. There was no anti-Inca reaction at the time of the Spanish conquest, either. There were Spanish glass beads in three of the burials excavated by Uhle, and their contents are not significantly different from those of the graves which lack evidence of Spanish contact.

The evidence for the Nasca drainage is especially meager. It consists chiefly of surface collections made at looted cemeteries and at a few habitation sites, plus observations made on whole vessels collected by Uhle in 1905 and Kroeber in 1926. There are no associations which permit chronological distinctions in the Poroma style and related materials. Nasca seems to have had the same range of styles and style mixtures which we noted for Acarí: its own native tradition, Inca style pieces, local combinations of Inca and other elements, and the widely distributed bird plate. We have also noted the presence of influences from Ica and Acarí.[22]

Even with our present unsatisfactory evidence for Nasca and the virtual absence of information for Pisco and Yauca, some general observations may be hazarded with respect to the reflection of cultural events in south coast pottery during the Inca occupation. In Chincha there seems to have been a very sharp break in the native pottery tradition about the time of the Inca conquest. Elsewhere, the local pottery traditions continued through the Inca period and into early Colonial times, the continuity being most marked in the small settlements away from the centers of Inca administration. At Ica the native tradition had such vitality that it became the basis for a spectacular artistic revival after the fall of Inca power, a revival which led to the purging of all features associated with Inca rule.

The Inca conquest brought some Cuzco pottery in trade to all of the south coast valleys, and Inca models were everywhere imitated by local potters. This fact could have been predicted without archaeological study. More interesting is the evidence for the development of a series of new eclectic styles. In each south coast

---

22 The fact that even this much information is available on the Nasca area we owe to the pioneer survey of David A. Robinson (ms.).

valley the local potters developed an original style which included some traditional elements, some Inca influences, an occasional feature borrowed from local pottery of centuries earlier, and traits from a variety of other areas, some apparently as far away as the Titicaca basin and Pachacamac on the central coast. All these new styles have much in common, but each is a distinctive combination of elements. These new styles were associated in people's minds with Inca rule and shared some of the prestige accorded to genuine Inca pottery.

## CONCLUSIONS

Archaeological data provide much new evidence regarding the significance of the Inca occupation on the south coast of Peru. We have reviewed the evidence of architecture and pottery in some detail and can now summarize the cultural information which we have extracted from it.

There seem to have been marked differences in social and political organization among the south coast valleys at the time they were conquered by the Incas. Chincha had a powerful centralized government, while Pisco was probably divided. Ica had a centralized organization of some kind, but we cannot be sure whether it was political or religious in nature. There was, however, a concentration of wealth and prestige at the site of Old Ica. Ica also had more cultural prestige than any of the other valleys, and its decorated pottery was sought and imitated throughout the whole area. There is no evidence now available suggesting centralization in the Nasca drainage. Acarí seems to have had no central authority and no point at which there was a concentration of prestige.

The Incas took advantage of existing centralization in Chincha and Ica, building their administrative centers at the focus of native authority. They probably ruled through the native nobility in both valleys. In the valleys in which there was no centralized authority already, the Incas imposed their own, constructing an administrative center at some convenient point to serve as the focus of Inca control. These administrative centers were located on the Inca coast road, a fact which emphasizes the military and administrative significance of the road system. No effort was made in this area to concentrate the population in towns, and existing patterns of settlement were not seriously interfered with. Even in the case of Acarí, where the Incas encouraged or permitted the settlement of some groups of natives near their administrative center, the native houses are in small separate clusters, not laid out on a regular plan.

Inca influence can be traced most widely in those valleys like Acarí where there was no native centralization to start with and no highly organized native nobility.

In contrast, in Ica the native nobility succeeded in monopolizing whatever "advantages" Inca rule may have brought to the valley, and little Inca influence seems to have filtered down to the ordinary farmer. The Ica nobility supported the Inca regime enthusiastically as long as it remained powerful. When it disintegrated, however, the nobles of Ica reacted against their Inca tradition with extraordinary violence, unparalleled elsewhere in the area studied.

The Inca conquest did not simply bring a mechanical addition of Cuzco influence to south coast culture. It led to some original developments in monumental architecture and in pottery. The architectural innovations are seen in the Inca administrative centers, which were probably built under the supervision of Inca architects; a more or less uniform "coast Inca" style was developed. The new developments in pottery are more spectacular and involve the creation of important new local styles. These styles combine elements gleaned from a wide variety of pottery traditions and some which were probably outright inventions. The mixture is different in each valley, however, a fact which suggests that the new styles were the work of local potters working more or less independently. It is possible that the development of these new styles was deliberately fostered by the Inca government as a means of weakening local loyalties symbolized by the earlier native traditions; at any rate, the new styles were closely associated with the prestige of the Inca regime.

The amount of new information on the cultural significance of the Inca occupation on the south coast which we have succeeded in extracting from the odds and ends of archaeological information now available suggests the remarkable possibilities which this type of study offers. Instead of lamenting the absence of written records in the Andean area, we have only to look closely at the abundant evidence which has survived from the past in the form of archaeological associations. The answers to many of our questions can be found in the ground.

## BIBLIOGRAPHY

CABELLO BALBOA, MIGUEL
    1945    *Miscelánea antártica* (Obras, vol. 1, pp. 91-443: Editorial Ecuatoriana, Quito).

CASTRO, CRISTÓBAL DE, AND DIEGO ORTEGA MOREJÓN
    1936    *Relacion y declaracion del modo que este valle de chincha y sus comarcanos se governavan Antes que oviese yngas y despues q(ue) los vuo hasta q(ue) los(christian)os e(n)traron en esta tierra* (Quellen zur Kulturgeschichte des präkolumbischen Amerika, herausgegeben von H. Trimborn, Studien zur Kulturkunde, 3 Band, pp. 236-246: Strecker und Schröder Verlag, Stuttgart).

CIEZA DE LEÓN, PEDRO DE
1922   *La crónica del Perú* (Los grandes viajes clásicos, no. 24: Calpe, Madrid).
1943   *Del señorio de los Incas*. Prólogo y notas de Alberto Mario Salas (Ediciones Argentinas "Solar," Buenos Aires).

KROEBER, ALFRED LOUIS
1944   *Peruvian Archaeology in 1942* (Viking Fund Publications in Anthropology, no. 4, New York).

KROEBER, ALFRED LOUIS, AND WILLIAM DUNCAN STRONG
1924a  *The Uhle Collections from Chincha* (University of California Publications in American Archaeology and Ethnology, vol. 21, no. 1, Berkeley).
1924b  *The Uhle Pottery Collections from Ica*. With three appendices by Max Uhle (University of California Publications in American Archaeology and Ethnology, vol. 21, no. 3, Berkely).

LOTHROP, SAMUEL KIRKLAND
1926   *La Centinela; an Inca Ruin on the Coast of Peru* (The Independent, vol. 116, no. 3944, Jan. 2, pp. 13-16, Concord, N. H.).

MENZEL, DOROTHY
ms.    *The Late Ica Pottery of Ancient Peru* (Ph.D. dissertation in Anthropology, University of California, Berkeley, 1954).

ROBINSON, DAVID A.
ms.    *An Archaeological Survey of the Nasca Valley, Peru* (M.A. thesis in Anthropology, Stanford University, 1957).

ROWE, JOHN HOWLAND
1944   *An Introduction to the Archaeology of Cuzco* (Papers, Peabody Museum of American Archaeology and Ethnology, vol. 27, no. 2. Cambridge).
1945   *Absolute Chronology in the Andean Area* (American Antiquity, vol. 10, no. 3, pp. 265-284, Menasha).
1956   *Archaeological Explorations in Southern Peru, 1954-1955; Preliminary Report of the Fourth University of California Archaeological Expedition to Peru* (American Antiquity, vol. 22, no. 2, pp. 135-151, Salt Lake City).

TSCHOPIK, MARION HUTCHINSON
1946   *Some Notes on the Archaeology of the Department of Puno* (Papers, Peabody Museum of American Archaeology and Ethnology, vol. 27, no. 3. Cambridge).

UHLE, MAX (A. L. KROEBER, ED.)
1924   *Explorations at Chincha* (University of California Publications in American Archaeology and Ethnology, vol. 21, no. 2, Berkeley).

URTEAGA, HORACIO H.
1939   *Tambo Colorado* (Boletín de la Sociedad Geográfica de Lima, tomo 51, trimestre 2, pp. 85-94, Lima).

BERKELEY, CALIFORNIA

# THE INCA BRIDGES IN THE HUÁNUCO REGION

DONALD E. THOMPSON AND JOHN V. MURRA

## ABSTRACT

Ethnohistorical, archaeological, and ethnological data are combined in a discussion of Inca bridges in the Huánuco area. A colonial document provides the details of how a major bridge on the Inca highway was constructed by placing a series of logs over projecting *canes*. The division of labor in providing the logs was described as being divided among neighboring communities, with the river itself as a significant dividing line. The section of the Inca highway in question is still in use today and the bridge still exists, apparently much the same as it was in the Colonial Period and probably in the Inca Period. Other bridges in the area are discussed from the point of view of function and maintenance and as an example of the persistence of an ancient tradition of bridge building.

COMMUNICATIONS and their maintenance have been a major concern of Andean peoples from Inca times and probably earlier. In Andean conditions, roads, trails, and bridges were probably as essential to the political cohesion of the Inca state and to the redistribution of goods within it, as they are today to political integration or economic development. At present, modern or colonial roads are still but a small part of the total communication network. Trails for horses, burros, and llamas and simple log bridges prevail, and these are maintained by the local communities with only occasional and quite recent aid from the national governments. As is to be expected, in a number of cases, the back country trails coincide exactly with the ancient Inca highway, and some bridges and sections of the royal road have been in continuous use from probably before the Inca period through Colonial times and up to the present day (Von Hagen 1955).

It may thus be feasible to approach the study of Inca communications through a combination of archaeological, ethnological, and historical techniques. A recent study (Mellafe 1965) published in the first issue of a new Peruvian scholarly journal, *Historia y Cultura*, had its starting point from the details of 16th century litigation between two groups of Andean communities over who was responsible for the maintenance and repair of what had been a major Inca bridge.

Testimony had been collected in the field and in Quechua. Accompanied by representatives of the feuding communities, the royal investigator, Diego de Espinoza Campos, a local man who spoke the language, travelled for six weeks over the area inhabited and controlled by said communities. Between them, they examined at least 32 bridges, measured and described most of them, indicated their local, regional, or pan-Andean functions and inquired into the "order they had in the distribution" of the maintenance chores. At the end of the trip, in December 1596, the group arrived at the "bridge of Huánuco Viejo," the object of the dispute. The measurements and inquiries were resumed, but in more detail; witnesses were interviewed on the spot, but if absent were sought out at towns two and three days' journey away. We have been fortunate to have this account available to us before publication, while we were doing field work in the area, through the courtesy of Rolando Mellafe, research professor of history in the University of Chile. It was he who located and has since edited the account (Mellafe 1965).

Because of the interesting material contained in this document, we made an effort to locate the bridge while studying Inca state installations in the Huánuco region. Fortunately, the bridge proved to be on a section of the Inca highway, which not only continued to be used during the Colonial period but also is still being travelled today. As a result, the bridge has been maintained and is probably still very similar to what it was in the Inca period. Located only a few miles north of a great regional administrative center, known today only as Huánuco Viejo, on the main royal road from Cuzco to Quito, it was of obvious interest since it permitted us to examine in detail the local manifestations of a major Andean complex (Murra 1962). By combining archaeological techniques with data from early eyewitness sources, we hope to know not only the physical installation but also the patterns devised by Inca rule to utilize peasant energies in the building and maintenance of the communication network.

## THE ROAD AND THE BRIDGE

The section of the road studied runs from Huánuco Viejo to Taparaku, the first important tambo to the north. Part of a major royal highway, this segment was followed by a number of early Colonial travellers and chroniclers, in-

Reprinted from AMERICAN ANTIQUITY, Vol. 31, No. 5, 1966. pp. 632-639.

Fig. 1. The Tambo of Taparaku. Well preserved, long, symmetrical building to the left;
part of a plaza and dwelling area to the right.

cluding Miguel de Estete, an eyewitness of the European invasion. The most complete early description of the road, however, is that of Vásquez de Espinoza (1948: 458–9), who in 1616 said of the trip:

From Pincos one travels 7 leagues over very rough, cold country to the Tambo of Taparaco, which belongs to the Province of Los Huamalies; from there, 4 leagues of bad road over the slopes of a sierra, keeping on one's left a deep river which comes down from the snowfields. At the end of these grades one crosses another river by a bridge and comes to a wide plain covered with cattle and llamas; at the end of it there are large buildings, with the Tambo of Huánuco Viejo . . .

Sketchy though this description is, it covers the main highlights of the journey, and there can be no doubt that this section of road is the one travelled by us and that the bridge mentioned is the bridge of Huánuco Viejo.

Even today, despite more than 400 years of use, this part of the Inca road is in quite good condition. The extensive ruins of Tambo Taparaku are still perfectly visible, though they are in poor shape because local people have been dismantling the walls to build modern houses and corrals (Fig. 1). The high percentage of Imperial Inca pottery scattered about the ruins leaves no doubt about the date of occupation, and certain sections of the site are sufficiently preserved to allow the walls of plazas, houses, qollqa, and other buildings to be traced. Today the area still bears the name Taparaku, a Quechua word meaning "large butterfly."

The Inca highway passes just to the west of the tambo and follows the right side of the valley almost down to the point where it joins the Viscarra River (formerly known as Orqomayu). In flat areas the road is well marked by lines of stones and, in places, is up to 12 meters wide. In more difficult terrain the road is narrower, and more elaborate construction supports it. On sloping ground retaining walls buttress the downhill side and the slope has been artificially flattened. Similarly, where it runs close to the river, dike-like retaining or defense walls keep the current from eroding the highway. Where swampy ground made travel difficult, the road was paved with stone, and all places where water flows across the road are equipped with stone-lined drains of careful workmanship (Fig. 2).

FIG. 2. A stone-lined drain crossing the Inca Highway between Huánuco Viejo and Baños.

Just before the juncture of the tributary (variously known as Rio de Taparaku or Rio de Iscu) with the Viscarra River, the road turns slightly away from the valley and descends sharply, somewhat upstream from the juncture of the two rivers (Fig. 3). The sharp descent of the road is managed by a set of quite well preserved stairs (Fig. 4). At this point, the road is slightly less than 3 meters wide. The steps average

about 10 centimeters high and 150 centimeters wide or deep. At the bottom of the stairs, the bridge of Huánuco Viejo crosses the river. On the other side of the bridge, the Inca road is destroyed for a short distance by the modern highway to Huallanca and some cultivated fields. It can be picked up again, however, ascending by more steps to the pampa above the Viscarra Valley. About one kilometer from the edge of the pampa lies the large city of Huánuco Viejo, with its hundreds of storage qollqa, large residential barrios, and impressive monumental architecture in the Imperial Inca style (Fig. 5).

In summary, this section of the royal road joins two major Inca sites and exhibits many of the features for which the road is famous: markers, drains, retaining walls, steps, and paving. The construction of the road must have required a large expenditure of time and effort, and the quality of that construction is borne out by the fact that it is still in quite good condition after over 400 years of use. The high visibility of the road, hence the ease with which it could be traced, allowed us to locate what are almost certainly the foundations of the bridge of Huá-

FIG. 3. The Inca Highway and the Viscarra River. The Inca Road can be seen to the left of the tributary valley, which it follows. It zig-zags down to the Viscarra River, which it crosses by the Bridge of Huánuco Viejo. Photo by Peter Jenson.

FIG. 4. Steps on the Inca Highway. These steps lead directly down to the Bridge of Huánuco Viejo.

nuco Viejo (Figs. 6 and 7). The bridge, unlike the road, contains perishable materials and had to be maintained if it were to continue in use.

## INCA BRIDGES: THEIR BUILDING AND MAINTENANCE

In addition to the well-known state highways (Von Hagen 1955; Strube 1963), the Espinoza Campos survey of bridges in 1596 revealed the location of many local and regional roads and paths. Mellafe (1965: 78) has noted that of the 32 spans inspected only five were of major significance; others were purely local. The one called Hupayguaro, built of poles by the villagers of Pachas, allowed them to cross a river "to their fields and there are some of maize and other vegetables. In wintertime [the rainy season] they cannot be without it and the old and the children go over it . . ." (Espinoza 1965: 101). Others, like the rope bridge at Morca, were said by four aged witnesses to have been built

in the time of the Inca. There were three baskets with their pulleys and ropes which served as bridges for the dealings of the Indians in the Andes where the Indians of the provinces of this region went, and from where they brought for the Inca feathers and cotton, and cocaleaf and other things which are taken from the said Andes. (Espinoza 1965: 84.)

Depending on their uses, bridges were built and maintained by varying segments of the social organization.

A fourth of a league 'from town, the Indians of Puños built it; it was necessary for the road and even more for the winning of salt as they carry the water across to pour it over some cliffs where salt curdles" (Espinoza 1965: 93).

The one at Llincaypucroc was built jointly by the villagers at Punchauraca and those from Miraflores "since it was between the two towns."

The wider spans were built under Inca auspices and involved much larger groups of local peasants. The Espinoza Campos text does not reflect the local, ethnic, political organization. The inspector treated each village as a separate unit, and the only authorities he mentioned were village leaders. He ignored the wider political affiliations which, from other, slightly earlier sources, we know had existed in the area (Ortiz 1920–25, 1955–61; Murra 1961). Such authority may have weakened by 1596, though two of these chiefs were still exempt from bridge duties at Morca, and five at Pachas (Espinoza 1965: 85, 99; Murra 1964: 438).

Espinoza, however, was aware of moiety divisions, common here as elsewhere in the Andes. Whereas the upper-lower complementarity (Hanansaya vs. Urinsaya) was usual in the South, in the Huánuco region we find it but rarely, mostly in the settlements of mitmaq colonists, such as Hanan Pillao vs. Urin Pillao, located down the

FIG. 5. Huánuco Viejo. One of the gates in the eastern quarter of the city.

Huallaga, where the Inca had settled them near the montaña. In Huánuco the moieties were thought of in terms of right bank and left, following a river's course: Allauca Rumar vs. Ichoc Rumar, Allauca Wari vs. Ichoc Wari (a different explanation for these terms is given by R. T. Zuidema 1964: 41). The local witnesses told Espinoza (1965: 104) "The river separated them; those of Allauca Guanuco were on the side toward Huánuco Viejo and those of Ichoc Guanuco on the side of the river where the tampu of Taparaku is located. . . ." This confirms the accuracy of Guaman Poma's (1936: 345, 1073) information about the country of his ancestors.

This dual division can be seen functionally in the alternating work pattern. The bridge of Huánuco Viejo, "the most necessary bridge in this province," was built, according to Gonzalo Cachas or Cahas (Espinoza 1965: 105), in the following way:

Of the seven tree trunks of which the said bridge is built . . . the first, of the upper part [was laid down] by those of Allauca Guanuco, the Collana [highest status segment]; next the other, thicker one, by those of Cinga [Ichoc Guanucos] . . . . Next, another by the same Indians of Allauca Guanuco, who in the beginning put down the first timber. Next, the fourth trunk, the Indians of the town of Pachas (see below discussion of their moiety affiliations), which was as thick as that of the Indians of Cinga. Next, the fifth timber, the Indians of the town of Llata [Ichoc Guanucos] . . . . Then follows the next one which is the sixth; the said don Gonzalo says it is the *guaica* of those of Ichoc Guanuco beginning with Pachas. . . . *guaica* [the work] was shared out among all those towns. Next, the seventh log was laid down by the Allauca Guanucos. . . .

The text is not clear as to whether the *guaica* timber was portioned out among both moieties or to only the Ichoc side. Mellafe (1965: 79) thinks that both shared it, and for aboriginal conditions this is likely. The pattern of Andean reciprocity tried for lineage and moiety equivalence in sharing the burdens of public works. If Pachas be counted with the left bank moiety, where it belongs physically, the first, third, and seventh timbers were laid down by the right bank side, while the second, fourth, and fifth fell to the left; the sixth would then be shared by both sides. By 1596, however, more than sixty years after Pizarro, Pachas was a major contender in the litigation and had sided with the right bank, for reasons which had probably more to do with the European partition of the countryside than with Andean moieties (Mellafe 1965: 73). The drawing up of *encomienda* lines

had generally ignored both ethnic and moiety lines. This may explain the suggestion in the text that the sixth trunk was the contribution of the Ichoc Guanucos alone, now that Pachas had shifted sides. While the left bank moiety admitted that (Espinosa 1965: 104) "their fathers and ancestors had attended to it [the bridge] and not by force since in the time of the Inca they had all done it," they saw no reason to do it any longer, since there were so "many bridges and obligations in their own country," as a result of a new order of things.

Mellafe (1965: 78) mentions one further reason why the left bank people were so reluctant to participate in the maintenance of the bridge as to sue for relief in the distant Lima court: in Inca times, they had been granted lands in the vicinity of the bridge, but they lost these lands when the *encomienda* lines were drawn. The evidence for such land grants by the Inca is not available in the Espinoza text at our disposal, but Mellafe's point fits what we know of Inca land tenures. This also brings up the matter of bridge custodians and their livelihood; they may or may not have been the same people as those responsible for the construction of the bridge. One of the very earliest of eyewitnesses recorded that "on each side of the bridge there were people who lived right there who had no other trade, nor duty but to repair and maintain the bridges" (Anonymous 1937: 74). Such full-time custodians, in the Andean economic system, would be assimilated in status to the *mit-maq* colonists who guarded fortresses and other state installations, and who would have had their fields nearby, to supply their food. The existence of such full-time custodians is not really confirmed by later observers who thought that bridge maintenance was undertaken in rotation by the various settlements in the region

FIG. 6. The Bridge of Huánuco Viejo.

Fig. 7. The Bridge of Huánuco Viejo. Construction details of abutments and *canes*.

(Ortiz 1920: 179; 1925: 222; 1955: 198; Garcilaso 1960: 94, 105; Cobo 1956: 129). Both systems may have co-existed, depending on the strategic importance of a given bridge. Under favorable circumstances this could be tested archaeologically (Murra 1962).

Espinoza Campos (1965: 87) reported at least one case in which the care of a bridge was related to state-sponsored settlements. Six elders from the vicinity testified that

from what they had seen and heard from their fathers and ancestors, in this settlement [*asiento*] of Chuquibamba, there were in the time of the Inca some *curicamaioc* Indians. These are Indians who took out gold from the well which is at this bridge; [these men] were from different nations and were settled on both sides of the river, and for these and for the passage to the provinces of Huánuco and those of Pariarga and the trade to the country of the montaña . . . and particularly for those who took out the gold . . . by order and indication of the Inca. It [the bridge] was built by those of Ichoc Guanuco . . . and those from Pariarga [on the Allauca Guanuco side] and these were helped by [men from] other parts [sent in by] the Inca and his captains and his governors . . .

A major part of the labor involved in building and maintaining any bridge was the providing of tree trunks. The bridge of Huánuco Viejo was located at 3,200 meters (10,800 feet); the towns feuding over it were usually even higher, most of them well above the tree line. In his travels, Espinoza (1965) noted repeatedly: "there are some small alder trees but not fit for a bridge in need of repairs," or "this is in cold country, there is no timber to make a bridge." While one of the many spans was built of *kinual*, a high altitude, slow growing, not very tall hardwood, the rest of the lumber had to be brought from very far away: "they carry them from more than four leagues, from the slopes of Vichun, in Allauca Pincos" (Espinoza 1965: 92).

The difficulties of obtaining wood affected the kind of bridge that would be built and embittered the controversy over responsibility for maintenance.

As they had no timber in their country, they have built it of ropes; [the straw for the rope] is available in the lands of the Shaca Indians . . . it seems to grow wild . . . and they buy it for their bridges . . . . The rope bridges are built every two years . . . but if they were made of wood, they say they could be renewed [only] every eight years (Espinoza 1965: 85–6).

Perhaps these rope installations were the ones requiring permanent maintenance personnel, whereas log bridges such as the one at Huánuco Viejo, could be maintained on rotation by the neighboring peasantry. At Huánuco Viejo, the Allauca moiety insisted (Espinoza 1965: 103–4) that "if built well and with good timbers it would last from four to six and more years," while the Ichoc villages argued that "all they know was that if it was well taken care of, it seemed to them it would last twenty years or more." The area around Llata, on the Ichoc side, was particularly short of wood before the eucalyptus was introduced.

## The Bridge of Huánuco Viejo

The earliest mention of the bridge at Huánuco Viejo is to be found in the description of the trip made by Hernando Pizarro to the coastal shrine of Pachacamac while his brother was still at Caxamarca. Miguel de Estete (1853: 342), who accompanied Hernando reported:

On the last day of the above mentioned month [March 1533], the captain departed with his companions from this town [apparently Huánuco Viejo], and they arrived at a bridge over a torrential river, made of very thick timbers, and on it there were gatekeepers who had charge of collecting the toll, as is the custom among these people.

Estete, then, establishes the fact that the bridge was built of large logs and adds the interesting sidelight that even such a small bridge as that of Huánuco Viejo had its guards. The Espinoza Campos text (Espinosa 1965: 103), however, provides us with the fullest and most precise early description:

. . . I walked from one side of the bridge to the other and I saw the abutments of it, which appear to have been securely and very well made in the time of the Inca, and so far as one can see they are permanent from being well finished, and [I] measured the said bridge and its timbers with a rope and a *vara* sealed with the seal of the city of Huánuco, and I counted the timbers and *canes* of it." (*Canes* are supports for the bridge which project slightly over the river from the abutments.)

The timbers of the bridge: there are seven logs [each of which] a man could enfold by stretching both arms around them; these cross the river from one side to the other over the *canes*. The two in the lower position are broken, and the five which are whole, or seem to be seen from below, were measured with the rope and *vara*. They are 17 and ¾ varas because they rest on top of all the *canes* and they are recessed into the wall; the bed of the river from wall to wall is 15 varas and 4 inches.

The timbers of the *canes*: on both sides it has three tiers of thick beams, five beams in each tier. The tier in which the ends of the beams were most readily visible, and which they say are of the same size as all the rest, were each six varas long. Of these [six] varas, four penetrate into the wall, and the *canes* project two varas over the river, and this totals 30 thick timbers of six varas each.

The timbers which they place over the *canes*: there are more than six thick logs which cross over the *canes*, three on either side of 2 and ⅓ varas each and this is the width of the bridge, of the seven said timbers, which rest on the *canes* and which make up the said bridge.

The present-day foundations or abutments of the bridge (Figs. 6 and 7) are built, in part, of rough rock and, in part, of dressed stone. The masonry is quite well fitted and there is no evidence of mortar having been used at any time. According to an elderly informant, Sr. Exaltación Luna, who lives next to the bridge, at a place known today as Colpas, and has worked on its upkeep, the bridge has been kept in repair recently, over the last fifty years or so. It is also likely, though not absolutely certain, that the bridge has been continuously maintained since 1596 when the Espinoza Campos hearings were held. In the course of these centuries it is possible that sections of the abutments may have been partly rebuilt; we would, nevertheless, suspect that much of the foundation is original Inca work, especially toward the bottom. These abutments or foundations provide an adequate defense against erosion by the river in addition to a foundation for the bridge itself. We were unable to find confirmation for the reports that Inca bridges were frequently built and manned in pairs, one for the officials, the other for the peasantry (Murra 1962: 3).

Today the bridge measures about 11 meters and 20 centimeters, from abutment to abutment. As in the Colonial period the bridge spans the river by means of thick logs resting on top of projecting supports or *canes*. The bridge is narrower than it used to be; now only three main logs, instead of seven, span the river. On top of these main timbers are smaller cross-logs which, in turn, are covered with a thin layer of stones, earth, and sod. The center of the bridge is strong enough to support men and animals (Fig. 6), but toward the edges it tends to be somewhat weak. Watching a herd of sheep cross, we saw one fall through between the cross-logs near the edge. While the main timbers are still supported by *canes*, today the *canes* consist of only two tiers of three logs each (instead of three tiers of five), plus the stone construction between the tiers (Fig. 7).

The basic principles of construction, then, remain essentially the same as they were in Colonial times and probably earlier in the Inca period. Since the peasantry themselves were

Fig. 8. Modern copy of an Inca stepping stone type bridge near Taparaku.

responsible for upkeep of the bridge, the absence of any great changes in construction is understandable, especially in places like Ripán and Aguamiro, nearby villages, which are so far from the centers of European settlement. Along the same section of the Inca road, near tambo Taparaku, in pastures belonging to the town of Llata, we found other examples of ancient types of bridges still in use today, and, according to local herders, they are modern copies of Inca bridges. Some of them are simple stepping-stone affairs, a series of small masonry piers, leaving *ojos* or eyes between them for the water to flow through (Fig. 8). Such self-conscious copying of ancient models in our time indicates again the strength of a tradition and an essential continuity in the methods of bridge construction used.

*Acknowledgments.* The field work on which this report is based was supported by the National Science Foundation. We are also greatly indebted to Rolando Mellafe for providing us with a copy of Espinoza Campos' document before publication. In our field research we were aided by Dr. Ramiro Matos, Sr. César Fonseca, Mr. Craig Morris and Mr. Robert Bird.

ANONYMOUS

1937 *Las Relaciones Primitivas de la Conquista del Perú; el anónimo sevillano de 1534,* edited by Raúl Porras Barrenechea. Paris.

COBO, BERNABE

1956 Historia del Nuevo Mundo [1653]. *Biblioteca de Autores Españoles,* Tomo 92. Madrid.

ESPINOZA CAMPOS, DIEGO DE

1965 Los Indios del Repartimiento de Ichochuánuco contra Los Indios Pachas, sobre el Servicio y Mitas del Puente del Río Huánuco. Los Reyes, Febrero 9 de 1592 [1596]. In "La significación historica de los puentes en el virreinato peruano del siglo XVI," by Rolando Mellafe. *Historia y Cultura,* Vol. 1, No. 1, pp. 65–113. Lima.

ESTETE, MIGUEL DE

1853 La relación del Viaje que hizo el Señor Hernando Pizarro . . . desde el Pueblo de Caxamalca a Parcama y de alli a Xauxa. In "Verdadera Relación de la Conquista del Perú y provincia del Cuzco, llamada Nueva Castilla." [1534], by Francisco de Xerez. *Biblioteca de Autores Españoles,* Tomo 26. Madrid.

GARCILASO DE LA VEGA

1960 Obras Completas del Inca Garcilaso de la Vega II. *Biblioteca de Autores Españoles,* Tomo 133. Madrid.

MELLAFE, ROLANDO

1965 La significación histórica de los puentes en el virreinato peruano del siglo XVI. *Historia y Cultura,* Vol. 1, No. 1, pp. 65–113. Lima.

MURRA, JOHN V.

1961 Social Structural and Economic Themes in Andean Ethnohistory. *Anthropological Quarterly,* Vol. 34, No. 2, pp. 47–59. Washington.

1962 An Archaeological "Restudy" of an Andean Ethnohistorical Account. *American Antiquity,* Vol. 28, No. 1, pp. 1–4. Salt Lake City.

1964 Una Apreciación Etnológica de la Visita. In *Garci Diez de San Miguel, Visita Hecha a la Provincia de Chucuito* [1567], pp. 419–42. Casa de la Cultura del Perú, Lima.

ORTIZ DE ZUÑIGA, IÑIGO

1920–25, 1955–61 Visita fecha por mandado de su magestad . . . [1562]. *Revista del Archivo Nacional del Perú.* Lima.

POMO DE AYALA, GUAMAN

1936 *Nueva Coronica y Buen Gobierno* [1615]. Institut d'Ethnologie. Paris.

ROWE, JOHN HOWLAND

1960 The Origins of Creator Worship among the Incas. In *Culture in History,* edited by Stanley Diamond, pp. 408–29. Columbia University Press (for Brandeis University), New York.

STRUBE, ERDMANN LEON

1963 Vialidad Imperial de los Incas. *Serie Histórica,* No. XXXIII. Instituto de Estudios Americanistos, Universidad Nacional de Córdoba. Córdoba, Argentina.

VAZQUEZ DE ESPINOSA, ANTONIO

1948 Compendio y Descripción de las Indias Occidentales [1629]. *Smithsonian Miscellaneous Collections,* Vol. 108. Washington.

VON HAGEN, VICTOR W.

1955 *Highway of the Sun.* Duell, Sloan and Pearce, New York.

ZUIDEMA, R. T.

1964 The Ceque system of Cuzco: The Social Organization of the Capital of the Inca. *International Archives of Ethnography,* Supplement to Vol. 1. Translated by Eva M. Hooykaas. E. J. Brill, Leiden.

INSTITUTE OF ANDEAN RESEARCH
Huánuco, Peru
July, 1965

# SOME POST-COLUMBIAN WHISTLING JARS FROM PERU

## Geoffrey Bushnell

The coming of the Spaniards to Peru meant the end of aboriginal culture as a whole, but the survival of individual traits, material and spiritual, in the pacified area was widespread and it deserves more study than it has hitherto received. A notable example was the cult of the dead, of whom many were removed secretly from Christian graveyards to caves or niches in the mountains and some were made into mummy bundles. Although a good deal has disappeared in the course of time, some features are still with us. An example is given by the small models of alpacas which are used in fertility ceremonies in the Cuzco region; before the Conquest these were made of stone, but they are now made of pottery at Pucára, and I found two examples in Cuzco market in 1951, among a multitude of bulls made for tourists.

The traits of material culture fall mainly into two hybrid types as Dr. S. K Lothrop has pointed out to me. Some, like the early post-Conquest tapestries, show the use of an essentially aboriginal technique to produce articles which are decorated predominantly but not entirely with Spanish designs. Into this group falls a gold arm band of aboriginal technique with repoussé designs of monkeys, pumas and a Spaniard on a horse; this example, in the Art Institute of Chicago, was noticed by Dr. Lothrop, who called my attention to it. Others, like the pottery with which I shall be chiefly concerned here, show the use of European materials for the production of purely aboriginal forms.

The pottery vessels to which I wish to call particular attention are mainly of Chimú Inca form, made after the Conquest of light-coloured glazed ware. Reason will be shown for ascribing two unglazed painted examples to the same period. One of these vessels is in the Cambridge University Museum and it was the acquisition of this which provoked me to pursue the matter. Naturally, I sought the help of Dr. Lothrop, who produced the examples from museums in the United States, together with a good many

Reprinted from ACTAS DEL XXXIII CONGRESO INTERNACIONAL DE AMERICANISTAS, 1959. pp. 416-420.

of the ideas put forward here. He really should be considered as the joint author of this paper. We are jointly indebted to Mr. Junius Bird for finding the examples in the American Museum of Natural History, producing photographs and making suggestions. Other examples are known to exist in Peru, in the Museo Nacional at La Magdalena Vieja, near Lima, and in the Municipal Museum at Piura, the latter collected locally. Doubtless there are many more, and I hope that this preliminary notice may lead somebody to undertake a fuller study.

The double whistling jars shown in plate 1 a-c are closely similar in form, the tall spouts being characteristic, on blackware vessels, of the Chimú-Inca period. That shown in plate 1 a, in the American Museum of Natural History,

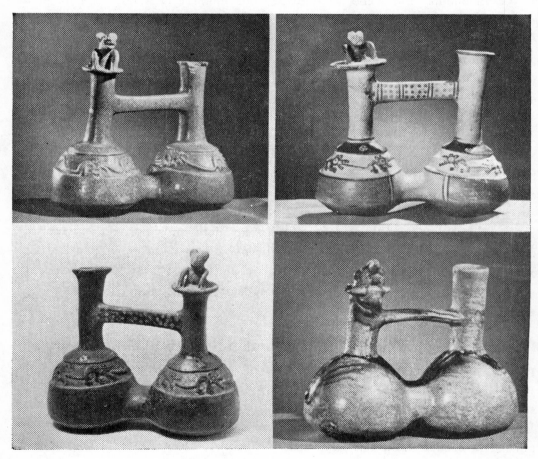

Pl. 1. a. Green glazed jar. Height 7¼ inches. American Museum of Natural History. (Courtesy of Junius Bird.)
b. Painted jar, Ht. 7¼ inches. American Museum of Natural History. (Courtesy of Junius Bird.)
c. Painted Jar. Ht. 7³/₈ inches. Peabody Museum, Harvard University. (Courtesy of Dr. S. K. Lothrop.)
d. Glazed Jar. Height 5½ inches. American Museum of Natural History. (Courtesy of Junius Bird.)

is of whitish paste with quartz sand temper and a greenish glaze with fine cracks. The whistle is under the belly of the freely-modelled cat on the closed neck, opening aft, and there is a frieze of animals (mice?) in relief encircling the base of each neck, facing anti-clockwise. That in · plate, 1 b, in the same Museum, is practically identical in size and of similar paste, but is painted in white, terra cotta, red and brown over a light buff slip, instead of being glazed. The whistle opens forward instead of aft and one frieze of animals faces clockwise. In that on plate 1 c, in the Peabody Museum at Harvard, the whistle again opens forward, but the animals face anticlockwise on both friezes. The interior is terra cotta in colour, and the outside is painted in white, red and brown over dirty cream and red slips. It was in fragments, and before repair it could be seen that it had been made in a pair of moulds running longitudinally, still showing finger marks where it had been pressed into the moulds from the inside. All three are so similar, even to the style of freehand modelling of the cats on the spouts, that they are probably from the hand of one potter, though the differences in direction in which the animals face on the friezes make it unlikely that the same pair of moulds was used for all. At the same time it is worth recalling that vessels from the same pair of moulds generally developed minor differences while being finished. The moulds themselves are, of course, made of pottery, a very suitable material since it absorbs water from the unfired cast, allowing it to shrink slightly and come away easily from the mould. Information about the provenance of these vessels is insufficient to give any clue to the question of common authorship. Of the first nothing is known, the second was bought from a dealer and is said to have come from Recuay in the north Highlands, and the third is from Churín, near Huacho, in the Huaura Valley, but the style points to manufacture further north.

Three other double whistling jars, all glazed, are of the same general type but they lack the friezes of animals. The first, (plate 1d), in the American Museum of Natural History, has the whistle in the breast of a bird. It of grayish paste tempered with quartz sand, and the glaze is yellow streaked with brown, carelessly applied so that it does not cover the whole surface. The second, in the Peabody Museum, has lost its whistle; it is thin and light, and has a good dark green to almost black glaze. The third, (plate 2 b), in the Cambridge Museum, is light in weight and of pinkish buff sandy ware with an olive green glaze mottled with dark brown and irregularly streaked with yellow. The glaze is missing in a few places and is deeply pitted in others, the pits sometimes extending down into the body. The whistle is in

Pl.  2.  a.  Green glazed stirrup-spouted jar.  Height 6⅝ ins.  Peabody Museum, Harvard University.
(Courtesy of Dr. S. K. Lothrop.)
b.  Green glazed jar.  Height 6¾ inches.  Cambridge University Museum of Archaeology
and Ethnology.

the lower part of the human figure, which carries a cat with a strong family likeness to those on the first three vessels described, and the opening is at the back.   Nothing is known of the antecedents of any of these, except that the second was bought in a pawn shop in Lima by Lothrop, who remarks that there is nothing to indicate that it had ever been buried.

Another late Chimú type is exemplified by a stirrup-spouted jar representing an animal (pl. 2a), probably a dog, with four lumps on the face; it has a bird in the angle of the stirrup.   The glaze is light olive green and has not fused properly at the back.   Like one of those already mentioned, it was bought by Lothrop in a pawnshop in Lima.   It is now in the Peabody Museum.

When and from whom did the natives learn the art of glazing?   At present our answers can only be in general terms, but the discovery of more examples and the excavation of early Colonial sites will doubtless make them more precise in time to come.   The green glaze on the Cambridge jar would not look out of place in mediaeval England, and there are English examples from the 14th to the 16th century in the same Museum which resemble it closely.   The paste also of some  English vessels is similar in colour to that of the Peruvian one.   These mediaeval lead glazes, coloured green with copper, were applied to the vessel before firing, so the elaboration of double firing did not have to be learnt, and the Indians with their long tradition of skilled potting could soon have learnt to practice the technique of glazing and to appreciate its advantages. The more elaborate of the old forms and the old style of painting which sometimes went with them (cf. plate 1 a-c) are unlikely to have survived the generation of potters which was working at the time of the Conquest, so vessels with these features should not be much later than the middle of the 16th century. It could be otherwise with a glazed jug or pitcher from Piura in the Peabody Museum. This is European in form with a type of handle common in mediaeval England, and though some relief ornament on the body is doubtless a reflexion of the painted "tree" on Cuzco Inca pottery, it could perhaps have survived for a longer time. The glaze on this pot is of the usual green colour but most of it has crumbled away. Mr. Arthur Lane, of the Victoria and Albert Museum, has told me that green lead glaze, used especially in conjuction with moulded decoration in relief, was very popular in Spain from the 14th to the 16th century.

In seeking to answer the question of who taught the Indians the craft, it must be remembered that the lead in introducing new techniques came from the religious orders. I must leave to others the investigation of the history of the first monasteries in north-west Peru and what they taught, but I can give a possible parallel. Fray Jodoco Ricke, who entered Quito with Benalcázar, founded the Franciscan convent there in 1535, and soon afterwards founded a small school where both natives and sons of colonists received not only religious instruction but also teaching in "artes y oficios". In 1553 this became the Colegio de San Andrés, whence issued the first painters, sculptors, architects, singers and musicians of the Colony, and in the publication I quote, Don José Gabriel Navarro, the Ecuadorian scholar, expressly included the Real Audiencia of Lima in the Colony, so some of the new artificers may have gone to the coast of Peru. Glazing of pottery is not specifically mentioned in my sources of information, but it was an everyday requirement of the colonists so it was probably taken for granted. Besides the things already mentioned Fray Jodoco taught the Indians how to plough with oxen and to make carts. He also brought the first wheat to Quito in an earthenware pot; this was kept as a precious relic in the monastery until it was given to General Flores, the first President of Ecuador between 1831 and 1834. Humboldt saw it at the beginning of the 19th century, and translated its inscription in old German for the friars "You who empty me, forget not your God". An inscribed late mediaeval jar of this sort would surely have been glazed, and who knows if it served as an example to the first potters to use glaze in South America!

# THE CULTURAL SEQUENCE AT YARINACOCHA, EASTERN PERU *

## Donald W. Lathrap

DURING May, June, July, and August of 1956 I was engaged in archaeological field work near the city of Pucallpa on the Ucayali River in eastern Peru. The project was sponsored by the American Museum of Natural History as a part of its long term program of anthropological work in the Peruvian Montaña. The Museum grants permission to present this preliminary statement, and it will publish the final report on this work.

The middle and lower sections of the valley of the Ucayali River, though not far east of the Andean highlands of Peru, are within the Tropical Forest Region of the Amazon Basin and are at an elevation of less than 500 feet above sea level. At the point where it passes Pucallpa, the Ucayali is already a monstrous river whose course is characterized by a low gradient and numerous meanders. This course frequently changes and leaves in its wake countless swamps, sloughs, and oxbow lakes. Yarinacocha is a typical oxbow lake located a few miles to the northwest of Pucallpa. At certain places along the lake shore there are clearings marking the sites of Indian and Peruvian fields, but for most of its length the lake is lined by dense jungle rising in a green wall to as high as 200 feet. The quantity and variety of fish within the lake is truly remarkable and the lake is a major source of food not only for the inhabitants of its immediate banks but also for the people of Pucallpa.

The present Shipibo village of San Francisco de Yarinacocha stands at the north end of the lake. In 1925 Günter Tessmann spent 2 months here doing ethnographic work. In the course of his studies he made a small collection of sherds which were of types obviously different from those made by the modern Shipibo. He illustrated some of these sherds in his book *Menschen ohne Gott*, but at that time not enough was known about the archaeology of

Lowland South America for the true importance of this material to be recognized (Tessman 1928: 26).

More recently the late Harry Tschopik, Jr., spent some time here in 1953, in the course of an ethnographic reconnaissance of the Ucayali drainage. He also made a small, surface collection of non-Shipibo sherds and recognized the possible importance of the locality as an archaeological site. It was on his recommendation that the Department of Anthropology of the American Museum of Natural History undertook to sponsor archaeological work at this spot.

I lived in the Indian village of San Francisco de Yarinacocha and hired a crew of Shipibo as workmen. My time in the village was spent in midden excavation in the hope of recovering stratigraphic evidence for a sequence of ceramic types. Excavations were conducted in 2 localities only. One of these was the high ground around the schoolhouse. This area is the nucleus of the modern Shipibo village. My workmen suggested Hupa-iya as the best name for this particular locality and so it was applied both to the site and to the most prominent archaeological complex there. This was the spot where both Tessmann and Tschopik made their collections.

The other place was a slightly lower knoll about a mile and a half to the northwest and at a considerable distance back in the jungle from the shore of the modern lake. This knoll stands beside a slough which the Shipibo called Tutishcainyo and that name has been applied both to the site and to its most important archaeological complex.

Surface collections were made at 3 other sites, all of which yielded the ceramic complex which has been called Pacacocha.

*The Ceramic Sequence.* The following remarks are of a tentative nature as two-thirds of the collections were still in transit from Peru at the time this paper was written. These comments are based on a fairly thorough analysis of the part of the collection which had arrived, the major part of the collections from the Tutishcainyo site, and on a preliminary analysis in the field of the most productive strati-

* This article is an expanded version of a paper read before the annual meeting of the Society for American Archaeology, Madison, Wisconsin, on May 3, 1957. I wish to thank Gordon R. Willey who read and criticized the original version and Robert J. Squier who read and criticized the present version. Their suggestions have been most constructive and helpful.

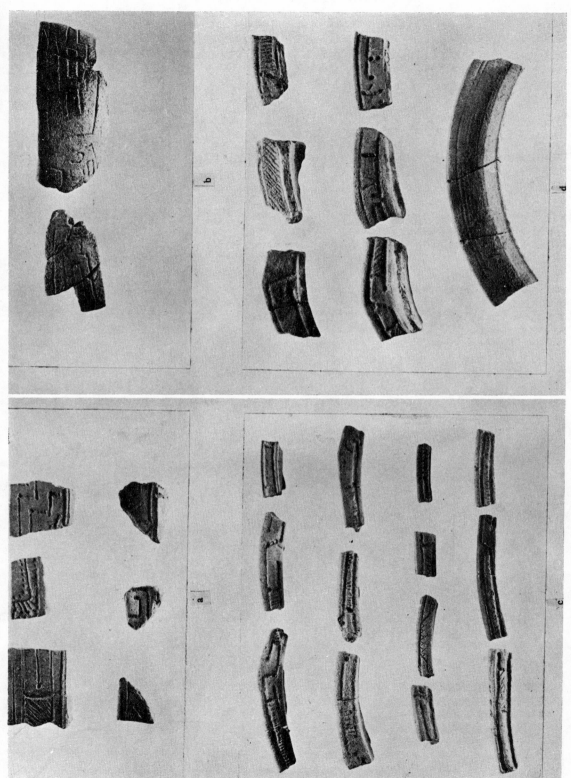

Fig. 1. Early Tutishcainyo pottery. *a*, body sherds; *b*, fragments of bowl with cat head; *c*, typical rims; *d*, typical decorated basal flanges.

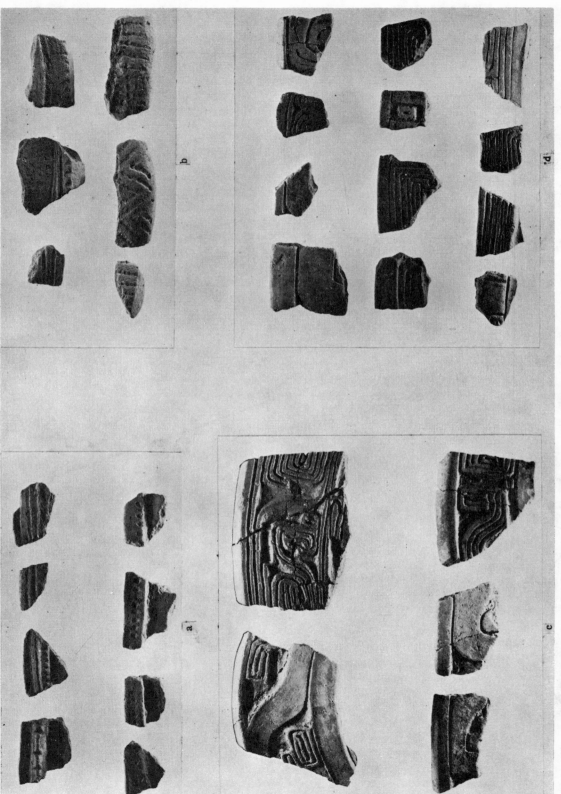

Fig. 2. *a* and *b*, Late Tutishcainyo pottery: *a*, typical rims; *b*, typical basal angles. *c* and *d*, Shakimu Excised pottery: rim and body sherds.

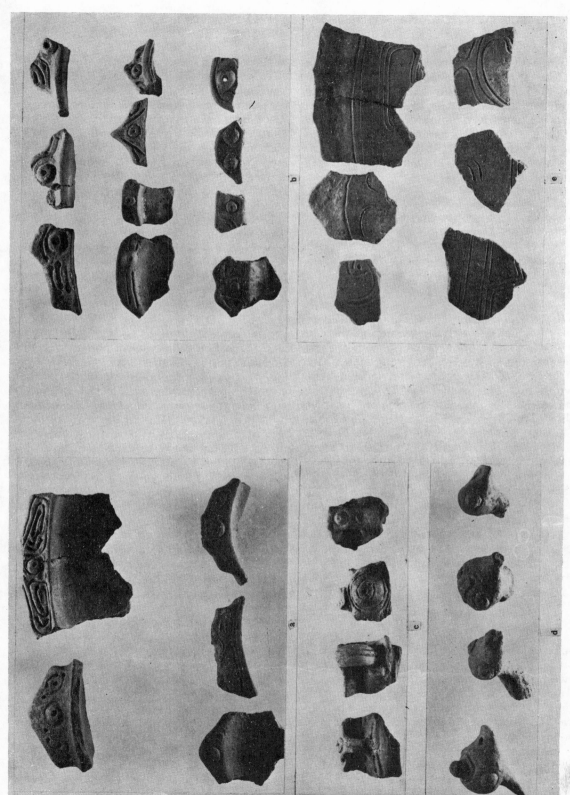

Fig. 3. Hupa-iya pottery. *a, b,* lugs; *c,* handles; *d,* adornos; *e,* body sherds.

graphic excavation at the Hupa-iya site. The biggest drawback in writing up this preliminary paper was the impossibility of comparing these 2 parts of the collection.

The only type of evidence used in constructing the sequence now to be presented is stratigraphic evidence, that is, the direct superposition of one pottery complex over another. The sequences at the 2 sites are not identical and the problem of their alignment can best be visualized when the 2 sequences are presented in tabular form.

| TUTISHCAINYO SITE | HUPA-IYA SITE |
|---|---|
| Modern Shipibo (only traces) . . . . . . . | *Modern Shipibo* |
| Thick, coarse, dark ware | |
| Pacacocha (only traces) | Pacacocha |
| | *Hupa-iya* |
| *Yarinacocha* | |
| | *Shakimu* |
| *Late Tutishcainyo* | |
| Early Tutishcainyo . . . . . . . . . . . . . . . . | *Early Tutishcainyo* |

The italicized names represent ceramic complexes which are well represented in the cuts and the relative stratigraphic position of which seems established beyond any reasonable doubt. It can be seen that there are certain problems which are unresolvable on the basis of this statement. For instance, the temporal relationship of the Yarinacocha complex either to the Shakimu complex or to the Hupa-iya complex is not clear. It is hoped that a more thorough analysis of the material will resolve these problems but at present it is best to acknowledge their existence openly.

1. The earliest ceramic complex at both sites, Tutishcainyo, may represent the oldest ceramic assemblage in this area but we can not be sure at present. At least 2 periods can be distinguished within this group of ceramics on the basis of certain modes of decoration. The following remarks deal specifically with *Early Tutishcainyo*; the Late variant will be treated separately. The most common vessel form is a large, relatively shallow bowl with a hemispherical base and walls which are concave, straight, or composite in profile. The break between the sides and base is sharply marked, in some instances by a simple ridge but more frequently by a broad horizontal flange. The typical rim is expanded outward in a broad, horizontal extension.

Decorated ware was the rule rather than the exception. Decoration was by incision and involved a variety of step-fret and step-scroll motives. Zoning was the basic concept in almost all of the design layouts. Areas of the pot's surface were demarcated by fairly deep incisions and these zones were textured by one of several techniques, including hatched shallow incision, crosshatched shallow incision, punctation, reed punctation, and occasionally zoned red painting. Frequently the incisions of such decoration were filled with a dry red pigment. Such decoration occurs on one or more of 3 zones of the vessel: on the flat upper surface of the rim, on the upper surface of the basal flange, or in a zone on the wall of the vessel.

Except where thickened at the rims and flanges, this pottery is very thin. The firing is uncontrolled and the core is typically intensely black. A significant percentage of this pottery has a heavy shell temper, while another portion is very heavily tempered with sand. The majority of the pottery has a slightly sandy paste and there is some evidence that some form of vegetable material was also added.

2. The *Late Tutishcainyo* pottery deviated from the norms described above in the following ways: the horizontally expanded rim became less frequent and was partially replaced by another form with crude, broad-line incision; the incised decoration tended to be more slovenly done and in some instances approached what might be called brushing; the flanges tended to become shorter and thicker while a specific form of notched, basal angle was diagnostic. A type of zoned decoration involving parallel rows of dots is confined to the Late period of Tutishcainyo. It seems highly probable that this type of texturing was done with a dentate roulette. (This point was brought to my attention by Richard MacNeish.) The Late Tutishcainyo pottery tended to be thicker and more completely oxidized.

3. At the Tutishcainyo site, Late Tutishcainyo is overlaid by the *Yarinacocha* complex consisting largely of thicker, plain ware. This type of pottery is sherd tempered and was smoothed while the clay was somewhat wet, giving a floated finish. The surface of this pottery tends to be relatively free from firing clouds; the interior surface is typically a bright, even orange, while the exterior surface ranges from orange to a medium, reddish brown. Characteristic forms include large, flat-bottomed, vertical-sided urns with simple rolled rims and very large, flat, circular platters with

straight, outsloping sides about 2 inches high. The rims of these platters are absolutely plain. Associated with this plain pottery are occasional sherds with red, black, or white painted lines on an unslipped base. These painted sherds are too small to permit an adequate characterization of the designs.

4. The *Shakimu* complex, which overlies the Tutishcainyo materials at the Hupa-iya site, is defined by the presence of a highly distinctive ware with excised decoration. With the possible exception of the modern Shipibo pottery, this excised ware was the most skillfully made pottery found in the course of the excavations. At least it was the only pottery which aroused the aesthetic interest of the modern Shipibo potters. The decoration consists of highly complex scroll and step motives standing in high relief against an excised background. Such decoration typically occurs on the outside of bowls with straight or slightly concave walls, but occasionally is found on the upper surfaces of basal flanges. Another plain but very well made and highly polished ware is clearly associated with the excised ceramics.

5. The ceramic complex which has been called *Hupa-iya* has been found only at the center of the modern Shipibo village, but the refuse containing pottery of this type is both thick and widespread here suggesting a density of population and intensity of occupation not equaled before or after that period. Hupa-iya is another incised ware complex. The incision seems to have been done when the clay was still soft and the incised line tends to a broad U-shaped cross section. The designs are curvilinear and have a free-flowing quality which is more easily perceived than defined. The decorated field is more likely to be the whole outer or inner surface of a vessel rather than being confined to a narrow zone. The incised lines usually end in expanded pits. Adornos, horizontal lugs, and vertical strap handles are common features. Another peculiarity is the persistent use of small, round, appliqué pellets with a central punctation and encircling, incised groove. Typical shapes are simple, hemispherical and oval bowls, and plates with incised decoration both inside and out. The surface color is usually an even, grayish brown. The paste of this pottery frequently contains small iron concretions which are only rarely found in the paste of the earlier ceramics.

6. There seem to be at least 2 and possibly more ceramic complexes consisting almost entirely of very thick, coarse wares. One of these, the *Pacacocha* complex, occurs abundantly at the center of the modern Shipibo village and is the only ceramic complex at several other sites where only surface collections were made. While the chronological position of this complex is, as yet, not absolutely clear, the available evidence would suggest a position subsequent to Hupa-iya. Huge, flower pot shaped urns are the common form. A crude style of adorno was a rarely used decoration on the otherwise plain ware. Another ware, thick, crumbly, and blackish, was found in small quantities very near the surface of the Tutishcainyo site. This sometimes has heavy thumb print corrugation. Large pointed-bottom urns occur.

7. Many areas of the modern Shipibo village are covered with a thin but dense layer of refuse containing *Shipibo* pottery. Shipibo fine ware is thin, hard, and well fired and polished. The 2 basic color schemes used are white-on-red and red-and-black-on-white. The white slipped ware is typically coated with a layer of resin applied immediately after firing while the vessel is still hot. The shapes include huge brewing urns, water ollas, and smaller bowls and cups. The utility ware is unslipped, but always decorated with a variety of incised, corrugated, and punctate decorations whose basic motives are the same as those of the painted decoration on the fine wares. The basic form of the utility ware is a large, open mouthed, cooking pot. All Shipibo pottery is tempered by the addition of finely divided, charred, silicious bark. The general style of modern Shipibo pottery has been well illustrated elsewhere (Tessmann 1928; Steward and Métraux 1948, Pl. 52 a, Fig. 87 a; Farabee 1922, Pl. 10) so that examples have not been shown here.

*Other Cultural Remains.* Cultural remains other than ceramics were extremely rare in all of the excavations. In part this is due to the complete disappearance of such materials as shell and bone from all but the most recent Shipibo middens and in part it may be the result of the lack of natural stone in this flat, alluvial valley. What was found can best be reviewed briefly in terms of materials.

Ceramic artifacts other than pottery include such items as spindle whorls, "fire dogs" (pot supports), and pot polishers. Modeled spindle whorls first appear in the Hupa-iya ceramic complex and are decorated in the same fashion as the pottery. In somewhat different forms they continue through the Pacacocha complex and are a part of the modern Shipibo ceramic complex. Perforated sherd discs which might have served as spindle whorls were found in the Early Tutishcainyo complex. Fragments of large, cylindrical "fire dogs" were recovered in association with the Pacacocha complex at the Hupa-iya site. Well-shaped ceramic pot-polishers are part of the modern Shipibo ceramic complex.

Amorphous lumps of fired clay were found in large numbers in most of the refuse excavated, but were especially large and frequent in the deposits containing Early Tutishcainyo ceramics, where they made up a large part of the volume of the midden. Such lumps may have served in various ways as stone substitutes in this completely alluvial region.

A single type of polished stone ax was recovered from all periods of the sequence. It has distinct lateral projections, or ears, and is the type of tool which in Highland and Coastal Peru has often been referred to as the "Inca ax." No other examples of standardized types of stone artifacts were recovered though there were a few flakes of cryptocrystalline rock which might have served as scrapers.

Only one bit of metal was recovered in the course of the excavations. It is a fragment of what appears to be electrum foil, found associated with Early Tutishcainyo material at the Hupa-iya site. It has been submitted for metallurgical analysis.

One burial was definitely identified as such but the bones were so far deteriorated that only traces of white, fibrous material remained. It was possible to note that it had been a primary, flexed inhumation without grave furniture but no other data could be obtained. From its position in the midden it seems most likely that it was buried at the time when the Yarinacocha complex was in use at the Tutishcainyo site.

No direct evidence of architecture was recovered but the impressions on certain clay fragments recovered in association with Early Tutishcainyo pottery suggest that wattle and daub walls may have been constructed during the earliest period of the sequence.

*The Affinities of the Ucayali Ceramics.* There are certain facts which should be kept in mind while reading the following remarks.

This work in the Ucayali Valley was the first systematic archaeological excavation done in the Peruvian Montaña and, with the exception of Nordenskiöld's work in Lowland Bolivia, the first systematic work within the Upper Amazon Basin (Nordenskiöld 1913). It is possible that this scarcity of pertinent comparative materials has resulted in a tendency for the writer to grasp at straws.

Only the 4 ceramic complexes, which are most clearly defined and the relative chronological positions of which are firmly established, need be considered at this time. The Yarinacocha and Pacacocha wares are too lacking in distinctive features to make long-distance comparisons possible, let alone profitable. The complexes to be considered are, proceeding from earliest to latest: 1st, Tutishcainyo with its emphasis on zoned decoration; 2nd, the Shakimu complex with elaborately excised wares and well-polished plain wares; 3rd, Hupa-iya with its broad line incision and modeling; and 4th, modern Shipibo pottery with its polychrome painting.

Before suggesting what other ceramic complexes Tutishcainyo might resemble, it is well to state at the outset that it is a somewhat outré configuration of ceramic traits when compared with other known assemblages in South America. With the various Chavín horizon ceramics of highland and coastal Peru, Tutishcainyo shares an emphasis on zoned decoration of several varieties, but specific stylistic similarities are few. The one representation of a jaguar on Tutishcainyo pottery more closely resembles those of Canapata and Pucara than it does specifically Chavín renderings of this subject. There are similarities between certain Chanapata rim forms and those of Tutishcainyo (Rowe 1944, Fig. 10, 4, 7; Fig. 11, 3; Fig. 12, 3). The site of Kotosh near Huánuco is the nearest truly highland site which is known archaeologically. It has produced 2 styles of pottery which are said to be contemporaneous there. One closely parallels such typical Chavín horizon wares as the Early Ancón series. The other style emphasizes zoned hatching filled with red pigment and in this respect as well as in certain design motives is similar to Tutishcainyo (Tello 1943, Pl. 19 b).

In the northern Andes and adjoining lowlands there are a number of features of ceramic style which resemble those found in Tutishcainyo. Such similarities are most numerous and specific in the Momíl collections from the north coast of Colombia recently described by the Reichel-Dolmatoffs (1956). Such shared traits are most numerous in Levels 5 and 6 of the Momíl cut.

Even farther afield are resemblances which may be noted between Tutishcainyo and certain ceramics of the Middle and Late Preclassic of Lower Mesoamerica. Specifically I am thinking of the large labial and medial flanges and the zoned crosshatching which are features of Provedencia in the Guatemala highlands and the rim and vessel forms common in the polished red and Usulutan wares in the late Preclassic of Copan and the Petén. (These comments are based more on an examination of the actual type collections in storage at the Peabody Museum of Harvard University than on the relevant published materials, that is, Shook 1951; Longyear 1952; Smith 1955). Some of these Mesoamerican similarities are quite striking but there must be a great increase in our knowledge of all of the intervening areas before the probability of historical connection can be evaluated.

Of the ceramics of the Shakimu complex, only the excised wares are sufficiently distinctive to require comment at this time. In their work in the Río Napo region of Ecuador during 1956-57 Evans and Meggers found that a series of excised wares is associated with the previously known but imperfectly described pottery of this area (Howard 1947: 42-7). Evans and Meggers kindly permitted me to examine their unpublished material, but it proves to be unlike the Shakimu excised wares. Compared to Shakimu Excised the Río Napo pottery has large and rather simple designs which were executed in a careless technique. In complexity of design and care of execution, the excised series in the Marajoara phase on Marajó is closer to the Shakimu pottery than is the Río Napo material, but a detailed comparison of design elements has not yet been made between Shakimu and Marajoara. The third and most striking comparison is with further collections from the latest work of Estrada (1956) and Evans and Meggers, on the coast of Ecuador. The ceramics of the Valdivia phase which underlies the already described Chorrera phase (Evans and Meggers 1957) contain an excised series which in vessel shape, technique, care of execution, and even to a degree in design elements is markedly similar to Shakimu Excised.

A full discussion of what these similarities might mean had best wait until complete descriptions of both complexes have appeared in print.

Hupa-iya shares a large number of its distinctive features with the Barrancoid materials from the Lower Orinoco Basin in Venezuela. The Barrancoid ceramics comprise a series of temporally distinct styles within a single tradition, rather than a single phase, but all of the details of this sequence have not yet been published (Rouse 1951). Rouse was kind enough to show me his type collections for the full range of the Barrancoid ceramics and it is my impression that Hupa-iya is most similar to Los Barrancos. In spite of the great geographical distances, the similarities between Hupa-iya and the Barrancoid ceramics are far closer than any of those discussed for the other complexes. There are certain ceramic styles which have been cursorily described and a number of isolated pieces which have been illustrated, which occupy a more or less intermediate position geographically and which show stylistic relationships to both of the complexes under discussion. There are, for instance, the "Unrelated Ware" of Easby (1952: 64, 67) in the area near the mouth of the Tapajos and the "Estilo Globular" of Hilbert in the area of the Río Trombetas (Hilbert 1955: 65-9).

On the basis of my work it is clear that the style of pottery now made by the Shipibo Indians did not develop in this region, but is a relatively recent introduction. The similarity of Shipibo pottery to that made by the Cocama farther down stream on the Amazon suggests that this style moved upstream from the central Amazon Basin. It has often been suggested that modern Shipibo pottery is somehow related to the polychrome style found on Marajó in the Marajoara phase (Kroeber 1949: 488; Willev 1949: 148). If there is a valid historical link between the 2 styles, it can be demonstrated only by further work in the central Amazon Basin. The work of Evans and Meggers (1950) has completely excluded Marajó as the point of origin for this polychrome tradition and my work has been equally conclusive for the Ucayali Valley in this respect.

*Speculations.* At the present state of knowledge concerning these materials, any broad statements about their significance must be of highly speculative nature. Nonetheless 2 such conjectures will be offered as possible stimulants to further research.

It seems possible that the origins of the Tutishcainyo complex may be somehow related to the spread of Middle Preclassic culture from Mesoamerica into South America which has been suggested in recent works by Porter (1953), Willey (1955), Evans and Meggers (1957; 243-6), and the Reichel-Dolmatoffs (1956). But there may have been a time lag in the more distant areas of the Tropical Forest, such as in eastern Peru, so that Tutishcainyo may be of lesser antiquity than some other South American cultures which suggest Mesoamerican influences.

The other hypothesis is that the spread of modeled-incised ceramics, such as Hupa-iya, throughout much of the Amazon Basin may in part be a result of the wave of migration which spread the Arawak languages throughout many of the same areas. All of the scraps of evidence which suggest this hypothesis will not be reviewed here as I intend to follow out this possibility in a more systematic way in future publications. There is, of course, a large block of Arawak speaking peoples in the Ucayali Valley who seem to have been pushed back from the main streams by the Shipibo and other Panoan speakers.

The number and disparate nature of the ceramic complexes recovered in these rather limited excavations are perhaps the most significant features of my work in the Ucayali Valley. They indicate considerable time depth for agricultural peoples and a diversity of cultural influences acting on this area. In short, the prehistory of this part of the Upper Amazon Basin seems to have been anything but simple in its general outlines. Since it is possible, even probable, that I failed to encounter other cultural complexes which may exist in the region, the picture is likely to become even more complicated before we have a full understanding of the prehistory of the Upper Amazon Basin.

EASBY, E. K.

1952 The Pre-Conquest Art of Santarém, Brazil. M. A. Thesis, Department of Fine Arts and Archaeology, Columbia University, New York.

ESTRADA, EMILIO

1956 Valdivia, un sitio arqueológico Formativo en la Provincia de Guayas, Ecuador. *Publicación del Mueso Victor Emilio Estrada*, No. 1. Guayaquil.

EVANS, CLIFFORD AND B. J. MEGGERS

1950 Preliminary Results of Archaeological Investigations at the Mouth of the Amazon. *American Antiquity*, Vol. 16, No. 1, pp. 1-10. Menasha.

1957 Formative Period Cultures in the Guayas Basin, Coastal Ecuador. *American Antiquity*, Vol. 22, No. 3, pp. 235-47. Salt Lake City.

FARABEE, W. C.

1922 Indian Tribes of Eastern Peru. *Papers of the Peabody Museum, Harvard University*, Vol. 10. Cambridge.

HILBERT, P. P.

1955 A cerâmica arqueológica da região de Oriximiná. *Instituto de Antropologia e Etnologia do Pará*, Publ. No. 9. Belem.

HOWARD, G. D.

1947 Prehistoric Ceramic Styles of Lowland South America, Their Distribution and History. *Yale University Publications in Anthropology*, No. 37. New Haven.

KROEBER, A. L.

1949 Art. In "Handbook of South American Indians," edited by J. H. Steward, Vol. 5, pp. 411-92. *Bureau of American Ethnology, Bulletin 143*. Washington.

LONGYEAR, J. M., III

1952 Copan Ceramics: A Study of Southeastern Maya Pottery. *Carnegie Institution of Washington, Publication 597*. Washington.

NORDENSKIÖLD, ERLAND VON

1913 Urnengräber und Mounds im Bolivianischen Flachlande. *Baesseler-archiv*, Vol. 3, pp. 205-55. Berlin.

PORTER, M. N.

1953 Tlatilco and the Pre-Classic Cultures of the New World. *Viking Fund Publications in Anthropology*, No. 19, New York.

REICHEL-DOLMATOFF, GERARDO AND ALICIA DUSSÁN DE REICHEL

1956 Momíl, excavaciones en el Sinú. *Revista Colombiana de Antropología*, Vol. 5, pp. 109-334. Bogota.

ROUSE, IRVING

1951 Prehistoric Caribbean Culture Contacts as Seen from Venezuela. *Transactions of the New York Academy of Science*, Series 2, Vol. 13, pp. 342-47. New York.

Rowe, J. H.

1949 An Introduction to the Archaeology of Cuzco. *Papers of the Peabody Museum, Harvard University*, Vol. 28, No. 2. Cambridge.

Shook, E. M.

1951 The Present Status of Research on the Pre-Classic Horizons in Guatemala. In "Civilizations of Ancient America," edited by Sol Tax, pp. 93-100. *Selected Papers of the XXIXth International Congress of Americanists* [New York, 1949]. University of Chicago Press.

Smith, R. E.

1955 Ceramic Sequence at Uaxactun, Guatemala. *Middle American Research Institute, Tulane University, Publication* No. 20. 2 vols. New Orleans.

Steward, J. H. and Alfred Métraux

1948 Tribes of the Peruvian and Ecuadorian Montaña. In "Handbook of South American Indians," edited by J. H. Steward, Vol. 3, pp. 535-656. *Bureau of American Ethnology, Bulletin* 143. Washington.

Tello, J. C.

1943 Discovery of the Chavín Culture in Peru. *American Antiquity*, Vol. 9, No. 2, pp. 135-60. Menasha.

Tessmann, Günter

1928 *Menschen ohne Gott*. Strecker und Schröder, Stuttgart.

Willey, G. R.

1949 Ceramics. In "Handbook of South American Indians," edited by J. H. Steward, Vol. 5, pp. 139-205. *Bureau of American Ethnology, Bulletin* 143. Washington.

1955 The Interrelated Rise of the Native Cultures of Middle and South America. In "New Interpretations of Aboriginal American Culture History." *75th Anniversary Volume of the Anthropological Society of Washington*, pp. 28-45. Washington.

Harvard University
Cambridge, Mass.
August, 1957

# PERUVIAN METALLURGY

## Samuel K. Lothrop

At the time of the Discovery, most American Indians who had access to metals also had some knowledge of metals. But the higher skills, based on casting rather than hammering, became widespread only about a thousand years ago.

There is a certain uniformity in the spread of metallurgy. Excavations have shown that the Maya became acquainted with metal near the end of their Classic period. The inhabitants of central Mexico began to hammer gold and to cast copper bells in Tula-Toltec times before 1000 A.D., and this knowledge of casting spread to the southwestern United States before 1100 A.D., as is established by tree-ring dating. In Costa Rica and Panama, all kinds of metals are associated with the historic tribes, but earlier cultures, recently discovered, had no metals. At present we can say nothing about dating in Colombia. In most of Bolivia, in Chile, and in Argentina no metals earlier than the Tiahuanaco horizon are on record.

In several parts of Peru, however, metal was worked perhaps more than two thousand years ago. There are two principal regions where the development of metallurgical techniques can be followed in considerable detail and over this long period of time. One is on the south coast, embracing the valleys from Chincha to Acarí, approximately the area covered by the Nazca culture. The other is on the north-central coast, including the region between Lambayeque and Virú. Professor W. C. Root (280) has recently published a detailed study of the southern area.

The archeological knowledge of north-central Peru extends back to about 3000 B.C. At that time, there were villages near the mouths of the Chicama and Virú rivers. The natives had developed agriculture, basketry, and weaving. Pottery seems to have been introduced about 1800 B.C. and the complex culture known as Chavín was developed over a thousand years later. These dates are estimates of Mr. Junius Bird, based on geological data and on a carbon 14 test. The earliest metal now known comes from three Chavín tombs, two found near Chongoyape and the third in the interior. The objects recovered include crowns, circlets, ear spools, finger rings, necklaces, nose pendants, gorgets, pins, spoons, and tweezers. They are of a sheet gold, except two specimens which are partly of gold and partly of silver. Designs follow the classical sculpture of Chavín de Huántar (200, 201).

As there are no known antecedents to Chavín metallurgy in either style or technique, the presumption is strong that we are confronted with new inven-

Reprinted from THE CIVILIZATIONS OF ANCIENT AMERICA: Selected Papers of the XXIX International Congress of Americanists, 1951. pp. 219-223.

tions. After noting the presence of gold and silver nuggets, the natives must have learned that they were malleable and could be hammered in sheets, which they found could be cut in various shapes. Then followed the discovery of decorative techniques: embossing or making raised patterns, champlevé or driving in the background of a design, incising, and various combinations of these.

In addition there followed the discovery of certain effects of heat. This resulted in annealing, which made it possible to soften metal and thus to hammer it into more elaborate forms, and in the use of solder, which made it possible to join sheets of the same or different metals. Molds and the art of casting remained unknown.

This is a formidable list of inventions, but there were many basic processes left for future discovery. Chavín craftsmen could make hollow beads or hollow figurines by soldering together the parts. They were ignorant, however, of copper, tin, lead, the use of alloys, open and closed molds, gilding, and silvering. Although objects of great artistic merit were produced, the Chavín workmanship, apart from soldering and annealing, is definitely primitive.

Turning now to the south coast, the Necropolis culture discovered at Paracas was in part contemporaneous with Chavín, as established by certain art motives shared in common. Paracas produced beaten gold ornaments which were embossed. Root (280, p. 12) has shown that the process of annealing, or recrystallization of metal which had become brittle from hammering, was understood at that time. The other techniques of Chavín were not practiced.

The Nazca culture on the south coast of Peru also produced articles of sheet gold at an early period. These include masks, head ornaments, huge nose pendants, plumes, belts, cut-out figures to be sewn on clothing, and hollow beads (199). Comparison with pottery designs suggests that the gold dates from the latter portion of the period. The beads were made in two parts which were soldered together.

It is possible that casting in molds became known in late Nazca times. The evidence is based on some graves opened by my wife at Chaviña between Nazca and Chala. Typical late Nazca pottery was found together with spear throwers tipped with solid copper pegs in the form of animals. Analysis will show whether these were cast or hammered from nuggets. Casting never became common in the subsequent periods on the south coast of Peru.

The Nazca period was followed by Early Ica. The only metal object found by Uhle in twelve graves of this date was a copper earplug. Root suggests that this specimen was imported and that all knowledge of metallurgy may have been lost throughout the Early Ica and the subsequent Middle Ica I periods, a span of several centuries.

In the Middle Ica II period, metalwork again became common on the south coast of Peru. New artifacts such as cuffs, earplugs, tweezers, bowls, and jars were introduced, as well as new designs. In earlier times, most objects were of high grade native gold, but this later was replaced by gold-silver and silver-copper alloys. The latter became predominant in Late Ica times. Tumbaga, a gold-copper alloy, apparently never was employed on the south coast.

Turning again to the north-central coast of Peru, we find that the history of metallurgy partly parallels the evolution we have described in the south. While metalwork was rare in the Chavín period, it became almost extinct in the subsequent Salinar period. Only a few crude objects of sheet gold were manufactured, and technical processes were limited to simple embossing and occasional cut-out patterns (182, Fig. 203; 33, Pl. 68). Why the metal industry should have been almost completely obliterated in both northern and southern Peru we cannot say. The facts now known, however, indicate that few if any metal objects were manufactured over a period of centuries.

The renaissance of metallury in north central Peru took place in the Gallinazo period. Some of the old Chavín techniques were revived, and new metals and processes came into use. Occasional embossed ornaments of sheet gold continued to be manufactured, and silver again appeared. The great technical advance, however, was represented by simple castings of copper in closed molds. The oldest New World bells now known date from this epoch. Soldering also reappeared, gilding was discovered, as well as the use of metal sheets for overlays.

Technically, Gallinazo produced a great advance in metalworking. These growing skills, however, did not reach a high esthetic level until the Mochica period, an epoch when all the arts flourished. Delicate castings, probably by the *cire perdue* method, were produced. Bimetallic objects again appeared. Tumbaga, a copper-gold alloy, was discovered. Both gilding and silvering were mastered. Although bronze did not come into use until later (171, Appendix C), tools and weapons were now manufactured and became progressively more common and more complex.

The Early Tiahuanaco period in the Lake Titicaca basin differs from other Peruvian cultures because copper rather than gold was the first metal to be utilized. In the Classic Tiahuanaco period, gold and silver objects were manufactured and a copper-tin alloy, or bronze, came into use. Tiahuanaco influence, as is well known, later spread over most of Peru. In spite of its proximity, however, Tiahuanaco had practically no effect on south-coast metallurgy, notwithstanding the introduction of Tiahuanaco pottery and weaving styles. It seems probable, though, that the use of bronze on the north coast was the result of Tiahuanaco penetration.

In the Chimu period, shortly before the Conquest, the north-central coast enjoyed all known Peruvian metals, alloys, and technical processes, except the inlaying of one metal in another. This was practiced only in the mountains of southern Peru during the Inca period.

In this discussion we have said little about the influence of one region on another. Root has suggested that the renaissance of metals on the south coast was due to the influence of the central coast. This seems quite possible. Although

## TABLE 1

### DEVELOPMENT OF METALLURGY IN NORTHERN PERU

| Period | Metals | Techniques | |
|---|---|---|---|
| Chavín | Gold <br> Silver (rare) | Hammering <br> Embossing <br> Champlevé <br> Incising <br> Cut-out designs | Annealing <br> Welding <br> Soldering <br> Strap joining <br> Bimetallic objects |
| Salinar | Gold (rare) | Hammering <br> Embossing <br> Cut-out designs (rare) | |
| Gallinazo | Copper <br> Gold (rare) <br> Silver (rare) | Hammering <br> Embossing <br> Simple casting | Soldering <br> Gilding <br> Overlays |
| Mochica | Gold <br> Copper <br> Silver (rare) <br> Tumbaga? | Hammering <br> Embossing <br> Cut-out designs <br> Casting <br> Soldering | Gilding <br> Silvering <br> Bimetallic objects <br> Tools |
| Tiahuanaco | Gold    Silver <br> Copper    Tin   ? | Mochica techniques, plus bronze? | |
| Chimu | Gold    Silver <br> Copper    Tin <br> Lead (rare) | All Peruvian metals, techniques and processes except metal in metal in-lays | |

## TABLE 2

### DEVELOPMENT OF METALLURGY IN SOUTHERN PERU
#### (After Root, 1949)

| | Paracas | Nazca | Early Ica | Middle Ica I | Middle Ica II | Late Ica I | Late Ica II | Inca |
|---|---|---|---|---|---|---|---|---|
| Gold......... | X | X | ........ | ........ | X | X | X | X |
| Silver........ | ........ | ........ | ........ | ........ | X | X | X | X |
| Copper....... | ........ | ? | ? | ........ | X | X | X | X |
| Gold-silver.... | ........ | ........ | ........ | ........ | X | X | X | X |
| Silver-copper.. | ........ | ........ | ........ | ........ | X | X | X | X |
| Bronze........ | ........ | ........ | ........ | ........ | ........ | ........ | X | X |
| | | | | | | | | |
| Hammering... | X | X | ........ | ........ | X | X | X | X |
| Embossing.... | X | X | ........ | ........ | X | X | X | X |
| Engraving.... | X | X | ........ | ........ | X | X | X | X |
| Annealing.... | X | X | ........ | ........ | ? | X | X | X |
| Casting....... | ........ | ? | ........ | ........ | ? | ........ | X | X |
| Soldering..... | ........ | X | ........ | ........ | X | X | X | X |
| Welding...... | ........ | ........ | ........ | ........ | ........ | ........ | ? | X |
| Gilding....... | ........ | ........ | ........ | ........ | ........ | ........ | ........ | ........ |

the sequence of metallurgical development in the Lima region is uncertain, it is known that objects of Classic Tiahuanaco style have been found at Pachacamac (297, p. 370). This indicates that metal either was imported or manufactured on the central coast precisely during the period when it was not produced in the south.

The discovery of tin and the invention of bronze cannot yet be definitely placed. Obviously a stanniferous region was involved (251). Data now available indicate that the use of bronze was confined largely to the Inca period.

Peruvian metallurgy probably contributed to the metalwork of Ecuador but the reverse is not true. On the other hand, it seems that a gold-copper alloy, mis-en-couler gilding and complex cire perdue casting were developed first in Colombia, and later influenced Peru, perhaps as early as the end of the Mochica period. In the Lambayeque region during the Late Chimu period, delicate filigree castings became very popular (12).

Finally, a brief word should be said about possible Peruvian influence on Mexican metallurgy. It has been suggested that the entire Mexican knowledge of metals was acquired as a unit from Peru by sea. The chief arguments in favor of this hypothesis are that silver and bronze were used commonly in both countries but rarely or not at all in intervening regions. Against this theory we may point out that no silver alloys are known in Mexico, although they are common in Peru. Bronze was used only for tools in Mexico, but its value in making sharp castings for ornaments was understood in Peru. Objects of pure lead were cast in Peru, but in Mexico lead was alloyed with copper. Thus it appears to me that both countries had discovered the same five basic metals and shared many of the same techniques, but each used them in ways suited to their own needs.

# BIBLIOGRAPHY

Antze, Gustav

(12)    1930    Metallarbeiten aus dem nördlichen Peru; ein Beitrag zur Kenntnis ihrer Formen. Mitteilungen aus dem Museum für Völkerkunde in Hamburg, XV. Hamburg.

Bennett, Wendell Clark

(33)    1946    The archeology of the Central Andes. Handbook of South American Indians, Bureau of American Ethnology, Bulletin 143, vol. 2, pp. 61-147. Washington.

Kroeber, Alfred Louis

(171)    1944    Peruvian archeology in 1942. Viking Fund Publications in Anthropology, number four. New York.

Larco Hoyle, Rafael

(182)    1941    Los Cupisniques. Casa Editora "La Crónica" y "Variedades," Lima.

Lothrop, Samuel Kirkland

(199)    1937    Gold and silver from southern Peru and Bolivia. Journal of the Royal Anthropological Institute, vol. LXVII, no. 2, July-December, pp. 305-325. London.

(200)    1941    Gold ornaments of Chavín style from Chongoyape, Peru. American Antiquity, vol. VI, no. 3, January, pp. 250-262. Menasha.

(201)    1951    Gold artifacts of Chavín style. American Antiquity, vol. 16, no. 3, January, pp. 226-240. Salt Lake City.

Nordenskiold, Erland

(251)    1921    The Copper and Bronze Ages in South America. Comparative Ethnographical Studies, vol. IV. Goteborg.

Root, William Campbell

(280)    1949    The metallurgy of the southern coast of Peru. American Antiquity, vol. XV, no. 1, July, pp. 10-37. Menasha.

Schmidt, Max

(297)    1929    Kunst and Kultur von Peru. Im Propyläen Verlag, Berlin.

# POTTERY STAMPING AND MOLDING ON THE
## NORTH COAST OF PERU

### Donald Collier

This paper is concerned with two Peruvian traditions of pottery construction and decoration. The first of these is the tradition of concave one-and two-piece molds; this is found on the southern portion of the North Coast. The second, typical of the far North Coast, is characterized by paddle-and-anvil construction and stamped decoration.

While making archaeological investigations in Casma Valley in 1956, I visited the pottery-making village of Mórrope, near Chiclayo.[1] I had heard that pottery molds were still used there and hoped that by observation of their use I might gain insight into the prehistoric molding techniques used to the south. Instead, I found the potters using the paddle and anvil; a convex mold functionally associated with paddling; and pottery stamps.

### Pottery Making at Mórrope

Mórrope lies about 30 km. northwest of Lambayeque on the southern edge of the Desierto de Mórrope. There are ten families of potters in Mórrope, all living in the northwest sector of the town—an area known as "Barrio la Otra Banda". The men are the potters but each is assisted by his family. The markets in Lambayeque, Chiclayo and nearby towns are the main outlets for the red, oxidized pottery of Mórrope. The potter's clay comes from a deposit about 30 km. north of Mórrope.

The molding is the first stage of construction. A stand consisting of a tall, inverted jar is set firmly in the sandy floor of the potter's shady patio. The up-ended bottom of this jar is then covered with sacking, to prevent the mold from slipping. The mold, which I shall call a convex pot-mold to distinguish it from other types of molds, is an ordinary pottery jar (*cántaro*).

Reprinted from ACTAS DEL XXXIII CONGRESO INTERNACIONAL DE AMERICANISTAS, 1959. pp. 421–431.

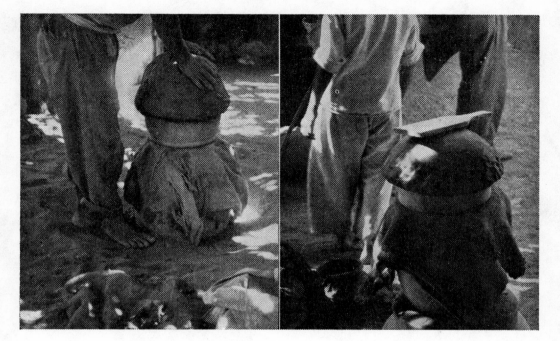

Fig. 1. Molding the clay over the base of an inverted jar to form the bottom half of a jar.

Fig. 2. Clay molded over an inverted jar and ready to be thinned and smootherd with a wooden paddle. Note that the mold stand consists of two jars.

It is placed upside down on the stand with its mouth resting on the sack-covered upper surface of the stand (fig. 1). The top of the mold is then about 75 cm. from the floor. The stand is sometimes elevated by embedding in the mouth of another jar that is set firmly in the floor and filled with sand. In this case the stand is either set mouth down so that its base supports the mold, or it is set base down and filled with sand flush with the rim so as to form a platform for the mold (fig. 2).

The potter stands while he works. He picks up a previously prepared "tortilla" of soft clay and dusts it and the mold with dry, powdered clay, which serves as a separator. He slaps the "tortilla" onto the mold and beats it down with his hands, moving continuously around the mold as he works and adding blobs of clay as they are needed (fig. 1). The final thinning and smoothing of the clay on the mold are done with a wooden paddle (fig. 2). He lets the clay dry for about ten minutes, then removes the partly formed vessel from the mold and sets it aside for further drying.

If the vessel is to be a bowl, the potter finishes the rim by adding a fillet of clay, which he shapes and smooths with his fingers and finally wipes with a wet cloth. If the vessel is to be a jar. it is placed bottom down on a finishing stand consisting of a tall, upright jar with sack-covered mouth. The walls are then further thinned and worked upward and inward by blows struck on the outer surface by a wooden paddle. A stone anvil is held on the inside, opposite the paddle. Fillets of clay are added to the upper edge of the walls as needed. The potter constantly circles around the vessel as he shapes and thins it. When making large jars, he continues this process until the neck opening is reached. But a different procedure is followed with small and medium-sized jars. After the vessel wall has been formed well above the shoulder, the potter places the jar on its side with its shoulder resting in the depression on top of the finishing stand. He holds the anvil against the inner side of the upper wall and paddles the wall on the outside from above (fig. 3). As the work progresses, instead of circling the jar as he did previously, he stands still and continually revolves it on its shoulder by slight motions of the paddle and anvil at the end of each stroke. The axis of revolution varies from nearly horizontal to 45 degrees, depending on which portion of the wall is being paddled.

When the jar has been finished up to the neck opening, it is set aside for further drying. The neck is then formed by applying a fillet of clay, which is smoothed with the fingers and then wiped with a wet cloth.

Fig. 3. Finishing a small jar with a paddle and an anvil. The paddle appears thicker than it is due to blurring.

The flat wooden paddles at Mórrope are rectangular, about 12 cm. wide, 20 cm. long, and 15 mm. thick (fig. 2). Both a plain paddle and a paddle with fine, diagonal, parallel grooves are used. The former produces a smooth vessel surface that later may be polished with a bivalve shell. The latter makes a surface covered with overlapping series of faint parallel ridges, which are left unpolished. This ridged surface is visible on the large bowl held by the girl shown in figure 6, where it contrasts with the smoothed band above that was produced during the finishing of the rim. The anvils are polished, ovoid river cobbles.

Carved wooden combs with four or five teeth are used to make diagonal groups of parallel incisions on jar shoulders just below the necks.

Stamps of fired clay are used at Mórrope to press designs into the still plastic shoulders of jars, but they are not employed as frequently today as formerly and are not valued or preserved by the potters, who say it is easy to make others when they are needed. Mórrope stamps are pear-shaped in outline, flat on both surfaces, and about 11-12 cm. long, 6-7 cm. wide and 2-2.5 cm. thick. The designs are incised or punctated on the stamp while the clay is still plastic. We saw three stamps (fig. 4): The first had

Fig. 4. Three pottery stamps from Morrope, showing both faces.

a plant with leaves and flowers on one face and a butterfly-like figure on the other; the second had two flowering plants on one face and an overall pattern of parallel incisions and rows of punctations on the other; the third had a cluster of circles with reed-punctate centers surrounded with circles of punctations on one face and no design on the other.

Fig. 5.  Fig. 8.

Fig. 6.

Fig. 9.

Fig. 7.  Fig. 10.

Fig. 5. Unfired pots drying in the sun.

Fig. 6. Repairing defects in sun-dried pots.

Fig. 7. Jars drying over smoldering dung.

Fig. 8. Jars drying over smoldering dung.

Fig. 9. Loading jars in pit for firing.

Fig. 10. The firing pit almost completely loaded. Large sherds cover the pile of jars.

Finished pots are dried first in the shade and then in the sun (fig. 5). After sun-drying they are inspected, and the imperfections in the surface are smoothed over with wet clay (fig. 6). The pots are then placed on top of piles of smouldering dung for two or three hours to remove the remaining moisture from the clay (figs. 7 and 8). They are repeatedly turned so that they will dry evenly. The firing takes place in a shallow pit about two by three meters and 25 cm. deep. The bottom of the pit is covered evenly with a layer of finely broken sticks and branches. Large jars are placed upright on the branches in contiguous rows. Then another layer of large jars is stacked on the first with the mouths down and positioned so that portions of the mouths of the lower jars open into the interstices of the upper layer, thus assuring a free circulation of oxygen during firing (fig. 9). Bowls and smaller ollas are stacked in two or three layers along the sides and ends of the central pile (fig. 10). There were 120 pots in one firing that we observed, and 70 in another. The whole pile is covered with large potsherds, then with a layer of broken branches, and finally, after the ignition of the wood, with a layer of dung. Firing is usually done in the afternoon and the pots are allowed to cool overnight before being taken to market.

A rather similar pottery industry exists at Simbilá near Piura, some 150 km. north of Mórrope (Christensen, 1955). The Simbilá potters, who are men, shape vessels from a lump of clay with wooden paddle and stone anvil, but they do not use the convex pot-mold. Their fired-clay stamps are similar in shape and designs to those of Mórrope. In addition to the standard domestic red ware, they produce mold-made black effigy pots for sale to tourists. These are either copied from ancient pots (*huacos*) or the molds are made from the latter. No description of the molding techniques is available.

The practice of molding the lower half of a vessel over the base of an inverted pottery jar, which I am calling the convex pot-mold, has also been reported from Colombia (Riechel-Dolmatoff, 1945), El Salvador (Lothrop, 1927, p. 116) and Jalisco and Colima in Mexico (Taylor, 1933; Foster, 1955, p. 4). In Cuernavaca, Mexico, specially made thick-walled jars are used in inverted position as molds (Foster, 1948, pp. 363-64). Only in Jalisco is this molding technique associated with paddling on the mold (pottery or wooden paddles) and the paddle-and-anvil technique (wooden paddle, heel of left hand used for anvil) for finishing the upper half of a vessel placed on a pottery stand. But the Jalisco potters do not use incised paddles or stamps for decorating pots.

## Two Ancient Pottery Traditions

The archaeological importance of stamped pottery on the far North Coast of Peru was first brought to notice by Kroeber and Muelle (1942). Throughout the region, from Pariñas Valley in the north to Jequetepeque Valley in the south, the most common pottery found on prehistoric habitation sites is a red ware bearing a great variety of simple and complicated stamped designs (Kroeber, 1930, p. 87; Kroeber and Muelle, 1942; Lothrop, 1948, pp. 64-65). In spite of its abundance on living sites this stamped red ware is rarely seen in museum collections. Evidently it was primarily for domestic use and was rarely placed in graves. The stamped designs were made with incised paddles and stamps of fired clay, of which a number have been found (Kroeber and Muelle, pp. 7-10, figs. 1-3). This stamped ware was fully developed on the far North Coast at least as early as the Coast Tiahuanaco period, was abundant during the Chimu period, and continued to be used until the Spanish conquest.

The modern pottery stamps used at Mórrope and Simbilá are similar in form and designs to the prehistoric pottery stamps, although there has been a reduction in design complexity, and a flower design of European origin has been added. The modern wooden paddle is similar in form and probably in function to the prehistoric pottery paddle. Whether there has been a complete shift in material from clay to wood or whether wooden as well as pottery paddles were formerly used can be settled only by further investigation. It might be possible to distinguish on the ancient pottery between designs originally incised on clay paddles and those carved on wooden ones.

There is no evidence at present to indicate that inverted jars were used for molding the bottoms of jars in prehistoric times. If the ancient potters did use the molding and paddling techniques of Mórrope, it should be possible to detect on the sherds a difference of surface finish on the interior of the basal and upper walls. The former would show the paddle-marked or smoothed surface of the mold, whereas the latter would be scraped or would have faint, concave facets left by the pressure of the anvil[2]. A quantity of large body sherds sufficient for such a study could probably be obtained only by excavation.

The interpretation of the archaeological evidence in terms of the modern pottery techniques at Mórrope and Simbilá leads to the following conclusions about the ancient pottery tradition of the far North Coast. 1) The paddle-

and-anvil technique was a basic mode of construction, which may have been combined with the molding of vessel bases on inverted jars. 2) Pottery paddles were used in vessel construction and for imparting all-over patterns to vessel surfaces. It is not known if wooden paddles were used. 3) Pottery stamps were used for making all-over patterns or for stamping design series around vessel shoulders.

On the southern half of the North Coast, from Chicama Valley to Casma, a contrasting tradition of pottery manufacture persisted. This was the tradition of one and two-piece concave molds. These molding techniques were already well developed during the Mochica period,[3] when they were used to make elaborate effigy-vessels for funerary use, but they did not reach their greatest degree of elaboration and extent of use until the post-Classic epoch (Collier, 1955, pp. 124-31). By Chimu times molds were used to produce all pottery except the largest storage jars, and ceramic manufacture reached the stage of mass production. The stipple-relief and figure-relief surface decoration so characteristic of the Chimu pottery made for both ceremonial and everyday use were entirely products of these molding techniques.

## Conclusions

The paddling-stamping techniques and the piece-mold techniques are parts of two historically distinct pottery traditions found on the North Coast of Peru. At present the molding tradition of the south is thought to be older than the stamping tradition of the north, but when the far North Coast is better known archaeologically the stamping tradition may prove to be equally old. I am inclined to believe that the rocker stamping of Chavin ceramics is historically unconnected with the later paddle stamping of the far North Coast, but proof of this must await more knowledge of the late Formative and Classic pottery of the northern region.

These two traditions did not exist in isolation. Simple check stamping spread to the south during the Coast Tiahuanaco period, probably as a part of the backwash of influence from the far North Coast following the spread of the Tiahuanaco style. The direction of the spread of check stamping is clear, for it reached Chicama in middle Tiahuanaco, but did not appear in Virú and in Casma, its southernmost extension, until late Tiahuanaco (Bennett, 1939, p. 88; Collier, 1955, p. 110). From Chicama southward check stamping was used to decorate the shoulders of black, *mold-made* jars (Collier, 1955, p. 176). These check-stamped vessels were not common.

Sometime during the Coast Tiahuanaco period the two-piece, concave mold spread to the far North Coast, where it was used to make effigy vessels, usually in black ware. Incised paddles or stamps were occasionally used to decorate the shoulders of these fancy molded vessels (Kroeber and Muelle, 1942, p. 21 and fig. 8). Thus there occurred here a slight blending of techniques from the two traditions. But the concave mold was never applied to domestic ware, which continued to be paddled and stamped and fired red. The old stamping tradition of the far North Coast continued undiverted until the coming of Pizarro, and it survives today in the pottery industries of Mórrope and Simbilá. Whether the molding of effigy vessels at Simbilá is a continuation of the old molding tradition is unclear.

It is a pity that on the southern half of the North Coast there is no surviving pottery industry that could deepen our understanding of the old molding tradition.

The closest contemporary parallel with the pottery techniques of Mórrope is found in Jalisco, Mexico. The numerous archaeological parallels between western Mexico and the coast of Ecuador lead one to wonder if any part of the paddling-stamping tradition of northern Peru diffused from Mexico by way of Ecuador, or in the reverse direction. The first step in testing this idea would be to investigate modern pottery techniques in coastal Ecuador and to look for evidence of paddling and stamping on the ancient pottery there. But these speculations lead far from the potters of Mórrope, who carry on a very old ceramic tradition that appears to have developed independently on the far North Coast of Peru.

---

## N O T E S

1 This field work was carried out on an expedition of Chicago Natural History Museum financed by a grant from the National Science Foundation. I am indebted to José Eulogio Garrido, Director of the Museo de Arqueología de la Universidad Nacional de Trujillo, for guiding me to Mórrope, and to Donald E. Thompson, my field assistant, for augmenting my observations at Mórrope.

2 Muelle reports anvil marks on the interior of a mold-made jar from Lambayeque (Kroeber and Muelle, 1942, p. 5, n. 5).

3 Larco Hoyle has stated that Cupisnique grave vessels were made in two-piece molds (Larco Hoyle, 1941, pp. 35-36), but he has not presented the evidence for this conclusion. The matter needs further investigation in view of the Classic date for the earliest molds in Mesoamerica.

# BIBLIOGRAPHY

BENNETT, WENDELL C.
1939 Archaeology of the North Coast of Peru. An Account of Exploration and Excavation in Virú and Lambayeque Valleys. Anthropological Papers, American Museum of Natural History, vol. 37, pt. 1. New York.

COLLIER, DONALD
1955 Cultural Chronology and Change as Reflected in the Ceramics of the Virú Valley, Peru. Chicago Natural History Museum, Fieldiana: Anthropology, vol. 43, Chicago.

CHRISTENSEN, ROSS T.
1955 A Modern Ceramic Industry at Simbilá near Piura, Peru. Chimor, Boletín del Museo de Arqueología de la Universidad Nacional de Trujillo, Año 3, pp. 10-20. Trujillo.

FOSTER, GEORGE M.
1948 Some Implications of Modern Mexican Mold-made Pottery. Southwestern Journal of Anthropology, vol. 4, pp. 356-70. Albuquerque.

1955 Contemporary Pottery Techniques in Southern and Central Mexico. Middle American Research Institute, Tulane University, Publication 22, pp. 1-48. New Orleans.

KROEBER, A. L.
1930 Archaeological Explorations in Peru. Part II: The Northern Coast. Field Museum of Natural History, Anthropological Memoirs, vol. 2, pt. 2. Chicago.

KROEBER, A. L., and MUELLE, J. C.
1942 Cerámica Paleteada de Lambayeque. Revista del Museo Nacional, tomo II, pp. 1-24. Lima.

LARCO HOYLE, RAFAEL
1941 Los Cupisniques. Lima.

LOTHROP, S. K.
1927 The Potters of Guatajiagua, Salvador. Indian Notes, Museum of the American Indian, Heye Foundation, vol. 4, pp. 109-118. New York.

1948 Pariñas-Chira Archaeology: A Preliminary Report. American Antiquity, vol. 13, no. 4, pt. 2 (Memoir no. 4), pp. 53-65. Menasha.

REICHEL-DOLMATOFF, G.

1945   La Manufactura de Cerámica entre los Chami.   Boletín de Arqueología, vol. 1, pp. 425-30.   Bogotá.

TAYLOR, PAUL

1933   Making Cántaros at San José Tateposco, Jalisco, Mexico.   American Anthropologist, vol. 35, pp. 745-51.   Menasha.

# THE CULTURAL SIGNIFICANCE OF PERUVIAN TEXTILES:
## PRODUCTION, FUNCTION, AESTHETICS

A. H. Gayton

In writing this article I am indebted to two great predecessors: Alfred L. Kroeber for his comprehensive and perceptive appreciation of Peruvian art as a cultural expression, and Lila M. O'Neale for her objective analysis of textiles as a measure of Peruvian technical development. Neither of them was indifferent to the values which the other emphasized. In assessing the Andean arts Kroeber recognized the technical limitations of the textile medium, while O'Neale frequently commented upon aesthetic aspects such as color and design. The former saw in textiles, as in ceramics, differentiating elements of style that would aid in establishing the time sequences of Andean subcultures; the latter perceived the technical data she must extract to aid in elucidating the chronological distinctions. As pioneers who advanced the systematic study of ancient Andean culture, they have been succeeded by able scholars whose investigations are continuously broadening and clarifying our knowledge of that civilization. Yet, so far as textiles are concerned, the developments largely have followed the basic interests of Kroeber and O'Neale--the significance of art styles and techniques as time-indicators.

Outside the professional field Peruvian textiles have received their share of acclaim from the current popular interest in "primitive art" which has been publicizing by turns of fashion Oceanian, African, North Pacific Coast, Andean, and Mexican native arts. Through exhibitions and illustrations the finest of Peruvian textiles have been presented to a public pleased by their beauty but indifferent to their original sense or their sundering from their cultural context. Such display textiles are selected for their aesthetic values alone. Often unable to represent a specific time-place style because of dubious provenience, neither do they exemplify the general quality range of textile products from which they have been extracted. However appreciatively Peruvian textiles have been regarded for their utility in providing chronological clues, their technical distinctions, and their aesthetic worth, the use and meaning of the fabrics to those who wove and wore them have somehow been lost to sight.

The aim herein is to engender some comprehension of Peruvian textiles as tangibles, as necessities, and as pleasures in their former human context. This approach is compatible with Kroeber's interests in Andean prehistory which were always those of the culture historian. He regarded "all native Peruvian civilization as a unit--a larger historical whole, a major areal culture with time depth." That the materials were archaeological and the ordering of their stylistic data a methodological necessity were but incidental to his prevailing objective--an understanding of the manifold nature of culture through time. As he has said, "The data on the major South American arts are inextricably intertwined with archaeology." The archaeological research and related textile analysis which Kroeber initiated in the 1920's have continued to accumulate, through succeeding decades, sufficient ramifying data to support reconstructive thoughts on the role of textiles in ancient Andean life.

Reprinted from KROEBER ANTHROPOLIGICAL SOCIETY PAPERS, No. 25, 1961.
pp. 111-128.

Like all products of human hands, the textiles of Peru were enmeshed with material and social aspects of the culture which created them. Technical developments can nourish yet delimit the product as a substance. The numerous ways in which cloth can be utilized can encourage production. If the decorative possibilities serve not only aesthetic aims but political and religious ends as well, as was the case in Peru, the role played by the medium can become entrenched and even powerful enough to keep rival media in abeyance. In this articulation of material and social factors, as exemplified here by fabrics, the interplay may be such as to reinforce social aspects and possibly in periods of simplest beginnings even to initiate them.

However much the finest of Peruvian fabrics have been exhibited, illustrated, and lauded in print, they represent but one extreme of an enormous range of quality. A large proportion of textiles, while not lacking in simple touches of embellishment, were made primarily for rugged uses. Coarse, burlap-like cloths were the usual outer wrappings of mummy bundles; similar cloths must have been employed in many ways--as containers for carrying in the harvests, baling goods for markets local or distant, as household utility cloths, and as garments by the poor. From north to south and east to west in the Andean area through twenty centuries, many thousands of sturdy, homely fabrics were produced as a normal necessity in the ordinary business of living. Ignored by collectors, this huge class of textiles is now known only in a small percentage of its original bulk as extracted from modern, controlled excavations--worn, patched, dirty and ragged.

Of domestic furnishings in ancient Peruvian homes we still know little, yet occasional specimens offer clues suggesting that people of some status, not only the elite, had padded quilts, small cushions, and cradling cloths. Fabrics hung in tombs may represent similar usage in dwellings; certainly some decorative textiles, because of their size or odd shapes, could hardly have been costume parts. Triangular, patterned cloths hung from the feathered canopy of the Inca's litter, as drawn by Guamán Poma de Ayala. A specimen in the Uhle Collection at Berkeley brings to mind portières because of its construction, length, and painted lower ends; this is a guess, of course. Yet to imagine the textile-conscious Peruvians in bare rooms would be an even stranger fancy. The general lack of capacious baskets or wooden chests implies that bulky goods such as extra clothing and ornaments were wrapped in cloths for home storage.

It is as clothing and its accessories that Peruvian textiles are best known. Here at least is abundant evidence that the potentialities of weaving were fully realized in the many-faceted role which dress plays in an advanced society. The basic garments were few: breechcloth, kilt, shirt, and mantle for men, and a one-piece dress and mantle for women. Additions of scarfs for the head, hair ties, and belts were usual. Cloth pouches were a general accessory for men, possibly for women too, as in Inca times. Specialties occurred which were characteristic of particular periods or places, such as the Paracas shoulder yoke, the Tiahuanacan four-pointed cap, or the Inca feathered poncho, but these were extrinsic to the standard forms which persisted through the centuries. Within the standardized forms a tremendous stylistic range was made possible by the variables of the textile content. The stylistic components of Peruvian garments were dimensions, fibers, colors, weaves, designs, and superstructural embellishments such as embroidery, passamenterie, reserve dyeing, and painting. Each component had many variables which by permutation permitted diversified styles to emerge in spite of the continuous adherence to basically simple garment forms. The styles which characterized areal and temporal planes in Peruvian history represented selections or constellations of preferences from innumerable possibilities for variation.

In the following discussion place and time labels have been kept to the minimum and esoteric textile nomenclature avoided whenever possible. The overall time span is roughly 2,000 years: from 500 B.C., by which time weaving was well developed, to 1532 A.D., date of the Spanish conquest. For temporal locations the terms early, middle, and late have been used loosely to cover approximately 500 B.C. to 700 A.D., 700 A.D. to 1200 A.D., and 1200 A.D. to 1532 A.D. They are time segments which encompass but do not delineate certain of the major cultures referred to by name. Thus Mochica, Paracas, and Nazca are within the early span, Tiahuanaco-Huari in the middle span, and Chimu and Inca of late times. (The newest archaeological timetable for prehistoric Peru is in the 1960 edition of Bennett and Bird, Andean Culture History, p. 112).

## Production

Of occupations at large, whether domestic or institutionalized, undoubtedly food production, ceramic manufacture, and textile fabrication were the three which consumed most of the time and energy of the Andean people as constant concerns. With cloth, production consists of many successive stages, each requiring particular knowledge and skills contributing toward a successful culmination as united in the end product. In the sophisticated civilization of Peru hundreds of persons were primarily engaged in various phases of cloth production. While many coastal families grew their own cotton, acquired a little wool (perhaps already spun and dyed), and wove sufficient cloth for their humble needs, the quantities of high-standard fabrics from Peru imply a marked degree of specialization--and not of weavers alone.

The prime desideratum was production of raw materials in sufficient quantity for the textile needs of a fairly dense population. A notion of quantity needs may be understood by imagining a simple example, a very coarse cotton cloth which might have been used by a laboring family. It is one yard square, woven in tabby or "plain weave square count" with 10 warps and 10 wefts per square inch. This means that within its dimensions there are 360 yards of warp crossed by 360 yards of weft, total yarn content 720 yards. For various purposes such a family might have five similar utility cloths in use, representing 3,600 yards of yarn. A hamlet of twenty hearths, as a reasonably small, humble community, then would have 72,000 yards or roughly 41 miles of the crudest sort of yarn employed in its low grade utility cloths alone. One could multiply this community many times over in coast and highland at any moment from the time of Christ onward. And, of course, in addition, the fiber requirements for medium and fine quality domestic cloths, garments, accessories, and grave offerings of all classes of persons must be conjured up as the normal, maximal requirement of fiber-in-use all at the same time.

Agricultural and pastoral pursuits produced the cotton and alpaca fibers which constituted the bulk of Peruvian textiles; llama as the coarsest wool and vicuña as the finest represented lesser quantities at each end of the quality scale. Indigenous to coast and highland, respectively, cotton and wool have been one of the major evidences for an early established trade system between these regions. Cotton was the fiber with which weaving began on the coast in preceramic times, yet the advent of wool and its incorporation in textiles in increasing amounts from pre-Christian times onward indicate that this fiber already had been used in weaving in the highland area to which wool was indigenous. Unless wool had its own history of usefulness in textile production it would not have come down to the coast as a commodity. All alpaca wool in coastal textiles was imported from the highlands; under primitive and prehistoric conditions acclimatization of these high altitude animals to a lowland habitat was unlikely.

Planting, tending, and harvesting of cotton was an occupation in itself, as was the breeding, herding, and fleecing of alpacas to supply the demands of consumption. The rounding-up and capture of vicuñas, never domesticated even in Inca times, probably called for a special class of hunters skilled in the pursuit of this shyest of all the wool-bearing cameloids. All the raw materials of textiles need preliminary processing. Both cotton bolls and fleeces must be cleared of refuse before deseeding or wool-washing can be done. Twigs, leaf bits, burrs, sand, and mud balls infest one or both fibers at the source. Color sorting, especially of wools from piebald pelts, might be done at this time rather than after marketing. Whether baling and marketing was done by the growers or by special middlemen vendors, distribution to spinners and weavers had to take place. In coastal valleys or highland districts, the native cottons and wools would move in small circuits; between highland and coast the humble llama, whose wool was disdained for good quality cloth, was the burden-bearer in caravans which continuously traveled the routes of communication exchanging commodities between the grossly different environments.

The spinner's role was a vital one in cloth production, requiring patient engagement in tasks onerous and monotonous. Even though the fibers were received in a partially cleaned state, their final preparation was necessary before spinning could begin. Remaining seeds and minute detritus must be pulled from cotton lints, and dirt and excessive grease washed from the wools. Standard Peruvian yarns show that paralleling of fibers was usually done; this to make a smooth, even yarn. Cotton fibers can be straightened by pulling small flocks apart over and over again. Laid together until a large pad of the prepared lints was formed, the pad became the stock from which the spinner drew forth fibers while spinning. A similar method may have been used with wool since wool cards were unknown and the combs found in ancient workbaskets are too delicate save for a final combing after preliminary finger straightening of wool fibers. (The combs are supposedly battens for pressing down tapestry wefts; they could have served both purposes.)

Even allowing for the fact that drop-spindle spinning can be carried on while walking about--as to fields, market, or a neighbor's house--the amount of time devoted to yarn-making must have been very great. Medium to fine quality yarns required the supported-spindle method whereby the operator sat on the ground with the spindle tip resting in a bowl or gourd to obviate strain on the forming strand. This was not a side occupation, especially when hundreds of yards of fine thread were to be produced. Rates of hand-spindle spinning differ so much by fiber and quality that it is fruitless to estimate even roughly what the production rate might have been.  But the quantities of good-grade cloths, not to mention those of luxury quality, indicate that Peruvian spinners probably formed a group distinct from both the suppliers of raw materials and the weavers.

Spinning is a skill which even in its highest proficiency can scarcely be called an art, yet that skill is an essential contribution to any textile which has artistic status.  Notable Peruvian tapestries with 250 wefts or more per inch are popularly credited to the weaver's art, while the spinner whose deft fingers produced yarn 1/250 of an inch in diameter goes unrecognized.  Length of yarn is impressive when the hundreds of yards necessary for even one crude cloth are realized.  But consistency of diameter with a uniform degree of twist--whether loose, moderate, or tight--is the criterion of perfection.  Delicate cotton threads are the most difficult to make uniform while retaining sufficient tensile strength to withstand the strain of weaving.  Yet such threads are far from rare in Peruvian fabrics.  Wools, with their longer staple often up to several inches, have the advantage of greater overlap in spinning.  On the other hand, alpaca and vicuña filaments are somewhat slippery and less prone to stabilize by intertwisting on themselves than are cotton lints.

Beside the initial spinning of single strands, doubling or respinning singles into two-ply thread was common practice, this task being a further time-consumer for the Peruvian spinner.  Yarns of multiple ply, such as those for loom strings, sewing, tassels, and other special purposes, may well have been made by the weaver as they were needed for work in hand.  However, compared to single- and two-ply yarns for cloth construction, the amounts of these special yarns were negligible.  It was the gross yarn needs for cloth in use and under construction, as well as the standards of excellence, which suggest that spinners formed a separate occupational class in the old Andean culture.

Color is an outstanding characteristic of Peruvian textiles.  Dyes were applied to cleaned fiber stock before spinning, to hanks of spun yarn, and to cloths taken from the loom (piece-dyeing).  The last method apparently was the least used for quality fabrics except when resist treatments were first applied to reserve areas of the cloth from the dye bath in order to create designs.  The enormous range of tints and shades, estimated by analysts as more than 150, was an early achievement in Peruvian textile history and one requiring expert knowledge.  Cottons are not amenable to the full absorption of dyes, although wools are.  With either fiber and with dye sources which varied chemically, the successful production of uniform colors for large quantities of yarn and which did not fade or bleed depended upon consistent dye decoctions and mordants that set the dye in the fibers.

Long periods of experimentation with many materials must have preceded the stage of security demonstrated by polychrome textiles made some three hundred years before the time of Christ and continuously produced throughout the pre-conquest centuries.  Of specific dye sources little is known as yet since the necessary laboratory analyses can be done only by a few experts.  Of dyes so proven the roster is surprisingly small:  indigo, relbunium, cochineal and shell-fish, with alum and iron mordants.  The varying hues of the natural fibers, both cotton and wool, account for much of the color range possible in combination with a few dyes. It seems probable that more dye sources will eventually be revealed. Whatever the circumstances, the procuring of raw materials, the extraction, preparation, and composition of dye solutions, together with their effective mordants, was an exacting task not haphazardly performed by amateurs. That the base fiber colors were different in subtle degrees made a further variable which the dyer had to take into account to achieve the desired tone. Wherever dyeing was done in quantity and with competence in ancient Peru a skilled artisan class can be postulated from the evidence of the textiles which their art enhanced.

Catering to spinners' and weavers' needs may have been special occupations too. Their equipment included an assortment of spindles with decorated whorls, hardwood battens, bone awls and picks, combs, and workbaskets. These objects are profuse not only in the general archaeological remains but sometimes in single graves as well. A burial yielding over 250 stone, pottery, and horn whorls certainly suggests that the individual had been a maker or vendor of these small, essential accessories.

Thus, before the weavers began their own distinctive tasks, there were numerous other persons involved in the preweaving stages. People on coastal farms and in mountain pastures, in spinning centers and dye establishments, on the paths to distribution—all were engaged in the production of textile materials which the weavers could coordinate and transform into cloth. In modern terms this is "the textile industry." In terms of a prehistoric culture it was a coordinated activity representing a large segment of the population's economic resources and productive enterprise.

The weaver's part in textile production is the one most familiar to us today, yet it is often taken for granted without any real understanding of the obstacles overcome in the actual construction of a cloth—more particularly when the weaver worked with few manual aids and a loom lacking treadle attachments. The Peruvian home-weaver as well as the professional was faced with certain common problems when making cloths for specific uses. By and large, most of their fabrics consisted of two identical webs seamed together to make up the desired width. Warp length could extend to several yards, if so wanted, but weft width on the backstrap loom in general use throughout the Andean world was limited to the weaver's reach. The loom required the insertion of the battening sword, a heavy wooden slat always at least two handbreadths wider than the warp plane. About 27 inches was the practical limit for width, and most woven webs were narrower than that. Consequently, even the crude cloth one yard square used above as an example of yarn needs, would have been woven in two strips 18 inches wide and 36 inches long, then sewn together. For the weaver this means that planning for finished dimensions must be calculated for two warpings and two weftings, and that patterned fabrics must be woven so that their parts will match when seamed together.

Since all clothing was made to size the length and number of warps had to be estimated for all webs composing a garment, e.g., for a shirt, two webs for the body, two others if it were to have sleeves, and three more if there were to be decorative bands on the sleeves and around the bottom of the body. Warping, the winding of the warp yarns before shifting them to the loom beams, is one of the most tedious parts of cloth-making. Length could be gauged when the warping posts were set up, but each turn of the yarn around them must be neither slack nor taut but of exactly uniform tension. Further, the heddle leases had to be lashed precisely to every other warp; a lease loop too long or too short would create trouble for the weaver when opening a shed and passing through the bobbin and battening sword. A covert virtue of Peruvian fabrics is the perfection of the original warping before weaving was begun, a seldom recognized skill of the weaver.

The weaving techniques at a competent weaver's command were several, and a choice of the one or more to be employed would have been made when assembling the yarns needed and setting up the warp. A cloth with a smooth surface, in which the warps predominated, required that the warps be set close together, or, for an opposite effect, as in tapestry weave, they would be spaced slightly apart. Complex weaves such as gauze, doubleface, doublecloth, or interlocking warp demanded excessive care in particular warping methods. These more difficult weaves were not uncommon and two or three techniques were often combined in one fabric.

Obviously, the qualities of yarns as fine or coarse, colored or natural, make differences in the physical nature and visual effects of a fabric. Another potent visual factor is the construction used--the ways in which the wefts interlace with the warps in the weave. This determines the texture of the surface, the visual emphasis of warps or wefts, the intensity of colors, and the adaptations of motifs. The weave or construction thus is not merely a necessary mechanical procedure in order to build a cloth of warps and wefts but engrosses factors of function and of aesthetics. This potency of structure, sufficient to enhance or mar the qualities of yarns, colors, and designs, was a major motivation for developing the different methods of interlacing warps and wefts which distinguish one weaving technique from another. In their severalties or in combination they augmented the satisfactions the Peruvians derived from their textiles. The weavers independently developed and perfected a roster of techniques which matched that of the Old World, adding a unique one of their own, the interlocking-warp technique. Plain weaves, tapestry, brocade, gauze, and doublecloth were already in use before the Christian era (in the Paracas Cavernas period), indicating a prior experimental period in which cloth structure had been explored in conjunction with the potentials of fibers, spins, and colors to result in a fabric production with controlled, professional competence.

That the home-weaving of cloths and garments ranging in quality from shoddy to excellent was a normal household activity in ancient Peru may be taken for granted. Nevertheless, the abundant remains of distinguished workmanship, often to the degree of virtuosity, indicate the existence of a class of specialists. The group of expert weavers, screened for their proficiency, who served the Inca rulers probably represent but one known instance of professionalism which had been long established in Peru. Quality and quantity as known from Paracas times onward make it inconceivable that such textiles were the products of part-time home-weavers whose thoughts and energies were claimed by multiple household duties. Whether these professional weavers worked commercially, were subsidized, or enforced to labor as for the Inca, there is no telling. The famous Mochica vase showing women at looms, a male supervisor, and a higher ranking man seated on a dais is usually interpreted as a "factory" scene. It

could as well be a training establishment or the working quarters in a great
household like those of Egypt and Medieval Europe. In any case, weavers are
depicted there as a discrete group, implicitly separated from housewifely rou-
tine of the ordinary sort.

Even further specialization within the professional class is implied by
the perfection of the complicated designs executed in the more difficult techniques. A weaver might master a technique and produce several exquisite fabrics
of that structure within a lustrum or decade but would hardly produce master-
pieces in all construction methods within the same period. Either as a life
work or by periodic changes the finest weavers must have concentrated on not
more than one or two techniques to produce, from planning to execution, textiles
of supreme quality. Collaboration of specialists may explain the finest composite specimens, such as a magnificent shirt from Supe containing twelve separate webs employing beside plain weave, tapestry, open-work tapestry, and interlocked warp and weft techniques.

While the most splendid textiles and other objects were the possessions of
an elite class or of the upper degrees of a graduated society as evidenced by
their grave furnishings, it is clear that textile production was the concern of
large numbers of Andean people: growers, processors, distributors, spinners,
dyers, weavers, and finally the owners and wearers who clung to their fabrics
even in death. In short, cloth manufacture formed a significant economic and
occupational integral of ancient Peruvian culture.

## Function

Every material is idiosyncratic in its services to man. Clay, wood, stone,
metal, ivory, bone, fur, feathers and fibers--each has advantages and disadvantages for specific purposes and visual pleasures. The sub-species, so to say, of
each medium are proliferated variations of the virtues and vices of the parent
class. When incentive exploits the potentialities of many sorts of fibers the
resulting mats, baskets, ropes, nets, threads, and cloths perform a multiplicity
of services. The Peruvians early recognized these potentialities and exploited
them with increasing perspicacity from preceramic times onward. Their talent
for textile development is evident from the oldest findings; these predate successful utilization in an equal degree of any other material then available in
coastal Peru.

The presence of a native cotton plant made this possible, but a recognition of the possibilities--if no more than by trial and error--was fundamental
to the initial progression from the use of thigh-spun bast fibers to thigh-spun
cotton. That is, from a stronger, harsher, more refractory material to a weaker,
smoother, more amenable fiber for new purposes. The familiar basketry and matting technique, twining, was continued with cotton yarns, resulting in a flexible fabric pleasant to the touch. The pliant yarns permitted easy manipulations
for designs and this virtue was early realized in the twined cotton cloths made
at such preceramic coastal sites as Huaca Prieta and Asia before 1000 B.C. The
numerous fragments recovered by excavation offer little indication of their
specific uses, yet they do show a recognition of and an esteem for the function
of cloth in the large sense: that it is a plane of soft, agreeably tactile

material which can be a vehicle for decorative motifs.  The eventual abandonment of twined cloth construction for the more versatile techniques of true
weaving multiplied the advantages to be derived from cloth, advantages extending beyond the utilitarian into the less palpable realms of social and aesthetic
values.  The advent of wharved spindles, the heddled loom, wool fibers, and
superior dyes hastened the development of textile functions into full status in
coast cultures by at least 500 B.C.

The practical utility of cloths as containers, dress, bedding, or hangings needs no elucidation.  That aesthetic pleasures come from color and design
is clear too.  Other functions are less obvious--those of social significance,
especially as embodied in dress.  Like costume of the Old World, that of the
higher civilizations of Middle and South America communicated several sorts of
cultural meanings.  An aggregate of basically conforming costumes, varying only
in minor details, marks the nucleus of areal and temporal unity, i.e., a community, district, or region through a period of time (in historic costume terms
"national" or "period" dress).  Through form, fabric, color, and design content
several sorts of social conditions may be manifest:  economic (by quality and
amount), political (by prescribed or proscribed materials, colors, or motifs),
religious (by materials, colors, and symbolic motifs), and military (by practical adaptations and symbolic motifs).  Degrees of social rank, classes of occupation or of servitude can be distinguished by the textile components.  Distinctions of sex, age level, and marital condition are often shown by major or
minor differences in dimensions, materials, colors, or motifs.  Whether or not
these diversities are governed by regulations or merely by custom, the apparel
as a totality of the tangible ingredients is also an expression of intangible
aspects of the society in which it is worn.

By no means all of these intangible components of costume are discernible
in the remains of Peruvian dress even though textiles were the prime conveyors
of social implications; a large share is known through information of different
sorts.  Inca dress and social regulations were pictured and described by Guamán
Poma de Ayala and the Spanish chroniclers.  North coast culture left a pictorial
ethnography in its modeled and painted pottery from Mochica through Chimu times.
And much can be safely inferred from the circumstances of burial, grave associations, and the textiles themselves from exhumations on the central and south
coast dating through the major chronological periods.  Gross areal and temporal
differences in ancient Peruvian apparel have long been known, as well as indications of economic, official, priestly, and military diversities.  Social categories as expressed in costume can be augmented and better defined as systematic
study is applied to the accumulating archaeological evidence.  Alas, the separation of artifacts and cadavers from sites and graves for specialized research
has left, so far, a wide gap in our knowledge about dichotomy of the sexes,
especially as it might be seen in dress.  If the more subtle badges of age level, marital status, or other personal conditions existed in Peru, they probably
never can be clearly recognized from the archaeological materials: too much and
too detailed bearing evidence would be needed.

The totality of men's dress as we know it from all Peru followed particular styles which characterized major sub-areas and time periods.  Differential
features include relative dimensions and proportions of length to breadth, presence or absence of sleeves, location of design areas, and nature of decorative

motifs. Readily recognized examples are the sleeved shirts of the north coast, the shirts with heavy fringing at armholes and bottom edges from the south coast (both of early period), the tapestry woven large shirts with vertical panels of Tiahuanacan motifs (middle period), and the Incan tunics with triangular yokes and checkerboard patterns woven in tapestry (late period). Systematic study of clothing undoubtedly would show more nuclear styles for places and times, as well as determine degrees of variation in those already known.

The burial of miniature or token garments with the dead which correspond in style with their normal-sized counterparts ramifies the importance of identification through dress, or at least the adherence to a contemporary style, which held through most of Andean history. For instance, examples from Paracas, Vista Alegre, and Moche represent three coastal locales in early, middle, and late times.

Regional differences like those mentioned above are significant not only politically, as when Inca law forbade changes in community styles, but psychologically as well: visual identification with family and fellow citizens of a community or area. Clothing that is practically uniform is still worn by village women of Guatemala, each village being distinguished by elements of proportion, weave, color and design in the home-woven blouses. These discrete styles persist in spite of long social and trade intercourse between the towns. No such close differentiation between sites is ever likely to emerge from any archaeological materials, even those of Peru, but it is not unreasonable to assume that a sense of community attachment was an adjunct of local regional styles, as known in Incan times.

Persons of high rank, priestly or official (possibly both-in-one) have been identified by their rich accouterments in the graves of the Paracas Necropolis. The custom of executing deity figures in cloth was already established in an earlier Chavinoid phase of south coast culture. The florescence of this art in the Necropolis phase is expressed in the costume--mantles, yokes, shirts, kilts, turbans--bearing extravagantly fantastic renderings of composite anthropomorphic felines, birds, and serpents. Quality is manifest in the laborious polychrome embroidery of fine-spun wool, while quantity in excess of any normal need is apparent in the huge mantles and the kilts which wrapped in several layers around the hips. Status was communicated through costume, a status that might have been based in religious concepts, in a governmental structure, or in domination by wealth. Whatever the basis of superiority, luxury fabrics made it known to fellow citizens. Other media, however beautifully executed, were but minor in the sepulchral bundles, subordinate to the textile furnishings of the deceased. Rarity of metals, especially gold, on the south coast in pre-Christian times might explain one discrepancy of materials, but not the lesser quantities of ceramics as possible status symbols of equal importance.

Relatively greater abundance of other possessions, especially of gold ornaments and utensils, by Inca times did not weaken the role of textiles as status symbols. On the contrary, some of the best evidence of the function of cloth qualities as prestige indicators, as a material art valued for social meaning and for personal elegance comes from this period. Preserved clothing and documentary information show the concern felt by the aristocratic class for impressive costume for themselves and adequate dress for the populace, when cloth production, as all else, became a state monopoly. As in previous periods it was the shirt, now of tunic proportions, which embodied not only elements of a distinctive period style but those of rank as well. Gone were the decorative designs depicting or referring to mythological deities and natural animal and vegetal forms. The clothing of noble persons depended, rather, upon refinement of quality, the over-all organization of design areas, these areas incorporating a roster of small motifs executed in tapestry weave to communicate the wearer's status. Organized in a checkerboard patterning, the series of small, glyph-like devices covered part or all of Inca noblemen's tunics.

An analysis of these devices and their association with qualities of wool, colors, and workmanship might reveal an hierarchical symbolism within the elite class. That is, whether all, some, or few of the motifs appear in particular types of tunics, suggesting the wearer's right to use certain of the devices. Other interpretations are possible, of course: that, merely, the finest tunics have the most complicated patterns and this proliferation of devices was meaningful only in terms of the weaver's artfulness. But this is a side problem.

The textile medium as used in clothing also distinguished particular social groups; two may be mentioned, first military units, second liveried servants. Mochica warriors wore clothing differentiated from that of every day life: short shirts without sleeves, very short kilts, protective padded panels for the body and thick cloth-covered helmets. Bold geometric motifs on the shirt, panel armor, and helmet were matched. The outfit was an ensemble implying through its textile decoration a totemic, heraldic, or political allegiance. The north coast custom of stripping weapons and all clothing from prisoners of war indicates the value of clothing both as loot and as personal symbols of dignity and rank. (Mayan prisoners, as seen in the Bonampak murals, were permitted to retain at least their breechcloths.)

Livery--matched clothing for groups of servants--is familiar in Old World civilizations, but not necessarily a concept to be taken for granted. Inca litter-bearers, as shown in Guaman Poma's drawings, were dressed identically, even to the position of their tied mantles. The use of livery may have been a late practice, yet the Inca were not wholly innovators, and elite households of prior date well may have had domestic servants in particular styles of dress.

Knowledge of women's apparel in ancient Peru is so deficient at present that it cannot merit discussion nor support inferences. In brief, from early periods (Paracas, Nazca, Mochica) and the late period (Chimu, Inca) there is visual or actual evidence that the basic dress was a wrapped rectangle of cloth pinned or sewn on one or both shoulders--like the dress of Pueblo women or the chitons of classical Greece. Decoration was similar to that of the contemporary masculine clothing but much reduced in amount. Short mantles and veil-like headcloths completed the costume in the Paracas and Inca cultures. That quality and quantity of their garments distinguished women of superior class or nobility can be safely assumed, but nothing more. It is conceivable that women wore shirts or tunics in some places or times of the old Andean civilization, as is the habit now with the women of some tribes in eastern Peru. Until the sex of cadavers and their clothing from many grave lots are made known the ancient dress of Andean women remains largely enigmatic.

Distinctions of age levels by dress are known for boys and youths in Incan times. Occasional child-size garments appear in collections, but without accompanying physical remains, no fixed practices about age-grading by costume can be postulated for earlier periods. Again, excavational data are needed and are quite unlikely to emerge in sufficient quantities for accurate information.

Textiles played their final role at death when the deceased, together with garments, pouches and cloths filled with food and coca leaves, was wrapped in several layers of fabrics and baled for burial. Ranging from ostentatious to modest, the grave accompaniments indicate the importance ascribed to textile possessions in the future life. Nor were all grave cloths practical: a neat bundle from a central coast burial revealed, when opened, many cloth scraps of good quality in decorated styles. Were these little rags "token" fabrics (like miniature garments) or pattern samples a deceased weaver was taking along for future reference? We shall never know. A currently popular assumption that sepulchral clothing was superior to or different from that actually used is difficult to prove. Certainly, elegant garments may have been made solely for interment and never donned--by those who could afford the luxury. Nevertheless, the Peruvian conception of a splendid afterworld surely was but a reflection of the values in their culture as known and experienced. Ostentatious furnishings, if somewhat "larger than life," were still expressing the basic realities of a former existence as well as beliefs concerning the future.

The function of textiles in the ancient Andean world were many. They served several practical purposes as containers, furnishings, and dress, and signalized by their quality and embellishment the social status of their possessors. Other uses as yet unknown may be recognized eventually. That cloth or garments were made for tribute before Inca times seems highly probable. Enormous fabrics emanating from the south coast are still cryptic; one of these is 12 by 87 feet, another about 23 by 162 feet, both have Paracas period associations. Except as tent-like ramada coverings or other temporary shelters their practical utility is doubtful. Huge dimensions to express wealth or prestige occurred in ancient Mexican paper and in Polynesian tapa cloth; for the same reasons the monstrous Peruvian fabrics might have had display value in processions, as offerings at temples, and found final service as mummy bundle shrouds. In spite of such mysteries--and there are many others with respect to cloth--present evidence is quite sufficient to indicate that the Peruvians fully exploited the textile medium to perform a myriad of services which aided and enriched their daily lives.

## Aesthetics

The separation of aesthetic aspects of textiles from their substantive and functional characteristics seems artificial. Peruvian fabrics clearly demonstrate that one of their major functions was to give visual pleasure. While medium, function, and aesthetics all interplay as inherent ingredients of a textile object, the artistry merits separate consideration like that given to materials and functions.

A visual art is basically material. Whatever its purpose and however informed with a grandiose concept, its execution is through a physical medium having qualities which are at once its advantages and its fetters. The artist's talent enhances the virtues and coerces the recalcitrancies of the material, exploiting them both to satisfy predetermined aims. The creative act of weaving is like that of other arts in that materials are transformed into a new entity, an object that did not exist before. Like a painter, with fixed dimensions of canvas or wall, the Peruvian weaver began with an established plane of warps limited in length and breadth. But unlike the painter, who can tentatively set the total composition by sketched lines and work progressively in any part of the field, the weaver builds the cloth by incremental weft additions. Initial errors in judging the space to be occupied by design units will dislocate the patterning throughout. Either what has been woven must be unravelled or the remaining design units be modified in some unobtrusive way. So too with any other misapprehensions, as of yarn quality, color combinations, or the construction technique; they become apparent and are fixed in the fabric as it grows. Errors cannot be painted over, chipped away, hammered out, or covered with a glaze. The manifest expertise of a high percentage of Peruvian fabrics indicates their weavers' absolute control of all the materials, manipulations, color and space relationships by preconception--the assurance that knows what should happen will happen in the process of fabric-making.

The physical qualities of the generally superior fabrics will be discussed before proceeding to a consideration of their designs in relation to the cultural context.

Yarns, whether of cotton or wool, were spun to an extraordinary degree of perfection. The aesthetic aim seems to have been just that: uniform diameter, tension, and color perfection in all grades including those of exquisite fineness. Such yarns are found in all types of textiles but are most apparent in the gauze weaves, the lace-like veils of spider web delicacy. Compact tapestry weaves indicate by their smooth surface that the wool wefts are hard and fine though individually barely visible, and their color interest serves as a barrier to immediate perception of them as yarn. When heavier grades of yarn were desirable, uniformity of diameter and color were still maintained. In fact, this rigidity of standards evidently prevented the exploration of other attractive possibilities in yarn construction. These are, for example, the combination of differently colored strands in one yarn, nodular color flecks, and intentional irregularity of diameter. Such yarns can add interest to plain weave fabrics and are the backbone of modern weaving to achieve subtle color and tactile effects. Only in the Paracas embroideries were two-toned yarns employed with any frequency and, even there, less for merits of their own than for expansion of the color range of the embroidery threads. Apparently, irregularly colored and spun yarns were associated in general with the poorest quality cloths (e.g., infants' "diapers," breechcloths, and crude work cloths) for which randomly mixed white and brown cotton fibers were given hasty, slipshod spinning.

Nature provided cotton and wool fibers in tones from white to brown, augmented to deep brown and black in the wools. In addition, Peruvian experimentation developed dyes to create numerous tints and shades of every hue. An addiction to strong color began early, as seen in Paracas fabrics, and continued unabated through the centuries. Regardless of how many hues were used in one fabric, they were never incoherent nor incongruent, owing to the weaver-artists' resourcefulness in making adroit juxtapositions and balanced color values in their textile compositions. The problem was to devise new combinations of interest to eyes surfeited with chromatic ingenuities. One solution, conveniently termed "color juggling," was to suddenly vary the color order which had been soberly followed through several repeats of a design unit. Rhythmically, this is syncopation--seemingly whimsical, yet intentionally and instantly obviating the danger of monotony. Although best exemplified in Paracas embroideries, the device recurs in later periods, notably in Tiahuanacan and Incan tapestries.

Relief from blatant hues came in the late Tiahuanacan-Huari tapestries, when color schemes were reduced to a series of muted colors centering around red, yellow, black, and white. Reds ranged from garnet to rose pink, the yellows from clear light to tawny browns, often infused with green, resulting in mossy tones. Sparked by black and white with an occasional touch of blue, this color scheme is one of the most restrained and sophisticated in Andean textile history. That it was employed with idiomatic abstract motifs makes it especially appealing to our contemporary taste.

Paralleling the brilliantly colored textiles and often in use at the same time were others dependent upon two markedly contrasting tones, usually brown and white. They emphasized bold geometric or interlocking patterns which covered the cloths. Such fabrics were a counterpoise to the richly colored creations. At the opposite extreme were the gauze-woven fabrics which were seldom colored or, if at all, as a monotone. Recognizing that the primary aesthetic interest lay in the lace-like structure, warps and wefts of mixed colors were eschewed. When colors were added to gauze fabrics, they usually were supplementary, that is, in alternate bands of another weave or as separately woven borders sewn around the edges, where they could not conflict with the gauze patterns.

So remarkable and varied was the color factor in Andean textiles that only these major characteristics can be mentioned here. A negative aspect serves to emphasize the color quality. Namely, that in no period of Andean history was a delicate or pastel color scheme in vogue, one of that sensitive or effete sort which marks the eighteenth century in Europe. However miniscule, precise, clever, or fantastic Peruvian color-entries might be, they always had strength: they were brilliant and complex, or dark-light and bold, or nothing--meaning natural fiber color.

This commitment to forceful color schemes does not altogether explain another rarity in Peruvian weaving: the use of warps of one color and wefts of another in tabby woven cloth. This device is frequently employed by modern Guatemalan weavers and is a forte of the handweavers of India. Warp-weft crossings of two colors produce either a muted overall tone or the opposite, a more intense effect. Occasionally Peruvian cloths of middle or late periods exhibit this feature, such as a deep green crossing violet (muting both), or a cerise crossing henna (intensifying the redness), or black crossing white (appearing as speckly gray). But such specimens are notable for their rarity and, apparently, were not greatly favored by Peruvian consumers.

Like color, the complex subject of design can be only briefly characterized. The roster of designs through the centuries divide into two major classes, representational and geometric. The former range from mythical creatures of elaborate fantasy to naturalistic humans, animals, birds, serpents, marine life, and food plants. Renderings of these supernatural and natural forms were realistically curvilinear in embroidery and tapestry weave, but were reduced to abbreviated angular lines in the more rigid weaving techniques. Geometric forms are the expectable blocks, triangles, diamonds, and zigzags, with heavy emphasis on stepped triangles and frets. Interlocking or reciprocal motifs, made by combining opposed stepped triangles, frets, and stylized bird and fish heads were stand-by solutions for borders or over-all patterns throughout most of Andean history.

Organization of design, like the distribution of color, was symmetrical. Or, when rarely deviating to the asymmetrical, was always in perfect balance. For example, large color areas were sometimes opposed diagonally in late period shirts, in a manner reminiscent of Medieval parti-coloring. Spot motifs were usually evenly spaced in vertical, horizontal, or diagonal rows. A variation of late times, especially Incan, filled the field with contiguous, rectangular compartments in which motifs changed form and color in a diagonal direction.

Floral motifs were almost entirely ignored except in Paracas and Nazca fabrics; even there, food plants and their products were the vegetal themes of interest. The Nazca flower-and-bird embroideries were the chief exception in centuries of fabric designing which never utilized the full graces of plant forms. The design potentials of flowers, leaves, stems, and tendrils, such as undulate in trellis patterns over Old World textiles, were left unexplored. Generally absent too were medallions, confronting animals, and interlaced bands which were the standard devices of Persian, Byzantine, and later textile designers of Europe. While Peruvian weavers independently developed structural techniques (tapestry, brocade, doublecloth, gauze) identical to those contemporaneously in use in the other world, their motivations for design were grounded in different aesthetic ideals. The historic bases of design concepts differed in the two hemispheres and ensuing developments continued to exhibit their disparate ancestry.

In combination, then, perfect yarns, energetic color schemes, and a roster of supernaturals, humans, felines, birds, fish, stepped triangles and frets, reciprocal motifs, and symmetrical organization were recurrent features of Peruvian textile art. On the whole, the styles which distinguished the fabrics of periods or areas from one another were never entirely novel. They were readaptations of old themes, stressing some components of style and repressing others, rearranging or recombining elements of design, narrowing or expanding color schemes, and favoring particular weaves to the partial neglect of others. This continuum through some fifteen to twenty centuries is remarkably stable. No want of imagination or assiduous application to textile design was the cause. On the contrary, the tremendous variety of design within this framework resulted from continuous ingenuity in devising permutations of traditional ingredients. The persistent core of aesthetic ideals seems to have been a form of Classicism wherein canons of quality, design, and color usage were early established and never wholly abandoned in spite of periodic mutations.

The weavers' pursuit of superlative qualities in their products was probably engendered, at least in part, by the elite class for whom they wove. A class composed of connoisseurs who, without being practising artists themselves, were yet aware of the means employed to achieve special effects and who were quite capable of making critical judgments on the style embodied in a fabric. The nature of Andean life was such that even the noble, rich, or official personages did not live in isolated unawareness of their artisans' methods--particularly not those of weavers and potters. There was not the abyss of ignorance which separates consumer from producer in a modern industrial society. Hence, one suspects, that the search for the peerless was stimulated by a clientele cognizant of the general methods of production and appreciative of the niceties in superior fabrics. The degree of excellence reached very early in Peruvian textile history, a few centuries before the time of Christ, intimates that even then weavers and embroiderers were being pushed to new levels of proficiency. Regardless of the conditions of demand--forced labor or benign patronage--the response is palpable in the artistry of the fabrics from early to late times. Interactions between weavers and patrons could have been of many sorts, and were sufficiently close and vital to make the textile arts a constantly dynamic factor in their culture.

Clothing and other textile appurtenances of public and private life were important visible evidences of authority. The expediency of "keeping up appearances" would consciously or unconsciously motivate the acquisition of impressive fabrics by those who could command them. Other potent reasons may well have been mere habituation to luxury and a true aesthetic enjoyment of the beauty of such possessions. Standards of the ruling class are usually emulated to whatever degree is possible by those of lesser ranks. Thus directly or indirectly the general excellence of average quality Peruvian fabrics is probably attributable to the extremely high standards, the absolute virtuosity, of the best. Sumptuary laws controlling certain usages in dress and possessions, as in Incan times, are in themselves evidence of ascending standards. Sumptuary laws are invoked to protect upper classes from imitation by the lower orders; that in general they have been ineffectual and new devices of prestige must be sought was probably as true in the New World as in the Old.

From the earliest known soft fiber textiles, those of twined cotton, it is evident that the medium was recognized as having potentials for aesthetic pleasures and communications of ideas. The designs done in twining techniques were the forerunners of an art which, with ceramics, bore the burden of conceptual meanings in Peruvian civilization. Because textiles could serve many purposes, were sizable, flexible, colorful, and transportable, their capacities as symbol-bearers and eye-pleasers were more versatile than those of ceramics or any other medium in the restricted technological stage in which the Andean area remained up to the Spanish conquest. The head start, so to say, which textiles had over ceramic, metal, and mural decoration may have established a lasting priority for the textile art as the primary means of visual communication.

Interplay between textile design and religious concepts is evident in Andean fabrics. The art style of Chavin, appearing early in ceramics, goldwork, and architectural decoration on the north coast, and in diminution in ceramics and gourds of the south coast, is represented on the central and south coast by a few surviving textile examples. The dominant figure of this style was a creature with feline characteristics. From roughly 500 B.C. to 1200 A.D. this protean figure recurrently appears in new guises as a textile motif. Other associated motifs came and went in varied forms. How often these were significant as religious or cult symbols and how often dissociated as purely profane decorative elements cannot now be known. But in their most fully developed forms as supernatural or "deity figures" in Chavin, Paracas, Nazca, and Tiahuanaco-Huari art it seems safe to assume that they carried meanings as visible manifestations of mythological concepts.

This periodic recurrence of highly elaborated supernatural creatures implies contact between textile designers and erudite persons such as priests or sages: the former illustrating by their art the principal legendary characters in the dogma of the latter. The weaver or embroiderer precipitated palpable forms out of the vaporous oral traditions. Whether such visualizations served cult propaganda, were purely devotional or liturgical in purpose, or merely expressed a fashion for mythological themes cannot be conjectured. The important inference is this: that once the practice of illustrating myth is established the inter-action between "verbalizers" and "visualizers" may be reciprocal. The artist may omit details because of technical problems, or may add others out of creative exuberance. In the absence of written records, the pictorial form can serve as the control or authority from which the priestly-narrators (and especially less learned viewers) draw inspiration. Eventually the verbal formulation may be augmented or modified "to fit the picture." For example, the feline-bird-serpent combination as a deity seems indubitably derived from religious lore, whereas the mass of subsidiary elements composing these figures in embroideries and tapestries are unlikely to have been fantasied item by infinitesimal item in verbal form. But the details added in the cloth could then be interpolated in the verbal rendition. At the same time that art--textile or other--was stabilizing and publishing myth it may have been unintentionally and gradually influencing the body of knowledge from whence it derived. Such interplay is not exclusively that of textile art; wherever myth is made manifest by god impersonation, ritual drama, and graphic media, inter-stimulus is expectable. While a reciprocal influence cannot be proven in a prehistoric, preliterate culture, it leaves open the probability that Peruvian textile art was not merely a passive recorder of ideas from the realm of cosmical knowledge.

Textile decoration of the Tiahuanaco-Huari style shows a change from pictorial representation of deity figures in full form to an abstract style composed of shattered elements of the supernatural, mainly eyes, nose, and teeth arranged in rectangular compartments. This disintegration of an entire, coherent design into a mosaic of remnant elements is one of the most fascinating transpositions in Andean art; although most apparent in tapestries of the period it is paralleled by designs of contemporary ceramics. The implications are as mysterious as they are manifold, suggesting rebellion against an imposed style, or the opposite, continuation in covert form of prohibited motifs, or again, just gradual deterioration of a style on the wane. Whatever the motivation, the conversion resulted in a new sub-style, one of the handsomest in Peruvian textile history.

This discussion is not meant to imply that meaningful designs in textiles always preceded their appearance in other media. Initial use of particular motifs may have been in one medium or another in different times and places. Borrowing of motifs between crafts requires adaptation to the technical limitations of the new material. Certain florid motifs of Late Nazca ceramics have been adapted by weavers to tapestry and interlocked warp weaves with a resultant reduction and angularization of the original curves. In the case of certain geometric patterns on ceramics these are, perhaps, too often attributed to textile sources of inspiration without sufficient proof. Mutual stimulation between craftsmen was probably as active as that between the craftsmen and the aristocratic consumers for whom they produced their best work. Common themes reflect the tastes and interests prevailing at the time.

As we see Andean textiles today, the individual specimens draw admiration for their beauty and skilfull execution. How much more impressive must such fabrics have been in the aggregate, as worn by rulers, priests, their retinues of retainers, acolytes, and musicians at public ceremonies. Spectators of lesser ranks were aware of the refinements and values of the costumes so exhibited. The mass effect would be one of grandeur for a people who were seeing the ultimate in perfection of an art which was but a household skill as practised in their own homes. As spectacular apparel, only one material could rival cloth on such occasions--the ponchos veneered with a mosaic of feathers imported from the eastern Andes. The sheen and color of the plumage gave these garments a luxurious glow analogous to that of the silk and goldthread vestments amongst the dull wools and linens of Medieval European dress. Yet the feather-surfaced ponchos were few and ritual in purpose, and alone could not outbalance the amplitude of fine cloth in costumes and accouterments of the elite class on festival occasions. At public ceremonies or on pilgrimages the commonality too presumably wore their best, good quality even though not magnificent. One sees a mass of well-dressed people to whom cloth was not merely a necessity but a pride, a pleasure, and an inspiration.

From grower to spinner, from weaver to wearer, in poverty and in wealth, in the home and in the tomb, textile materials were intermeshed with the individual lives and the daily habits of every Peruvian. The production of cottons, wools, dyes, spinning and weaving equipment, and cloth itself were part of the basic economy. Improvements in weaving techniques fusing with social developments raised artisans to specialists of professional status. As symbols of prestige fine fabrics were as much a necessity to the aristocracy as were merely serviceable garments to the poorest laborers. When informed with theosophic meanings textiles were the transmittors of religious concepts. This intensive integration with many aspects of Andean culture made textiles one of the primary stabilizing factors in a civilization notable for its progressive conservatism through the centuries.

## Bibliographic Note

A summary article does not permit itemization of all the publications which have contributed to its contents; grateful acknowledgment is made to their many authors. Pertinent works of A. L. Kroeber and Lila M. O'Neale are to be found in the excellent bibliographies of Peruvian sources appended to:

Bennett, Wendell C., and Junius B. Bird. Andean Culture History. (American Museum of Natural History, Handbook Series No. 15, 1960.)

Mason, J. Alden. The Ancient Civilizations of Peru. (Pelican Book A395, Penguin Books, Ltd., Baltimore, 1957.)

# URBAN SETTLEMENTS IN ANCIENT PERU

## John Howland Rowe

There were urban settlements in ancient Peru which were comparable in size and cultural importance with the great cities of antiquity in the Old World. Large urban settlements were built in Peru much earlier than is generally recognized; one preceramic site of this character is known from the central coast. The story of the urban pattern in Peru in later times is not one of simple expansion through the growth of existing settlements and the establishment of new ones, however. Many sites of large urban centers were occupied for relatively short periods and then abandoned. Whole districts with a flourishing urban tradition lost it and shifted to other patterns of settlement. The most striking example of the loss of an urban tradition is found in the southern sierra, where there was a general abandonment of urban settlements toward the end of the Middle Horizon which invites comparison with the abandonment of Roman cities in the Dark Ages. At the time of the Spanish conquest the only parts of Peru where there were large urban settlements were the central sierra and the north coast.

The evidence relating to the rise and fall of urban settlements in Peru is still scattered and fragmentary, and any interpretation of it is bound to be tentative. A review of the subject may, however, serve to clarify the problems involved and suggest fruitful lines of research for the future.

Two introductory digressions are necessary before we can discuss the evidence from specific sites. We need an explanation of the system of dating to be followed and a discussion of what we mean by an urban settlement.

In this review dates will be given in terms of the system of periods of relative time which I have used in earlier publications.[1] The periods are defined with reference to a master sequence, the sequence of changes in the pottery style of the valley of Ica. There are seven periods in all in this system, covering the span of time from the introduction of pottery at Ica to the abandonment of the traditional cemeteries a little over a generation after the Spanish conquest. The periods are named Initial Period, Early Horizon, Early Intermediate Period, Middle Horizon, Late Intermediate Period, Late Horizon, and Colonial Period.

The Early Horizon begins with the beginning of Chavin influence in Ica pottery and ends when slip painting replaces resin painting in this valley as a method of executing polychrome designs on pottery. The Early Horizon can be subdivided into ten smaller time units (epochs) on the basis of a recent analysis of the Ocucaje pottery style.[2] The Early Intermediate Period, which follows the Early Horizon, is characterized by the presence of Nasca style pottery in Ica and can be divided into eight epochs on the basis of L. E. Dawson's studies of Nasca pottery. The next period, the Middle Horizon, begins with Phase 9 of the Nasca style, which, elsewhere

---

Reprinted from ÑAWPA PACHA 1, 1963. pp. 1-27.

on the coast, is associated with strong influences from the Ayacucho area
in the sierra.  It lasts until the beginning of the Chulpaca style at Ica
and can be divided into four epochs.  The Late Intermediate Period lasts
from the beginning of the Chulpaca style at Ica to the beginning of the
Tacaraca A style, an event which apparently coincides rather closely with
the conquest of Ica by the Incas in about 1476.  The Late Horizon is the
period of Inca domination at Ica and of the Tacaraca A phase of the local
pottery tradition.  It ends with the beginning of the Tacaraca B style,
close to the time of the Spanish conquest of Ica, an event which took place
in 1534.[3]

Archaeological units from other parts of Peru are dated to one or
another of these periods or their subdivisions on the basis of evidence
that the units in question are contemporary with a particular unit of pottery style at Ica.  Direct evidence for dating of this kind is available in
those periods labelled "horizons," because in these periods there was an
expansion of trade; certain highly distinctive pottery styles were distributed over large areas, and imported vessels in these styles are found associated with ones in the local traditions.  In the Early Horizon the Chavin
and Paracas styles were widely distributed in this way, while in the Middle
Horizon a spread of the Pacheco-Conchopata style is followed by an even
wider distribution of the style of Huari.  One phase of the Cajamarca pottery tradition had a wide distribution at the same time that the Huari
style did.  In the Late Horizon Inca style vessels from Cuzco were widely
traded and imitated, and a number of other styles had a more restricted
spread.

In the periods which lack the "horizon" label trade was much more
restricted, and arguments for contemporaneity are generally indirect, except when closely neighboring valleys are involved.  As more local sequences become known, however, there is no reason why detailed cross-dating on
a valley to valley basis cannot be achieved.

The Colonial Period and the Late Horizon can be dated by historical
records and reliable traditions.  Our only source of dates in years for
earlier sections of the Peruvian chronology is the method of radiocarbon
dating.  Relatively few radiocarbon determinations are available for ancient
Peru, and not all the determinations which have been announced are on reli-
ably associated samples and consistent with one another.  The most consistent determinations available in June, 1962, suggest the following approximate dates for the beginning of the periods named:

>1400 B.C. - Initial Period
>
>600 to 700 B.C. - Early Horizon
>
>100 to 150 A.D. - Early Intermediate Period
>
>800 A.D. - Middle Horizon
>
>1100 A.D. - Late Intermediate Period

The determinations used for these estimates are based on the Libby half-
life value of 5568 years for radiocarbon.

The assignment of cultural units to periods in this study is based on archaeological evidence independent of radiocarbon dates, except in a few cases which will be discussed individually.

This study is concerned with urban settlements in ancient Peru. For the purposes of the present argument, an urban settlement is an area of human habitation in which many dwellings are grouped closely together. The dwellings must be close enough together to leave insufficient space between them for subsistence farming, although space for gardens may be present. In the case of a site where the foundations of the dwellings have not been excavated, an extensive area of thick and continuous habitation refuse provides a basis for supposing that the settlement was an urban one.

The intent of this definition is to exclude clusters of dwellings so small that they could be interpreted as belonging to the members of a single extended family. Twenty dwellings is perhaps the minimum number which would provide this exclusion.

It will be convenient in our discussion to distinguish four kinds of urban settlements, according to whether or not they include residents who are engaged full time in occupations other than hunting, fishing, farming and herding, and whether or not there is a separate rural population in the area. I am proposing to use the word "pueblo" to designate an urban settlement in which all the residents are engaged in hunting, fishing, farming or herding at least part of the time, and "city" to designate one which includes residents engaged in other activities (manufacturing, trade, services, administration, defense, etc.). If the urban settlements have around them a scattered rural population, I propose to call them "synchoritic," a term coined from the Greek word chorites, countryman. If all the people engaged in rural occupations reside in the urban settlement itself, so that the countryside has virtually no permanent residents between the settlements, I propose to call the settlements "achoritic." The four kinds of urban settlements, then, are the synchoritic pueblo, the achoritic pueblo, the synchoritic city and the achoritic city.[4]

People who live in an urban settlement but are engaged in hunting, fishing, farming or herding must travel to work, and they can only work effectively in the immediate neighborhood of the settlement. The productivity of land and water in the accessible area therefore limits the number of people engaged in these rural activities who can live together in a single urban settlement. The maximum figure under favorable conditions in native North America seems to have been about 2,000; at any rate, the largest pueblo-type settlements in the Southwest and on the Northwest Coast apparently did not exceed this figure. There is no reason to think that the limit was higher in ancient Peru.

The population limit just discussed sets a ceiling for the total population of pueblos but not for that of cities, since cities also include residents engaged in occupations which can be carried on within the city itself. We thus have reason to suppose that any urban settlement with a population in excess of 2,000 is or was a city and not a pueblo, even though specific evidence relating to the occupations of the inhabitants is

295

not available.  Unexcavated archaeological sites with habitation areas of great extent fall into this category.  I propose to refer to urban settlements estimated to have had less than 2,000 inhabitants as "small," and ones estimated to have had more than 2,000 as "large."

The distinction between synchoritic and achoritic urban settlements has a bearing on the problem of the destruction of cities.  By definition, some of the residents of a city are not themselves directly engaged in the production of food and raw materials of animal and vegetable origin, and these people must obtain such necessities from the producers.  In the case of synchoritic cities, some or all of the producers live outside the city proper.  The spatial distinction facilitates the development of a social distinction between urban and rural residents.  If the urban residents control the market, as is usually the case, they are in a position to exploit the rural residents in various ways, arousing thereby an understandable resentment and hostility  among the latter.  Then if the cities are weakened by political and economic instability the countrymen may take a violent revenge, destroying the cities which have become a symbol of oppression. In the case of achoritic cities, resentment between the producers of food and raw materials and the rest of the urban population might also arise and could easily lead to violence.  The producers, however, being themselves city dwellers, would be more likely to try to take over the city government than to destroy their own homes and shrines.  As a pattern of residence, the pattern of synchoritic cities contains an element of potential instability which is not present in the achoritic city pattern or in any of the other patterns of urban settlement.

This general theory is a development out of Michael Rostovtzeff's more specific argument that the antagonism of the rural population to the cities in the Roman Empire was the major factor in the destruction of Roman cities in the west in the 3rd and 4th centuries A.D.[5]  The best documented example is the destruction of Augustodunum (Autun) in 269 by a coalition of local "peasants" and Roman soldiers, the soldiers themselves having been recruited from the rural population.

Any discussion of urban settlements in ancient Peru necessarily involves reference to ceremonial centers as well.  Ceremonial centers occur in Peru; they may be combined with urban settlements in various ways or provide a kind of alternative to them.  A ceremonial center is a grouping of public buildings housing common facilities, such as shrines, meeting places, markets, and law courts, which is used seasonally or at prescribed intervals by the population of a considerable surrounding area.  Between the occasions when a ceremonial center is used it is either closed and empty or houses only a small permanent population of caretaker personnel. The general population which makes use of the center may be entirely dispersed in the surrounding countryside, or it may be clustered in urban centers.

Ceremonial centers may be found even in an area where large cities also occur.  In the Andean area today there are a number of rural churches which attract very large numbers of people once a year for a religious festival and fair, and some of these ceremonial center churches are located

not far from major cities.  Cities do generally provide competing facilities, however.

We can now turn to the archaeological evidence for urban settlements
in ancient Peru.  The story begins on the Peruvian coast before the first
appearance of pottery in this area, but after cotton began to be used as a
textile fiber.  In the stage bounded by these two events the coast dwellers
drew their subsistence primarily from hunting sea mammals, fishing, and
gathering shellfish, although some plant cultivation was practiced as well.
Many of the known habitation sites are on waterless sections of the coast
which were attractive because of the abundance of shore resources.  Small
urban settlements of the pueblo type are very common, the best known being
that at Huaca Prieta in Chicama.  At a few of these sites public buildings
can be identified.  At Rio Seco, for example, there are two mounds about
4 m. high, each consisting of two levels of rooms which had been deliberately filled with stone to provide a raised substructure for an important
building.[6]  The preceramic population of the coast did not live exclusively
in pueblo type settlements, however; there are also many very small habitation sites.  At Ancón, where Edward P. Lanning and I have been making a
systematic survey, some of the small sites are set back from the shore,
probably to take advantage of supplies of Tillandsia, an epiphytic plant
which was used for fuel in dry areas.

The possibility that there were also preceramic cities is suggested
by the size of the Haldas site, situated at Km. 329 north on a dry shore
just south of Casma.  Lanning tells me that the preceramic occupation
refuse at Haldas covers an area about two kilometers by one and averages
50 cm. in thickness.  There is also a complex and imposing temple structure
at this site, and part of it was built before the introduction of pottery.
The University of Tokyo expedition of 1958 secured a sample for radiocarbon
dating consisting of cane used to wrap stones laid in the floor of the
temple, and this sample (Gak-107, run in 1960) yielded a date of 1631 B.C.
± 130.[7]  If the area covered by preceramic refuse at Haldas is continuous
and was all occupied at the same time, the population of the site must have
been well over 10,000.  Further excavation at this site is urgently needed.

The temple at Haldas was enlarged in the Initial Period, but there
are only about 300 square meters of Initial Period habitation refuse.  The
shrinkage of population which this figure suggests may be the result of a
shift to the Casma Valley following the introduction of maize[8] cultivation.
Maize appears in the refuse at Haldas shortly before pottery.[8]  In any
case, Haldas appears to have become a ceremonial center rather than an urban
settlement in the Initial Period.

There were urban settlements elsewhere on the coast in the Initial
Period, however.  The Hacha site in Acarí is one; it has habitation refuse
covering an irregular area about 800 by 200 m. along an abandoned channel
of the Acarí River.  This occupation is dated by two radiocarbon determinations:  UCLA-154 (1962), 1297 B.C. ± 80, and UCLA-153 (1962), 997 B.C. ±
90, both run on charcoal samples.[9]  At this site there are remains of several structures with walls of packed clay which were probably public buildings; one of the structures is earlier than the 1297 B.C. charcoal sample.

Ordinary dwellings were probably constructed of flimsier materials, as they were in later times. Pottery is common and distinctive. Although the Hacha site is located about 21 km. from the sea, marine shellfish are prominent in the refuse. In the refuse associated with the radiocarbon date of 997 B.C. the cultivated plants represented, in approximate order of abundance, are cotton, gourds, lima beans, squash, guava, and peanuts.[10] No trace of maize has been found. Relatively little excavation has been carried out at Hacha, and the data are still insufficient to determine whether it was a pueblo or a city.

In the sierra the site of Qaluyu, located in the northern part of the Titicaca basin near Pucara, probably also qualifies as an urban settlement of the Initial Period. Qaluyu is a stratified site with two distinct phases of occupation. The later one, associated with Pucara style pottery, is Early Horizon in date. The earlier occupation is characterized by a distinctive pottery style called Qaluyu which occurs in a stratigraphically early position at Yanamancha, near Sicuani, as well as at Qaluyu itself. Although there is no way to relate the Qaluyu style to the Ica valley sequence directly, its consistently early position in local sequences and the absence of common Early Horizon stylistic features argue for a date in the Initial Period. There are two radiocarbon dates from Qaluyu based on charcoal samples associated with Qaluyu style pottery, namely P-156 (1958), 1005 B.C. ± 120, and P-155 (1958), 565 B.C. ± 114.[11] The two samples were taken from about the same depth in a short test trench and should not be so far apart; they cannot both be accepted in the first sigma. The earlier one fits the archaeological evidence better.

The accumulation of habitation refuse at Qaluyu forms a low mound several acres in extent. A road has been cut through the mound, and the Initial Period occupation is exposed in the road cut. The extent of this exposure suggests that Initial Period refuse underlies virtually the whole mound, but further excavation would be necessary to establish its limits. No buildings have been excavated at this site, and the case for its being an urban settlement of some kind rests on the probable extent of the refuse.

The site of Marcavalle near Cuzco yields pottery in a local version of the Qaluyu style. The refuse covers at least an acre.

For the Early Horizon, many sites have been recorded which qualify as urban settlements, both on the coast and in the sierra. Several are large enough to be considered large cities, the ones now known being located in the Titicaca basin, in the Ica Valley on the south coast of Peru, and in the Mosna Valley in the northern sierra. Let us discuss the large sites first.

At Pucara in the northern part of the Titicaca basin are the ruins of a very large urban settlement with imposing public buildings. Pucara is a "one period" site and the type site for the Pucara pottery style. No earlier pottery has been found there, and there was no later occupation until the Late Intermediate Period. There is no direct evidence by which to relate the Pucara style to the Ica sequence, so radiocarbon dates provide

the only basis for correlation.  Six radiocarbon determinations have been
made on charcoal samples from a refuse deposit at Pucara (P-152, P-153,
P-154, P-170, P-172, and P-217).[12]  Five of these determinations agree
very well and suggest a date in the first century B.C.  The sixth, P-154,
agrees only if taken in the second sigma.  A date in the first century
B.C. should fall in the latter part of the Early Horizon, perhaps Early
Horizon 8 or 9.

Both public buildings and private houses at Pucara were built of
adobe on stone foundations, and the collapse of the adobe superstructures
has buried the foundations so that only the largest buildings can be distinguished on the surface without excavation.  There were at least three
large buildings, probably temples, on a terrace called Qalasaya at the
foot of the great Rock of Pucara.  The residential area was on the flat
plain between this terrace and the river and was apparently very extensive.[13]

The area around Pucara is good farming country where potatoes and
quinoa can be grown, and there are catfish in the Pucara River.  Good pottery clay is available near the river, and there is a considerable pottery
making industry at Pucara today.  If ancient Pucara was a city, as its size
suggests, its economy probably involved pottery manufacture, trade, and
religious activities as well as farming.

The Pucara settlement at Qaluyu, only three or four kilometers
away, also covers a substantial area, though a less extensive one than at
Pucara itself.  As the local farmers have recognized, the mound at Qaluyu
is shaped like a catfish, a fact which suggests some deliberate planning.
According to Manuel Chávez Ballón, there is another very large Pucara site
at Tintiri on the road from Azángaro to Muñani.  No one has yet looked for
small habitation sites between these urban settlements.

The site of Tiahuanaco, at the southern or Bolivian end of Lake
Titicaca, covers an area at least 1-1/2 by 1-1/4 km.  The full area over
which sherds occur on the surface has never been mapped, but the reports
of visitors indicate that it is immense.  The surface remains represent a
Middle Horizon occupation, but there is evidence that the site was already
important in the Early Horizon.  Since this evidence has never been brought
together, a review of it is in order.

Bennett apparently dug into an occupation level of Early Horizon
date at the bottom of his Pit V, located east of the Acapana, the level in
question being his Level 9 (4.00 to 4.60 m.).  It was set off from the
deposit above by a thin layer of clay.  Bennett collected 116 sherds from
Level 9, 111 of them being plain ones.[14]  The most significant of the
decorated sherds was a small one with a stepped design in red and black,
the color being outlined by incision.  When I examined this sherd in
Bennett's collections at the American Museum of Natural History in 1941 I
identified it as Pucara Polychrome.[15]  The identification was based on the
colors, surface finish, and technique of decoration, the design being too
simple to be diagnostic.  It may be, of course, that the sherd in question
belongs to a local style related to Pucara rather than to the Pucara style

proper, but, as Bennett noted, it is quite different from later Tiahuanaco pottery.

The evidence of radiocarbon determinations confirms the early date here assigned to Level 9. Alfred Kidder II and William R. Coe dug another pit adjacent to Bennett's Pit V in 1955 to secure samples for radiocarbon dating. Sample P-150 (1958), animal bones from 3.25 to 3.50 m. depth, corresponding to the lower part of Bennett's Level 7, gave a date of 246 A.D. ± 104. Sample P-123 (1958), damp charcoal from 3.50 to 3.75 m. depth, corresponding to Bennett's Level 8, gave a date of 141 A.D. ± 103.[16] In the light of this evidence, a date in the first century B.C. for Level 9 is entirely reasonable.

Some sculpture in the Pucara style has been found at Tiahuanaco also, notably the two kneeling figures in red sandstone which stand at the sides of the door of the Tiahuanaco church. These are ancient statues which were reworked for Christian use early in the 17th century. The reworking did not extend to the backs of the figures, however, and enough is left of the back of the headdress on one of them so that we can recognize it as a work in the Pucara style or in a style closely related to it. The Spanish chronicler Bernabé Cobo gives a circumstantial account of the finding of these statues, and his account suggests that they were dug up near the church, rather than in one of the areas where there were ruins on the surface.[17] Perhaps the reason why more remains in the Pucara style have not been found at Tiahuanaco is that the area of the modern town has not been explored.

In 1858 the Swiss naturalist J. J. von Tschudi purchased a small stone carving in the purest Pucara style at the town of Tiahuanaco.[18] This carving, now in Bern, was in use as a cult object at the time of Tschudi's visit and consequently lacks provenience. It may very well have been dug up at Tiahuanaco also, however.

Since 1957 Carlos Ponce Sanginés and Gregorio Cordero Miranda have been excavating at Tiahuanaco for the Bolivian government, working mainly in and near the Qalasasaya. They have found a new pottery style in their lowest levels which is probably of Early Horizon date also. Ponce assigns the new style to his "Epoca I" and describes it as very distinctive, including painted pieces, plain polished pieces, and modelled ones. The painting is most commonly in red on yellow, with some incised motifs and feline designs drawn in black and white.[19] I propose to call the new style Qalasasaya for convenience of reference. The head of the principal figure on an incised and painted bottle of this style illustrated by Ponce has a number of features which occur in the same combination at Ica, where they are limited to Early Horizon 10.[20] This observation suggests a date immediately following the Pucara occupation. On the other hand, a radiocarbon sample which is supposed to date "Epoca I" materials gives a date of 239 B.C. ± 130 (GaK-52, organic carbon from Qalasasaya Pit E-14, Layer 6).[21] The radiocarbon determination suggests that the Qalasasaya style is earlier than Pucara. More evidence is clearly needed to settle the problem of dating, but the indications are that the Qalasasaya style belongs sometime in the Early Horizon.

So far we have no evidence regarding the extent of the Early Horizon occupation at Tiahuanaco, but if there were urban settlements at the other end of the lake at this time there may very well have been an important one at Tiahuanaco also.

The Ica Valley is one of the larger valleys on the Peruvian coast, but its water supply in ancient times was very limited. The Ica River carried water for three months of the year at most, and in some years it carried no water at all. On the other hand, one good soaking of the land a year was enough to ensure a crop of maize and squash.

In the earlier part of the Early Horizon the population of Ica seems to have been distributed in numerous small settlements along the edges of the valley. Some of them were certainly large enough to qualify as pueblos. In Early Horizon 9 times, however, there was an abrupt concentration of the population in a few very large urban settlements. Two of these settlements have been located, namely Tajahuana, on a dry plateau beside the river, about half way down the valley, and Media Luna in the oasis of Callango, far below. According to L. E. Dawson, who discovered it, Media Luna is an area of continuous, concentrated habitation refuse over a kilometer across, with fifteen small adobe mounds and some remains of adobe walls on the flat. The mounds presumably represent temples or other public buildings. There are no fortifications at this site. The Tajahuana site is only slightly smaller. The whole area is covered with stones representing the foundations of small rectangular houses, and there are a number of mounds about the same size as the ones at Media Luna. Tajahuana is elaborately fortified with multiple walls and a dry moat on the side of easiest access.

Both of the sites described were occupied only during one epoch of the Early Horizon, perhaps for a century or a century and a half, and then never occupied again. They apparently represent achoritic cities, without smaller settlements between them, but we have no evidence of the nature of their economic life. In the next epoch, Early Horizon 10, settlements were substantially smaller but very numerous, suggesting that there had been a redistribution of the population rather than a decline in numbers. Whether pueblos or small cities, the new settlements were synchoritic. The situation suggests that the striking concentration of population in Early Horizon 9 reflects some kind of political planning.[22]

There is no indication that the urban settlements of Early Horizon 9 depended in any way on large scale irrigation works. There was probably never enough water at Callango to irrigate any very large area, while the Tajahuana site is located close to the river bank and adjacent to a marshy area. The sites in the Ica Valley which depend on major irrigation canals all date to Early Intermediate Period 7 or later.

In the northern sierra of Peru we have evidence of urban settlements in the Mosna Valley east of the Cordillera Blanca. The principal site in this valley is Chavin, where there is an impressive temple which is famous for its stone sculpture. Archaeological research has been largely concentrated on the temple. Wendell C. Bennett, who excavated there in 1938, suggested that the temple was a ceremonial center for seasonal use with a

very small resident population.[23]  However, Marino Gonzáles Moreno, the
Peruvian government commissioner at the site, who is a native of Chavin as
well as a very able archaeologist, showed me evidence that the whole area
occupied by the modern town, which is adjacent to the temple on the north,
is underlain by Early Horizon refuse and constructions.  An area perhaps a
kilometer long and half a kilometer wide is involved.  There is also a considerable area of habitation refuse on the other side of the river.  Chavin
thus appears to have been a large city.  There are reported to be a number
of smaller sites of the same period within a few kilometers of Chavin itself, so it was probably a synchoritic city.

Chavin was certainly a religious center, and it has a favorable
location for trade.  The Mosna Valley is a natural route of communication
between the sierra to the west and the tropical lowlands along the Marañon.
Whether the site was also a manufacturing center cannot be determined on
the basis of the evidence now available.  A city the size of Chavin is
likely to have had considerable political power.

Chavin was not a ceremonial center in the settlement pattern sense
during the Early Horizon, but it may have become one during the Early Intermediate Period.  Most of the habitation area of the city had been abandoned
by the end of the Early Horizon, but later structures and refuse around the
temple indicate continued use of the ceremonial part of the site.

If Tiahuanaco was already a city in the Early Horizon it may have
had a continuous urban life through the Early Intermediate Period.  All the
other known Early Horizon cities, however, were either entirely deserted or
at any rate had ceased to exist as cities before the end of the Early Horizon.  The break is particularly remarkable in the northern Titicaca basin,
because we have no idea what followed it there.  Although a certain amount
of exploring has been done, no habitation sites have been found which can
be attributed to the Early Intermediate Period; we do not even know what
kind of pottery was in use.

Apart from the large city sites we have been discussing, the known
Early Horizon habitation sites are mostly small urban settlements, probably
of a pueblo character.  Some examples are Llawllipata, near Pomacanchi;
Chanapata, at Cuzco; Pozuelo, in the Chincha Valley; and the Tank Site at
Ancon.  There are also, of course, many important sites which I do not have
sufficient information about to discuss from the point of view of this survey; Kotosh, La Copa, Pacopampa, and Chongoyape fall into this category.

For the Early Intermediate Period many sites representing large
cities are known from southern and central Peru, but none has been reported
in the north.

There are large urban sites of the Early Intermediate Period in the
south coast valleys of Pisco, Ica, Nasca, and Acarí.  The site of Dos Palmas
in Pisco comprised an area of habitation nearly half a kilometer long and
some 300 m. wide when it was photographed from the air in 1931 by the
Shippee-Johnson Expedition (Plate I).  By 1957, when Dwight T. Wallace visited it on the ground, the area had been brought under irrigation and the
site largely destroyed.  The photograph of 1931 shows the habitation area

densely packed with the fieldstone foundations of small rectangular rooms, interrupted by four or five small open plazas. The pottery is in a local style datable to Early Intermediate Period 3.

In Ica there is a great habitation site of Early Intermediate Period 1 and 2 on the slopes of a hill at the edge of the Hacienda Cordero Alto. The population then seems to have shifted to the other side of the valley, where there is an equally large site of Early Intermediate Period 3 to 5 on the slopes of Cerro Soldado. The Cerro Soldado site consists of the fieldstone foundations of small houses scattered over the slopes of a large rocky hill overlooking the Ica River. A shrine can be identified on one of the spurs of the hill. No habitation site attributable to Early Intermediate Period 6 has yet been found in Ica, although burials of this period are known there. In Early Intermediate Period 7 there was a large city on the Pampa de la Tinguiña, a broad alluvial fan subject to occasional flooding. The surviving area of habitation is just under 600 meters across and was probably originally half again as large, the missing sections having been washed out in flash floods. The ruins consist of fieldstone foundations of buildings, a number of small mounds, and at least one plaza. An imposing adobe palace associated with this site was destroyed by the owner of the neighboring hacienda in 1959. Tinguiña is a "one-period" site, abandoned before the end of Early Intermediate Period 7 and never reoccupied.

The story of settlement in the ravine of Nasca has not been traced systematically, and only one large urban site is known there. This site is Cahuachi, which comprises shrines, plazas, cemeteries, and habitation areas extending along the side of the valley for over a kilometer. Strong's excavations there in 1952 indicated an occupation from Early Horizon 10 to Early Intermediate Period 3.[24] It is not easy to determine how much of the area of Cahuachi was used for habitation. The houses were constructed of perishable materials, so that their foundations do not show on the surface, and some of the surface pottery is derived from looted tombs rather than from refuse. Nevertheless, the habitation area was clearly extensive.

The largest urban site in the valley of Acarí is Tambo Viejo, at the south edge of the modern town of Acarí. The Early Intermediate Period habitation area at this site is about a kilometer in length and half a kilometer in width, comprising fieldstone foundations of small rectangular rooms, a number of small mounds, probably representing shrines or public buildings of other kinds, and plazas. The site is surrounded by fortification walls of fieldstone and adobe. The earliest occupation is represented by pottery datable to Early Intermediate Period 2 and representing an old local tradition. The site seems to have been rebuilt and enlarged in Early Intermediate Period 3 and abandoned before the end of this epoch. The Early Intermediate Period 3 occupation is associated with Nasca style pottery and very likely represents an actual Nasca invasion.

Further up the Acarí Valley at Chocavento is another fortified habitation site, closely similar to Tambo Viejo but about half as large. Still further up valley there are two additional sites of the same sort,

one at Amato and the other at Huarato. Both are smaller than Chocavento.
All of these sites appear to have been built and abandoned in Early Intermediate Period 3. It is not unlikely that all these Acarí sites represent
achoritic urban settlements, that is, ones in which the farming population
of the valley was concentrated; their size bears some relation to the amount
of farm land available nearby. The size of Tambo Viejo indicates that it,
at least, was a city. These sites of Early Intermediate Period 3 represent
the peak of urbanization in the Acarí Valley. In all subsequent periods
the habitation sites in this valley were relatively small.

        The fact that Cahuachi in Nasca and the urban settlements in Acarí
were deserted at about the same time is suggestive, in view of the evidence
that the fortified settlements in Acarí represent an invasion from Nasca.
Perhaps Cahuachi conquered a little empire on the coast which was destroyed
after a generation or two. The situation could be clarified by further
study of habitation sites in the Nasca area.

        There are a number of Early Intermediate Period sites in the area
around Ayacucho in the sierra which are large enough to qualify as large
cities. The extent of these sites must be traced from the distribution of
pottery fragments; there are no architectural remains of the Early Intermediate Period visible at the surface. In the immediate environs of Ayacucho
there are three large habitation sites of the Early Intermediate Period,
Acuchimay, Chakipampa (Tello's "Conchopata"), and Ñawimpukyu. All three
continued to be occupied into the Middle Horizon, and the last two have remains of Middle Horizon buildings. The great site of Huari, about 25 km.
north of Ayacucho, also had an extensive Early Intermediate Period occupation as well as the Middle Horizon one for which it is famous. At Churukana,
a short distance east of Huari, there is a very large Early Intermediate
Period habitation site which is not obscured by any later occupation.

        Tiahuanaco either continued to be occupied or was occupied again in
the Early Intermediate Period. The Early Intermediate Period pottery style
at this site is the Qeya style, the major component of Bennett's "Early
Tiahuanaco" category, corresponding to Ponce Sanginés's Epoca III. The
name Qeya is derived from the name of the type site, Qeya Qollu Chico on
the Island of Titicaca, where it was found isolated in burials excavated by
A. F. Bandelier in 1894. Bandelier's collection from this site is at the
American Museum of Natural History; it is referred to but not described in
his report.[25] The two pits, V and VIII, in which Bennett got "Early
Tiahuanaco" refuse are located half a kilometer apart, a fact which suggests
the presence of an extensive habitation area. Ponce Sanginés dates the
construction of the Qalasasaya to his Epoca III, so the site also had large
public buildings in the Early Intermediate Period.

        On the central coast the sites of Pachacamac and Cajamarquilla were
large urban settlements in the Middle Horizon and the Late Intermediate
Period, and at both sites the occupation can be traced back to the Early
Intermediate Period. We do not know the area involved or the character of
the early occupation, however. The site of Maranga, between Lima and
Callao, includes a cluster of great temple mounds which were built during
the Early Intermediate Period and abandoned early in the Middle Horizon.
No extensive habitation area has been found associated with these mounds,
and it is very likely that they constituted a ceremonial center.

There was a moderate sized settlement of urban character at Playa Grande, on the desert coast south of Ancon.[26] The habitation area at this site was about 400 m. across and included at least seven public buildings. There was no water available for irrigation at Playa Grande, and the population must have been engaged in fishing, gathering shellfish, and hunting sea mammals, like the inhabitants of the settlements along the desert coast before the introduction of pottery. I hesitate to argue that the existence of an urban settlement at Playa Grande implies general use of this pattern in the neighboring valleys. Occupational convenience might encourage the formation of urban settlements by fishermen, even though contemporary farmers preferred a different pattern of residence.

Schaedel has argued that urbanization began on the north coast in the Middle Horizon or Late Intermediate Period, and that the earlier pattern in this area was one of ceremonial centers.[27] He reached these conclusions on the basis of a survey of major architectural remains on the north coast carried out between 1948 and 1950. The procedure followed was to locate large ruins on aerial photographs and then to visit the sites on the ground. This procedure provides an excellent basis for studies of monumental architecture, but it yields only part of the information needed for the study of settlement patterns. Many habitation areas on the coast cannot be identified at all on aerial photographs and can be recognized on the ground only by the presence of ancient pottery, bone fragments, and shell. Except in areas where stone was very abundant, ordinary houses on the coast were generally framed with poles and closed with matting or with canes smeared with mud. Such houses leave no remains except a floor and some post holes which, if not covered by a layer of refuse, weather away within a few centuries. Generally the floors are covered with refuse and can be found by excavation. The data for the Early Intermediate Period collected in Schaedel's survey may reflect the pattern of scattered residence and ceremonial centers which he suggests, but they could also result from a pattern of urban residence in flimsy houses which left no remains of the sort he was mapping.

Apart from Schaedel's survey, data on north coast settlements in the Early Intermediate Period are not abundant. The problem is complicated by the fact that, for certain valleys (e.g., Casma and Lambayeque), the pottery of the Early Intermediate Period has not been identified.

The extensive survey of ancient sites carried out in the Virú Valley by J. A. Ford and Gordon R. Willey in 1946 indicated what Willey has called a small or medium sized village pattern for settlements of this valley in the Early Intermediate Period.[28] The Huaca Gallinazo, which is the largest habitation site associated with Gallinazo style pottery, is described as covering an area of 400 by 200 m.[29] These relatively small settlements may have been associated with ceremonial centers, if that is the function served by the so-called "castillos." The Virú evidence can hardly be said to contradict Schaedel's generalization. On the other hand, it does not support his interpretation very strongly, because Virú, which is not a very large valley, had no major urban settlements even in the Late Intermediate Period when such settlements were fairly common on the north coast.

The fact that later sites on the central coast, such as Pachacamac and Cajamarquilla, were already occupied in the Early Intermediate Period leads us to ask whether the same might not be true of some of the large late urban settlements on the north coast. Heinrich Ubbelohde-Doering did some digging at the great site of Pacatnamú in the Pacasmayo Valley in the hope of finding an early occupation. The earliest pottery he found, however, dates to Middle Horizon 1.[30]

The Middle Horizon was marked by a great expansion of the Huari culture centering in the Ayacucho area, an expansion which probably involved military conquest. Its traces have been found through most of Peru, in the sierra from Sicuani to Cajamarca and on the coast from Ocoña to Chicama. There was a parallel expansion of the Tiahuanaco culture in the basin of Lake Titicaca and in northern Bolivia, reaching the coast in the extreme south of Peru and in northern Chile. These expansion movements are significant for our story, because the Huari culture certainly had a well established tradition of large cities by the beginning of the Middle Horizon, and the Tiahuanaco culture probably did also.

There seems to have been a concentration of population and probably also of power at Huari in the Middle Horizon. The great urban settlements in the environs of Ayacucho were abandoned at the end of Middle Horizon 1, while the major occupation at Huari dates to Middle Horizon 2 and 3. The site of Huari is enormous. According to Bennett, the "major core" of the ruins covers an area at least 1.5 km. square. The masonry structures represented by the ruins now visible above ground were probably public buildings; the habitation area around them can only be traced from the distribution of surface sherds.[31]

Tello reports the existence of another large site like Huari at Hatun Wayllay on the Lircay River in Huancavelica.[32] A 16th century writer describes what appears to be another such site at Cabana in the province of Lucanas in the southern part of the modern Department of Ayacucho.[33]

A striking feature of the Huari expansion was the construction of very large building complexes consisting of plazas, corridors and rectangular rooms laid out according to a formal plan. The walls are very high, with few doors and windows, and refuse is virtually absent. These elaborate complexes probably housed government stores rather than people. There is a comparatively small complex of this type at Huari itself, in the Capilla Pata sector. The larger ones are Pikillaqta, at the lower end of the valley of Cuzco, Wiraqocha Pampa, near Huamachuco, and a site on the Pampa de las Llamas in the valley of Casma on the north central coast.[34] The existence of these formal storage complexes provides evidence that the expansion of Huari was not simply a matter of peaceful penetration or raiding. It represents the formation of an imperial state with a well organized administration.

Pikillaqta has an extensive Middle Horizon habitation site associated with it. The habitation site is located on the next hill (Raqch'i), an elevation formed by an old lava flow. Here there are pockets of soil, including some fairly extensive fields, among the outcrops of lava, and

Middle Horizon sherds occur on the surface.   Presumably the buildings
were of adobe.

There are many Middle Horizon habitation sites of various sizes in
the area of Huari expansion, usually marked by refuse without standing
ruins.  Waywaka, near Andahuaylas, is relatively extensive; Yanamancha,
near Sicuani, and Zukzu, at Urcos, are small.[35]  Evidently, the entire
population was not concentrated in large cities.

On the south coast there is a small Middle Horizon 1 habitation
site at Pacheco in the ravine of Nasca, associated with a shrine of
Ayacucho type.  No really large Middle Horizon habitation site has yet
been identified on the south coast, although some extensive cemeteries of
this period are known, particularly in the Nasca drainage.  However,
little enough survey work for habitation sites has been undertaken in this
area so that it would be dangerous to infer that no large Middle Horizon
site exists.

Pachacamac continued to be occupied throughout the Middle Horizon,
but the occupation of this period is covered by later construction and
could only be traced by excavation.  Many Middle Horizon burials have
been found at Pachacamac, however, and the pottery in them represents a
local variant of the Huari style.  This Pachacamac variant is distinctive,
and its influence can be traced over most of the central coast and as far
south as Ica.[36]  Since Pachacamac was a great city in the earlier part of
the Late Intermediate Period, it is reasonable to suppose that it was already one in the Middle Horizon when it was such an important center of
influence.

The north coast was an area of large cities in the Late Intermediate Period.  One of them, at any rate, namely Pacatnamú in the Pacasmayo
Valley, can be traced back to the beginning of the Middle Horizon, as we
have already noted.  If Schaedel is right in claiming that there were no
large cities on the north coast before the Middle Horizon, the easiest way
to account for the rather abrupt appearance of such cities is to suppose
that they represent a pattern of settlement introduced by the already
urbanized conquerors from Huari.

Tiahuanaco reached its greatest extent in the Middle Horizon, and
most of the famous sculpture from this site is of Middle Horizon date.  No
other really large Middle Horizon city has been found so far in the area
of Tiahuanaco expansion.  This fact may be significant, or it may simply
reflect inadequate exploration.  There has been relatively too much attention paid to carved stones and not enough to house foundations and habitation refuse.  For example, when Bennett was excavating the cut stone ruins
of a Tiahuanaco temple at Lukurmata he noted the presence of house foundations and habitation refuse but did not trace the area of habitation.[37]
Some small Tiahuanaco habitation sites are known; there is one on a hill
at Juliaca, for instance.

Both Huari and Tiahuanaco were abandoned toward the end of the
Middle Horizon, and there was no sizable later settlement at either site.

Furthermore, in a large part of southern Peru and Bolivia the abandonment of cities was general; there were virtually no large cities in this area in the Late Intermediate Period and the Late Horizon. The entire pattern of settlement in large cities was eliminated and not reintroduced until after the Spanish conquest.

The abandonment of the great cities in the south coincides approximately with the decline and eventual elimination of Huari and Tiahuanaco influence in local pottery styles. The Late Intermediate Period was a time of marked local cultural diversity and relative isolation, contrasting in both respects with the Middle Horizon. Some evidence regarding political conditions in the Late Intermediate Period can be derived from Inca traditions, and these traditions describe a situation of extreme political fractionation in the sierra at the time of the beginnings of the Inca dynasty. Evidently, the great imperial states of the Middle Horizon fell at about the time that the cities were abandoned. There thus appears to be a formal parallel in Peru to the situation in western Europe at the time of the abandonment of the Roman cities.

The general absence of large cities in the south in the Late Intermediate Period was noted by the University of Tokyo field party which surveyed the area in 1958. The expedition report, in discussing the site of Churajón in the Arequipa area, says that it is "the only city site of the Urbanist period that has ever been recognized in the southern Andes."[38] The "Urbanist period" of this statement is approximately equivalent to the Late Intermediate Period. There is some question, however, whether Churajón qualifies as a city in terms of the criteria used in this study. The Tokyo party reports two habitation areas at Churajón, one of 2,000 square meters and the other of 5,000 square meters. The 5,000 square meter area, however, includes tombs and agricultural terraces as well as dwellings. The habitation areas described sound like small urban settlements, and probably pueblos rather than cities.

The largest urban settlements in southern Peru datable to the Late Intermediate Period which I have visited are Mallawpampa at Curahuasi, Qaqallinka and Timirán near Arequipa, and Sahuacarí and Otaparo in the Acarí Valley.[39] Probably all of these sites continued to be occupied in the Late Horizon. They cover areas at least 300 m. across and include the remains of fieldstone foundations as well as habitation refuse. These sites need be no more than relatively large pueblos. The sites which Max Uhle visited at the southeast end of Lake Titicaca between Achacache and Huaycho sound similar.[40]

In the area around Cuzco many Late Intermediate Period sites have been identified. Some are very small, representing perhaps no more than half a dozen houses, while others have an area of refuse 200 to 300 meters across and evidently represent pueblos or small cities. Examples of the larger sites are Qencha-qencha in the valley of Cuzco and Kuyu (Pukara Panti-lliklla) near Pisac.

The Ica Valley seems to have had a pattern combining small settlements and imposing ceremonial centers in the Late Intermediate Period. The

major ceremonial center was at Old Ica in the Pago de Tacaraca where there
is a large cluster of adobe temple mounds but little habitation refuse.
Smaller clusters of mounds, probably representing subsidiary centers, occur
at Macacona and Chagua (La Venta).  The habitation sites of this period are
numerous but small in area and scattered all over the valley.

In central Peru there are some Late Intermediate Period cities of
large size.  I have visited two near Huancayo, Patan-qotu and Qotu-qotu.
The University of Tokyo expedition estimated that Patan-qotu extended for
two kilometers along the bank of the Mantaro River, and Qotu-qotu may be
nearly as large.  The latter site continued to be occupied into the Late
Horizon.[41]

Pachacamac on the central coast was a very large city in the early
part of the Late Intermediate Period.  Indeed, most of the buildings now
visible in the central and southern part of the site appear to be Late
Intermediate Period constructions.  The city declined in size, however,
and was at least partly in ruins when the Incas took it.  The best evidence
for this fact is provided by the excavations which Arturo Jiménez Borja
carried out in the central part of the site in 1957-58.  Jiménez cleared a
small temple of the Late Intermediate Period in this area and found the
courtyard filled with over a meter of very dirty Inca refuse.  Part of the
facing of the south wall of the courtyard had fallen out, perhaps during an
earthquake, and the layers of Inca refuse continued into the gap in the
face of the wall.  There is thus no question that this building was in a
ruinous condition when the Incas began to use it as a dump.  Miguel Estete,
who accompanied the first Spanish exploring party to reach Pachacamac, in
1533, reported that much of the city was in ruins in his time.  He says:
"It must be something very ancient, because there are many ruined buildings,
and the town has been walled, although most of the wall has now fallen in;
it has its main gates giving access to the interior and its streets."[42]

Cajamarquilla, in the valley of Lima, was a large city in the Late
Intermediate Period, as we have already noted.  No one has succeeded in
identifying early Spanish references to it, and its ancient name is unknown.
No evidence of Inca occupation has been found there.  It is thus at least
possible that Cajamarquilla was abandoned before the end of the Late Intermediate Period.

The north coast was the most highly urbanized part of Peru in the
Late Intermediate Period, with many large cities of imposing size.  I have
not explored this area myself and have nothing to add to the descriptions
of north coast city sites published by Schaedel and Kosok.[43]

For the most part, the patterns of settlement of the Late Intermediate Period carried through into the Late Horizon.  Whatever changes
occurred were the result of Inca planning, so we need to add some comments
on Inca practice.

As we have seen, the Cuzco area, where the Inca state began, had a
pattern of small urban settlements and even smaller clusters of houses in
the Late Intermediate Period.  Cuzco, the Inca capital, was a small urban

settlement at the time the Incas began their expansion; Inca traditions were
quite explicit on this point.  Pachakuti, the first great Inca conqueror,
who ruled from about 1438 to about 1471, rebuilt Cuzco to make it a more
appropriate capital for the new empire.  He planned a core of palaces, temples, and government buildings with a ring of small urban settlements around
it.  The residential settlements were separated from one another and from
the core area by open fields.  Since the service personnel in the core area
probably grew to number at least 2,000, the core itself was technically a
large city by the criteria we are using.  However, Pachakuti's intent appears
to have been to build a ceremonial center with a cluster of small urban settlements dependent on it.

        The administrative centers which the Incas established in the prov-
inces tended to follow the model of Cuzco, except when they were attached
to already existing native settlements.  The Inca administrative center in
Acarí, for example, consisted of government buildings with satellite settlements located some distance away.[44]  If there were any Inca settlements
which were planned as large cities, they were some of the great regional
centers in the north, such as Pumpun, Wanuku (Huánuco Viejo), and Tumipampa.

        Where the native population was very scattered, the Incas tried to
consolidate it in urban settlements to facilitate government control, but
the settlements so formed were not large and had a minimum of public buildings, aside from a shrine or two.  The settlements established for the col-
onization of uninhabited country were likewise small.  Machu Picchu, which
was the largest of a group of Inca colonies in the rough country between
Ollantaytambo and Vilcabamba, contained a total of only about 200 rooms for
all purposes.[45]  The Incas were not city builders in the sense that their
predecessors of the Middle Horizon had been.

        Such, then, is the record of urban settlement in ancient Peru as
it appears in the present state of archaeological knowledge.  There are
still great gaps in what we know and extensive areas where no archaeological
survey has ever been undertaken, but the present record is sufficient to
support a few conclusions and to make it possible to ask some useful new
questions.

        In the first place, Peru has a long and persistent tradition of
urban settlement.  From far back in preceramic times the urban pattern is
found generally wherever patterns of residence have been investigated.
Scattered settlement in family groups is also found, but in combination with
urban settlement rather than as an alternative to it.  There are a few cases
of what appear to be achoritic urban settlements, as in Ica in Early Horizon
9, in the Lake Titicaca basin at the time the Pucara cities were flourishing, and in Acarí in Early Intermediate Period 3.  In Ica and Acarí the
achoritic pattern is associated with fortification of the settlements and
may be a deliberate military measure.

        So little excavation has been carried out in Peruvian urban settle-
ments that it is usually not possible to distinguish a small city from a
pueblo.  We can only be sure we are dealing with cities when we find habitation areas so extensive that they fall into the "large" category.

Large cities are not as generally characteristic of Peruvian settlement patterns as small urban settlements.  Some large cities were built at
some time or other in most parts of the sierra and the coast, but usually
only part of the area was urbanized at any one time.  The concentration of
population in large cities appears to have been most general during the
Middle Horizon.

The earliest large city so far known is preceramic Haldas on the
coast, an isolated phenomenon in the present state of knowledge and one
which deserves careful investigation.

The basin of Lake Titicaca was the home of a long tradition of large
cities.  This tradition goes back to the Initial Period (Qaluyu) and was
very likely continuous from that time until the end of the Middle Horizon.
There may have been a general abandonment of large cities in the northern
part of the basin near the end of the Early Horizon, bringing an end to such
cities as Qaluyu and Pucara, but it is at least possible that the occupation
of Tiahuanaco was not interrupted until the general crisis at the end of the
Middle Horizon.

There was a large city at Chavin in the Early Horizon, but it is not
yet clear whether it was unique or merely one of many such settlements in
the northern sierra at that time.  If the latter, it may be possible to
find links between the northern tradition and the Lake Titicaca one.  Similar difficulties attend the interpretation of the occurrence of cities on
the south coast in the Early Horizon.  A large unexplored area separates
the south coast from Lake Titicaca.  The south coast urban tradition appears
to have been continuous until the Middle Horizon, although individual sites
were abandoned on many occasions.

The expansion of Huari in the Middle Horizon is the expansion of a
culture of cities which had its center in the Ayacucho area.  Large cities
in this area can be traced back well into the Early Intermediate Period,
and designs on pottery indicate contacts with the urbanized south coast in
Early Intermediate Period 7 and with Tiahuanaco in Middle Horizon 1.  The
origins of the urban tradition in the Ayacucho area are still obscure, because there has been so little exploration in the sierra.  Large cities may
well go back to the Early Horizon here, in which case a link with other
Early Horizon occurrences of cities should be sought.

It was probably the influence of the Huari culture which was responsible for the introduction of large cities to the north coast.  This area
appears to have had only small urban settlements and ceremonial centers in
earlier periods.  Once it accepted the large city pattern, however, the
north coast became highly urbanized and maintained its urban tradition until
the time of the Spanish conquest.

The power of Huari and Tiahuanaco collapsed at the end of the Middle
Horizon, and their fall was accompanied by a general abandonment of cities
in southern Peru.  Thereafter, the prevailing pattern of settlement was one
of small urban settlements and dispersed dwellings.  The fact that the abandonment of cities was general over a large area suggests that there was a

reaction against cities as such, and we are reminded of the hostility of the rural population to the cities in the later Roman Empire.  Like the Roman cities, the Peruvian ones of the Middle Horizon did have a rural population around them.  It is interesting that the reaction took place in the areas where the urban tradition was very old and not on the north coast where large cities were a new phenomenon.

The story of ancient Peruvian cities has some important implications for general theories of the development of cities.  In the first place, in Ica, where I have had an opportunity to study the relationship between cities and irrigation, large cities appear first and major irrigation canals were only built later.  It would be difficult to argue that there was any relationship between irrigation and the development of cities in this area, unless it was that the growth of cities produced a pressure on the land which was met by irrigation projects on an unprecedented scale.

In the second place, the Peruvian data throw some light on the relationship between cities and ceremonial centers.  Except for the late and somewhat peculiar case of Cuzco, there is no example in our Peruvian data of large cities developing out of ceremonial centers.  When large cities replaced or were added to ceremonial centers, as occurred on the north coast, the cities represent the intrusion of foreign ideas coming from another area where the urban tradition was much older.  The ceremonial center, therefore, is not a necessary stage in the development of the city.

The Peruvian evidence also shows very clearly that the large city is not such an advantageous institution as to spread consistently at the expense of other patterns of residence.  We have seen how large cities disappeared over a considerable area in southern Peru at the end of the Middle Horizon and were replaced by a pattern of small urban settlements.  At Ica an urban pattern was replaced by a ceremonial center one in the Late Intermediate Period.  During this same period Pachacamac was transformed from a large city into a ceremonial center, which is all it was when the first European visitors saw it.  Something similar had happened at Haldas in the Initial Period.

The ceremonial center is obviously in some sense an alternative to the city, providing the kinds of public institutions and services which are present in large cities, but without a permanent concentration of population. It would be possible to argue from the Peruvian data that ceremonial centers represent a secondary development out of cities.  They clearly do so in some cases, but it would be going too far beyond the evidence to maintain that the prior existence of cities is a necessary condition for the development of ceremonial centers.

Berkeley, California
October 23, 1962

Acknowledgments. This study is based on research supported in part by a grant from the National Science Foundation. Except as otherwise noted in the text, the data used are derived from my own field work, guided on many occasions by the expert knowledge of Manuel Chávez Ballón, Oscar Núñez del Prado, Arturo Jiménez Borja, Dwight T. Wallace, Lawrence E. Dawson, Dorothy Menzel, and Edward P. Lanning. Lanning read an earlier version of the text and provided valuable criticism. I take this opportunity to express my thanks to Dr. Paul Fejos and the Wenner-Gren Foundation for Anthropological Research for providing access to the unpublished aerial photographs of the Shippee-Johnson Expedition of 1931.

## NOTES

[1] Rowe, 1960a, 1960b, 1962b.

[2] Menzel and others, ms.

[3] A summary of the archaeological sequence in the Ica Valley is given in Rowe, 1962a.

[4] As the reader will note in the text which follows, this study suffers to some extent from the fact that the categories used in it grew out of my attempts to compare and interpret field data. The field observations were not made with these particular distinctions in mind and often fail to include the most pertinent details. Such deficiencies can be taken care of by further fieldwork, however, and the inductive approach calls for no apology.

[5] Rostovtzeff, 1957, vol. 1, pp. 496-501.

[6] These mounds are described by Engel, 1958, pp. 89-90. My data, however, were provided by E. P. Lanning, who participated in the excavations at Rio Seco.

[7] Kigoshi and others, 1962, p. 91, and information provided by Rosa Fung de Lanning. See Engel, 1958, fig. 4, for an inaccurate plan of the Haldas temple.

[8] Information provided by E. P. Lanning.

[9] Sample UCLA-154 was collected in 1961 by J. H. Rowe and Dorothy Menzel and consisted of wood charcoal and carbonized seeds associated with a thin layer of ash on a clay floor at the foot of and continuous with the longest section of packed clay wall at the south end of the site. The ash represents the remains of a substantial fire which burned the face of the wall. The construction of the wall should, therefore, be earlier than the date of the sample. Sample UCLA-153 was collected in 1959 by Gary S. Vescelius, Hernan Amat Olazabal, and Dorothy Menzel, all at that time working on the joint archaeological project sponsored by the U.S. Educational Commission in Peru and the University of San Marcos. It consisted of wood charcoal from a layer of undisturbed refuse on the lee side of a sand hill

at the north end of the site.  Both samples were submitted to the laboratory by J. H. Rowe.  Since the site had been dated in the Initial Period on the basis of the archaeological relationships of its pottery, textiles, and stone work, both dates are acceptable.

[10]Preliminary identifications by J. H. Rowe and L. E. Dawson, not checked by experts.

[11]Ralph, 1959, p. 57.

[12]Ralph, 1959, p. 57.

[13]For photographs of the Pucara site see Kidder, 1943, and Rowe, 1958.

[14]Bennett, 1934, pp. 378-385 and Table 1.

[15]Rowe, 1944, p. 56.

[16]Ralph, 1959, p. 55.

[17]Cobo, lib. XIII, cap. XIX; 1956, Tomo 92, p. 197.

[18]Rowe, 1958, pp. 260-261.

[19]Ponce Sanginés, 1961, pp. 33-35.

[20]Ponce Sanginés, 1961, p. 22, top figure; comparison with Ica by Dorothy Menzel.

[21]Kigoshi and others, 1962, p. 91.

[22]Early Horizon 10 was also a time when the Ica Valley had a relatively unified pottery style.  See Menzel and others, ms.

[23]Bennett and Bird, 1949, pp. 133, 136-137.

[24]A sample of the pottery from the Cahuachi excavations is illustrated by Strong, 1957, who also provides a plan and aerial photograph of the site.  Strong generously permitted L. E. Dawson, Dorothy Menzel, and me to examine his original sherd collections, and the dates here assigned to Strong's materials are based on Dawson and Menzel's observations.  I have also visited Cahuachi personally.

[25]Bandelier, 1910, pp. 172-173 and plate XXI.

[26]Stumer, 1953, pp. 44, 48, and fig. 1; Tabío, 1957, p. 5.

[27]Schaedel, 1951a, p. 22; 1951b, pp. 234, 242-243; and compare Willey, 1953, pp. 412-413.

[28]Willey, 1951, p. 198.

[29]Willey, 1953, pp. 132-133; Bennett, 1950, pp. 25-29.

[30]Ubbelohde-Doering, 1959, pp. 6-26. The excavator's stylistic attributions of the pottery found in burials E-I, M-XI and M-XII are erroneous. These are all Middle Horizon I burials, dated by the Moche V style vessels they contained. All dark incised ware is not Chavin; all utilitarian face-neck jars are not Gallinazo, and so forth. The eclecticism reflected by the variety of decorated vessels in these burials is a common characteristic of Middle Horizon 1 burials elsewhere on the coast as well.

[31]Bennett, 1953, p. 18 and fig. 2.

[32]Tello, 1942, pp. 683, 684.

[33]Monzón, 1881, p. 210.

[34]McCown, 1945, pp. 267-273, figs. 5 and 13; Rowe, 1956, pp. 142-143; Kubler, 1962, plate 162; Tello, 1956, pp. 49-51 and fig. 2. Pikillaqta is dated by a find of small stone figures in Huari style. Wiraqocha Pampa is dated by its resemblances to Pikillaqta and to the Capilla Pata sector of Huari. The site on the Pampa de las Llamas is the group of rectangular plazas and associated buildings lying northeast of Huaca Mojeque at the foot of Cerro San Francisco. I know it only from Tello's plan and description, which provide very inadequate evidence for dating. My grouping of this site with the sierra ones is no more than a guess based on certain features of its formal plan.

[35]Waywaka and Yanamancha are discussed briefly in Rowe, 1956, pp. 143 and 144.

[36]Menzel, 1958, pp. 40-41.

[37]Bennett, 1936, pp. 491-492 (sections K and L)

[38]Ishida and others, 1960, p. 468.

[39]Qaqallinka ("Casa Patac") and Timirán ("Dos Cruces") are described briefly in Ishida and others, 1960, pp. 467 and 462. For Sahuacarí and Otaparo, see Menzel, 1959, pp. 130-131.

[40]Rowe, 1954, p. 107.

[41]Ishida and others, 1960, p. 471.

[42]Estete, 1938, p. 87.

[43]Schaedel, 1951a, 1951b; Kosok, 1960.

[44]Menzel, 1959, p. 130.

[45]Plan in Bingham, 1930.

# BIBLIOGRAPHY

Bandelier, Adolph Francis Alphonse
1910    The islands of Titicaca and Koati.  The Hispanic Society of
America, New York.

Bennett, Wendell Clark
1934    Excavations at Tiahuanaco.  Anthropological Papers of the American Museum of Natural History, vol. XXXIV, part III, pp. i-ii, 359-
494.  New York.

1936    Excavations in Bolivia.  Anthropological Papers of the American
Museum of Natural History, vol. XXXV, part IV, pp. i-ii, 329-507.
New York.

1950    The Gallinazo group, Viru Valley, Peru.  Yale University Publications in Anthropology, no. 43.  New Haven.

1953    Excavations at Wari, Ayacucho, Peru.  Yale University Publications
in Anthropology, no. 49.  New Haven.

Bennett, Wendell Clark, and Bird, Junius Bouton
1949    Andean culture history.  American Museum of Natural History, Handbook Series, no. 15.  New York.

Bingham, Hiram
1930    Machu Picchu, a citadel of the Incas.  Memoirs of the National
Geographic Society.  Yale University Press, New Haven.

Cobo, Bernabé
1956    Historia del Nuevo Mundo.  Biblioteca de Autores Españoles desde
la formación del lenguaje hasta nuestros días (continuación), tomo
91, pp. 1-427; tomo 92, pp. 5-275.  Ediciones Atlas, Madrid.

Engel, Frédéric
1958    Sites et établissements sans céramique de la côte péruvienne.
Journal de la Société des Américanistes, n. s., tome XLVI, 1957,
pp. 67-155.  Paris.

Estete, Miguel
1938    La relación del viaje que hizo el señor capitán Hernando Pizarro
por mandado del señor gobernador, su hermano, desde el pueblo de
Caxamalca a Pachacama y de allí a Jauja.  Los cronistas de la
conquista; selección, prólogo, notas y concordancias de Horacio H.
Urteaga.  Biblioteca de Cultura Peruana, primera serie, no. 2, pp.
77-98.  Desclée, De Brouwer, Paris.

Ishida, Eiichiro, and others
1960    Tōkyō Daigaku Andesu chitai gakujutsu chōsa dan 1958 nendo
hōkokusho.  Andes; the report of the University of Tokyo Scientific
Expedition to the Andes in 1958.  Bijitsu Shuppan sha, Tokyo.

Kidder, Alfred II
1943    Some early sites in the northern Lake Titicaca basin.  Papers of
the Peabody Museum of American Archaeology and Ethnology, vol.
XXVII, no. 1.  Cambridge.

Kigoshi, Kunihiko, and others
    1962    Gakushuin natural radiocarbon measurements I.  Kunihiko Kigoshi,
            Yoshio Tomikura and Kunihiko Endo.  Radiocarbon, vol. 4, pp. 84-
            94.  New Haven.

Kosok, Paul
    1960    El valle de Lambayeque.  Actas y trabajos del II Congreso
            Nacional de Historia del Perú (época pre-hispánica), 4-9 de agosto
            de 1958, vol. I, pp. 49-67.  Centro de Estudios Histórico-
            Militares del Perú, Lima.

Kubler, George
    1962    The art and architecture of ancient America; the Mexican, Maya,
            and Andean peoples.  The Pelican History of Art, Z21.  Penguin
            Books, Baltimore.

McCown, Theodore Doney
    1945    Pre-Incaic Huamachuco; survey and excavations in the region of
            Huamachuco and Cajabamba.  University of California Publications
            in American Archaeology and Ethnology, vol. 39, no. 4, pp. i-x,
            223-400.  Berkeley and Los Angeles.

Menzel, Dorothy
    1958    Problemas en el estudio del Horizonte Medio en la arqueología
            peruana.  Revista del Museo Regional de Ica, año IX, no. 10, 20 de
            junio, pp. 24-57.  Ica.

    1959    The Inca occupation of the south coast of Peru.  Southwestern
            Journal of Anthropology, vol. 15, no. 2, Summer, pp. 125-142.
            Albuquerque.

Menzel, Dorothy, and others
    ms.     The Paracas pottery of Ica; a study in style and time, by
            Dorothy Menzel, John H. Rowe, and Lawrence E. Dawson.  (submitted
            for publication in University of California Publications in
            American Archaeology and Ethnology).

Monzón, Luis de
    1881    Descripción de la tierra del repartimiento de los Rucanas
            Antamarcas de la corona real, jurisdicion de la ciudad de Guamanga.
            - año de 1586.  Relaciones geográficas de Indias.  Publícalas el
            Ministerio de Fomento.  Perú.  Tomo I, pp. 197-215.  Tipografía de
            Manuel G. Hernandez, Madrid.

Ponce Sanginés, Carlos
    1961    Informe de labores, octubre 1957 - febrero 1961.  Centro de
            Investigaciones Arqueológicas en Tiwanaku, Publicación no. 1.
            La Paz.

Ralph, Elizabeth K.
    1959    University of Pennsylvania radiocarbon dates III.  American
            Journal of Science Radiocarbon Supplement, vol. 1, pp. 45-58.
            New Haven.

Rostovtzeff, Michael Ivanovitch
    1957    The social and economic history of the Roman Empire.  Second edi-
            tion, revised by P. M. Fraser.  At the Clarendon Press, Oxford.
            2 vols.

Rowe, John Howland

1944     An introduction to the archaeology of Cuzco. Papers of the Peabody Museum of American Archaeology and Ethnology, vol. XXII, no. 2. Cambridge.

1954     Max Uhle, 1856-1944; a memoir of the father of Peruvian archaeology. University of California Publications in American Archaeology and Ethnology, vol. 46, no. 1, pp. i-viii, 1-134. Berkeley and Los Angeles.

1956     Archaeological explorations in southern Peru, 1954-1955; a preliminary report of the Fourth University of California Archaeological Expedition to Peru. American Antiquity, vol. XXII, no. 2, October, pp. 135-151. Salt Lake City.

1958     The adventures of two Pucara statues. Archaeology, vol. 11, no. 4, December, pp. 255-261. Brattleboro, Vt.

1960a     Cultural unity and diversification in Peruvian archaeology. Men and cultures; selected papers of the Fifth International Congress of Anthropological and Ethnological Sciences, Philadelphia, September 1-9, 1956, pp. 627-631. Philadelphia.

1960b     Tiempo, estilo y proceso cultural en la arqueología peruana. Segunda edición, corregida. Tawantinsuyu K'uzkiy Paqarichisqa - Instituto de Estudios Andinos - Institute of Andean Studies, Berkeley.

1962a     La arqueología de Ica. Revista de la Facultad de Letras, Universidad Nacional "San Luis Gonzaga" de Ica, año I, no. 1, primer y segundo semestres de 1961, pp. 113-131. Ica.

1962b     Stages and periods in archaeological interpretation. Southwestern Journal of Anthropology, vol. 18, no. 1, Spring, pp. 40-54. Albuquerque.

Schaedel, Richard Paul

1951a     The lost cities of Peru. Scientific American, vol. 185, no. 2, August, pp. 18-23. New York.

1951b     Major ceremonial and population centers in northern Peru. Civilizations of ancient America; selected papers of the XXIXth International Congress of Americanists, pp. 232-243. University of Chicago Press, Chicago.

Strong, William Duncan

1957     Paracas, Nazca, and Tiahuanacoid cultural relationships in south coastal Peru. Memoirs of the Society for American Archaeology, number thirteen. Salt Lake City.

Stumer, Louis Michael

1953     Playa Grande: primitive elegance in pre-Tiahuanaco Peru. Archaeology, vol. 6, no. 1, March, pp. 42-48. Brattleboro, Vt.

Tabío, Ernesto E.

1957     Excavaciones en Playa Grande, costa central del Peru, 1955. Arqueológicas; publicaciones del Instituto de Investigaciones Antropológicas, I-1. Museo Nacional de Antropología y Arqueología, Pueblo Libre, Lima.

Tello, Julio César
  1942    Orígen y desarrollo de las civilizaciones prehistóricas andinas.
          Actas y trabajos científicos del XXVII Congreso Internacional de
          Americanistas (Lima, 1939), tomo I, pp. 589-720.  Lima.

  1956    Arqueología del valle de Casma; culturas:  Chavin, Santa o
          Huaylas Yunga y Sub-Chimú.  Informe de los trabajos de la Expedición
          Arqueológica al Marañón de 1937.  Publicación Antropológica del
          Archivo "Julio C. Tello" de la Universidad Nacional Mayor de San
          Marcos, vol. I.  Editorial San Marcos, Lima.

Ubbelohde-Doering, Heinrich
  1959    Bericht über archäologische Feldarbeiten in Perú. II.  Ethnos,
          1959, nos. 1-2, pp. 1-32.  Stockholm.

Willey, Gordon Randolph
  1951    Peruvian settlement and socio-economic patterns.  Civilizations
          of ancient America; selected papers of the XXIXth International
          Congress of Americanists, pp. 195-200.  University of Chicago
          Press, Chicago.

  1953    Prehistoric settlement patterns in the Virú Valley, Perú.
          Bureau of American Ethnology, Bulletin 155.  Washington.

Plate I. Dos Palmas in the Pisco Valley, photographed from the air by George R. Johnson in 1931 (photo courtesy of the Wenner-Gren Foundation for Anthropological Research, N.Y.).